Hitler's Panzer Generals

Germany's success in the Second World War was built upon its tank forces; however, many of its leading generals, with the notable exception of Heinz Guderian, are largely unknown. This biographical study of four German panzer army commanders serving on the Eastern Front is based upon their unpublished wartime letters to their wives. David Stahel offers a complete picture of the men conducting Hitler's war in the East, with an emphasis on the private fears and public pressures they operated under. He also illuminates their response to the criminal dimension of the war as well as their role as leading military commanders conducting large-scale operations. While the focus is on four of Germany's most important panzer generals – Guderian, Hoepner, Reinhardt and Schmidt – the evidence from their private correspondence sheds new light on the broader institutional norms and cultural ethos of the Wehrmacht's *Panzertruppe*.

David Stahel is a leading authority on German military history in the Second World War. He is a senior lecturer in history at the University of New South Wales in Australia. His previous publications include *Operation Barbarossa and Germany's Defeat in the East* (2009), *Kiev 1941* (2012), *The Battle for Moscow* (2015) and *Retreat from Moscow* (2019).

Hitler's Panzer Generals

Guderian, Hoepner, Reinhardt and Schmidt Unguarded

David Stahel

CAMBRIDGE
UNIVERSITY PRESS

Shaftesbury Road, Cambridge CB2 8EA, United Kingdom

One Liberty Plaza, 20th Floor, New York, NY 10006, USA

477 Williamstown Road, Port Melbourne, VIC 3207, Australia

314–321, 3rd Floor, Plot 3, Splendor Forum, Jasola District Centre,
New Delhi – 110025, India

103 Penang Road, #05–06/07, Visioncrest Commercial, Singapore 238467

Cambridge University Press is part of Cambridge University Press & Assessment,
a department of the University of Cambridge.

We share the University's mission to contribute to society through the pursuit of
education, learning and research at the highest international levels of excellence.

www.cambridge.org
Information on this title: www.cambridge.org/9781009282819

DOI: 10.1017/9781009282802

First published 2023

Printed in the United States of America by Sheridan Books, Inc.

A catalogue record for this publication is available from the British Library.

ISBN 978-1-009-28281-9 Hardback

For Craig, Candice, Carly, Bianca and Samantha

CONTENTS

FIGURES

ACKNOWLEDGEMENTS

I am indebted to a number of scholars for their expertise in the transcription and translation of the private correspondence that formed the basis of this study. Daniel Schneider, Dr David Hamann, Dr Alex J. Kay and Dr Madeleine Brook were all instrumental to this process. Generous funding was provided by my home institution, the School of Humanities and Social Sciences at the University of New South Wales, Canberra. Feedback and corrections on an early draft were provided by Dr Jan Tattenberg, Dr Roman Töppel, Dr Jeff Rutherford and Associate Professor Eleanor Hancock. I would also like to thank the three anonymous reviewers engaged by Cambridge for their helpful comments, corrections and new lines of enquiry. Finally, to Michael Watson and the team at Cambridge University Press I extend my continued thanks for their unflagging professionalism.

INTRODUCTION

During the Second World War the German panzer generals were the subject of a great deal of myth-making, both in German and in Allied propaganda. After the war this entered a new phase with the publication of self-exculpating memoirs, studies for the US army historical division and uncritical biographies. Only relatively recently has a great deal of research been done to reassess their role both in a professional military capacity and in terms of their individual participation in Germany's war of annihilation in the East. We therefore know a great deal more about what these men did and how they did it, but that does not always provide the answer why. If the image of the German panzer generals was built on a myth, then who were these men beyond the stylised propaganda images and resolute military orders?

For the great bulk of German generals in the Second World War there are no private wartime papers (letters or diaries) to study. Whether this is because families have withheld such evidence or because it has simply been lost is largely unknown. From what does exist, it can be hard to generalise too much about a common service culture for a number of reasons. Like any army, there were numerous and distinct branches of service (infantry, artillery, panzer, intelligence, supply, etc.); there were four ranks of general entailing very different duties and responsibilities; there were many theatres, some much more active than others; and, finally, the different periods of the war contrast hugely from each other. Much of the commentary about the German generals in the Second World War overlooks these differences and attributes to them a generic set of experiences as well as a mindset that is as often false as it is correct. This study attempts to establish a more complete picture of one of the most important groups: the command of the *Panzertruppe*, particularly in 1941 on the Eastern Front.

In total there were six German generals who served as panzer group/army[1] commanders in 1941, and this study assesses four of them based on their private wartime correspondence. These include Colonel-General Heinz Guderian (Panzer Group 2), Colonel-General Erich Hoepner (Panzer Group 4), General of Panzer Troops Georg-Hans Reinhardt (Panzer Group 3 as of October 1941) and General of Panzer Troops Rudolf Schmidt (Panzer Group 2 as of late December 1941). The two other panzer group commanders in 1941 were Colonel-General Ewald von Kleist (Panzer Group 1) and Colonel-General Hermann Hoth (Panzer Group 3 to October 1941). Since the latter two generals have no known wartime letters that have been made available for research, I have excluded them from this study.

While a traditional biography seeks to chart a life story, this is not what I am attempting here. The focus is on the period in which the letters were written (1941) and the many new insights they offer. By way of introduction, I will briefly outline the early career of each man, but the central discussion of this study will be the private correspondence of the generals (Chapter 1), who they were as individuals (Chapters 2 and 3) and how they conducted themselves in their commanding roles (Chapters 4 and 5).

The most famous of our four subjects is undoubtably Heinz Guderian. He came from an established military family, attended a cadet school (with mediocre grades)[2] and formally entered the army in 1907 at the age of nineteen. He attended the War School at Metz and was commissioned into the 10th Hanoverian Jäger Battalion in 1908. Guderian's exposure to technology began early, with his being selected for detached duty to a telegraph battalion (1912–1913), but his education and career prospects leapfrogged when he was selected as the youngest officer of his cohort for general staff training in Berlin. The outbreak of the First World War, however, interrupted these studies and he had to serve as a provisional general staff officer until early 1918, when he was sent to Sedan, France, on an abbreviated month-long general staff course. Guderian passed his exams and was admitted to the elite officer corps of the German army, an achievement which only added to his already burgeoning self-confidence. As Guderian later recalled, 'I felt capable of mastering any task which the future might hold in store for me.'[3]

Guderian's appointments during the war reinforced his affinity with technology. He served as a signals officer first with the 5th Cavalry Division and then with the Fourth Army. From the outset, Guderian witnessed the futility of men against fire with his division being badly mauled at the first battle of the Marne (September 1914). Later, at the first battle of Ypres (October–November 1914), Guderian began to lament the army's loss of mobility, an experience dramatically reinforced in the attritional struggle he later observed at Verdun (1916). Guderian also served as an intelligence officer and was among the first to recognise and embrace the use of aeroplanes to gather information and survey enemy positions.[4] The appearance of British and later French tanks was, however, another matter. Guderian does not appear to have shown any special interest in these new weapons, which reflected both their lack of early success and their general dismissal among the German high command, who initially saw them as a mere novelty weapon.[5] Of course, that changed for Guderian after the war and while he was not the much-lauded 'father' of armoured operations, he did play a key role in their development and use in Germany. The interwar debates in which Guderian engaged did not always reflect his foresight and prudence. He bitterly opposed a more general mechanisation of the army to support armoured operations, believing his panzer forces alone would suffice to win wars. He also dismissed the new artillery assault gun (*Sturmgeschütz*), which would prove so cost effective and efficient in the coming conflict. Beyond any strategic decisions, Guderian's rash personality and fiery temper did much less to advance the cause of the emerging *Panzertruppe* than his immediate superior Lieutenant-General Oswald Lutz. Although Guderian's post-war memoir claimed the limelight, it was in fact Lutz's more measured and calculating approach that succeeded in establishing Germany's panzer forces as a strong and coherent branch of the Wehrmacht by the late 1930s.[6]

Erich Hoepner was the son of a Prussian medical officer who attended the Kaiserin-Augusta school before admission to the Schleswig-Holstein Dragoons Regiment in 1905. From 1911 to 1913 he was a regimental adjutant and qualified for general staff training in the same cohort as Guderian. Hoepner's training was also incomplete at the outbreak of war in 1914, but he secured an appointment as the first orderly officer to the Ia (the first general staff officer) of the XVI Army Corps. This exposed him to the complex workings of a high command

and Hoepner even performed secondary duties for the Ib (supply officer), which sufficed for him to be admitted into the general staff as early
as 1915.[7] Although Hoepner enjoyed a relatively safe staff position, he
seized opportunities to move up into the frontlines. In one of his surviving letters from the First World War, dating from February 1916, he
wrote: 'We crawled around in the [underground] positions and sapped
for 5 hours. The French [underground mines] blew up twice while we
were there. In the second blast, I was just in the front position and
suddenly flew against the wall [...] It's a mean warfare, 25 mtr. under
the earth.'[8] Clearly, Hoepner exemplified the 'hands-on' style of command that was a hallmark of the German military tradition. In the
autumn of 1916, Hoepner was transferred to a new post on the general
staff of the First Army and then in 1917 to the Seventh Army. Being even
further to the rear, Hoepner had less and less contact with the front, but
in the summer of 1918 that changed when he became the first general
staff officer (Ia) of the 105th Infantry Division and remained in that
position until the end of the war.[9] Like Guderian, Hoepner served the
entire war on the Western Front, which helped convince many such
officers that Germany's most worrisome enemies were the Anglo-French
powers.

In the interwar period Hoepner served on the general staff of the
cavalry inspectorate in Berlin and then, from 1923, he was on the staff of
the 1st Cavalry Division. Although the cavalry has been simplistically
framed as a recalcitrant service, dismissive of reforms, Hoepner was
a progressive voice increasingly seeing horses as a means for rearward
transport, not forward combat.[10] Hoepner was still a captain at the
beginning of 1926, but rose seven ranks in fourteen years, which speaks
to the rapid expansion of the army under Hitler, but also to Hoepner's
military acumen as well as his embrace of opportunities under National
Socialism.[11] In the interwar debates over armoured doctrine, motorisation and resource allocation Hoepner was at best tangentially involved.
He was strongly committed to the concept of movement over fire, which
he saw as the quintessential lesson of the First World War, but this was
hardly a controversial view.[12] Hoepner, perhaps wisely from a career
perspective, kept his head below the parapet of factional wrangling and
concentrated upon his command appointments. In a twist of fate, his
command for the invasion of Poland in 1939 was at the head of the XVI
Army Corps, the same corps he had served in at the beginning of the
First World War.

Rudolf Schmidt's family included a proud (Bavarian) military heritage on his mother's side, while his father was a high school principal. Schmidt finished his schooling in 1905, graduating with outstanding grades, and the following year he joined the army as part of the 3rd Hessian Infantry Regiment 83, based in Kassel. Schmidt demonstrated an interest in technology and his natural aptitude was rewarded in 1911 with an assignment to a telegraph battalion. This experience proved to be formative for Schmidt and just before the outbreak of the First World War he found himself on the staff of the telephone detachment of the 1st Reserve Corps, which would find itself serving on the Eastern Front against Russia. Schmidt took part in both the German victories at Tannenberg (August 1914) and the first battle of the Masurian Lakes (September 1914). Schmidt's performance was rewarded in April 1915 with command of the telephone detachment of the 1st Landwehr Division, and then in October of the same year he became the adjutant of the telegraph department within the Twelfth Army. All of this experience was accrued on the Eastern Front and it was not until April 1916, when Schmidt received the joint command of the telegraph and telephone detachments of the Guards Corps, that he transferred to the Western Front. Here he experienced the Allied offensive on the Somme, which demanded the constant movement of German reserves as well as the coordination of artillery fire support, placing a huge burden of responsibility on Schmidt and his men. His proficiency led to a short appointment on the staff of the chief of the field telegraph service within the Supreme Army Command. This lasted from April to June of 1917 and was followed by a succession of appointments that finally exposed Schmidt to more general duties within a command staff. He was first on the staff of the 28th Reserve Division and then, from January 1918, worked within the intelligence section of the XIV Reserve Corps. Schmidt had been due to start his general staff training at the War Academy in October 1914, but the war ended that opportunity and he had to wait until he received a place at the abbreviated short-course in Sedan. This finally took place in September 1918, and he qualified in October. Schmidt was then posted to the command of the Fourth Army, but in the dying days of the war as revolt broke out in northern Germany, Schmidt was sent to Hamburg at the head of a battalion, presumably to restore order.[13]

After the war Schmidt returned to staff positions in communications, rising in 1931 to chief of staff of the Signal Inspectorate in the

Reichswehr ministry. Despite no armoured background whatsoever, Schmidt's reputation as a forward-thinking and highly adaptable officer saw him placed in command of the 1st Panzer Division in October 1937.[14] Schmidt belonged to an emergent group of innovative officers embracing technology and motorisation. Moreover, their small number was already wielding disproportionate influence and proving highly effective in shaping army doctrine.[15]

Georg-Hans Reinhardt was the son of a banker. In 1907 he joined the 8th Infantry Regiment 'Prince Johann Georg' of the Saxon army in Leipzig. Reinhardt would be the only senior army commander in Operation Barbarossa to have started his career in the Saxon army. He served mainly in the infantry during his early years of service and was a regimental adjutant by the outbreak of the First World War. Advancing as part of the XIX Army Corps through Belgium and into northern France, Reinhardt took part in the first battle of the Marne.[16] Over the coming nine months the continued attrition of positional warfare took a huge toll on Reinhardt's regiment until in June 1915 it was judged no longer combat-worthy, with one report stating: 'A large part of the troops were in a state of complete physical and mental exhaustion, which manifested itself in fits of crying, anxiety, insomnia and loss of appetite.'[17] Reinhardt's service on the regimental staff may well have shielded him from the worst of these conditions, but the suffering must have been all too apparent. In May to June 1916, he was transferred to serve on the staff of the 58th Infantry Division, before completing his general staff training in July and August of that year. In the autumn of 1916 Reinhardt served in a German logistics unit in support of the Austro-Hungarian Seventh Army in the Carpathian region of South-Western Europe. This new assignment brought him to the Eastern Front and in January of 1917 he moved to Courland, at the other end of the Eastern Front, to serve in a similar role for the 8th Cavalry Division. In September 1917 Reinhardt was transferred back to the Western Front, where he saw out the remainder of the war as the first general staff officer (Ia) of the 192nd Infantry Division.[18]

After the First World War, Reinhardt's service record demonstrated that his skill in command was complimented by a genuine desire to learn. Alongside his military duties he became a 'guest student' at the University of Leipzig, studying history, philosophy and economics. His passion for education led to formal teaching roles within the army, first as an instructor of tactics at the Ohrdruf infantry school, and then, from

1927, as part of the T4 department of the *Truppenamt*. Reinhardt taught military history and army tactics for four years with outstanding results. His willingness to embrace new ideas made him a natural fit for the pioneering clique that were pushing for both the modernisation of the army and the incorporation of new weapons and doctrines. Reinhardt joined the *Panzertruppe* in 1937, serving first under Schmidt in the 1st Panzer Division, before securing command of the newly created 4th Panzer Division in 1938.[19]

As diverse as their early experiences were, there was in fact much more that united the future panzer generals than there was that divided them. Exploring this nexus between individuality and institutionalisation is one of the key considerations of this study. Each of the five chapters of this book explores a different thematic area. The first chapter critically considers the letters themselves and asks questions about their veracity as historical sources. This chapter does not just probe the information provided within the available correspondence, but points to the noteworthy absences they disguise. Importantly, this chapter, as well as the study generally, also considers the unique collection of letters written by Guderian's wife (Margarete) in 1941. This is the only known surviving collection of letters from a general's spouse, offering a contrasting viewpoint to the generals and revealing a woman who both conforms to and confounds the National Socialist ideal of womanhood.

The second chapter explores the private 'inner' world that the correspondence represents, asking fundamental questions about the core beliefs and priorities of the generals. It pertains to external events, such as their conception of command responsibility in the new war in the East, but also to their personal role within their families as loving husbands and fathers. It considers who these men were individually and how they responded emotionally in the face of ever mounting pressures. The chapter is an attempt to get beyond the well-known veneer of the German panzer generals as tough, self-assured military professionals. While their reputations and achievements no doubt formed an essential part of their self-conception, they still experienced doubts, fears, hopes and longings. With so much riding on their shoulders during Operation Barbarossa, the question becomes how these men coped, or did not cope, with the awesome weight of responsibility.

The third chapter deals with the public side of holding high command, which reflects the fact that the generals were very much popular figures, not just for the tens of thousands of men who directly served under them, but for the wider German nation. It explores the extent to which the generals were aware of their public standing and the degree to which they prioritised and propagated this to advance their own self-image and career prospects. Indeed, the concentration of time and energy that the generals directed towards their representation in the media as well as their jostling for awards and promotions leads one to the conclusion that their behaviour, and even their military decisions, was to some extent affected by the pursuit of celebrity.

The fourth chapter deals with the criminal aspect of the war in the East and how that is dealt with, or silenced, in the letters. Using a wide variety of sources and studies, the chapter is partly concerned with establishing the degree of culpability each of the individual generals has, but also considers how each man reconciled his participation in a genocidal war with a self-conception of being good, righteous and moral. In fact, the act of writing to their wives and being lovingly connected to, and validated by, a non-military world functioned to maintain the requirements of the 'righteous self', which social psychologists emphasise as fundamental to emotional equilibrium, even when perpetrating or participating in violent acts. Analysis of language, presentation, context and justification provides one set of insights, while the exclusion of many topics, and the crimes in which they are known to have taken part, suggests an awareness that their behaviour was aberrant and contravened accepted moral values.

The fifth and final chapter in this study looks at the military campaign as represented in the correspondence. This probably represents a more familiar aspect of the men under discussion here, but the fact that there is so much detail about the 1941 campaign that has been overlooked in available histories makes it a valuable discussion. The candour and openness of the panzer generals discussing their operations in such detail make a mockery of the strict secrecy ordered by the army, but whatever the imprudence of such disregard for military security, the result offers invaluable perspectives on the operational history of Barbarossa and Typhoon. Moreover, the command disputes, both among the generals and with the high command, reveal the agenda-driven politics of individual commanders, which in many respects reveals the corrupted culture of the *Panzertruppe*.

This study is first and foremost about the four men who achieved panzer group/army command during 1941 and directed some of the most significant battles in the German invasion of the Soviet Union. During the course of the Second World War the number of men who reached the senior ranks of the *Panzertruppe*, men who obtained the rank of General of Panzer Troops or above, came to fifty-eight. Yet beyond their service records only a handful of them left private papers from which we might better understand their wartime role and view of events. If we took a much larger sample size and included every active service army officer who reached the rank of Major-General or above, we would be dealing with some 1,858 men. Yet for the vast bulk we know little to nothing about their wartime service and have simply no documentation to reconstruct how they individually made sense of the war. Clearly, therefore, personal letters from four of the most senior German commanders all active in the same service and at the same time in the war are rare.[20] We can also then consider the value of these letters beyond what they tell us about the men who wrote them. Indeed, the analysis of 'ego-documents' has long encouraged a broader utility than the narrow sub-set of individuals who wrote them. As Kaspar von Greyerz noted: 'For all practical historical purposes, what we are looking at in self-narratives are primarily persons in their specific cultural, linguistic, material and, last but not least, social embeddedness.'[21] How the panzer generals privately understood and represented the new war in the East tells us much about how Hitler's officer corps coped with the pressures of command, rationalised violence, justified losses and conducted manoeuvre warfare.

1 THE LETTERS OF THE PANZER GENERALS

After eighty years of intensive historiography surrounding the personalities and actions of leading German military commanders, any new study must be able to present its readers with something original. This is especially true for an author who has already written at length about generals in the context of Operation Barbarossa. Yet an expert knowledge of a subject as well as the available literature is the best starting point for identifying new material. The panzer generals' private letters are a unique and remarkable set of documents. My past operational studies had captured the men in uniform in stark focus, but much less so the men beyond the uniform. Previous biographical studies had largely failed to make good use of the letters and the opportunity was suddenly presented both to record what I had found and, in a sense, to complete, or at least complement, my earlier work on the German panzer operations in the East. The letters capture a human dimension to directing the Eastern campaign. They address very real fears, doubts, hopes and motivations, little of which is ever found in official records, and yet it is instrumental to explaining the actions and behaviour of individuals. Moreover, having a group of men to compare allows one to determine what is simple personality and what is better explained by institutional culture or the ethos of the *Panzertruppe* command.

Validity, Veracity and Verification

Importantly, there has never been a substantive study of the panzer generals' letter collections. Despite their seemingly obvious importance, they have seldom been used in historical studies of Operation Barbarossa, although they have been cited in a number of biographical works. There are two related problems that have militated against use of the letters. First, any scholarly study of Operation Barbarossa confronts the imposing problem of source material. The *Ostheer* (Eastern Army) in 1941 fielded more than three million German soldiers, generating tens of thousands of historical records that make true expertise in this area a more ambitious claim than for any other theatre of the Second World War. The paper trail is simply immense, and while every military historian is forced to impose limits on what they can reasonably access, a scholarly study of the Eastern Front forces an even more judicious approach to primary material. This alone should not preclude study of the generals' letters, but it has been compounded by a second problem. Most of the letters were written in *Kurrentschrift*, sometimes referred to simply as 'old German script', a handwriting form based on late medieval cursive writing. Individual letters of what we know as the Latin alphabet were formed differently. Indeed, some might be thought to emanate from a completely different language. Making matters worse, *Kurrentschrift* is only an umbrella term. In practice different German states, and even regions within states, taught their own unique variants of cursive handwriting with widespread differences. It was only in 1911 that a single uniform handwriting script was introduced in the state of Prussia, which was slowly adopted throughout the rest of Germany, becoming mandatory for every school curriculum in 1935. Even this new standardised *Sütterlinschrift* would be sufficiently foreign to most present-day Germans for it to be unreadable, and it was only in 1941 that another nationwide reform adopted what today is identified as handwriting based on the familiar Latin alphabet. In short, without specialist training and a lot of practice, reading cursive handwriting in the *Kurrentschrift*, which the German generals learned in their youth, is exceedingly difficult.

For this study I had all of the letters transcribed from *Kurrentschrift* by a professional palaeographer (Daniel Schneider) and then had the results checked by a second palaeographer who is also an historian (Dr David Hamann). The exceptions to this were Reinhardt's letters, which had already been transcribed using a typewriter without the original letters being available to consult. Once the letters of Guderian, Hoepner and Schmidt had been transcribed, I worked with a professional translator and historian of National Socialism (Dr Alex J. Kay) to translate them. Schmidt's letters were translated separately (by Dr Madeleine Brook).

While historians of Germany's 1941 campaign in the East have typically overlooked the generals' letters, biographers have shown more interest, although the results have not always advanced our understanding and, in many respects, have only further entrenched post-war mythologies. In the early 1970s the British historian Kenneth Macksey was the first to seek access to Guderian's letters, contacting his son Heinz Günther Guderian. Heinz Günther was Guderian's eldest son, who followed in his father's footsteps and became an officer in the Wehrmacht, ending the war as the operations officer of the 116th Panzer Division. Macksey himself had been commissioned in the Royal Armoured Corps for service in the war, and the common ground that the two men shared allowed them to strike an immediate chord. Macksey was given access to Guderian's private papers and in return he allowed Heinz Günther to read and comment upon his drafts.[1] Not surprisingly, Macksey's 1975 biography closely followed Guderian's own narrative as established in his 1952 memoir *Panzer Leader*. Importantly, however, Macksey's discussion of the Barbarossa campaign was limited to just thirty-three pages, and his use of Guderian's letters was limited to a handful of favourable excerpts. The result was an idealised portrayal that only perpetuated Guderian's already towering mystique in the Anglo-American world.[2]

Research for the first German-language biography of Guderian was under way even before Macksey's book appeared. Written by Karl J. Walde, it appeared in 1976, with Walde also having access to Guderian's letters through Heinz Günther. Like Macksey, Walde forged a warm relationship with Guderian's son, no doubt encouraged by the tremendous admiration Walde felt for his subject. Indeed, according to Walde, Guderian's picture hung 'not just in the barracks of the West German *Bundeswehr*, one found it in the military halls of all Europe, America and Asia'. Walde's advocacy was followed by the insistence that his biography would 'capture the whole Guderian critically', but then Walde conceded: 'It is based on his memoir, the credibility of which is proven.'[3] Guderian's letters are therefore treated as a confirmatory tool for Guderian's own post-war reconstruction of events, rather than a unique set of documents that reveal far more about the man behind the wartime propaganda and post-1945 embellishments.

In a somewhat different category is Dermot Bradley's 1986 *Generaloberst Heinz Guderian*, which offered a more scholarly treatment of the subject, but one that still divorced Guderian's military achievements from his political, moral and criminal activities.[4] Bradley's focus on Guderian was also linked to his investigation of the 'origins of modern Blitzkrieg', which meant the emphasis was overwhelmingly on the pre-war period, with just ten pages devoted to Guderian's participation in Operation Barbarossa.[5] Guderian's letters constituted the backbone of the primary source material, but Bradley's limited analytical engagement and neglect of archival verification (where it would have been possible) granted Guderian's claims far too much scope within the text.

The best biography of Guderian is Russell A. Hart's 2006 addition to the Potomac Books 'Military Profiles' series.[6] Hart offers a clear-sighted depiction of Guderian, making excellent use of the available contextualising literature. The only limitation is the formulaic scope of the series, which restricts authors to a succinct 120 pages of text. Accordingly, Hart's coverage of the Barbarossa campaign was squeezed into thirteen pages, meaning that, while the book remains a candid and insightful portrayal, it provides no coverage of Guderian's wartime correspondence.

Relative to Guderian, the wartime activities of Hoepner, Schmidt and Reinhardt have been the subject of much less attention, but each of them has been the subject of a German-language biography. The first was by Heinrich Bücheler, who made liberal use of Hoepner's letters for his 1980 study, but the result only served to confirm the author's agenda for writing the book.[7] Bücheler saw Hoepner as a German war hero and dedicated anti-Hitler conspirator. The violent aspects of Nazi policy in the East and Hoepner's role in them are nowhere to be found in his study. Not surprisingly, Hoepner's letters were selectively read and interpreted, rendering Bücheler's biography of limited use.

Rudolf Schmidt only became a panzer army commander at the very end of 1941, following Guderian's dismissal. He started the Barbarossa campaign as a panzer corps commander in Panzer Group 3 and progressed to command of the Second Army in November. His German biographer Klaus Woche incorrectly assumed that Schmidt's wartime letters had been seized and destroyed by the Gestapo, but this oversight is symptomatic of the book's poor research and apologist narrative.[8] Even though the book appeared in 2002, when a much more critical literature about the Wehrmacht and its senior commanders had emerged, Woche simply ignored scholarly critiques. The result was not only a flattering portrayal of Schmidt, but Woche's determination to present the Wehrmacht in the best possible light led him to ignore evidence of criminality and cast the Germans as victims of Allied bombing and Soviet terror.[9]

The only biography of Reinhardt was written by Christoph Clasen and appeared in 1996.[10] Clasen's comprehensive 720-page text made liberal use of Reinhardt's private letters, citing them at length. He also engaged directly with Reinhardt's National Socialist affiliation and post-war conviction for war crimes committed in the Soviet Union. There is no attempt to isolate or idealise Reinhardt's military career, making it a valuable and underutilised biography.

The only study to make use of all the generals' letter collections was Johannes Hürter's majestic 2006 study *Hitlers Heerführer* (*Hitler's Army Commanders*), which unfortunately has never appeared in English.[11] This encompassed twenty-five of Hitler's leading generals in the East throughout 1941–1942.[12] The research and analysis are impeccable, but the number of subjects necessitated a very wide lens, meaning that the panzer group/army commanders, and especially their letters, could not be given particular emphasis or attention.

The intention of this study is to place the generals' private letters in the foreground and consider these documents as a unique source not simply to chart the momentous events under way, but to consider how and why the panzer generals behaved as they did. Importantly, unlike later generations of wartime generals, who might well suspect that any 'private' letters or records would one day enter the public record, there is little suggestion that the panzer commanders wrote with such ideas in mind. Allowing for the exception of Reinhardt's personally transcribed collection, the authenticity of the letters and the fact that they were not written with a view to any future historical purpose provides a view of the generals that moves us beyond wartime representations or post-war justifications. That the letters served as an ostensibly private outlet for the generals' thoughts and emotions underscores the importance of the collections.[13] Even one of Reinhardt's letters candidly admitted: 'Outwardly, I do not lose my composure and I also retain my faith in victory, but inwardly, I wrestle with myself and suffer.'[14] Clearly, there was a dichotomy between the public and the private self, which the letters capture. Yet, while the letters provide many tantalising private insights, we must be mindful that the generals still intended to project a certain self-image, albeit a less guarded one. Notions of early twentieth-century German masculinity cannot be ignored and appear, to varying extents, as a constant theme in both what was expressed and how it was represented. For example, after Reinhardt's open admission of inward suffering, he quickly qualified his remarks with the reassurance: 'In no way should my letter create the impression that I am subdued or that we are failing or despairing.'[15] Maintaining an appropriate disposition before his wife, even in the face of his evident anguish and pain, was clearly essential.

Reinhardt's letters have been available the longest, having been donated to Germany's Military History Research Office (*Militärgeschichtliches Forschungsamt*) in 1962, a year before the general's death.[16] Hoepner's letters were not donated to the federal German military archive until 1983, some thirty-nine years after his death. The donation of Schmidt's collection of letters took until 1999 and Guderian's until 2001. Previous to these donations researchers had to gain family permission, which appears to have affected the conditions of use.

While the authenticity of the letters raises few concerns, this is not to say a degree of manipulation has not occurred. We must consider that individual letters may have been destroyed or at least withheld from the public record to avoid incriminating the generals or tainting their post-war image of honourable and decent men serving in a 'clean' Wehrmacht. To determine if this was the case, I averaged the frequency of each general's correspondence for 1941 and checked this against the individual dates of letters in order to identify behaviour patterns and therefore any anomalous irregularity. Guderian wrote his wife thirty-one letters between 27 June and 16 December, which overall equates to an average frequency of five and a half days between letters. Yet, when one checks the actual dates of his letters, unexplained gaps appear. In September, for example, there is a conspicuous gap of seventeen days between his letters of 8 and 25 September. There is another gap of twelve days in late August and two further periods of ten days between letters. On the surface none of this need raise particular suspicion; there could have been numerous explanations that do not involve a suggestion of wilful manipulation. If we focus on the seventeen-day gap in September, Guderian was no doubt busy conducting the final stages of the Kiev encirclement, but there had been plenty of frantic periods previously in which the general had studiously maintained his correspondence. It is also noteworthy that in his letter of 25 September, Guderian made no attempt to excuse or explain his unusually long absence from writing. This is because Guderian had in fact written to his wife at least once during this seventeen-day period, but no trace of the letter exists in the general's personal papers that were donated to the archive. The reason we know Guderian wrote in this time is a letter in reply, from his wife Margarete, on 19 September thanking him for his letter 'of the 13th', which had arrived that morning.[17] Not only is there no letter from Guderian from 13 September; there is none in his collection written on the thirteenth day of any month. So what happened to this letter? Clearly, it was received by Margarete in Berlin and she was saving his letters. The Guderians were not subject to the usual delays in postal communication between the Eastern Front and Germany (often four to six weeks) because, like a lot of the senior commanders, they used privileged connections in the Luftwaffe to ferry their letters.[18] In fact, when Heinz wrote his letter on 25 September, he had already received Margarete's last letter from 19 September, written just six days before.

Whatever may have happened to Guderian's letter from 13 September, we can at least confirm that the panzer general's public collection is not complete and that the other long gaps in his correspondence strongly suggest that this is not the only example. If letters were deliberately excluded or destroyed (as opposed to simply being lost), it seems a reasonable hypothesis that they contained information that Guderian or his family wanted to suppress. In fact, on three occasions in 1941 Guderian included separate letters from third parties that he thought would interest Margarete, but on each occasion, he instructed her to destroy them after reading. For example, on 31 October he wrote: 'I'm enclosing a letter from Hirtenlein, which will interest you and which you should please destroy.'[19] There is never any mention of why these letters should be destroyed, but it shows Guderian was clearly sensitive about certain information.

A simple explanation might be that Guderian wrote about sensitive military matters, which even for everyday soldiers was strictly forbidden according to censorship rules, but this seems highly unlikely given that all four of the panzer generals flouted such regulations in letter after letter. In theory, letters were bound by the 'Ordinance on Communication', which was published on 12 March 1940 and stipulated that information was subject to secrecy regulations in six key areas, the most important being number 1: 'Distribution of information on army matters which are subject to secrecy'.[20] This required soldiers to withhold all specific details of their service, such as the composition, size and location of their units, the names of superiors and comrades, and information related to equipment and arms, military intentions and combat losses.[21] Indeed, one of the things that makes the correspondence of the panzer generals so fascinating is just how much confidential military information the generals shared with their wives (as will be explored in Chapter 5). Any one of the letter collections would have been a goldmine for Allied intelligence, but the generals, whose letters were excepted from censorship checks, clearly did not consider this a risk. If Guderian was not therefore worried about sharing military information, then what was it that proved so sensitive and potentially compromising?

Apologists might speculate, on the basis of Guderian's post-war claims, that he was perhaps destroying incriminating evidence of supposed anti-Nazi views, but, as this study will demonstrate, Guderian (and his wife Margarete) were committed National Socialists. While purely speculative, it is not unreasonable to consider that Guderian was sharing some form of information about Germany's killing programme in the East (a subject he also chose to exclude from his memoir). Such a hypothesis may also fit with the period of time in which Guderian's correspondence becomes noticeably sparse. Between 18 August and 25 September Guderian's public record includes just three letters for the entire thirty-seven-day period, well below his usual average. In this same period, post-war statements from members of *Einsatzgruppe B*, the SS killing squads operating in Guderian's rear area, identify mid-August as the point when they received instructions to mass murder entire Jewish communities.[22] By the end of October *Einsatzgruppe B* had already murdered 45,467 Jews.[23] Senior army commanders were no doubt aware of what was happening in their rear area; if Guderian communicated any of this information to Margarete, especially if the framing suggested a justification or even endorsement, the whole post-war image of Guderian would have been ruined. Of course, this is pure supposition, but it is hardly an implausible hypothesis, given Guderian made antisemitic remarks even after the war.[24]

Hoepner's collection of letters contains the same anomaly. Hoepner wrote his wife Irma thirty-one letters between 23 June and

23 December 1941, giving him a statistical frequency of one letter every 5.9 days of the campaign. Yet in November the collection has only three letters, with a notable break of twenty-two days between 5 and 27 November. Hoepner's letter from the 27th also confirms the incomplete inventory of the archival holdings. The letter opens: 'Tomorrow, an air force officer on my staff is flying to Lötzen. I want to quickly use the opportunity to send my regards and pictures to you, although I wrote only the day before yesterday.'[25] Needless to say, there is no letter from Hoepner on 25 November. There are no letters from Irma to gauge her response, but if she had not received the letter her husband had referred to, she would presumably have mentioned this to him. Yet nowhere in Hoepner's subsequent correspondence does the general respond to a missing letter and the personal couriers that they used meant letters were much less likely to disappear on route. Thus, it seems likely that this letter did indeed reach Irma, which again raises the question of why it was not included in the public collection. Indeed, even with knowledge of a letter written on 25 November, there was still an unusually long gap of twenty days since the previous known letter. Moreover, the statistical average of one letter every six days is only based on letters we have in the collection. The more letters, the higher the frequency of correspondence, making interruptions of the length that we see in November all the more conspicuous.

In Reinhardt's case, the fact that he did not submit his original handwritten letters, but rather a typed document purporting to be his wartime correspondence, poses its own problem. This may simply have been to reduce the problems of reading his handwriting, but we cannot ignore the potential this poses for manipulation. Importantly, a close reading of Reinhardt's letters against wartime records does not suggest that the available content has been falsified, but his periodic use of ellipsis makes clear that choices were made about what content was included. The general absence of any intimate exchanges with his wife or discussion of family matters suggests one likely aspect of Reinhardt's edits. This is by no means conclusive, though, given that Schmidt's handwritten letters are likewise completely devoid of personal remarks towards his wife. Since Reinhardt expunged details, even if only personal exchanges, it still reduces the overall value of his collection. Encouragingly, however, the last letter Reinhardt wrote before the beginning of Operation Barbarossa derisively asserted that the Soviet leaders were 'very Jewified'.[26] Such a flagrant characterisation not only reveals Reinhardt's penchant for antisemitism, but also that his post-war editing was not beyond the inclusion of such revealing, even if prejudiced, remarks.

While Reinhardt's letters concentrate mainly on military matters, subjecting the available collection to the same analysis of statistical frequency suggests further significant anomalies. Reinhard wrote thirty-four letters between 26 June and 31 December 1941, which on average equalled one letter every 5.1 days, but in practice the dates of Reinhardt's correspondence are extremely uneven. On nine occasions he wrote a letter the very day after having written, on four occasions he wrote after just two days and eight times the interval was three days. Thus, two-thirds of all his letters are written in close proximity to each other, while at the other end of the spectrum large gaps appear, the longest being a twenty-three-day break from 24 October to 16 November. Nor did Reinhardt's letter from 16 November offer any explanation or apology for the supposed interruption in his correspondence. Moreover, there are further gaps of sixteen, fourteen and two of thirteen days, suggesting a number of possibilities: Reinhardt's commitment to personal corres-pondence swung rather wildly, the demands of command dictated his haphazard results, letters were simply lost or, finally, not all letters were included in the submission to the archive.

Schmidt's collection of correspondence is unique in that many of the items he sent to his wife may not have been conceived as conven-tional letters. At the top of numerous letters, Schmidt prefaced the date with the words 'Report from' (*Bericht vom*), implying he saw the correspondence more as a record of what had happened in the campaign than a letter addressed specifically to his wife. Importantly, not all the letters are prefaced in this way and some of them do veer much more into the personal realm. Schmidt's letters are also on average much shorter than the other collections. In a few cases they consist of only a sentence or two. As Schmidt, however, explained in one letter early on in the campaign, 'things are not propitious for long letter-writing'.[27]

Statistically, Schmidt's correspondence was the most frequent, with an average of one letter every 4.8 days, but the collection started almost a month into the campaign on 21 July and ended on 29 December, condensing his thirty-three letters into a shorter period. Once again, however, the actual dates of the letters suggest there may be gaps in the available correspondence. After not writing anything for the first twenty-nine days of the campaign, Schmidt sent his wife Fridel a short letter on 21 July and then seemingly waited a further twenty-two days before writing again. From that point onwards Schmidt's correspondence markedly increased, with four letters in August, six in September, eight in October, six in November and nine in December. The first letter in Schmidt's archival collection was in fact to Guderian's wife Margarete requesting Heinz's field post number (without which one could not send letters on the Eastern Front). This letter was dated 14 July, whereas his first letter to Fridel took until 21 July. Although it may seem curious that Schmidt found time to write to Margarete Guderian (and wanted to write to Heinz) before his own wife, the explanation appears to be that Allied air raids on Münster, where the Schmidts had their family home, had forced Fridel to flee the city and stay with her cousin in Leipzig.[28] This is important context as it could plausibly explain the absence of letters from Schmidt in the summer of 1941.

Part of the problem in establishing details about these collections of letters is the lack of information surrounding them. The German authorities did not take the opportunity to ask why these collections were being donated, or whether they were complete, or to gather any other context about them. Perhaps letters were lost by the family, or some were purposefully withheld for personal reasons. Attempting to learn further details through the families has yielded nothing. Heinz Günther Guderian died in 2004 and while I was able to meet with Guderian's grandson, Jürgen Grub, before his own death, he was not even aware of the existence of his grandfather's wartime letters, let alone able to offer any further details about them. Schmidt had no children, and no descendants from Hoepner or Reinhardt's families could be located (or when contacted, opted not to reply).

While the correspondence sent by the generals constitutes the central focus of this study, there is another collection of letters that offered vital context. Margarete Guderian is the only one of the wives whose own letters to her husband were also made available to the archive. There are only thirteen letters spanning 31 August to 29 December, which, thanks to her husband repeatedly referencing the arrival of her letters, we know is only a fraction of what she sent to him.[29] Nevertheless, hearing from Margarete offers all kinds of important context for understanding Heinz, but also for the rare insight gained into the world of a leading German general's wife. Illuminating Margarete's unique relationship to the events under way in the East and considering to what extent wives were participants, rather than simply passive observers, offers further context for understanding the role of the family in Nazi Germany, especially among elites. Unlike the wives of soldiers, women like Margarete were privy to much more sensitive information and offered feedback on this, thereby becoming part of the conversation. Knowing something about how they engaged with their husbands, what advice they gave and how that might have sustained the men and impacted events is hardly of peripheral importance. Moreover, while there can be no generic characterisation of a general's wife based on Margarete alone, her letters offer at least an impression, filling something of the void left by the absent letters of Eva Reinhardt, Irma Hoepner and Fridel Schmidt.

The five letter collections studied here are directly comparable for the second half of 1941, given it is in this period that they all offer substantial contributions and are writing in relation to the same military campaign. Hoepner's letter collection begins in August 1939 and ends with his dismissal at the start of 1942 (his last letter dates from 4 January 1942). Schmidt's letters, on the other hand, only begin in July 1941 and continue to his own dismissal in early 1943. Guderian's collection of correspondence spans 1939 to 1944, but the Barbarossa campaign boasts more letters than the rest of the war put together. For example, there are no letters from 1942, only two from 1943 and three from 1944. However, Guderian's collection includes considerably more letters prior to Barbarossa, with eight letters from 1939 and nine from 1940. Similarly, the bulk of Margarete's letters date from 1941, with just three from 1940, none for 1942–1943 and nine for 1944. Reinhardt's collection spans the longest period, beginning in September 1939 and ending in January 1945, but June–December 1941 constitutes his greatest volume of writing as compared with any other six-month period of the war.[30] As a result, the role of the panzer generals in Operation Barbarossa, while not the exclusive focus, forms the principal backdrop for this investigation.

2 THE PRIVATE GENERALS

For all the drama, distinction, poise and posturing attributed to the German panzer generals, they were, at the end of the day, still men. As such, they were also complicated individuals. At times the sterling confidence of the well-crafted propaganda images reflected a reality. These men exuded a remarkable self-confidence, while accepting an unusual degree of risk both in the direction of their forces and in their own personal exposure to the enemy while visiting forward areas. Yet this is the much propagated, and sometimes exaggerated, side of the coin. Their willingness to accept so much risk was in no small part driven by a very real fear of failure, which in the Wehrmacht was typically understood to be a failure of command, whatever the odds or tangible realities. Commanders were expected to seek solutions, battle through adversity and find a path to victory. It was the firebrand, go-getter ethos of the *Panzertruppe* to break all resistance and impose one's will upon the enemy. Subordinates who questioned objectives or expressed doubts were seen as dubious command material. Not surprisingly, this fed a culture where few voiced reservations, no matter how well-founded. It also meant that as military assets diminished and resources dwindled, the prospect of failing to achieve objectives loomed ever larger as 1941 progressed. This placed a very personal degree of stress on German commanders, which has largely been obscured by the absence of source material concerning their private experience of the war.

Embracing Family and War

The confidence exhibited by the German generals was not just a product of army culture, but a reflection of the Wilhelmine society in which they came of age. Here purposeful, brave and determined men were considered the bedrock of a strong and healthy society.[1] Yet German masculinity also encompassed chivalrous ideas of discipline, virtue, devotion and gallantry, which in Prussia's hierarchical society encouraged careers in the military.[2] This military conception of masculinity did not change under National Socialism, but the tolerance for any deviations certainly did. As Lisa Pine has argued, the Nazis promoted 'an ideal type of masculinity, which sustained a hierarchical relationship, particularly conforming to norms of male dominance patterns'.[3]

The generals were therefore confirmed in their authority not only by their uniforms and ranks, but also in society and family life. The acceptance of their roles becomes abundantly evident in Margarete's first letter to Heinz.[4] Here she cautiously approached the topic of warfare and was suitably self-deprecating in addressing Heinz's professional role as a general: 'I dare not allow myself to think too much about the events of the war, above all not about the infinitely great tasks you are repeatedly given to solve in the war zone.'[5] Margarete's letters typically focused on family and home life, but in order not to ignore Heinz's persistent discussion of his day-to-day exploits, she delicately engaged with the military component, careful not to overstep her position by assuming any kind of remedy for his complaints. Her engagement with the military sphere was almost always determined by Heinz; he established the subject-matter and Margarete simply responded.[6] She even at one point explicitly described her support for Heinz as being 'the purpose and aim of my vocation as a woman'.[7] In this sense they both shared a sense of duty around separate, but clearly defined, gender roles. As Margarete viewed it, she was simply performing the obligations of a wife on the home front, which in no small part was connected to her letter-writing. As she wrote to Heinz in December: 'The fact that I give you joy and can help you with my love in difficult times, even when we are separated, gives me comfort, even in my loneliness, and spurs me on to continue living for you and to make you happy.'[8] As a 48-year-old woman in 1941, Margarete's letter-writing was not only directed towards supporting her husband in the East, as many other women were doing, but also towards supporting their two adult sons, Heinz Günther (born in 1914 and referred to as Heinzel in the letters) and Kurt (born in 1918 and referred to as Kurti in the letters).

Unfortunately, none of Margarete's correspondence with her sons is available, but from her letters to Heinz it is evident that she wrote to them often and worried constantly about their well-being. Heinz too cared about their welfare, but seemed to show much less interest in their day-to-day lives. His first mention of his sons came only after three weeks of the campaign, in his fifth letter of the war. The short reference at the end of the letter read only: 'Hopefully, you have good news from the boys.'[9] A week later he repeated this hope and then, remarkably, on 24 July, Heinz wrote to Margarete requesting that she send him the respective field post numbers of both boys, without which a letter could not be delivered within the German army.[10] Heinz casually played down the request, remarking offhandedly: 'I, of course, didn't write them down.'[11] This confirms that Heinz had not written to either of his sons since the beginning of the campaign and possibly some weeks before that, when he had last left Berlin. In fact, the impetus to write to his sons seemed only to have come after Kurt sent his father a congratulatory telegram for the award of the Oak Leaves to the Knight's Cross (which was announced on 17 July).[12] Even once Guderian had received the field post numbers for his sons, there were only two occasions throughout the remainder of his 1941 correspondence when he explicitly made reference to having written to one of his sons. Perhaps not surprisingly, therefore, Guderian seemed not to have received as much post in return as he might have liked. In a letter from 24 October, Guderian complained to Margarete: 'Please write me a long, kind letter with some good news from you and the boys, who don't get in touch. I hope they're well.'[13] While Guderian's panzer group was deployed in the middle of the Eastern Front as part of Army Group Centre, his sons served in the two neighbouring army groups. Heinz Günther served as part of Panzer Group 1 in Army Group South and Kurt in the Eighteenth Army belonging to Army Group North. To Guderian's mind, their areas of deployment were greatly preferable to his own; as he assured Margarete, 'both boys are experiencing interesting sections of the war and are getting to know an interesting region of Russia. There is little variety here in my area.'[14]

Figure 2.1 Heinz and Margarete Guderian at home in Berlin in 1940

One may wonder if Guderian's somewhat detached relationship from his sons was a symptom of his high rank and demanding position, although his numerous letters to Margarete and other free-time activities suggest that he simply did not prioritise the correspondence. Perhaps, therefore, Guderian's behaviour simply reflected a different generation in father–son relationships, one in which Guderian's limited contact was in fact unremarkable for its time. Yet there is an analogous contemporary to compare Guderian's behaviour against. Hoepner had two children, Joachim (born in 1913 and referred to as Achim in the letters) and Ingrid (born 1917). Like Guderian's sons, Joachim was serving on the Eastern Front in 1941 as part of the Sixth Army in Army Group South. With Hoepner's panzer group advancing northeast into the Baltic states, Hoepner lamented the distance between them, as he wrote to Irma on 30 June: 'It's a shame that his [Joachim's] division didn't retain its earlier function. Then I would already have been able to visit him.'[15] Unlike Guderian in this early period, Hoepner displayed a constant concern for Joachim's well-being and in nearly every letter remarked on the absence of post from his son. By the end of July, Hoepner made enquiries of an officer from the Army High Command (OKH), about the delay in receiving post from the southern part of the front.[16] In mid-August, in spite of having heard that Joachim was well, Hoepner began routinely using his connections in the high command to acquire news about his son. He even went so far as to contact the Sixth Army directly to request (and receive) telegrams personally from the chief of staff, Colonel Ferdinand Heim.[17] As Hoepner admitted to Irma, 'this kind of thing is not welcomed by the divisions. There is a general lack of friends in this war.'[18] Nevertheless, in stark contrast to Guderian, Hoepner displayed a significantly greater emotional investment in his son's activities and well-being, even to the point of improperly exploiting his position to gain whatever information he could.

Schmidt was childless and Reinhardt had two daughters (Eva Gisela born in 1920 and Eva Rosemarie born in 1922). Yet because many high-ranking German officers fostered long family traditions of military service, Guderian and Hoepner were hardly unique for having sons serving on the Eastern Front in 1941. There was also a sincere desire on the part of many young officers to serve in combat roles, rather than in staff or rear positions, despite the well-known dangers. In fact, a considerable number of high-ranking officers lost sons in the East, with the earliest example being the well-publicised death of Hans-Georg Keitel, the youngest son of the commander-in-chief of the Wehrmacht, Field Marshal Wilhelm Keitel.[19] On the same July day that Hans-Georg Keitel fell, Guderian reported to Margarete that the son of his comrade, General of Infantry Gotthard Heinrici, commander of the XXXXIII Army Corps in Army Group Centre, had been seriously wounded. The young man had been shot three times through his arm, chest and thigh, on which Guderian observed, 'hopefully the young lad will pull through.'[20] Less fortunate was the son of Lieutenant-General Horst Stumpff, the commander of the 20th Panzer Division, who, Guderian noted, was killed in July.[21] Schmidt's nephew was badly wounded on 17 July and as a result had lost his left arm.[22] Despite the apparent dangers, both of Guderian's sons had purposely sought combat duty, but, at least initially, were to be disappointed. Having seen first-hand the losses, especially among junior officers within his own panzer group, Guderian wrote to Margarete at the end of July:

> Perhaps it was a gift from heaven that our boys had to remain during precisely these weeks in positions that do not fully satisfy them. They are so young and the war will certainly last long enough for them to have the opportunity to distinguish themselves. Perhaps you can comfort them with that thought. It's their right to be dissatisfied with their current lot, and a good sign of their soldierly disposition.[23]

Interestingly, Guderian defers the communication of his 'comforting thought' to Margarete. It is also noteworthy that he judges the war to last long enough for them to see plenty of action.

Hoepner's son was to be transferred to a new position right before Barbarossa began, which only added to his father's concerns. 'He'll hopefully end up somewhere where he advances swiftly', Hoepner wrote to his wife on 30 June.[24] Subsequent letters suggest Joachim was in a 'forward' position as his father continued to gain information through his contacts in the high command. 'According to the last report of the OKH', Hoepner wrote to Irma on 26 August, 'Achim's division is now on the move, the advance party, to which he definitely belongs, is advancing towards Chernobyl in the lower Pripet [Marshes].'[25]

There can be no question that Hoepner and Guderian were concerned about the safety of their sons, but they also understood and accepted combat as an essential element of what Guderian referred to as the 'soldierly disposition'.[26] Thus, their letters oscillate between fatherly concern and professional pride in their service. In one letter from 24 September, Hoepner recounted the latest information on Joachim's activities in the field to Irma: 'Achim must have participated in the encirclement of Kiev from the Pripet [Marshes] via Dnieper, Desna and Yahotyn to the south [...] If he made it through alright, he'll have experienced a great thing. That would be really lovely after the prior efforts and disappointments.'[27] In Hoepner's mind there was clearly no consideration that weeks of combat might result in serious non-physical wounds, rendering Joachim's experience something other than 'a great thing'. When Guderian's oldest son, Heinz Günther, was finally given a combat command in November, Guderian wrote to Margarete of his satisfaction: 'I'm very pleased that Heinzel has received a command with the riflemen. It's the precursor to the general staff training.'[28] Guderian clearly saw this as a necessary means to an end for his son's military career, but the enhanced danger of this new assignment was not lost on him. 'Hopefully, he'll return safely from this undertaking [...] The smart boy [...] will certainly make a good general staff officer. The transfer in June was the right thing for his military development, even if he couldn't immediately see it himself.'[29]

It is clear from both generals' letters that they were subtly crafting careers for their sons, which by the end of 1941 led successfully to both Joachim and Heinz Günther obtaining prized staff positions, although not necessarily in accordance with each boy's own desires. In early December, Hoepner exploited his connections within the Army Personnel Office to discover that Joachim was slated for 'special assignment' and would serve as a first orderly officer, the right hand of the first general staff officer.[30] There is no evidence that Hoepner was unfairly influencing this process, but the general's name and standing within the army as well as the fact that he was making direct inquiries of a man named Bassewitz, who was himself compiling the final list of assignments, certainly suggests at least an indirect pressure to advance Joachim's case.

Guderian's letters offer no evidence that he improperly engaged in any administrative machinations on behalf of Heinz Günther; he certainly did not allude to contact with the Army Personnel Office or any other influential figures. Yet, as discussed, Guderian's letters to Margarete only infrequently mentioned his sons, which in itself suggests a somewhat more detached interest in them and their careers, at least relative to Hoepner. With little forewarning, and only a month after having received his new command with the riflemen, Heinz Günther was suddenly ordered to Berlin to begin general staff training in January. For a young man wishing to prove himself at the front, his reassignment left him deeply resentful. As Margarete wrote to Heinz on 17 December: 'I'm expecting Heinzel in the coming days; he wanted to depart on 15 December; his replacement had already arrived. He [the replacement] had been adjutant of 36 Panzer [Regiment, belonging to the 14th Panzer Division] and is now ranting just as much as Heinzel about his transfer.'[31] While Margarete knew it was not what her son wanted, she wrote Heinz of her 'endless joy' and began excitedly making Christmas plans. 'I'll then at least have one of my three beloved warriors with me.'[32] When Heinz Günther finally did arrive on 24 December, his anger had not abated and Margarete wrote nervously to Heinz, 'He looks fresh and well, though the difficult situation is really tormenting him inside and he is devising some remedy.'[33]

As men who had committed their lives to professional military service, it is not surprising that Hoepner and Guderian accepted that their sons would have to endure a certain exposure to danger in order to build a successful career in the army. At the same time, while Margarete lamented the hardship of separation from her menfolk, in none of her letters did she question the war itself, in spite of her closest kin being directly exposed to its many dangers. With Heinz supportive of the war and, at least initially, confident of Germany's success, one might conclude Margarete was reluctant to express any doubt in his judgement. As we have seen, her sons were also very eager to prove themselves in combat, especially with the name Guderian, which not only carried a military pedigree, but in Nazi Germany was already a name of household celebrity. Even without a very public profile, males in the National Socialist state were not only expected to serve out of a sense of national obligation and duty; enduring battle had become a powerful social proving ground of manly virtue, a rite of passage not only extolled in propaganda, but internalised and validated among males themselves. As René Schilling has described the prevailing sentiment: 'Men "belonged to war", because here was the place where the "defiant, hot, wild daring manhood" could prove itself.'[34] Margarete's sons were therefore driven to war by everything from state compulsion and social expectations to long-standing family tradition (Heinz's father, Friedrich Wilhelm Guderian, had himself risen to the rank of Lieutenant-General in the army). Beyond such cultural, social and family pressures, the sons of senior generals were probably extra-sensitive to any perception of 'special treatment', which unfairly advanced their careers and denied them their place as true war heroes who earned their pedigree among 'real men' at the front.

Margarete's willingness to support her menfolk in wartime was not, however, a reluctant act of powerlessness or passive acceptance determined by a subordinate gender role. Far from having any supposed stereotypical compulsion to protect her family above the requirements of the state or service to the army, Margarete took the opposite view and rejected such a protective instinct almost as if it were a selfish act. To her mind, duty in wartime, as a self-respecting German citizen and proud wife and mother, meant enduring adversity, hardship and sacrifice. The pain of separation and potential for loss were to be lamented, but borne. The confluence between front and *Heimat* was something Margarete strove for, as she wrote to Heinz in November: 'With the greatest sympathy, we are thinking of you in terrible, wintry Russia and we are grateful and ashamed that we are permitted to have a nice, warm, well-kept home here.'[35]

Margarete was not labouring under an imposed burden that took her husband and sons away from her; her burden was one that she understood and accepted, which may have made it somewhat more bearable. Nor was she naïve about the dangers. In a letter from 26 October Margarete related news to Heinz from their youngest son as a newly promoted lieutenant:

> Kurti was able to successfully take action during a breakout attempt by the Russians in front of Leningrad and he took forty prisoners with his platoon and counted thirty dead. It will be very gratifying for him that the Russian campaign has given him the opportunity for deployment accordingly, after all. May God keep him in good health. Heinzel's friend, Falkenberg, has been killed in action as a company commander in front of this city. Spanke in the same place, too.[36]

Given his close proximity to danger, Margarete eagerly awaited Kurt's letters, so when she had not heard from him for over a month by early December, she wrote to Heinz about the absence of post. Yet Margarete did not dwell on the subject, nor engage in any unfounded speculation about his well-being; in fact, her only comment on the matter was that 'perhaps the post was lost'.[37] In the same letter to Heinz on 4 December, she was also able to report that Heinz Günther was safe and well, having survived the German retreat from Rostov. This was somewhat curious given that the city was occupied by the Germans on 20 November and lost in a Soviet counterattack eight days later.[38] Thus, Margarete had information about her son which was, at most, six days old. While it is not impossible for a letter to have reached the family home in Berlin in that time, it would certainly have been highly unusual, prompting the question of whether the Guderian family, like the Hoepners, were the recipients of privileged information, especially given that Heinz Günther, unlike Kurt, belonged to the *Panzertruppe*. As Margarete explained to Heinz, 'I breathed a sigh of relief at the news of Heinzel's well-being; the evacuation of Rostov made me worry for him, as he had just written with delight about the conquest and I knew he was there.'[39] Yet the best illustration of Margarete's resilience to the dangers her sons confronted came from a letter Kurt addressed to his brother, which curiously was sent not to Heinz Günther's field post number, but rather to the family home, perhaps in the expectation that his mother would relay the letter as a faster alternative. This letter arrived on 17 December and was the first news from Kurt that Margarete had received since early November. 'I accidentally opened it', she wrote to Heinz, 'so happy was I to finally receive post from him.'[40] The contents of the letter must have made for shocking reading, which Kurt may not have anticipated would be read by his mother. Yet Margarete's description of these events appears remarkably nonchalant; even though she did express concern for Kurt, she appeared astonishingly unperturbed by the horrific conditions and mortal dangers to which her son was exposed. Writing to Heinz on 17 December, Margarete reported:

> Our young debutant [a reference to his promotion to lieutenant] has endured heavy fighting and we must be thankful to fate that he has survived it in good health. His unit is deployed near [. . . illegible], which is being attacked by the Russians with strong forces. Kurti writes: 'We had occupied a strategically important village; to our right and left, there were open hollows of 10 km and woodland all around, in some places right up to the outermost houses. Here, we were subjected for several days to a fantastic barrage and air raids, [. . . illegible], tank assaults, etc. Completely surrounded, three days without food, low on ammunition, vehicles shot to pieces, we were finally thrown out. One-third losses. Fifty per cent of my motorcycle platoon, thirty per cent of the scout platoon. In the past days, all houses were burned down, so that we were only able to dwell in foxholes etc.'
>
> The Russians blew up his vehicle with armour-piercing incendiary projectiles, so that all his belongings are burned. A great situation for our poor boy to be in. Hopefully, he'll receive warm things; such circumstances are worrying in the freezing cold. May God grant me that he remains healthy and in one piece; the deployment he so longed for has now become very tough.[41]

Perhaps even more surprising than her calm depiction of Kurt's situation is that the letter then pivots into lengthy discussions of utterly mundane family news, as if Kurt's exertions hardly merited much further thought. Her letter continues: 'Aunt Leni's visit was very nice, though it revealed in the long run an overly great bond with the other relatives. Too much was left undone and I felt very tied up. Aunt Leni will spend Christmas with Aunt Annie, so she won't be alone, either. Her departure – with a window seat – went smoothly.'[42] While no definitive conclusion may be drawn, what appears to be a parallel representation of the extraordinary and the mundane might simply illustrate the successful integration of war and *Heimat*. Another perspective might suggest that Margarete was 'performing resilience' by deliberately exhibiting composure in the face of adversity.[43] After all, role models presented by the regime to women like Margarete offered imposing examples. Annemarie Mölders, the mother of the celebrated fighter ace Werner Mölders who was killed in 1941, had also lost her husband in France in the First World War. She had two other sons, one of whom was already a prisoner of war and the other was serving at the front. After so much pain and loss she, nevertheless, offered herself to women as an example of stoic resilience, telling her audiences 'that man stands under a different law than does woman. And [...] so it must be. And [...] it is good so. As long as the world exists, woman will hate war and love the warrior – precisely because the best warrior is also the best man.'[44] The message was clear – if Annemarie Mölders could stand tall after all she had been through, what self-indulgent woman, who had lost no one, dared to fret over the mere prospect of loss?

Margarete was a devoted wife and mother, but she was also a proud German, which in times of war, as Nazi propaganda repeatedly extolled, trumped any individualistic impulse. War demanded sacrifices and that was never questioned in her letters, nor was it cause for an overly emotional response. Hitler himself glorified women who 'with iron discipline entered into the fighting German community'.[45] Gudrun Schwarz's study of an idealised SS wife suggests notable parallels: 'As "hero mothers" they should raise the offspring for the heroic fight, strengthen their men and sons in their enthusiasm for fighting and war, send them proudly and consciously into the fight.'[46] Far from the war being an exclusively male preserve, women were an integral part of the national struggle and were expected to play their own part. Even when Heinz Günther returned home at the end of the year, Margarete rejoiced for the time they could share together and, as she wrote to Heinz, '[I] can talk to him about the events of the war.'[47]

Of course, only Margarete's letters are available for study, so it is impossible to form a picture of how the other generals' wives might have compared, but in Hoepner's case one thing can be observed. His son also faced considerable danger on the Eastern Front and yet at no time did he write to Irma consoling her about the pain of separation or reassuring her about the heavy losses, which could not be hidden on the home front because of the proliferation of death notices in newspapers.[48] Even without a son in the war, Schmidt's letters are likewise devoid of explanation to his wife about the necessity of sacrifice, presumably because Irma and Fridel never wrote seeking reassurance or expressing concern because they, like Margarete, understood the war and did not give in to doubts or unbecoming emotional displays.

Reinhardt's letters to Eva, however, provide a contrasting example, which acts to further confirm the strength of social mores demanding universal support for men in wartime. It would appear Eva had written to her husband expressing profound concern for his well-being during visits to the front, which prompted a thinly disguised rebuke. Writing his reply on 4 October, Reinhardt's letter concerned itself solely with this matter and included no other topic or news. His tone was for the most part gentle, but the point was firmly stated. The letter opened: 'My dear should not worry too much about me. [...] I know, after all, that I do not have a cowardly wife and I am happy and grateful [for this] from my heart.'[49] The clear implication being that any fears associated with a 'cowardly wife' would be unacceptable, which is why he also reassured her that this was not the case. The statement was a clear admonishment as well as a reminder of the kind of behaviour he expected. This was followed by an explanation for why a general had to be seen at the front. That Reinhardt was having to explain himself and justify a military matter to his wife seems also to have been a source of some frustration. As he pointed out: '"Checking that everything is all right" and "helping out at the front" or, if necessary, "bucking them up" is my duty!'[50] There could be no question about a wife standing in the way of a senior German officer's duty, especially in times of war. Her role was not to question his behaviour, nor allow any self-indulgent fears to add to his already grievous concerns. As Angelika Tramitz observed of the traditional officer's code of conduct: 'Maintaining control over oneself and others in every conceivable situation was part of the self-image of the strong-willed officer.'[51] As the wife of a senior general, Eva was part of a privileged elite whose behaviour reflected upon her husband and whose position demanded that she maintain herself in a socially appropriate manner. The fact that subsequent letters from Georg-Hans to Eva did not revisit this issue suggests the point was well taken.

Body, Mind and Soul

While Guderian and Hoepner's sons faced profound danger as junior officers on the Eastern Front, one might assume that command of a panzer group or panzer corps was a comparatively safe assignment. At least in the modern era, generals should rarely be exposed to personal risk in warfare, not because they are not brave men, but because their loss jeopardises a great deal institutionally, intellectually and psychologically to an army. These considerations should have been no different in the Wehrmacht, but throughout the Second World War the German army suffered heavy losses even among its senior leadership. Some 342 German generals died during the war, with 214 of these being killed in combat or missing in action (presumed dead). Another fifty-eight died of natural causes, twenty-five of accidental death, twenty-five of suicide and twenty were executed.[52] The emphasis on forward command naturally accounted for the heavy losses among junior officers;[53] however, such was the cult of the offensive within the Wehrmacht that even the most senior officers can be seen to have personally exposed themselves to danger at the front, even to the point of leading local attacks.

Perhaps the most revealing instance of a senior German commander exposing himself to danger comes from a letter written not by one of the panzer generals, but by Field Marshal Walter von Reichenau, who commanded the Sixth Army in 1941. Writing in September during the battle of Kiev, Reichenau related his role in an attack on a Soviet position, explaining:

> I put speed into 44 Infantry Division's attack by personally leading the assault by 5 Infantry Regiment. I led the assault for three kilometres, quite literally not only with the first wave, but as the leading man in it. Enemy resistance was very stubborn, their mortar fire being particularly severe, and the only way we

could avoid it was to advance just as fast as we could. We
repeatedly passed through disintegrated groups of the enemy,
until I spotted some high ground some three hundred metres
away and made for it.[54]

The idea of a Field Marshal leading an infantry attack might say something about the élan of the German officer corps, but it is an equal
indictment of the imprudence of Reichenau himself. Whatever may have
been gained, the risk – not only of death, but the potential for capture and
interrogation – can hardly have been justified for a local tactical success.
Throughout the German army there was no service that valued such high-
risk forward leadership more than the *Panzertruppe*, which propaganda
stories routinely celebrated and thereby reinforced. Indeed, of the twenty-
seven German corps commanders killed in combat during the war, half
were in command of panzer corps.[55] In his post-war memoir Guderian
related a story in which his convoy was stopped by Soviet infantry firing
on the main road between Rozana and Slonim. The attempt to dislodge
them had proven unsuccessful until, as Guderian's account continued; 'I
joined in this action and by firing the machine-gun in my armoured
command vehicle succeeded in dislodging the enemy from his position;
I was then able to drive on.'[56] Guderian makes no mention of this action
in his letters to Margarete, which is not in principle cause to doubt the
story, but one wonders if his seemingly decisive personal intervention was
somewhat overstated. It was not the only attack Guderian claimed to have
taken part in. During a visit to the 17th Panzer Division at the end of
August, Guderian wrote: 'I went up to the front line, where Rifle
Regiment 63 was attacking, and participated in a part of their attack on
foot.'[57] In a separate incident the following day, a meeting with fellow
officers was suddenly subjected to Soviet shelling, resulting in five
wounded, including a major who had been sitting next to Guderian. 'It
was a wonder that I remained unhurt.'[58] Guderian mentioned the wound-
ing of his officers in a letter to Margarete, but without any details,
especially his own proximity to the event, which could be understood as
shielding Margarete from unnecessary worry.[59] Colonel Karl-Henning
von Barsewisch, the senior Luftwaffe officer at Panzer Group 2, confirmed
in his diary that Guderian did indeed participate in frontline action. At the
battle for Roslavl, Barsewisch noted that Guderian led the attack from the
lead position of a panzer division, and, as he approvingly observed: 'That
probably says it all!'[60]

In Reinhardt's letters to Eva, he tells of being so far forward that he was watching his tanks assaulting into Soviet positions and yet the fact that he did not lead the attack himself was almost something he felt he had to address: 'I would have most liked to have placed myself at the forefront of my panzer regiments and hurtled into the city yesterday, but I of course didn't do it; reason prevailed; we have to wait, because no one knows how the Russians will conduct themselves.'[61] Forward command did not have to include personal participation in attacks to constitute a danger; indeed, the pervasive combat environment, even at points well behind the front, was fraught with peril that did not spare the panzer generals. As a translator on Hoepner's staff wrote after the war: 'I was ordered to see Colonel-General Hoepner in a village near the front. In order to orient the situation, the generals repeatedly exposed themselves to personal danger.'[62] On only the second day of the war, Hoepner's chief of staff, Colonel Walter Chales de Beaulieu, decided that the panzer group command staff needed extra security and so he requested and received a platoon of Waffen-SS soldiers. As Hoepner wrote to Irma, 'Beaulieu is afraid for me.'[63]

Such concern was not unwarranted. Reinhardt, as one of Hoepner's two corps commanders in Panzer Group 4, wrote to Eva: 'The "higher-ups" haven't a clue [...] the daily fighting at the front, the uncertainty of being shot at from behind as well as from the side from bushes and woods, etc.'[64] Indeed, such was the danger of movement for senior commanders in the East that when Allied propaganda at the end of June incorrectly reported that a senior German panzer general had been captured, many believed this might be Guderian.[65] Schmidt, who was a long-standing family friend of the Guderians,[66] was initially unsure if the news was true, but once disproven he wrote a letter to Margarete in July telling her of his relief. 'Today's *Deutschlandsender* report has freed me from the great concern that your husband might have fallen into enemy hands, as the hogwash of the English and Russians of 14 days ago would have it.'[67] Irma Hoepner appears also to have heard the same propaganda broadcast and asked her husband about it; however, Erich had not heard the report and replied to her on 19 July: 'As far as I know, no panzer general has been captured.'[68] However, he then wondered if the report pertained to Schmidt because of a story he had heard about his near capture by the Red Army. As Hoepner explained: 'Schmidt, who received the Oak Leaves, did run into the enemy, but he was able to save himself by crawling through a ditch. The Russians kept his car, his overcoat and his maps.'[69] This experience is not detailed in any of Schmidt's letters to Fridel, but, as noted in the

Introduction, Schmidt's collection of letters to his wife includes very few from the early period of the war.[70] The only letter Schmidt sent to his wife in July did, however, include a passage detailing his commitment to forward leadership. Writing on 21 July, Schmidt told Fridel: 'So far I have always been at the forward-most point of the entire army by a long way.'[71] The risk this posed was illustrated in another letter from September, where Schmidt explained: 'Right now, artillery is firing close to my trailer. 3 fatalities. So I'll have to remove myself to another location.'[72] Without question, forward command brought incalculable benefits in leadership and morale for the *Panzertruppe*, but especially in the early months of the advance when lines were confused and headquarters persistently on the move, the physical risk to the generals remained constant.

Campaigning in the East naturally presented dangers related to the war, but as older men spanning the ages 53 (Guderian), 54 (Reinhardt) and 55 (Hoepner, Schmidt) there were sometimes additional health concerns. Even before the campaign began Guderian had suffered from sciatica, a nerve pain affecting the lower back, buttocks and legs, which caused him periodic discomfort. The condition is typically exacerbated by prolonged exposure to cold weather and, not surprisingly, in December Guderian wrote to Margarete that his sciatica was 'really playing up'.[73] He also had a bad heart, which months after his dismissal from command would lead to 'a complete collapse', which Guderian described as leaving him 'almost totally unconscious for several days'.[74] While his heart trouble is never explicitly referenced in his letters during the campaign, the implications of his condition may be evident in his complaints to Margarete about persistent fatigue. On 12 August Guderian wrote: 'Haven't I become very old? These hard weeks leave their marks on a person [...] Sometimes, I have an enormous need to sleep, which I can rarely satisfy. And yet, in myself I feel completely healthy and – when something happens – fresh and fit, too. As soon as the tension wanes, however, the setback strikes.'[75]

Hoepner had no known health problems prior to the campaign. By early July, however, he wrote to Irma about a painfully swollen leg, which he tried to rest, 'but it's impossible to take it easy.'[76] By 13 July he wrote that the diagnosis was an infection of the veins, which had incapacitated him and was being treated with ice-cold, acetic compresses. After four days of rest, during one of the most important periods of the campaign, Hoepner at last noted improvement and, encouragingly, was told by his doctor that a bandage would need to be worn for three more weeks.[77] Yet a month later the leg had not healed and, feeling frustrated by his restricted movement, Hoepner had given up wearing his bandage. As he explained to Irma on 18 August: 'I couldn't bear it any more in this heat. Underneath, a fungal infection had taken hold on the sole of my foot and, on top of that, blisters, which itched terribly. Yesterday, I was once more on the move the entire day and can therefore hardly walk today.'[78] Clearly, Hoepner was struggling, but after 18 August there is no further mention of problems with his leg, which may have become easier to care for once the summer heat abated and the pace of Army Group North's advance slowed.

Figure 2.2 Erich Hoepner (right) meeting Georg-Hans Reinhardt (left) during Operation Barbarossa in August 1941.

Reinhardt's health was good, but he wrote to Eva about how he suffered on the long car journeys between his units. The air was 'unimaginably dusty' and the ride on the abysmal roads was so wild that he claimed he emerged every time 'soaked to the skin'. Even with excellent driving, Reinhardt wrote on 12 July, 'we passengers are thrown about so much when we drive over potholes that everything in us is jostled about, so that we sometimes think that our intestines will be turned inside out, our backbone sprained, etc., not to mention the fierce heat.'[79] Yet Reinhardt could also joke about such arduous journeys, claiming at one point that they offered free sweating treatments and a strong massage for the entire body. Schmidt's behaviour indirectly referenced the same problem. As a great lover of classical music, to which the radio in his staff car was often tuned, Schmidt would sometimes insist that his car halt while an important piece played so that it might be enjoyed without the disruptive noise of a bouncing automobile.[80]

None of the four panzer generals reported stomach problems from the food available in the Soviet Union, but that is not to say it did not constitute a problem. Field Marshal Günther von Kluge, who is often portrayed as a kind of adversary of the *Panzertruppe* because of his frequent clashes with Guderian, was head of the short-lived Fourth Panzer Army (June–July 1941), to which Panzer Groups 2 and 3 were subordinated. Kluge's only letter from July 1941[81] attributed his recent poor health, which he described as a 'very bad attack', to poor Soviet food. He then explained to his wife Mathilde: 'Very many of my gentlemen had similar [digestive] conditions. The diet is too one-sided.'[82] Not everyone, however, lamented the available food. Schmidt and his officers apparently ate very well, with the general sometimes cooking for himself as well as his fellow officers. Fabian von Schlabrendorff, who attended some of Schmidt's dinners, even recalled: 'He knew the art of cooking like no other.'[83] Perhaps not surprisingly, in contrast to Kluge, Schmidt's letters do not report any digestive ailments during the campaign.

The letters of all four panzer generals reflect another problem that few other sources have discussed in any depth. While it may have been assumed that each of the generals was under enormous psychological strain, it has hardly been possible to measure that in any kind of meaningful way. What we learn from the generals' private letters is that the physical dangers and illnesses that they endured formed only one aspect of the psychological and emotional challenge demanded by campaigning on the Eastern Front. As one might expect, the initial weeks of the campaign were full of hope and optimism. The advance was rapid, Soviet forces were collapsing and victory was believed to be only weeks away. Already in July Hitler was bestowing the laurels of battlefield success, awarding no less than thirteen Oak Leaves to the Knight's Cross, including, as we have seen, to Schmidt and Guderian.[84] The pace of events was, however, beginning to take a toll on the commanders in the field. As Reinhardt wrote to Eva on 23 July: 'I think it's good that we accept and enjoy what a given moment offers us, some more consciously, some less so. Otherwise, we would have trouble coping with the strain, which is considerable as it is, and particularly that which weighs on our minds, the responsibility for the success of the fighting and, above all, for the human lives entrusted to us.'[85] Reinhardt was increasingly distressed by the number of casualties within his panzer corps. This became evident the following month when he wrote a long letter to Eva telling her how important it was for him to know that he was in her thoughts. As Reinhardt admitted, it was his one source of solace, 'especially when I experienced difficult times, when I had to be strong, also when driving past rows of graves tugged so strongly at my heartstrings, or when otherwise splendid commanders and troops threatened to waver'.[86] Such letters reflect the importance of wives like Eva and their role in sustaining commanders in the East. As Reinhardt explained, 'I knew how much I was with you in your thoughts and worries and hopes, and how much you desire our victory. This feeling has accompanied me.'[87] Just like Margarete, one gains the impression that Eva's day-to-day hopes and worries were naturally with her husband, but that she also understood and subordinated those needs to the higher purpose – a shared desire for victory. Reinhardt drew strength from this symmetry of purpose and steeled himself against an emotional outburst that the demands of the campaign constantly threatened to induce. As Reinhardt's letter continued:

> Perhaps it is these times that are most difficult for a leader who takes his responsibilities seriously: how hard the troops fight, how many sacrifices they make, how they then doubt whether they'll reach their objective after all, how some start to get pessimistic and ask themselves whether their efforts will pay off, and then, as a leader, not to go nuts and to bear up and to remain confident and strong, in spite of the most heartfelt compassion.[88]

Reinhardt was clearly witnessing, as well as experiencing, the emotional demands of the campaign: the losses, the suffering and the despair. Subordinate officers were being worn down and some were even questioning what could still be achieved, but Reinhardt, in spite of his sympathy, resolved to drive his men on, refusing, as he saw it, to 'go nuts', remaining 'confident and strong', and dismissing 'compassion'.

The fate of his men also troubled Schmidt, especially since the ethos of forward command not only incorporated visits to the front, but also included the horrors of overwhelmed field hospitals. In only his second letter to Fridel, on 12 August, Schmidt wrote: 'What misery and dreadful injuries you see in the hospitals. And with what patience and bravery the poor fellows bear their suffering. This war here simply cannot be compared with any other, it is so tough and bloody.'[89] It was a similar sentiment that disturbed Hoepner, who already at the end of July openly addressed 'the mental and professional burden of senior leadership'. Here Hoepner confided in Irma the toll that the war was having on him, especially the constant reports of losses, some of whom were well known to him. He took the time to list the deaths of young men from families Irma herself knew and then shared his pain at having to constantly write letters of condolence. Hoepner was not just reporting on sad events, but admitting the grief this caused him: 'I often suffer greatly from it. I'm constantly thinking about the dual task of practical and tactical leadership and the efforts to keep losses to a minimum.'[90]

Guderian too was grappling with the demands of the war in this early period, but did not focus on his men as much as on himself. On 24 July he wrote to Margarete that he longed to return home and leave 'this apathetic and barren land, after all the unpleasantness I've encountered here'.[91] Guderian had no doubt been buoyed by his early success and the public recognition that came with it, but, as his momentum flagged during the second half of the battle of Smolensk, his mood began to change. Part of the problem was Guderian's fixation with his nominal superiors, whom he chose to blame for all the problems he was encountering, although in truth they imposed little upon Guderian and were not infrequently rebuffed or simply ignored. In fact, it was not the growing weakness of Panzer Group 2, the army's strained logistical apparatus or the Red Army's unceasing resistance that were the subject of Guderian's frustration. As he told Margarete in early August, 'Your loving compliments on the Oak Leaves did me good, especially as the gruelling irritations are not yet over, despite my release from being subordinated to

Mr von Kl[uge]. They've now just shifted. I don't know how long my heart and nerves will be able to endure it. Right now, I'm running on empty.'[92] The aforementioned Fourth Panzer Army, which Kluge had commanded, was disbanded in late July, largely because Guderian's intransigence had rendered it redundant, but even so Guderian took exception at reverting to the command of Field Marshal Fedor von Bock as the commander of Army Group Centre.[93] Therefore personalities and strategic differences of opinion were what distressed Guderian at this early stage of the war. The ebb and flow of his operations were also factors affecting his mood. As he concluded a letter to Margarete on 7 August: 'My mood is fluctuating a lot; at present, I'm at a low point.'[94] Just how much the stress of command impacted Guderian's psychological well-being was captured in a letter at the end of August when he wrote: 'My health is good, but I'm otherwise unwell.'[95] Guderian's mental health was in decline and his letters from the autumn and winter would reflect just how far the deterioration would extend.

Managing the stress and responsibility of command consumed more and more effort the longer the campaign dragged on. After all, Operation Barbarossa was supposed to be a summer campaign; there had been scarcely any thought given to an autumn extension, let alone the frightful prospects of continuing into the winter. Thus, the burden for haste and results fell disproportionately on the panzer generals, who responded with one operation after the other, allowing little time to rest, rebuild or resupply their increasingly exhausted formations. It was always a case of having to do more with less, and since the National Socialist ethos emphasised individual leadership above material circumstance, stress became an inescapable consequence of command. On 8 August Reinhardt wrote to Eva:

> I'm still sitting in my omnibus, where I've been since this morning, with few interruptions, consumed by anxiety, tension and worry. [...]
>
> My nerves are of course really stretched sitting here. It's better when I can witness events with my troops and travel with them at the front. But there'll be no driving today; everything is attacking on foot, 'unfortunately' for the most part through forests and trenches, and the situation for us today is so difficult in multiple ways that I personally have to be constantly reachable at the command post, in order to contribute to

decisions of all kinds. Waiting for messages from the front, the ongoing uncertainty, the back and forth of good and bad news – all this was already the most gruelling thing imaginable for me as a general staff officer in the World War.[96]

The helplessness Reinhardt felt passively awaiting the outcome of events explains his vigorous embrace of forward leadership both for its recognised intrinsic merit and also for his own piece of mind in managing, or perhaps even avoiding, the stress of headquarters. What Reinhardt did not address on 8 August was his own role in pushing forward his under-resourced men in an attack on the lower Luga River that initially proved very costly and made little progress.[97] Yet panzer commanders were supposed to be indefatigable and indeed many of their successes were won by slim margins, meaning adversity and opposing odds were no reason to cower from, or call off, attacks.[98] German propaganda certainly never missed celebrating the bold and daring successes the panzer generals won, but the cautionary tale of attempting too much and failing was never publicised, and generals who did this were seldom reprimanded within the army itself.

Figure 2.3 Georg-Hans Reinhardt in April 1942.

Reinhardt's letter from 8 August never questioned his decision to push the offensive forward, in spite of encountering well-prepared defences in thick woods, interspersed with mutually supporting man-made and natural obstacles.[99] Even in the midst of such frantic activity for the panzer corps, Reinhardt's letter to Eva served a tangible function, providing a soothing remedy for the stresses of command. As Reinhardt explained:

> You're perhaps surprised that I'm taking the time to write to you at this length on such a stressful day. I'm doing it because I'm attempting to calm myself by seeking refuge with you in my thoughts, and I'm succeeding. When the waiting for news from the front becomes too long, I distract myself. I don't want to make enquiries at the front too often, otherwise I'll make them nervous or they'll think me nervous. But I'm not, at least not outwardly![100]

Far from the wives of generals being incidental figures serving only as domestic partners in distant Germany, they clearly played a crucial role sustaining and bolstering senior commanders in ways that conventional military histories have not been able to acknowledge. At its heart, Reinhardt's letter confirms the enormous psychological strain generals laboured under and the need they felt to mask this burden from their men, giving a false guise of confidence even in the face of distress. Of course, generals in all wars project a façade of command that is always more contrived than real, but on the Eastern Front this phenomenon was tested to an extreme as Germany's panzer and motorised divisions were whittled down to their barest bones over the course of 1941. This also explains why subordinates often complained that their officers did not understand the real situation at the front, not because the commanders were themselves oblivious, but because they felt inhibited in their reactions and always sought to project a veneer of unshakeable calm and steadfast resolution.

With the panzer generals enduring high levels of both physical and psychological stress, the letters provide some insight into how they coped with such challenges. A common set of beliefs that all four generals shared was their relationship to the Protestant Church and the significance this assumed in explaining their values and behaviour. Germany under Hitler was made up of 95 per cent Christians, and of these some 55 per cent were Protestants.[101] The elite of the German officer corps was overwhelmingly made up of Protestants. This predominance had its roots in the Protestant Kingdom of Prussia, which dominated the German officer corps before the First World War and constituted the birthplace of Hoepner (Frankfurt an der Oder, 1886), Guderian (Kulm, 1888) and Schmidt (Berlin, 1886). Reinhardt was born in the likewise predominantly Protestant Kingdom of Saxony (Bautzen, 1887). Indeed, in 1907 only some 16.6 per cent of German officers were Catholic, which not surprisingly predetermined an enduring dominance of Protestants in the German high command of the Second World War.[102] While one might assume a natural opposition between the Protestant Christian faith and the realities of wartime Nazism, the generals' letters reflect no hint of confusion or contradiction in that regard. All four generals alluded to God in their letters, sometimes in moments of open reflection, but also to buttress their periods of dejection and melancholy. Indeed, references to God in their letters show a remarkable increase as the year progresses. During the first fourteen weeks of the campaign (from June to the end of September) there were only nine separate mentions of God, but in the following nine weeks (October and November) this rose to thirteen references. Most remarkably, however, in December alone, when the harsh winter conditions took hold and the Soviet counter-offensive began, the number of references jumps to seventeen. This suggests an anecdotal correlation between adversity and religious motivation, a trend that parallels the decline of Germany's fortunes in 1941.

In order to ascertain the role and importance of religious belief among the generals we must look at context. While references to God are common to all of the letter collections, the devotion to faith was much less conspicuous in letters written by Hoepner and Schmidt. Both thanked God on a number of occasions, but less as explicit references to deeply held beliefs and more as simple turn of phrase. For example, in July Hoepner wrote to Irma: 'The heat has been unbearable for the last eight days, 30° in the shade, 48° in the sun. Thank God that we've found ice here.'[103] Similarly, on 27 November he wrote: 'We're advancing, thank God.'[104] Such casual allusions to God are instructive because they artificially inflate the number of recorded references without seriously engaging with the idea or meaning of faith. More to the point, Hoepner, unlike the other generals, never engages in anything more substantive. There is no further discourse on the importance of God or his faith, which, given the emotional demands and unrelenting pressures of the campaign, is suggestive of Hoepner's diminished faith or perhaps lack thereof.

Schmidt, by contrast, is somewhat more ambiguous. In his small number of letters from the early months of the war Schmidt made just one reference to God when, after a period of wet weather had ended in August, he noted simply 'thank God'.[105] Infrequent and cavalier usage would seem to fit with Hoepner's indifference, yet Schmidt seems to have fallen back more and more on his faith as the war dragged on and his position became steadily more desperate. Fighting against superior Soviet forces at Tikhvin in November, Schmidt for the first time included an explicit appeal to God's providence and good grace. After tallying the formidable Soviet forces arrayed against him Schmidt concluded, 'These will be difficult days. God willing, they will be successfully overcome.'[106] Later in the hard winter fighting, after detailing to Fridel his lack of strength and the impact of the cold weather, he concluded: 'It isn't easy ... But, God willing, it will come right.'[107] In such a context it is impossible to differentiate between a literal and a figurative meaning in Schmidt's mind, but importantly the references to divine intercession only appeared once the material strength of his forces had sunk so low that the enemy threatened to overwhelm him.

If Hoepner and Schmidt exhibited a more circumspect relationship to their faith, the letters of the Guderians and Reinhardt attest to far stronger religious feelings. Yet here too one can observe a progression both in the aggregate number of references to God and in the increasing earnestness of those discussions. In fact, throughout the summer months none of the generals engaged in a substantive discourse about God or their faith, rendering their portrayal of the German advance essentially a secular affair won exclusively through strength of arms. Unlike later periods, God was evoked neither to aid victory nor in gratitude for it. Yet as the campaign dragged on and the conditions worsened, Reinhardt found himself reflecting more and more on his faith and writing about it to Eva. At one point in early October, he implored her to follow his lead and 'trust, like me, that dear God will protect us, just as he has protected us thus far'.[108] In a later letter from December he opened with an unreferenced citation: '"When the need is greatest, God's help is nearest to you!"'[109] Clearly, in the midst of increasing hardship, Reinhardt sought the consolation and reassurance he found in his faith. Reinhardt again embraced his faith in 1948 when he found himself on trial for war crimes, gathering character witnesses who attested that 'he derived all his energy from his deep, profound belief in God'. This, the court was told, accounted for his 'irreproachable conduct' and 'chivalrous attitude'.[110]

Guderian also fell back on his faith in difficult times, although his writings reflect a somewhat more utilitarian use. As a general, Guderian had a well-earned reputation for ruthlessly exploiting any opportunity to gain scarce resources for his hard-pressed panzer group and later panzer army.[111] Perhaps not surprisingly, therefore, when the Soviet winter offensive opened in December Guderian turned to God for his army's deliverance and he appealed to Margarete to do the same: 'Pray to God that He preserves our army, our brave young German men, and that He spares us the fate of Napoleon and his soldiers.'[112] There is no question Heinz and Margarete were devout believers, with Heinz investing a perhaps surprising faith in divine providence despite his reputation for being a modern, self-reliant panzer general. Already in September he wrote: 'Only God now knows whether our task can be achieved,'[113] and he followed this in November by observing, 'How things will turn out, God only knows.'[114] Yet Guderian's recalcitrant character and often fraught relationships with higher authority even extended to chiding the Almighty when he felt unduly affected. Once the seasonal rains came in October, beginning the biannual *rasputitsa* (literally translated as 'quagmire season'), an event which was entirely predictable, Guderian reacted to the occurrence as if it were a malevolent act of divine intercession. Writing to Margarete on 11 October, Guderian complained, 'God has played dirty tricks on us.'[115] Reinhardt also felt cheated in this period and on 23 October attributed his lack of success to 'the weather gods with the elements!'[116] Once Army Group Centre resumed its offensive in November, Reinhardt repeated his assessment, writing to Eva on 19 November: 'We were the first to set off again, after the weather gods had forced us all to stop.'[117] The fact that the autumn rains were anything other than a miraculous event suggests that the generals were taken somewhat by surprise and, not for the last time, underestimated the impact of the Russian climate on their operations.

By comparison with Heinz, Margarete made more frequent reference to God in her much smaller volume of letters. In particular, she prayed for the protection of her family, writing to Heinz in October: 'I know that you are also closely united with me, and I ask God that this may remain the case and that He will again allow us to experience each other's company in health and peace.'[118] Such heartfelt sentiments also extended to her sons and, while no letters to them are available, she shared some of her reflections with Heinz. 'May God grant me that he [Kurt] remains healthy and in one piece.'[119] Unlike Eva Reinhardt's indiscreet airing of concern for her husband's well-being, which to Georg-Hans threatened the strict protocol of deference and composure expected from wives, Margarete may have more artfully expressed the same sentiment through the guise of prayer. The subtle act of asking the Lord's protection, as against any individual pleading or display of mawkishness, served to express heartfelt concerns, but couched them in a constructive and agreeable manner.

Membership of the Church community formed another pillar of Margarete's social and moral world, which advocated its own expectations of women that Doris Bergen has observed further reinforced a patriarchal order: 'The ideal German Christian wife offered her husband quiet support and respectability.'[120] There could be no question that Margarete adhered to respectable standards and deferred to her husband, but her support for the war effort ran deeper than an imposed patriarchy. Women in Margarete's circle of standing and privilege did not think of the war as a conformist gender issue, even if the conflict was almost exclusively started and prosecuted by men. Quite the contrary, it was precisely because soldiers stood in harm's way, upholding chivalrous ideas of protecting women on the home front, that wives and mothers owed their love, devotion and ceaseless support to their men in uniform. Margarete could scarcely conceive of warfare creating a rift between herself and Heinz; their separation was simply a necessary evil that could end only with victory. The Church, state, army and wider German society offered no framework to conclude anything else.

Whatever degree of faith the generals retained, it is worth considering what vision of Christianity they embraced. How did they reconcile their devotion to a religion that grew out of Judaism and espoused core principles of love and goodwill with the imperatives of a tyrannical regime that embraced murderous antisemitism?[121] The largest Protestant church in Germany was the German Evangelical Church, comprised mainly of the three major theological traditions that had emerged from the Reformation: Lutheran, Reformed and United. Most of Germany's forty million Protestants were members of this church, although they also provided the membership for newer groups like the radical German Christian Movement.[122] The latter was a predominantly Protestant organisation with some 600,000 members that relentlessly campaigned for a so-called 'racially pure' church. Indeed, these self-styled 'storm troopers of Christ' explicitly targeted perceived Jewish influences on Christianity in virulently anti-semitic church publications and public campaigns. In addition to drawing upon early Christian theological antisemitism, the movement also sought to highlight the visceral antisemitism of Martin Luther, who described Jews in language similar to that later used by Hitler, thereby adding a degree of legitimacy for pro-Nazi Protestants. Importantly, the movement's message and influence extended well beyond its limited membership and helped, according to Doris Bergen, 'to fuse Christianity and National Socialism' because 'the German Christians articulated a task that faced every Christian who accepted Nazism as legitimate.'[123]

For the panzer generals this was an essential point in reconciling their faith with National Socialist aims, especially given the kind of war being waged in the East. None of the letters offer a word of contradiction, or suggest any hint of moral conundrum, between faith and Germany's war of annihilation in the East. There is no known connection between any of the generals and the German Christian Movement, but the organisation's success was in blurring traditional church teachings to promote 'Aryan Christianity' and provide institutional support for National Socialist ideals, especially antisemitism. Of course, the German Christians were opposed within the Protestant movement by a dissenting alliance known as the Confessing Church who opposed any assimilation of the individual Protestant churches into a uniform 'Reich church'.[124] This led to the so-called 'church struggle' (Kirchenkampf), but the debates were based on theological disputes rooted in alterations the German Christians were making to biblical text, liturgy and catechism.[125] As Wolfgang Gerlach has documented, the Confessing Church did not seek to resist attacks on Jews, and indeed his research exposed their own anti-Jewish writings.[126] Not surprisingly, therefore, supporters of National Socialism and antisemites could be found on both sides of the church divide, with Doris Bergen concluding that 'the differences between the German Christians and many of their fellow Protestants were never very great after all.'[127] Thus, far from being any kind of institutional corrective or moral counterpoint to the worst excesses of Nazism, the Protestant Church instead provided the panzer generals with a reaffirming confirmation of their loyalty to the state as well as the righteousness of their religious convictions.

The Protestant Church was also vocal in its support for the war effort, releasing a public statement a day after the invasion of Poland that highlighted its identification with Hitler and the armed forces:

> The German Evangelical Church stands in true fellowship with the fate of the German people. The Church has added to the weapons of steel her own invincible weapon of the Word of God: the assurance of faith that our people and each individual is in God's hand, and the power of prayer which strengthens us in days of good and evil. So we now unite in this hour with our people in intercession for our Führer and Reich, for all the armed forces, and for all who do their duty for the fatherland.[128]

Devout Christians were therefore expected to be supporters of the war, offering the generals confirmation of their faith and affirmation – or even celebration – of their service. Moreover, the message of the German Christian Movement may have appealed to military men given their fondness for martial symbolism and a soldierly orientation. At public events the German Christians incorporated flags, marching formations, slogans and popular wartime rhythms and songs, while the language and imagery went so far as to depict physical violence, but always respectful of the heroic and noble German.[129] Accordingly, the army high command's overwhelming Protestant majority could hardly have hoped for a better ecclesiastical champion. The German Christians offered a new aggressive Christianity, uniting Germany against its foes, and no enemy was more despised than the Godless Bolshevik in the East.[130] Whatever exactly the panzer generals made of their divided Church is left unanswered by their wartime letters; however, the issues shaping perceptions of the war in the East provoked no controversy for Protestants and, if anything, offered a subject upon which they could unite. Indeed, the reopening of Soviet churches during Barbarossa gave the campaign a sense of religious liberation.[131] The communist foe was unequivocally reviled for his atheism, which a telegram to Hitler on 30 June 1941 from Protestant clerics explained:

> You, my Führer, have banished the Bolshevik menace from our own land, and now summon our nation, and the nations of Europe, to a decisive passage of arms against the mortal enemy of all order and all Western-Christian civilisation. The German

nation, including all its Christian members, thanks you for this deed. The German Protestant Church accompanies you in all its prayers, and is with our incomparable soldiery who are now using mighty blows to eradicate the source of this pestilence, so that a new order will arise under your leadership.[132]

For all that is written about the Protestant 'church struggle', the Church remained remarkably united in actively encouraging virulent antisemitism within German society. The new war in the East was portrayed as a struggle 'between the eternal Germany and the eternal Jew'.[133] If faith was a core belief of the panzer generals, the message that the Protestant Church promoted was indistinguishable from the Nazi state, countering whatever moral ambiguity Christians might otherwise have experienced for those with knowledge of the horrific events unfolding in the occupied Soviet territories. German military belt buckles proclaimed 'God is with us' (*Gott mit uns*), which, thanks to the Church, the panzer generals had no cause to doubt and from which, given all the difficulties with which they were confronted, they could in fact draw some solace.[134] The unity of shared purpose was underscored by Reinhardt's letter on 7 December, which expressed confidence despite the fact that his panzer group had become the initial focal point of the Soviet winter offensive: 'I have faith in God and faith in my troops that we will fulfil our mission in spite of all the adversity.'[135]

While the Protestant Church wholeheartedly endorsed Germany's war in the East, the church also legitimised the institution of marriage, which for a German officer of their generation was as much a personal choice as it was a professional arrangement. In the early twentieth century a German officer was to a large extent under the control of his regiment and was not permitted to choose his wife freely. A man had to first obtain a marriage consensus from his regiment, which demanded that any prospective wife meet certain social obligations. Nor were these simple formalities. The social selection criteria for an officer's wife were at least as strict as for the officer himself and it was not uncommon that incompatibility resulted in the tragedy of lost love or an abandoned military career.[136] Erich and Irma Hoepner were the first to marry in 1910,[137] followed three years later by Heinz and Margarete Guderian in 1913. Both wives were lucky not to lose their husbands during the First World War, although Erich and Heinz served mainly in staff positions away from the frontline fighting. Rudolf and Fridel Schmidt married in 1917, but

Reinhardt was still a bachelor when the war ended, despite being in his early thirties. Finding a wife was, however, made somewhat easier by the high losses of men resulting in an estimated two million German women never marrying, which somewhat absurdly was referred to in German society as the 'women's surplus'.[138] Finally, in 1919 at age thirty-two, Georg-Hans met and promptly married Eva.

Maintaining long-distance relationships through wartime was something that the Guderians, Hoepners and, to a lesser extent, the Schmidts had experience in. Letters naturally allowed communication, but to what extent did they serve as a conduit for any kind of intimacy? On one level we have already seen that the generals were prepared to discuss their at times fraught emotional states, which already reveal a level of trust in their correspondence and a willingness to communicate private sentiments. Yet these emotions were almost always tied to military matters and therefore flowed more naturally into their correspondence. Assessing their willingness to engage in intimate exchanges, not simply of a sexual nature, but reflective of physical and emotional need, offers a further insight into the burdens of separation. This can only have exacerbated the corresponding emotional stress of command. Importantly, a far broader assessment of German soldiers' letters, which I recently conducted for another book, would suggest that sexually explicit exchanges were less common than one might imagine.[139] Many men doubted the appropriateness of writing anything that might be construed as being of a sexual nature, a reluctance that stemmed in part from conservative Christian views typical of the period. National Socialist views of sexuality also frowned upon open displays of emotional or sexual need, although some in the party attacked this concept as reflective of medieval Christianity and 'eager clerical moralists'.[140]

Burdens of the Heart

One important factor that separated the generals' letters from those of their men was the prospect of censorship. The letters of soldiers were subject to an army-level screening process, although in practice only a tiny fraction of the mail passing to and from the front was ever checked.[141] The generals, however, were typically sending their mail via personal courier and were in any case free from censorship on account of their high rank. Such privacy can only have encouraged the generals to communicate more openly.[142] Without question, Guderian was the most forthright in his expression of intimacy. Even before his long absence and the difficulties of the campaign, Heinz was openly affectionate towards Margarete. In his first letter to her on 16 June he wrote:

> Now our lovely, long time together has really reached an end and I'm sitting wistfully in front of the first, small rose that you gave me after all, and which now gladdens me with its scent and reminds me of you.
>
> First of all, I'd like to truly thank you from the heart that you once again so beautifully organised our time together for me, and tell you that I'm happy about it and love you very much. Accept a long, tender kiss on your sweet lips and your small, dear hand.[143]

None of Margarete's early letters from the campaign are available, but she was sending Heinz assortments of dried flowers (ox-eye daisies and cornflowers) as a symbol of her own heartfelt affection.[144] These delighted Heinz and served as highly sentimental mementos. Indeed, it seems Guderian had a passion for gardening and may have grown these flowers himself, since Margarete's first letter stated: 'Your sweet flowers are still nicely in bloom, but they're already the last of this summer.'[145] Guderian not only thanked Margarete for her 'Blumengrüße' (floral greeting), but added: 'Unfortunately, that kind of thing doesn't exist here at all.'[146] Such a statement was patently untrue. Countless German soldiers from across the Eastern Front attested to enthusiastic floral tributes, welcoming them as liberators from Soviet tyranny.[147] Guderian's claim may therefore represent an early degree of melancholic lament or perhaps a reluctance to attribute such warm-heartedness to the much-reviled Soviet Union.

Beyond the symbolic exchange of flowers, Heinz and Margarete's correspondence shares some surprisingly romantic content. Concluding his letters, Heinz often expressed his love descriptively. On 29 June he closed with 'a sweet, long kiss on your red lips',[148] followed in mid-July by another 'long, sweet kiss, regrettably only in thought!'[149] By the end of July he wrote: 'Allow me, in thought, to kiss you fervently on lips and hand and know that I am thinking of you in abiding love.'[150] Heinz's willingness to elucidate such tenderness and emotional honesty probably gave Margarete licence to do the same. Her typically hardy exterior and otherwise dispassionate emotional responses suddenly crumbled in her declarations of reciprocal love and yearning for

Heinz. In the first letter of her collection, dated 31 August, Margarete's growing heartache at separation and fear of loss found expression. Responding to Heinz she wrote: 'My longing is just as huge; how I would love to look into your big eyes again and let you hold me in your protecting arms. Sometimes, I'm tormented by a feeling of terrible loss and abandonment.'[151] Michelle Mouton's research has charted the 'stark psychological burden' of long-term marital separation,[152] so we need not be surprised at Margarete's distress, but the fact that she expressed it so candidly is, according to Peter Knoch, exceptional. Knoch's study of social norms in German letters suggests that by the Second World War some soldiers were beginning to express sexual desires more explicitly, whereas women continued to use much more guarded language.[153]

Margarete's otherwise carefully maintained mask of dignified detachment and proud stoicism clearly had its breaking point, but, unlike Reinhardt, who corrected such improper behaviour from his wife, it seems Heinz understood and even appreciated her candour. Indeed, Heinz's letters show that his own psychological wellbeing was suffering as the campaign wore on, which beyond any explicit references to depressive thoughts, may be charted by his emotional withdrawal into home life and especially his love for Margarete. More and more his letters ruminate on their shared life together and, on the occasion of their twenty-eighth wedding anniversary, Heinz took the time to write an especially endearing letter:

> I don't want to let our wedding anniversary pass without paying tribute to you in abiding love and deep gratitude. You have brought so much happiness and sunshine into my life and stood at my side so faithfully and sympathetically in joyous and sorrowful times that I can no longer imagine existing without your presence. [...] I come today with empty hands. I cannot even place a flower on the table for you. But you should at least know that I'm thinking of you, in spite of all tempests that these weeks bring. [...]
>
> I am spending the evening of 1 October looking at your pictures and I'm comparing photograph and watercolour. Both of them convey your essence in different ways, and it is very interesting to agonise over it, which says a lot. The watercolour is certainly more complicated. The artist has captured

several moods; the photograph only the present moods, of course.

I'd prefer to have the model with me, then loneliness and worries would fade away. My darling, stay healthy and remain such a sweet, good, indispensable life companion to me, as always. For my part, I will attempt to thank you for it and serve you in abiding love, till death us do part. Fare well and, finally, accept a long, sweet kiss from your faithful Heinz.[154]

Margarete, of course, also marked the date with a heartfelt letter, but on this occasion her pain at separation and the fears she held for her family were kept firmly in check.

Today, 28 years ago, we two formed our happy alliance for life. With gratitude and deep joy, I think of our wedding day. When I gave myself to you in love and I was given great happiness as a wife. My love and my happiness have today only become deeper and more heartfelt, my dearest. I feel the same when I think of you today, and these sentiments greet you from the heart. [...] My most heartfelt wishes, in special love, are with you today for the new major battle you have embarked upon.[155]

Her words conveyed an earnest and loving sentiment, but no longer strayed into being emotionally overwhelmed. As René Schilling noted: 'Of course, a good German woman would not resist when her husband went to war.'[156] Such repressed feelings were, however, never too far from the surface. In a letter from 26 October, Margarete alluded to the internal struggle she felt in conforming to perceived expectations, but in doing so her loneliness again found expression and even concluded with a possible allusion to sexual desire.

Another lonely Sunday! The big house is eerily still; my desires and thoughts are with you, my dearest. When, oh when will you be with me again? I am living only in this hope and attempt to keep up my spirits in this way. I also force myself to be inwardly glad, in order that you will find a fresh woman upon your return, just as you would like her. I paint myself a picture of how lovely our reunion will be; much more beautiful and heart-felt than ever; our bond increases during all our separations and all our saved-up love must then be released.[157]

Heinz also afforded veiled indications of sexual desire: 'Your picture smiles at me and wakes the desire for a good word and a long kiss, for warmth, understanding, contentment, for conversation and love.'[158] Clearly, Heinz and Margarete shared a deeply loving relationship, which served both as a source of solace as well as despair in their separation. Increasingly, however, the tone of the letters suggests a pervasive torment at being apart, especially in Heinz's case as the parallel burden of command weighed more and more.

None of the other generals' letters included such sensual exchanges, although that is not to say they were devoid of intimate content. Hoepner addressed his letters to 'My dear heart'[159] or even on occasion used the nickname 'Dear Fusspot'.[160] He also closed almost every letter with variations on the same theme: 'A heartfelt kiss for you',[161] 'A special kiss for you',[162] 'a sweet kiss',[163] and 'Warmest wishes and a loving kiss!'[164] Such formulaic repetition and the absence of any further elaboration diminishes somewhat the sense of affection, but there is one notable exception. In an apparent response to Irma's inquiry about a potential Christmas gift, Hoepner wrote: 'I now have no special requests apart from that of the previous year: a picture of you.'[165] However strong his feelings for Irma, there can be no question that Hoepner prioritised his duty beyond all else. Even as a young officer during the First World War Hoepner admitted to Irma: 'The officer at war really should not be married.'[166]

However much more reserved Hoepner's letters were by comparison with Guderian, this seems less a commentary on his love for Irma than his unwillingness to commit such thoughts to paper. Angelika Tramitz's study of sexuality within the German officer corps found that a 'proper marriage was only possible with a more than decent woman, who at best even embodied the noble lady whom an officer could and should honour in a knightly fashion'.[167] Not surprisingly, therefore, such a chivalrous honour code dictated the decorum of officers when engaging with dignified ladies and this pervaded not only their courtship, but marriage itself. It placed limits on the open expression of intimate, especially sexual, content. Even common soldiers in the German army strove to balance their desire to express affection and intimacy without crossing into the socially taboo and often morally despised manifestation of overly sexual content. Heinz Rahe, a non-commissioned officer in the 13th Panzer Division, articulated this dilemma in a letter he wrote his wife in October 1941:

Yesterday, N. read me a sentence from a letter that a girl had written him: "You are my sweet, little, tubby, lovely Fritzerl!" Something like that. That made me realise again how very sober in fact my letters, or even our mutual letter correspondence is – at least compared with that. And yet! What does that girl find out from her "sweet Fritzerl" apart from a few smoochy phrases, naturally non-binding on both sides? [...] You know, the word love is such cheap coinage today that I do not want to use it for us, at least not in the manner of current speech.[168]

Reinhardt's letters cannot really be assessed for their intimacy, since he retyped and edited his wartime correspondence before submitting the collection to the West German Military History Research Office in 1962 (the collection was transferred to the Federal Military Archive in 1972). Reinhardt's use of ellipsis makes clear where content was selectively expunged. He no doubt recognised the letters for their historical value, but either did not think that personal details could be relevant or of interest to future historians or he regarded such content as off-limits and altogether private. As a result, blocks of text from each of his letters, and unfortunately even small details, like how he addressed his wife or how he closed his letters, have been removed. Nevertheless, Reinhardt's concentration on military matters at times surreptitiously converged with personal matters, allowing flashes of insight into his personal life. On 26 June, while revelling in the success of his early advance, Reinhardt framed the achievement as a gift to Eva. 'Our victory is almost a birthday present to you in its uniqueness, bought by my troops and all the strength I could give.'[169]

If there is an enigma within the group of generals, it is Schmidt. His letters are almost completely devoid of anything that might be characterised as intimacy or even personal content. Indeed, Schmidt has thus far hardly featured in this chapter dealing with the private side of these generals because his letters are so narrow in their devotion to military matters. The closest reference to a personal sentiment or feeling towards Fridel comes on 24 December (the highpoint of the German Christmas calendar) when Schmidt wrote: 'Herrmann has touchingly decorated a Christmas tree for me and placed it in my room. In addition, I've received one stollen cake and an apple cake from the army. And the lovely things from you. What more could I want?'[170] Unlike Reinhardt, we have Schmidt's handwritten original letters, so content has not been edited out. As noted in the introduction, many (but not all) of Schmidt's letters were headed 'report' followed by the date, which could indicate that they served a different purpose from what we might imagine a personal letter to contain. Yet there are clear instances that show Schmidt was also using the correspondence to communicate solely with Fridel. On 13 December, Schmidt wrote: 'Now I really ought to write you a long Christmas letter, but I can't get around to it because the Russians have broken through.'[171] Thus, it seems unlikely that the collection is simply one of reports and that there could have potentially been a separate collection of much more personal letters written to Fridel. Schmidt simply seems to have avoided almost any emotional content or even family news in his letters.

What is especially revealing is a separate set of two letters that Schmidt wrote to Lieutenant-General Friedrich Paulus in 1941. Importantly, these were discovered among Paulus's private papers; they were not part of Schmidt's collection, but they certainly cast the panzer general in a very different light. Schmidt's letter from 13 November opens:

> Dear Paulus!
> Thank you very much for your letter. However, my deeply felt outbursts of anger should in no way prompt you to give any instructions. I just had to have someone to whom I could secretly share my opinion, and you were the only person I trusted. So don't be angry with me because of the complaint. [...] In any case, I thank you warmly for always being so kind to me.[172]

In the first instance the tone here is already much more personal than almost anything Schmidt wrote to his wife. Secondly, since Schmidt's letters to Fridel are so matter-of-fact and devoid of feeling, it might well be that he felt better able to confide in Paulus, not just in a professional capacity, but emotionally as well. The state of Schmidt's marriage can only be a matter of conjecture, but if the existing correspondence represents the extent of his engagement with Fridel, it suggests a distant relationship, which the absence of any children might further confirm. As Sonja Hagelstam's study of wartime letters concludes:

> the writers were involved in an ongoing process of weaving together their lives. [...] this was done on a practical and everyday level, but the correspondents also employed different strategies in

order to keep up the marriage on an emotional level. [...] When a marriage is mainly maintained through correspondence it is of utmost importance to clearly and frequently articulate thoughts and feelings to ensure enduring love and support.[173]

By the same token, Claus-Christian Szejnmann noted that disruption, separation and mental strains made it 'crucial for the inner stability of soldiers to maintain personal relationships and to communicate their feelings'.[174] This process certainly came with many challenges for couples, as it necessitated the transposing of emotions from speech and gesture to a world of literary expression, which risked what Christa Hämmerle referred to as the private 'couple cosmos' (*Paarkosmos*) becoming public.[175] Yet it also offered the prospect of redefining communication, as Cornelie Usborne observed: 'In letters, couples could develop a narrative to help them to discover a better sense of their selves, to understand traumatic circumstances and to transcend pain with language.'[176] Similarly, Hester Vaizey concluded: 'Men may well have given voice to their emotions more easily on the page than in the flesh.'[177]

Figure 2.4 Rudolf Schmidt in November 1940

In Schmidt's case none of this was apparent. Beyond the absence of intimate content, we can also look at the length of Schmidt's letters to see a marked difference from the other generals. Although we know that Guderian wrote more letters to Margarete than his collection represents, the word count of Schmidt's correspondence is just 28 per cent of the size of Guderian's total (4,734 to 16,506 words). This is in spite of the fact that Schmidt's collection contains two letters more than that of Guderian (thirty-three to thirty-one letters). A similar trend is seen in comparison with Reinhardt and Hoepner. Schmidt's total number of words comes to less than half (44 and 45 per cent respectively) of his fellow panzer commanders, in spite of writing two more letters than Hoepner and one fewer than Reinhardt. Thus, in addition to the absence of emotional content, Schmidt was spending much less time on his wife's correspondence. The same, however, did not hold true for Schmidt's two letters to Paulus in July and November. His letter to Paulus in July was 448 words in length and the letter he wrote to Margarete Guderian in the same month came to 283 words. Yet the average of his four letters to Fridel in July and August comes to just 108 words.[178] Schmidt's November letter to Paulus was more than four times the length of his July letter at 1,891 words. This single letter is over 500 words longer than the total of Schmidt's seven letters written to Fridel in the same month. It all suggests a marked reluctance to write to his wife in comparison with both the other panzer generals and Schmidt's other addressees. Coupled with the lack of emotional content that Hagelstam identifies as necessary for a healthy relationship, it seems that Schmidt's correspondence with Fridel was more form than substance.

Understanding the nature of the generals' relationships at a personal level gives us a good indication of how honest and open the communication between husband and wife was. Certainly, for Guderian, but also for Hoepner and Reinhardt, the exchange of letters appears to have served as a unique source of emotional support, providing an outlet for grievances, fears and even self-doubt that cannot be found anywhere else. As a result, their letters chart a personal dimension to the war in the East that contrasts starkly with the tightly controlled wartime propaganda of brash, confident and decisive panzer generals. The fallacy of this representation was already becoming evident in the summer weeks of the campaign, but by the autumn the psychological cracks were becoming harder to mask and, for each of the four generals, the pretence was dropped altogether in December.

Burdens of Command

Guderian's reputation as the hard-hitting general who personi-fies the image of tough panzer commanders is not without merit. Guderian was remarkably strong-willed and could be a particularly striking figure both within the German chain of command and for his foreign adversaries. Yet the war in the East rapidly wore down even the toughest personalities and by 11 October Heinz wrote to Margarete of his need to 'unburden my heart to another human being'. Although Guderian appears to have enjoyed positive relations among his staff, he noted, 'as an older person – I am ever more isolated and the young people increasingly keep their distance. In spite of the very nice way of life in my staff, I feel this more and more.'[179] Four days later, Guderian admitted to experiencing 'many emotions' and found himself reminis-cing about 'lovelier and generally carefree times'. Yet Guderian was fighting the impulse for melancholy because, as he told Margarete, 'I don't want to give you a heavy heart' and because he was worried about the state of his men, for whom 'one must be a good example [...] and bring himself to merriment, a daily new struggle'.[180] Shortly thereafter, Guderian came down with a terrible cold, writing that it 'must also be endured in good spirits'. Privately his letters were drifting more and more into fantasies of home life, writing at length on 21 October about his envy for Margarete's life of 'peace and the contentment', concluding 'my longing for a reunion and our happy, blissfully sweet life together becomes ever stronger'. It was a stark contrast with his parallel por-trayal of life at the front: 'Here there is no personal touch, no spirit, no contentment. In this country, the beauty is just as tramped down as the spirit. Everything has become a bleak, mechanical, heartless machinery, hideous and squalid, indescribably feeble. One has to have seen it to know what it's like.'[181]

Guderian's downcast outlook was not only a notable contrast with his earlier letters, but a source of growing concern for Margarete. Writing on 5 November, she observed: 'Your report sounds very wistful and, unfortunately, not very hopeful and confident [...] I'm very troubled by that.' She too had been sustained by the hope that they would be reunited in the winter when German operations came to a halt, but was coming to the realisation that Heinz would not be able to leave his command. This was a crushing blow for Margarete, who confided in Heinz about her own fragile emotional state: 'I'd kept myself in good spirits with this feeling of expectation and focused all my thoughts and actions on it. Nonetheless, I won't yet abandon all hope, dearest; I want to retain the belief in order not to succumb to the despair of the moment.'[182] It is not clear when exactly Margarete's letter reached Guderian, but using personal couriers their correspondence was typically separated by only a matter of days. In any case, a week later, on 12 November, Guderian suddenly wrote to Margarete that he had tried to leave the front and return home for a visit, but had been prevented by snowstorms. He said he would try again on 13 November, but this attempt would also prove unsuccessful.[183] Guderian was already suffering emotionally and feeling the pain of separation, but the additional anguish of Margarete's isolation may well have pushed him to a breaking point. Granting oneself a leave of absence, however short, in the midst of operations was certainly an extraordinary liberty that, on the one hand, speaks to Guderian's disconsolate frame of mind, but on the other, highlights the hypocrisy of generals who expected and demanded so much more of their men. Only days before, Guderian had described the morning frosts and viscous mud as 'torture for the troops', but his emerging depression had become evident in every letter. 'Hopefully, I can soon adopt somewhat happier tones. Complaining does not come naturally to me. But at present it is difficult to be in good spirits.'[184] Compounding his psychological angst, or perhaps as a physiological manifestation of his emotional state, Guderian's health suddenly declined. In addition to a worsening of his long-standing sciatic condition, his stomach was upset and he also noted that he was suffering from 'severe headaches'. As a cure Guderian noted: 'Fasting for several days supposedly makes the rebellious stomach see sense. As long as I can stay in my well-heated general's apartment, I can endure anything, but if we have to change positions when operations progress, the matter will become difficult in this cold.'[185]

Guderian's autumn letters chart the most profound decline of mood among the panzer generals, but he was by no means alone in his suffering. Schmidt's panzer corps was fighting under particularly difficult circumstances, first to seize the Russian town of Tikhvin (8 November) and then to hold it against constant Soviet pressure. On the same day that Army Group Centre was surging forth with Operation Typhoon towards Moscow, Schmidt was desperately struggling to repel enemy attacks. 'It's bad here now', he wrote Fridel on 2 October. 'All the heavy Russian attacks are now concentrated on me. I sometimes don't know where my own head is.'[186] The pressure Schmidt felt was unremitting and by the end of the month he admitted, 'the last 3 weeks have worked on my nerves like nothing else before. I can't shake the agitation and the pressure of the enormous responsibility at all.'[187] Chief among Schmidt's responsibilities were his men, who suffered and toiled to carry out his every order, but could scarcely be protected from the freezing conditions or incessant Soviet attacks. While professing 'I simply love our people,' whom he lauded as 'brave and unassuming', this same devotion to his men made it all the more difficult for Schmidt to witness their sacrifices. On 1 November he admitted, 'the severe losses are deeply saddening'.[188] Two weeks later, on 15 November, Schmidt claimed he was in the midst of the 'toughest and bloodiest battles that I have ever fought', but he did not wish to burden Fridel with the details because, as he explained, 'It is difficult enough for me in the face of all the casualties.'[189] Just how tormenting the losses were for Schmidt is captured by a letter on 18 November in which he wrote: 'I can hardly express how much we must respect the men. The many fallen, who were sent to their deaths through my command, frequently appear to me at night.'[190] In a later world such disturbances would probably be diagnosed as a form of post-traumatic stress disorder, but such a concept was not known to psychiatry at the time.[191]

Empathy for the long-suffering troops was a basic emotion that troubled each of the generals, in part because it was a natural human response, but also because the scenes of physical horror and utter despair were so ubiquitous. On 22 October Hoepner alluded to the condition of his men, including those he encountered during a tour of inspection at two field hospitals: 'I now feel very sorry for the troops, because they are suffering a great deal from the weather and the abysmal roads. I visited two field hospitals today – a grave duty – and conferred the Iron Cross.'[192] Hoepner's account offers no further elaboration, but of course graphic descriptions could hardly have reassured Irma. An indication of what may have constituted Hoepner's visit is offered by a Catholic priest from the 18th Panzer Division:

> Ambulances come and go, unload their sad cargo and disappear again in the direction of the front. I go from room to room. All words fail here. Quiet whispering and groaning, usually silence, large, wide-open eyes. Only here and there a tired smile. Behind the building, in a shady corner, the dead: officers and men. The

numbers ever increasing. They are young people, barely come of age, for the division is, of course, comprised almost exclusively of active troops.[193]

Such scenes of pain and loss were no doubt the 'grave duty' Hoepner referred to, but unlike Guderian and Schmidt, his autumn letters betrayed little evidence of a psychological decline. Whether that was due to a more robust nature or a purposeful choice to shield Irma from the consequences cannot be known, but either way his resilience would fail in December. Yet Hoepner was not only confronted with death and suffering as an abstraction, among men he did not know; the autumn period also claimed his friend Colonel von Wolff and then, on 3 November, his long-time comrade and close personal acquaintance Colonel Georg von Neufville. Hoepner recounted this news to Irma, concluding: 'It is dreadful.'[194] In fact, Neufville was posthumously promoted to Major-General, which Hoepner may well have facilitated.[195]

Reinhardt's personal experience of the autumn campaign was boosted by his promotion to command Panzer Group 3, replacing Colonel-General Hermann Hoth on 9 October.[196] This prestigious appointment was a very public recognition of his performance thus far and no doubt buoyed Reinhardt's mood heading into the autumn *rasputitsa* and the many challenges that awaited. Thus, Reinhardt's letters are decidedly free of the pessimism, stress and at times dejection that characterise Guderian and Schmidt's writings.[197] This is not, however, to suggest Reinhardt did not experience difficulty. On 16 November he wrote Eva: 'This morning, my troops reported for duty. You'll understand how I feel. My thoughts are out there, with my troops, with all their desires and worries.'[198] Reinhardt's empathy for his troops was again emphasised on 23 November, when he wrote of his service at the front to inspire his men: 'In the past few days, I had to expose myself on multiple occasions, somewhat more than I would normally do.'[199] Such profound commitment to their men contributed to the esteem the generals gained as military commanders, but it is worth remembering that their great sympathy for the plight of the troops never sufficed to spare the men from their ongoing suffering. By the onset of winter, Reinhardt could not offer more than the example of his leadership and willingness to endure the conditions at the front, at least in part, as they did. Writing to Eva of the admiration he felt for his men, Reinhardt also confessed to the conflict within himself that all his assurances and demands would end in some form of victory:

> I am deeply moved by how much I must demand of my brave troops. In temperatures of [minus] 30 degrees, everything is twice as difficult to endure; problems emerge for men and vehicles alike that were hitherto unknown to us here. When, as a commander at the front, you can only express thanks and recognition, while moved to rejoice inwardly that everyone is pulling together, after all, and promise nothing in the way of help but must instead depart with the final words that you have to continue to have faith and demand that they hold out – well, that's tough. And yet, I have the feeling that it was important for me, today especially, to visit the front and at any rate better for me than to sit in my parlour and be subjected to one strain after the next on the telephone. Outwardly, I do not lose my composure and I also retain my faith in victory, but inwardly, I wrestle with myself and suffer until the victory will soon hopefully put everything right.[200]

Such a bold admission of inner conflict was an uncharacteristic disclosure for Reinhardt, who, like Hoepner, was about to have his remaining illusions of German victory shattered by the December retreats. Yet, for the time being, Reinhardt attempted to assure Eva, as he had assured his men, that there was no cause for alarm. Following on from the above passage, Reinhardt told Eva: 'If I provide you with these lines with an insight into the final thing that moves me today, then I do it not to reassure myself. In no way should my letter create the impression that I am subdued or that we are failing or despairing.'[201] It was almost a retrospective contradiction of his own plainly voiced self-doubt, or perhaps a rejection of the 'weakness' to which he had momentarily succumbed. Sonja Hagelstam's research into concepts of masculinity in the era suggests that for some men, wives could never be seen as a source of consolation because that would constitute too much of a perceived role reversal. As she explained, 'how could a husband who was expected to protect his wife, family and home openly express feelings of fear [. . . a] married man had to try to overcome possible feelings of anxiousness at least to some extent without the aid from the wife.'[202]

Whatever the general applicability of Hagelstam's analysis, Guderian certainly did not shy away from sharing his doubts and fears. Indeed, he gratefully accepted and even welcomed Margarete's letters of commiseration. Writing on 17 November, Guderian imparted his appreciation: 'You show much understanding and kindness for our situation out here, so that your words are always a big comfort and a true joy for me.'[203] Of course, Guderian was in a far more fragile state than anyone, aside from Margarete, could have suspected. The same letter of 17 November recounted a three-day tour of the front that confronted Guderian with the wretchedness of the conditions and the general misery of his men, which only compounded his own melancholy. 'I was able to deliver a number of Iron Crosses, the men were very pleased, but I gained an insight into their lives, which saddened me very seriously.'[204] Once again, Guderian's thoughts turned to home and he speculated about some of his divisions being sent back to Germany for replenishment. 'I don't yet know whether I'll stay here or receive another task; hopefully the latter.'[205] Given that the overwhelming bulk of Germany's armoured forces were deployed in the East and Guderian had always styled himself as the pre-eminent panzer leader, it was a telling admission. The sluggish progress of the campaign by the end of November and the unending hardships weighed tremendously on Guderian, and his letters of despair telegraphed his mood. On 21 November he admitted to Margarete, 'yesterday I was on the brink of despair and a bag of nerves. Today, the unexpected combat success of the brave tank divisions provided me with a new ray of hope; whether it can be sustained will become clear over the coming days.'[206]

More and more, Margarete's letters were responding to Heinz's emotional state, seeking to counter his dejection and boost his waning self-esteem because she alone recognised the depths to which he was sinking. Her letter of 27 November adopted a profound tone of responsiveness:

> Your last letter saddened me again, because I cannot help you in your present situation or even care for you. Your concerns for your loyal, brave men are no doubt very oppressive and can scarcely be remedied. [. . .] I hear from all sides that you possess the hearts of your soldiers. You can feel happy and proud of this! Even if you can't always accompany your brave men in their hardship, they know that you feel for them and that you

are doing your best for them. [...] If only I could give you the same feeling! How lovely our reunion will be, my dearest!²⁰⁷

On 4 December Margarete even admitted that her words of compassion were a reaction to Heinz's despondency. 'I am always with you in thought and I want to do and say many kind things for you, because I know that you need it, my dearest.'²⁰⁸

Another noteworthy indication of Guderian's decline is his increasingly illegible handwriting, which Katrin Kilian specifically identified as a symptom of 'war weariness' in her study of German soldiers' wartime letters. According to Kilian, such a tangible manifestation of stress was not uncommon: 'These symptoms are usually in style and diction, in rapid changes of subject, spelling mistakes, and increasingly poor handwriting (a tendency to produce a weak, shaky, uneven scrawl).'²⁰⁹ Atypically, Guderian's letter of 31 October included passages with numerous indecipherable words (and these were checked by two separate handwriting experts who had transcribed all of the letters in the collection). In most cases it is individual words that are illegible, but in others the handwriting appears to garble a whole string of words. In all such instances one can only insert an ellipsis, leaving only what can be reasonably verified. If 'war weariness' or stress was the cause of Guderian's deteriorating handwriting, then the result was telling because the most egregious example is so littered with gaps as to become incomprehensible. From what can be deciphered, Guderian wrote: 'I'm enclosing a letter from Hirtenlein, which will interest you and which you should please destroy, [...] an English magazine [...] for my war [...]. You can gather from the latter that in London I [...] of my [...] has cleaned up and that my imminent departure is desired.'²¹⁰ Of course, there could be alternative explanations for bad handwriting. Perhaps Guderian was overly tired or writing while in a moving vehicle, but whatever the exact cause, his distressed state of mind cannot be ignored.

When Colonel-General Wolfram von Richthofen, commanding the VIII Air Corps providing aerial support for Army Group Centre, visited Guderian on 7 December, he alluded afterwards in his diary to the shattered man he encountered: 'To Guderian. Very open discussion. He is only externally hard, otherwise made of jelly. I actually wanted to be consoled by him and instead had to do it myself for him! Bitter and difficult.'²¹¹ No longer was Guderian's thinly disguised depression hidden from view by the façade of a once indominable reputation for towering self-confidence. Indeed, his state of mind seemed to mimic the steady disintegration of his panzer forces as the casualty lists grew ever longer: 'Even among my faithful men here, implacable death has again wrought havoc and when I today inspected some withdrawn tank formations, among the officer corps it was sadly empty.'[212] Writing again on 10 December, as the Soviet winter offensive was only just beginning, Guderian lamented: 'I naturally make the greatest effort to do my duty, but it greatly aggrieves me not to be able to better remedy the hardship of the troops.'[213] The extent of that helplessness was explained in his last letter of 1941, written on 16 December: 'during the night I often lie sleepless and rack my brains for what else I could do to help my poor men, who must remain outside, unprotected in this winter weather. It is terrible, inconceivable. [. . .] The feeling of not being understood and being helplessly at the mercy of the circumstances is simply nerve-wracking.'[214] Finally, Guderian admitted to Margarete that he had reached an unprecedented low point: 'How we are supposed to come out of this again, I don't yet know myself. [. . .] I cannot recall having ever been so anxious for professional reasons as I am now and I only hope that I can endure it.'[215] Days later, Schmidt, who by this point was Guderian's neighbouring army commander and in frequent contact with him, observed his mood and on 19 December noted that the once 'great optimist' had reached 'the end of his hopes'.[216] Of course, Guderian was soon released from the torments of his command. Given the circumstances that surrounded his dismissal, which included flagrant acts of insubordination, he may have been consciously or unconsciously complicit in manufacturing his own departure from the Eastern Front and thereby avoiding the shame of deserting his post at a time of crisis.[217]

Schmidt's autumn campaign to capture Tikhvin had severely strained his nerves and he seemed to welcome his new command in the Second Army, not only because it constituted a promotion from corps command, but for the relative peace it afforded him.[218] A day after assuming his new appointment in Orel, Schmidt wrote to Fridel: 'There's much less to do than with the [XXXIX Motorised Army] corps.'[219] Without knowing it, Schmidt had actually left the frying pan for the fire, as the Second Army was the weakest army formation in Army Group Centre (seven under-strength divisions), held responsibility for one of the longest stretches of front (260 kilometres) and was dangerously overextended. It all meant that Schmidt's reprieve from the torments of

Tikhvin was to be short-lived once the Soviet winter offensive began. Accordingly, the crisis that beset the Second Army surpassed anything Schmidt had previously experienced. By 13 December, with his divisions already tumbling backwards, Schmidt listed some of the intractable problems he confronted: 'snowstorm, black ice, provisioning difficulties, no reserves'. As a result, his nerves were again stretched to breaking point and he wrote to Fridel, 'due to this crisis I am busy day and night. It has never gone so badly for me.'[220] By 24 December the situation had deteriorated further and Schmidt admitted, 'I often feel utterly dejected by all the suffering [...] but I can't change it.'[221] Perhaps uniquely, such helplessness took an especially heavy toll on the panzer commanders because their distinctive training, resourcing and experience had always emphasised dominating the enemy and dictating the terms of action. They were unaccustomed to the lack of control and freedom of manoeuvre, which under the circumstances greatly amplified the suffering of their men.

By December Hoepner had conducted two major campaigns, first capturing the Baltic states and sealing off Leningrad and, secondly, redeploying south to encircle the Soviet Western Front and lead the drive on Moscow. Although Hoepner faced periodic setbacks and neither city was captured, the summer and autumn were clearly marked by long advances and repeated victories. Accordingly, his letters to Irma reflect a sanguine self-confidence, troubled at times by losses and the suffering of his men, but overall maintaining a certain conviction that nourished and sustained his emotional well-being. December turned everything on its head. While it is clear that the armies of Guderian and Schmidt were fighting for their lives south of Moscow, it was actually Hoepner and Reinhardt whose vastly overextended panzer groups would meet the epicentre of the Soviet counteroffensive north of the city. Three days into the Soviet offensive, Hoepner, for the first time, alludes to his own failing health, telling Irma, 'I'm really in desperate need of a health cure.'[222] Hoepner made no mention of any physical ailments, but the emotional stress of his command became evident in every letter. On 12 December he wrote: 'Since 2 December, we've been in a state of considerable anticipation. We only ever receive bad tidings these days. The sound of the telephone is enough to make one jump. And it never stops ringing. [...] It is incredibly difficult to keep our nerves. The commanding generals [at the corps and divisional level] are crying out for help.'[223] Hoepner noted that his chief of staff,

Chales de Beaulieu, had become so nervous that he could no longer sleep at night. Days later, on 14 December, Hoepner admitted to the same affliction, which fed his 'horrible mood' and left him to conclude: 'My nerves are threatening to fail me.' Even when Hoepner did sleep, it seems the psychological pressure he was under evoked dark memories from the First World War, because for the first time he admitted to Irma: 'At night, my memories of 1918 torment me. But here, we are even more helpless in the struggle against the winter than we were back then against the enemy.'[224] Determining the situation in 1941 to be less favourable for Germany than the year 1918 is itself a remarkable comment on the decline of Hoepner's mental state. According to Colonel Hermann Balck, who visited Hoepner at this time, the hardest challenge 'came in situations where one had to muster all his personal powers to appear upbeat and confident in order to give his subordinates strength'.[225] Severe fatigue, anxiety and even trauma had become Hoepner's personal daily battle and it threatened to overwhelm him, but, as revealing as his letters were, there is also evidence that Hoepner restrained himself so as not to unduly worry Irma. On 21 December he wrote: 'The whole affair is dreadful. [...] It is tremendously draining in terms of nerves and work. This is now our Christmas festival! I don't want to cause you any more of a heavy heart with my concerns.'[226]

Like Hoepner, Reinhardt had endured the summer and autumn campaigns in reasonably good spirits, bolstered by his success at the head of XXXXI Panzer Corps and his promotion to panzer group command in October. It was, however, precisely Reinhardt's deep advance in Operation Typhoon that exposed his panzer group to the dangerous repercussions of an unanticipated Soviet counterstrike. Initially, Reinhardt's December letters to Eva spoke of being 'full of worries' about what was being reported at the front, but there is still a sense that the panzer general did not yet appreciate the scale and scope of what was beginning.[227] On 9 December that shocking realisation came as the panzer group's defensive front threatened total collapse and Soviet forces advanced to within six kilometres of Reinhardt's headquarters. That night Reinhardt wrote to Eva about the perilous ordeal he had been thrust into and the awful effect it was having on him:

> I cannot describe to you what I have suffered. For all the responsibility that I carry, to have to watch helplessly how the situation became increasingly desperate, despite having made

reserves available on time, who could have helped but were not able to get to where they should be due to the weather and the roads, was almost too much to take.[228]

Worse was yet to come, but unlike Hoepner, Reinhardt did not shield Eva from the frightening details of his nervous anguish. In fact, uncharacteristically, Reinhardt was sending almost daily letters, suggesting he found the writing a cathartic form of therapy or simply took solace from a virtual dialogue with Eva. In any case, he did not hold back on this suffering. On 10 December Reinhardt wrote:

> Today is awful. [...] I am now sitting here at 4 p.m. in my half-vacated room and trembling in anxiety and doubt about how things will proceed. It is awful to be alone, to do nothing, to be unable to do anything. [...] None of the help promised to us has arrived [...] When alone, I am afraid, not of the enemy, but of the back and forth of my thoughts. I involuntarily brood on whether I have made mistakes and how much I am to blame for the unfortunate turn of events in our advance, which had been so successful. I am confronted by the great pressure of the responsibility for the victims that these difficult days cost us.
>
> I see before me the pale, hollow-eyed faces of my men this morning, of whom I must expect superhuman feats. Do they condemn me for it?! I doubt whether I'll retain my command, whether a better man must not replace me. On the other hand, I would consider it desertion to throw in the towel here and now; now I must face the music.[229]

Reinhardt's candour introduces fascinating insights. Uniquely among the panzer generals, he appeared willing to consider his own responsibility for the events overtaking his command and leading to the suffering of his men. The fact that he asked if the men might 'condemn' him, and feared being left alone to confront 'the back and forth of my thoughts [...] on whether I have made mistakes', suggests Reinhardt harboured his own doubts, and even personal recriminations, about driving the overextension of his panzer group. He also called into question whether he would retain his command, as if his troops would not be the only ones casting an accusatory eye on his performance. Two days later, on 12 December, Reinhardt wrote again to Eva of his terrible loneliness, which, he noted, 'depresses me twice as much in my sorrows, which are still troubling me'.[230] Of course, Reinhardt's winter ordeal was only just beginning and the toll this took on his nerves was enormous. On 15 December he told Eva of how awaiting news from the front 'we trembled from hour to hour'[231] and by the end of the month he declared with resignation: 'You can imagine how gruelling this stressful game is [...] and have to constantly hope that everything will turn out well with God's help.'[232]

What is remarkable about the generals' letters is the contrasting picture they offer. The dash and flair of the panzer generals, who were celebrated both during and after the war for their supposed iron will and determination, were in fact suffering far more from the demands of the campaign and the pressures of command than has hitherto been recognised.[233] While they no doubt orchestrated some of the most remarkable victories of the 1941 campaign, as the tide of events turned and they reaped the same harvest of desperation and despair that they themselves had sown time and again amongst their enemies, the panzer generals proved scarcely better equipped to cope with the reversal. Without intending to unfairly disparage them or minimise the circumstances driving their psychological malaise, it is of course a much greater test of character, and any supposed 'iron will', to confront crisis and defeat successfully than to operate in the glow of victory. Of course, the generals had become accustomed to success and there was nothing in the military planning or state propaganda to prepare them for what the Eastern campaign would require. While their suffering at a personal level is an important indication of how they experienced events and what state of mind they inhabited, the panzer generals nevertheless remain principal instigators of the conflict in the East as well as enforcers of Germany's murderous policies (as will be explored in Chapter 4). Thus, one should not confuse the generals' letters and the narrative of victimhood that these at times suggest with the direct responsibility they bear for the untold misery and loss of life in 1941.

Investigating the private world of the generals is an essential starting point to begin a discussion of how they constructed their sense of self and oriented their core values. The answers are not always the same. Family assumed a questionable importance for Schmidt, who remained childless and appeared emotionally distant from Fridel. Guderian, by contrast, devoted himself to Margarete unconditionally, although he did not appear to have exhibited anything like the same dedication to his two sons. Hoepner and Reinhardt, in keeping with contemporary concepts of masculinity, adopted more circumspect approaches. Reinhardt largely edited personal and family content out of his letters, while Hoepner expressed affection, but in an emotionally guarded tone.

Family was not the only point of orientation; their Protestant faith as a measure of spiritual enlightenment and piousness offered the generals another fundamental point of reference. Yet, as we have seen, none of the generals engaged in a substantive discourse about God or their faith until the difficulties of the campaign mounted, suggesting a somewhat conditional devotion. At the same time, National Socialism's prejudicial propaganda about the Soviet 'East' received no moral corrective in the Church's teachings or public statements. Indeed, the eradication of 'Godless Bolshevism' and the embrace of zealous antisemitism were actively promoted by the Church, suggesting that the more devout declarations by Guderian, Reinhardt and, to a lesser extent, Schmidt by no means disassociated them from core Nazi beliefs.

The irony for the generals is that their professed devotion to Germany, family and God was the very thing perverted by their parallel adherence to National Socialism. As Sebastian Haffner observed as early as 1940:

> The Nazis, in the eyes of the loyal Germans, are not the breakers and destroyers of the family, but its protectors and champions. [...] Not the enemies but the saviours of Christianity and the Church [...] Thus, the Nazis have to persuade the majority of their countrymen to believe the opposite of almost everything that they are and want to do, in order to win and keep their loyalty. [...] They work constantly in two directions. They vaunt their humanity and humility as well as their ruthlessness and severity. They talk, almost in the same speech, of Germany's boundless love of peace and of the 'new division of the world'. And they know that they can count on applause in both cases.[234]

Haffner's concept of the 'loyal Germans' epitomises the contradiction of the panzer generals. They lamented the losses among their troops, but scarcely questioned the necessity of the war, nor their own role in the suffering of the men. They counted themselves dutiful disciples of God and evoked his benevolence and protection, but ignored the misery and murder their actions entailed for others. The generals exhibited their humanity through the tenderness of their letters home, but on the same pages depict a ruthless war that they themselves directed. They yearned for peace and an end to suffering, but worked only towards conquest and subjugation. If the Nazis could count on applause for their mixture of high-minded rhetoric and base savagery, the duplicity and contradictions were unwittingly embraced by the panzer generals, who – to adopt Haffner's metaphor – were both clapping enthusiastically from the stands and appearing on the stage to take a bow.

3 THE PUBLIC GENERALS

If the last chapter offered an unfamiliar 'private' view of the panzer generals in the East, then this chapter gives a contrasting insight into the 'public' image they sought to project. It explores their pursuit of reputation through a public profile, not simply for reasons of personal ambition and vanity – which certainly played a part – but for the professional benefit that fame played in advancing their respective careers. This is perhaps one of the essential elements in the success (or failure) of senior German military commanders that has remained largely obscured and underappreciated. For the most part, one would be correct in thinking that a career in the German army was built upon performance, ability, character and intellect. Promotion was governed by a regulated set of appointments and duties through which one progressed according to aptitude and proficiency. Patronage no doubt also played a role in building military careers, but to a lesser extent than in other European officer corps. The system, however, changed at the top of the hierarchical pyramid with the parameters for appointment and progression becoming more fluid and inexact. Certainly, under National Socialism, reputation, social status, leadership connections, ideological commitment and breadth of experience all played a role. Yet because these characteristics were malleable constructs, subject to interpretation, an individual's status became a crafted narrative built by word-of-mouth, notoriety and, perhaps most uniquely, military celebrity. This was a crucial difference from contemporaneous states: National Socialism did not just celebrate the military as an essential arm of the state, but incorporated martial ideals into the very fabric of the idealised society.

Military Celebrity

The basic conception of males and masculinity in Nazi Germany became inextricably interwoven with the warrior ethos, creating a popular image of the noble fighting man irrespective of age or occupation. Illustrative of this, Adelheid von Saldern observed, 'well-known pictures show, soldiers and workers had the martial appearance of the hard, masculine, militarized and racially "clean" man.'[1] Nor was it just the iconic propaganda imagery, as René Schilling's study concluded: 'The enduring idea of the German man as "hero" and warrior was evident on the linguistic level. The most popular attribute to illustrate strong and undisputed masculinity was still "hard as steel" or "steely". Everything about the ideal heroic man seemed hard and armoured.'[2] Thus, military prestige was by no means limited to the armed services, but the widespread indoctrination of males into a cult of the warrior turned the Wehrmacht into a hallowed institution and the senior generals into quasi-high priests of the much-vaulted profession of arms. As a result, the generals were not just recognised figures within military circles, but they also garnered genuine popular interest and celebrity appeal. This inadvertent audience opened the door for enterprising individuals actively to cultivate their public image, which, beyond nourishing egos, had the undeniable benefit of advancing their profile in professional circles. Of course, such self-indulgent behaviour was considered beneath many of the generals, especially for those with aristocratic backgrounds or conventional ideas about the professional conduct of senior officers.[3] On the one hand, the cavalry, as the precursor to the panzer corps, had been the more conservative arm of the army, but the embrace of new technology and doctrine had modernised the culture as well as the thinking, creating a more receptive attitude towards new forms of professional (and personal) development. After all, the panzer corps prided itself on innovative concepts and dispensing with long-standing conventions, especially if the results showed promise.[4] Not only were many of the panzer commanders amenable to marketing themselves as well as their service; the public embraced them as a coveted symbol of the new, modern, dynamic and seemingly unstoppable Germany, comparable within the Wehrmacht only to the highly popular Luftwaffe fighter aces and U-boat commanders. As Johannes Hürter observed in the aftermath of the victorious battle of France, 'Guderian, Hoepner, Hoth, Kleist, Reinhardt and Schmidt counted among the most popular German generals.'[5]

As Operation Barbarossa got under way and the panzer generals were kept busy at the forefront of the advance, they measured their success against a number of factors, some of which were objectively military, but others decidedly not. The public representation of their achievements was a feature of all four panzer generals' correspondence and from the earliest days they were evidently eager to see themselves recognised in published army reports as well as state media. Five days into the campaign Reinhardt wrote to Eva about the successful conclusion of the tank battle at Raseiniai. 'We are proud to have won the greatest and heaviest tank battle so far; perhaps it will be mentioned once in the army report [*Heeresbericht*]. My troops deserve it; they've suffered immensely.'[6] During the first week of the campaign the German people received almost no details about what was happening in the East. Public announcements spoke only of great victories and successful advances; it was not until 29 June that a much-anticipated broadcast of twelve 'special announcements' (*Sonderberichte*) was delivered at hourly intervals.[7] The importance of these special announcements was underlined by Howard Smith, an American correspondent in Berlin, who described the ritual event:

> The announcer interrupts programmes to announce a special communiqué is coming, and repeats this prologue every five minutes until it comes. The *Sondermeldung* is preceded by a moment of silence, during which all restaurants and cafes are required by law to turn up the volume of their radio sets so that people on the streets, too, can hear; waiters are forbidden to serve during the broadcast, and patrons forbidden to chat until it is over. It is not an announcement; it is a religious service. After the silence comes a long drawn out fanfare of trumpets, and the rolling of drums with the strain of *Die Wacht am Rhein* surging up through the clatter. This is repeated three times, then another silence. Then, in the voice of an apostle, the radio announcer sonorously reads.[8]

Writing on the morning of 29 June, Guderian was feeling very satisfied about his progress and was clearly looking forward to the public broadcasts. 'I am well, and operations are progressing to my satisfaction. The radio will make special announcements today, from which you can see that our undertaking has measured up to the high expectations.'[9] Hoepner had also keenly anticipated the broadcasts and on 30 June he wrote with particular pride to Irma about what he considered as his special recognition. 'I'm sure you've often waited a long time for news on the radio. Yesterday, among the first eight special reports two finally appeared that give you an account of my activities so far: the tank battles on the Dubysa [River] north of Kovno[10] and the capture of Daugavpils. In the larger picture of operations, the crossing of the Daugava [River][11] stands out very favourably.'[12] While Hoepner was grateful for any credit attributed to his panzer group, Reinhardt's hope for specific recognition of his panzer corps at the battle of Raseiniai was fully satisfied when one of the special announcements was devoted entirely to this encounter. As the propaganda report read: 'After a two-day period, on 26 June, the German panzers victoriously led a massive tank battle north of Kovno. Many divisions were encircled and destroyed, over 200 Soviet-Russian tanks, including twenty-nine of the heaviest models, more than 150 guns as well as hundreds of trucks fell into our hands.'[13] The panzer groups of Guderian and Hoth, in the centre of the German front, also received praise for their part in encircling two Soviet armies at Białystok and closing a major pocket at Minsk.[14]

While the generals savoured the tone of triumph that framed the first week of their campaign, behind the scenes Hitler's propaganda minster, Joseph Goebbels, bitterly complained that his propaganda machinery had effectively been hijacked by one of his rivals, the Reich's press chief Dr Otto Dietrich, to overplay the successes at the front.[15] Of course, Nazi propaganda was usually more show than substance, but it is worth briefly considering just how events at the front were reported and how distortion was built into the process. While the Wehrmacht's wartime accomplishments might appear to speak for themselves, during the 1930s no such assumption was made. The Wehrmacht's success was carefully scripted for domestic audiences and an inter-ministerial committee for civilian–military coordination, called the State Defence Council (*Reichsverteidigungsrat*), was set up under the direction of Major Alfred von Wrochem. Wrochem was the author of an influential book about the failure of German propaganda in the First World War, and his appointment charted a new course for wartime propaganda. The State Defence Council included a number of leading army officers, including at the time Guderian, who was Inspector of the Motorised Troops. Wrochem introduced the idea of sending war correspondents, photographers and film crews to the

front.[16] These would be organised into dedicated propaganda companies (*Propaganda-Kompanien* – PK), which by 1941 numbered just over
200 men each, providing not only material for the German radio,
cinemas and press, but also propaganda directed towards the enemy
to encourage defeatism and desertion. As Omer Bartov noted, it was 'the
first war which blended modern images and technology, which sold
itself as a media event'.[17]

For Operation Barbarossa, each of the German armies and
panzer groups had its own propaganda company, which was integrated
into the command staff, allowing it to forge close relations with the
senior commanders.[18] However, this was not always the case, as some
high-ranking officers displayed a marked mistrust and even scepticism
towards the PK men. Others, of course, realised the opportunity they
represented and took a very personal interest in their work. According
to Jochen Lehnhardt, it was especially the panzer commanders who
fostered close relations with the PK men: 'Rommel became the quintessential example, but Guderian was also especially active in advancing
his own personal celebrity. Other notable panzer commanders in this
regard were Hans-Valentin Hube and Walter Model, while in the wider
army were Eduard Dietl, Fritz Lindemann and Walter Reichenau.'[19]
Some of the PK men liked to frame their battle narratives around
dashing and bold individual commanders, which instantly appealed to
the panzer generals and reinforced their own sense of importance and
authority in the field. The gallant example of the dynamic frontline
commander not only functioned to bolster individual celebrity, but
also became a crucial element in driving the cultural conditioning of
the officer corps. As Felix Römer explained:

> The propaganda companies delighted in presenting athletic,
> determined-looking combat officers in command pose.
> Popular troop leaders like Erwin Rommel were held up by
> newsreels and field newspapers as icons, whom up-and-
> coming officers were supposed to emulate. Ambitious officers
> not only derived their expectations of themselves from these
> norms – they also had to live up to them vis-à-vis subordinates,
> officer colleagues and superiors. The fact that soldiers and offi-
> cers constantly observed each other was part of the social con-
> trol within the Wehrmacht – even troop leaders were subjected
> to this.[20]

Hoepner's correspondence with Irma shows that he was very conscious of the PK men in his panzer group and appeared especially keen that they capture his personal direction of the campaign. On only the second day of the war in the East, Hoepner noted: 'Today, a war photojournalist took photographs of us, while I watched a panzer regiment commence its attack.'[21] A week later, on 30 June, Hoepner began including copies of the propaganda photos in his letters home: 'Sch. recently took this marvellous picture. Voigts just photographed me writing this letter. Other than that, many photos are also taken wherever I appear. As I have my own propaganda company, you might see me one time in the newsreel. I won't speak on the radio though.'[22] By 19 July Hoepner was anticipating the publication of such material and called Irma's attention to this: 'Hopefully, you've now received the second series of pictures, too. I'm pleased that you enjoyed the first one. My propaganda company takes many photographs and develops films of our men. Perhaps you'll spot us sometimes in an illustrated magazine.'[23] In addition to posing for photographs, Hoepner also appeared to be able to direct some of the creative content for print articles, knowing that anything the PK men covered would be presented in a positive light. On 5 July he told Irma: 'The officers are fantastic. I have tasked the writer Ziesel, whom the OKH assigned to me, with writing about this.'[24]

While the propaganda companies were assigned to the panzer groups, the constituent corps and divisions were very much the focus of the day-to-day work. Indeed, the customary narrative of heroic individual commanders leading brave men into battle naturally favoured those closest to the action. Not surprisingly, therefore, the panzer generals tended to place themselves at the forefront of the advance in part because this was a proven formula for successful offensives, but also because commanders sought to meet the expectations of a wider social-cultural dynamic. The generals were highly visible figures, aware that their troops as well as fellow officers were observing them and deciding for themselves who did and who did not prove themselves to be worthy leaders. Most senior commanders in the *Panzertruppe* understood that leading by example at the front, getting their uniforms dirty or facing some element of danger developed trust among the lower ranks and earned the officer in question respect and sometimes widespread veneration. The addition of PK men as outside observers not only heightened the stakes, but offered the potential reward of individual recognition and acclaim well beyond one's own unit. Thus, the mixture of inspirational leadership for a tactical or operational advantage was inevitably fused with ego and vanity, encouraging senior officers to present themselves at the front and perform actions that were technically well beneath their rank. Such behaviour was driven by both professional and personal motivations, while at the same time allowing the propaganda companies to reaffirm the iconic cultural mythos that Germany's wartime leaders were invariably bold and fearless. The willingness of the panzer generals to lead from the front, risking their lives and even exposing themselves to the potential for enemy capture, might suggest this was no mythos or propaganda invention, but PK reports should not simply be accepted at face value.

In the Anglo-American world there has been something of a cottage industry among small-scale publishers of military history to reproduce German wartime PK reports uncritically for niche audiences looking for confirmation of the Wehrmacht's military prowess.[25] Such reports can help us understand the idealised self-conception of the German army, but it would be naïve to assume they were not embellished and even at times blatantly falsified. Of course, without dedicated study it is hard to know the precise extent of this, but the potential for self-aggrandising media exposure was certainly enough for the panzer commanders to forge close relations with the PK men. As an example, Schmidt at the head of his XXXIX Motorised Army Corps became the subject of a glorifying article by the war correspondent U. Maleiski:

> Since the beginning of the fighting in the East it has been the indomitable will of the general [Schmidt] to keep pushing his troops forward by all means and to achieve the daily goals, which sound almost unobtainable. On the first day of the war, he was with his troops at six o'clock in the morning and immediately drove his staff car to the focal points of the fight, regardless of the enemy fire. On a hill near the enemy, he meets the commander of the Panzer Group, Colonel-General Hoth, who greets him with the following words: 'Yes, that's right, I want to see my generals that far ahead.' The daring action of the general and the exemplary fighting spirit of the troops breaks the resistance in a very short time. The way to Olita is free. By taking advantage of this favourable location, it is possible to occupy the two bridges over the Nemen [River]. Despite lively fighting and strong fire on the main bridge near Olita, General Schmidt drives to the other bank to assess the battle for the bridges.[26]

The depiction of a panzer general risking all to lead his men at the front became the very embodiment of the National Socialist heroic trope, and in Schmidt's case this ideal pervaded both public as well as private representations of himself. In his first letter to Fridel of the campaign, Schmidt proudly explained: 'We usually sleep fully clothed, because of course the attacks and shooting are constant. So far, I have always been at the forward-most point of the entire army by a long way. But now I have had to stop and wait.'[27] According to Thomas Kühne, Schmidt was conforming to an archetypal ideal: 'The epitome of the hero was the charismatic leader who put his men under his spell and drew them magnetically into battle.'[28] Force of personality, fearless leadership and a willingness to sacrifice for his men qualified Schmidt for the highest praise, but this image was – at least in part – a purposeful construct necessary for any aspiring commander to build his reputation and career. Furthermore, one must critically consider how much time a corps commander should be spending at the front, where communications were no doubt more limited and pressing decisions could not always be made.

Figure 3.1 Rudolf Schmidt in August 1941

Another war correspondent, Hans Hertel from the *Thüringer Gauzeitung*, may even have been personally recruited by Schmidt, given that he volunteered for service as an orderly officer on XXXIX Motorised Army Corps' staff and came from Weimar, where Schmidt had previously been posted.[29] Hertel's dispatches mimicked those of Maleiski in bombast and bravado, but most importantly, at the core of his story stood Schmidt himself – indefatigable and unyielding. Publishing in the *Thüringer Gauzeitung* on 1 July, Hertel wrote:

> The troops continued their attack in the morning with undiminished speed and punched their way through enemy resistance everywhere. But the general [Schmidt . . .] knows that speed is everything in this offensive. So, he gives the order: Forward at all costs! And now an unparalleled hunt begins. The general, accompanied only by a few members of a reconnaissance detachment and a few men from his staff, positioned himself in the lead and drove ahead in an open staff car to explore the best routes. [. . .] Everywhere between the general's patrol and the troops advancing from behind is still teeming with Russians [. . .] The Russian is now fighting fanatically [. . .] the general himself drives everything forward. [. . .] The crews of the staff cars disappear into the ditch and have to watch as the Russians destroy the vehicles. General [Schmidt] is right at the front in the right ditch, and anyone who can, somehow works their way to him. The small group, which is just before the bend in a grove in the ditch, now receives not only shell fire, but also devastating fire from machine guns and constantly growing rifle fire. [. . .]
>
> A comrade from the propaganda company, who lived through that night with us, summed up his impressions when we all came out of the battle, dead tired and filthy [. . .] the general's example remains an incentive for the last man.[30]

It is impossible to know exactly how embellished such reporting was, but given the larger-than-life tenor of the stories and central role attributed to the commanding officer, it is not hard to see why the panzer generals embraced the limelight and perhaps at times felt obligated to risk so much. Certainly, National Socialist propaganda underlined why there was such a remarkable belief in the concept of individual 'will'. Given the centrality of Hitler to the Nazi state, and the pervasive influence of what historians refer to as 'the Führer myth', it is not surprising that his personal example also had a decisive impact upon the culture of the army. A cornerstone of Hitler's public speeches and writings was his own life story, in which his 'triumph of the will' conquered all adversity and led to his rise from army corporal to head of the German state. Practical considerations such as Germany's ruinous economic position, weak democratic institutions, the divisive political climate and widespread public disaffection after the loss of the First World War were not the emphasis: Hitler was the man who imposed himself on Germany's troubles and triumphed. After 1933, National Socialist propaganda took up a similar story of a nation reborn in Hitler's mould, united in purpose and deed by a common insuperable will.[31]

For the Wehrmacht the primacy of 'will' was a natural fit for the archetypal military commander who carried his army to victory with conviction and assertiveness. Notions of *Kampfgeist* (fighting spirit) and *Siegeswille* (desire for victory) were certainly not unique to the Nazi period[32] or even to the German military tradition.[33] Nevertheless, the concept of the *Siegeswille* was radicalised markedly under National Socialism. One aspect of this was the establishment of 'Wehrmacht psychology', which assessed officer candidates at some twenty-two testing sites around Germany in 1940. In addition to traditional notions of courage, decisiveness, self-control, perseverance, obedience and leadership qualities, 'Wehrmacht psychology' also placed heavy emphasis upon identifying *Willensstärke* (literally 'strength of will'). Colonel-General Walter von Brauchitsch emphasised this in December 1938 when he announced that future officers would need to be 'convinced go-getters' (*überzeugte Tatmenschen*) characterised by 'steel-hard personalities, strength of will and resilience'.[34] Jörg Muth's study of German command culture noted that *Willenskraft* (willpower) was 'paramount among the capabilities' of a German officer: 'the will to become a role model of an officer, the will to succeed in any given task, the will to force a tactical decision, the will to speak his mind, and the will to remain steady under pressure'.[35]

By the outbreak of the Second World War, *Willensstärke* had been internalised as the leading characteristic of the best German officers. It was not just a propaganda tool, but a system of belief that had acquired genuine agency within the army command. Illustrative of this, Reinhardt's letters to Eva often cast himself in a similar light to the propaganda, not so much in tone, but in placing the emphasis for success on his decisive intervention. On 5 October he wrote:

> It's good that I drove to the front in good time. Everything went wrong to begin with: delays, the late arrival of orders, missed roads, etc. I arrived just in time to galvanise everyone, drove ahead of some commanders, so that they were forced to hurriedly keep up; then everything gained momentum and we were then able to advance more than 50 km.[36]

No one can deny the importance of good leadership in warfare and there is no reason to question that at times Reinhardt made crucial interventions.[37] Yet the concept was rife for abuse as commanders compensated for matériel deficiency with ever increasing demands on subordinate officers to achieve more with less. Indeed, as we have seen, the panzer generals themselves felt this pressure from above, which contributed to their own psychological decline as they worked tirelessly for solutions to increasingly intractable problems and were never able to fully accept that too much was being asked of them, just as they were asking too much of their own men. The overestimation of the 'great captain' in understanding military campaigns has only relatively recently been identified as a problem in Western historiography,[38] so even beyond the German army's blinkered cultural context, which was impossible for men like Reinhardt to escape, generals of the era struggled to grasp the limitations of individual command.

In another letter Reinhardt wrote in November, he presented the changing fortunes of a poorly performing division as a direct result of his leadership, in spite of the fact that as the panzer group commander, he was a long way removed from the day-to-day operation of the division:

> Several weeks ago, a division was subordinated to me [handwritten note in the margin – 14th Motorised Infantry Division] that had somewhat lost faith in itself. It had been repeatedly split during the October hostilities, had been subordinated to others and been obliged to help them, and was severely weakened in the process and somewhat looked down upon. I, therefore, assumed control of it, as well as a new commander.[39] On the occasion of the takeover, I appealed to the commander [Major-General Heinrich Wosch], and shortly

afterwards the fighting started again. As it turned out, the division had received very little in the way of tasks; only now was there a, by no means easy but fine task, which I could and had to assign to it, of course, with a certain amount of trepidation as to how things would turn out, but in the hope that tangible, important objectives would entice it and boost its morale.[40] Today, I can say with great satisfaction that I was not deceiving myself. Everyone talks approvingly of the division, which adds to its successes day by day; it has also received thanks and recognition from the Field Marshal [Bock], and the most important thing is that the division itself is happy and proud and its faith in itself is restored.[41] For me, however, it was of course a duty to take care of this division more than others. Yesterday, I not only visited the division but also an infantry regiment [handwritten note – 11th Infantry Regiment] at the front that already knew me from Saxony. It was uplifting to see the joy – I almost want to say astonishment – in everyone's eyes at seeing army commanders so far forwards in their midst, and then to feel the joy when I was able to shake hands with the commander at the regimental command post and express my thanks to him and his regiment.[42]

Such self-belief in effecting radical change from above mimics the simplistic propaganda narrative that emphasised the decisive role of the commanding general to the exclusion of all else. Thus, the success of any given panzer group or panzer corps was a reflection of the general himself, not an exceedingly complex process with many competing factors, including enemy counter-measures and even good and bad luck. Accordingly, the panzer generals took public announcements detailing the achievements of their formations very personally, because it was generally understood to be an individual accomplishment. As Reinhardt excitedly wrote to Eva on 12 July: 'Tomorrow, on Sunday, there will likely be more important special announcements; it might be the case that we're involved in the conquest of a major city [Pleskau ...] worthy of mention.'[43]

That the panzer generals valued public recognition as highly as they did made them very conscious of what was reported from the front and who was given the credit for it. Feelings of jealousy and suspicion

Figure 3.2 Georg-Hans Reinhardt (second from left) meeting with his officers in July 1941

were never far from the surface because public profiles held real currency in the National Socialist state. While the panzer generals competed among themselves, there was an even greater sense of entitlement, and even at times antagonism, in relation to the slow-moving infantry. As Guderian objected to Margarete on 15 July: 'Every day claims new victims, and behind us there marches an enormous army that is yet to fire a shot! Considering that, there's all the more coverage of them in the press. Even more so than the French campaign, the Russian campaign – at least where our panzer group is concerned – has become almost exclusively an affair of the panzer troops.'[44] This was completely untrue and Guderian almost certainly knew it. While there could be no question that his panzer group was pushing the German front forward, Guderian's men were advancing mainly on the major roads, bypassing countless thousands of Soviet troops who were left to the following infantry to engage and capture. The idea that the hard-pressed infantry had not fired a shot in three weeks was wilfully disingenuous.[45]

Aware of her husband's predilection for public recognition, Margarete attempted to mollify Heinz after hearing a broadcast describing the German encirclement at Kiev without a personal acknowledgement of his role. Margarete not only anticipated Heinz's disappointment, but tactfully assured him that he would eventually receive the appreciation he felt he deserved. On 19 September Margarete wrote:

> On Wednesday, news of the great victory came from Führer Headquarters in confirmation of your report, unfortunately without mentioning your name or even the panzer formations, but only the 'strong units' of the army of Field Marshal von Bock.[46] The main thing, however, is that you managed it, my dearest, and that you are healthy and content; I'm sure your achievement will be properly recognised someday![47]

The announcement not only singled out Bock, but also named Field Marshal Gerd von Rundstedt (Army Group South), Field Marshal Albrecht Kesselring (Air Fleet 2) and Colonel-General Alexander Löhr (Air Fleet 4). What might have been particularly galling to Guderian was the fact that Bock had strenuously opposed the operation into Ukraine, advocating instead for Army Group Centre's continued drive on Moscow. Guderian had initially supported Bock, but changed his mind after a visit to Hitler's headquarters and complained thereafter that Bock withheld support for his drive into Ukraine.[48] To Guderian's mind, Bock being named at his expense as one of the heroes of the Kiev encirclement was nothing short of an injustice; however, recompense was soon made as the unprecedented scale of the Soviet disaster in Ukraine encouraged German propaganda to make more public announcements. On 21 September Guderian was personally named, along with Reichenau (Sixth Army) and Kleist (Panzer Group 1), as being instrumental in the success of the operation.[49]

It was not the first time that Guderian had been mentioned by name in the campaign. He was celebrated over two successive days on 6 and 7 August at the conclusion of the battle of Smolensk.[50] Likewise, Hoepner received a public acknowledgement on 6 August for breaking through the Soviet line south of Lake Peipus, but cannot have been impressed that in the published pronouncement his name was incorrectly spelled as 'Höppner'.[51] Even more irritating for Hoepner was that by August his panzer group's advance was faltering, which, like Guderian, he attributed to his superiors and their unwillingness to adequately resource him. Writing to Irma on 18 August, he complained at length before concluding: 'Thus, I suddenly have tasks that I have to fulfil with insufficient forces, are never fully realised and, therefore, receive no recognition.'[52] Hoepner desperately wanted to cap his summer offensive with the investment or even capture of Leningrad, which he knew would earn him a mark of distinction surpassed only by the capture of Moscow. Not only did Hoepner believe that his superiors were denying him the strength to reach his objective, but when he received the news that his panzer group would be diverted south for the autumn offensive (Operation Typhoon), he interpreted this as further evidence that his superiors were seeking to steal his glory. As he wrote to Irma on 12 September:

> The most important thing now is that I'll be taken out of here from 15 September. That's frustrating, because we are again deprived of the outward appearance of a victory. Since 9 September, we've broken through the outer line of fortifications. [...] Generally speaking, my campaign against Petersburg is thus over.[53] I won't be entering the city, either. It's the end of a frustrating chapter. Most recently, another spanner was thrown in the works, when they did not assign to me all envisaged troops, and they even reserved for themselves the influence over the deployment of the air fleet. One could assume that the senior authorities want to keep for themselves the glory of taking the city.[54]

Such suspicion and mistrust only serve to underline the significance attached to public acknowledgement. In the same letter, Hoepner included for Irma a copy of *Blücher*, a short four-page newsletter produced for the German soldiers at the front, which extolled the achievements of his panzer forces at Leningrad.[55] There could be no denying the panzer generals craved attention and tended to react very poorly when they felt ignored or overlooked.

Schmidt was the only one of the panzer generals not to be mentioned in any of the Wehrmacht reports for 1941, but that was not at all unusual for a corps commander (he only gained an army command on 15 November). Yet on 5 September Schmidt nevertheless felt it necessary to explain to Fridel that: 'For political and military reasons, nothing about us has yet appeared in the Wehrmacht's report.'[56] Three days later, a special announcement stated that the 'German–Finnish ring around Leningrad was closed', which provoked a contrasting response from Schmidt.[57] Having earlier made excuses for his lack of public recognition, he then took the opposite view. Although the special announcement made no reference to Schmidt or his motorised corps, he proudly wrote to Fridel: 'As you will have heard from the special reports and the military reports, I'm outside Petersburg.'[58]

Clearly, generals sought to advance their own prestige through the exploitation of propaganda, and we should not be surprised that Guderian, as the best-known panzer general in the Soviet campaign, was also the most skilled in advancing his own celebrity. Creating a genuinely popular following required reaching people beyond the tight constraints of state media, which Guderian had already success-fully done in 1937 when he published his bestselling book *Achtung – Panzer!*[59] While the book is typically described as a military treatise advocating for the concentrated use of armour, Guderian was not just presenting a series of lectures on strategic theories and technical innov-ations. As he wrote in the introduction, the aim of the book was 'to inspire veterans and young soldiers alike', and in places the book became a rallying cry for Guderian's brand of 'go-getter' panzer trooper with himself as their self-styled guru-general.[60] Beyond anything to do with military innovation, *Achtung – Panzer!* was a thinly disguised promotional book for service in the panzer forces. As Guderian wrote:

> Service in the panzer forces is fine and varied, and every tank-man is proud to belong to this new arm, which is dedicated to the offensive. But panzer service is also demanding; it requires young men of sound constitution and mind, with cheerful hearts and determined will. Tank service builds small unit cohesion in a quite remarkable way; there can be no distinctions – officers, NCOs and men alike share the same testing conditions of com-bat, and everyone must play his part to the full. [...] Actions speak louder than words. In the days to come the Goddess of Victory will bestow her laurels only on those who are prepared to act with daring.[61]

Without question, Guderian was by far the best known of the panzer group commanders in 1941 and if he had a rival in the celebrity stakes, it was actually the much more junior Erwin Rommel, who was still a corps commander and only a Lieutenant-General when Barbarossa began. Of course, Rommel's fame underlines the disproportionate importance of celebrity to career-building within the Nazi state and it is not surprising that he too had stolen a march on his contemporaries with his own bestselling book, *Infanterie greift an* (*Infantry Attacks*), also released in

1937.[62] Whatever the virtue of Rommel's observations about infiltration tactics and manoeuvre warfare, as David Grossman noted, it remains 'a self-promoting book in which Rommel tells how he won the *Pour le Mérite*, Germany's highest award in the World War I – also known as the Blue Max'.[63] Christian Adam's study of bestselling books in the National Socialist state noted: 'The war dynamized certain processes in the book market and brought about highly effective marketing concepts.'[64]

Since Guderian was nothing if not innovative in promoting his own brand, in 1941 he planned a masterstroke of public messaging by engaging Hans Gustl Kernmayr, a leading National Socialist propagandist, to write a glorifying biography of him. As Felix Römer has observed: 'Wartime biographies generated soldierly self-images: the documented relationship between career paths and mentalities proves how much military structures and events influenced the protagonists.'[65] Kernmayr's own profile was as important for selling books as his subject. An Austrian who claimed to have known Hitler since the First World War, Kernmayr became a dedicated National Socialist and had to flee Austria as a result. After the *Anschluss* he accompanied Hitler's victory tour, describing himself as Hitler's 'scribe' and releasing a fawning propaganda book *Ein Volk kehrt heim! Österreichs Kampf und Befreiung (A People Return Home! Austria's Struggle and Liberation)*.[66] Guderian was impressed and invited Kernmayr to join his staff in the East to observe the earliest days of the campaign. The two forged a bond and, if not already before, certainly in this period the plan for a biography was agreed. Kernmayr was already committed to a brief spell as a special war correspondent, so writing about Guderian fitted his own agenda. Returning to Berlin from Panzer Group 2, Kernmayr personally visited Margarete to deliver a letter from Heinz and no doubt pursue another source of information on his subject. Up until this point, the prospective collaboration served both men, and Guderian wrote confidently to Margarete on 4 July: 'He [Kernmayr] nicely implemented his tasks here and we were fond of him. He is due to return in around four weeks.'[67] It is unclear if Kernmayr did return to Panzer Group 2, but he did set to work on a manuscript, which, owing to his typically prolific output, was drafted by mid-September and sent to Guderian's home in Berlin. Margarete received it on 18 September and read it immediately. Her reaction was decidedly disapproving. Although she opened her description of the book to Heinz with the assurance that it 'contains many good and great things', she was less impressed by

Kernmayr's tangential discussions of what she considered unnecessary subject-matter. For example, she thought he spent too much time discussing 'the milieu of country roads, from which K[ernmayr] cannot entirely free himself'.[68] This is probably a reference to the difficulties of conducting rapid, mobile operations on unsealed Soviet roads. Margarete also took exception to his discussion of the soldiers, which at times included their civilian professions and lives before the war. This she felt was indulgent, 'a little too much drama for my taste, just as you can often sense that he is not a soldier himself'.[69] One suspects that Margarete's distaste was directed towards anything that distracted from Guderian the great man. After all, there were no complaints of overindulgence in Kernmayr's depiction of Guderian. Yet the issue that concerned her most was the depth of the discussion devoted to their private lives. As she protested to Heinz: 'For us ethnic Germans, with our Prussian and morally strict way of thinking and feeling, some things are absurd, but I will write to him and ask him to change some things, especially as regards our personal life. Perhaps you don't want anything at all to be included about that.'[70]

Margarete clearly had serious reservations and while she qualified these, no doubt knowing how important the project was to Heinz, she concluded her letter by advocating for a new approach. 'I am perhaps too critical, but a book that concerns itself with you must surely be seriously worked through, and K[ernmayr] does not have the stamina or the patience for that. His other books are also a bit lightweight.' Unfortunately, at this point Margarete had reached the bottom of her page and rather than continuing on a new piece of paper she opted to scribble her remaining thoughts along the long edge of the paper over her previous text, rendering words illegible. She suggested to Heinz the name of another biographer, which cannot be deciphered, and described him as 'a serious craftsman, both soldierly and [illegible word] as a person and a writer; I would have rather entrusted this book to him. [. . .] I am eager to hear your criticism; don't let yourself be influenced by me.'[71]

Margarete may have invited Heinz to make up his own mind, but she must have suspected that her condemnation of Kernmayr would spell the end of his involvement. Guderian's reply was swift and unambiguous. On 25 September he assured Margarete: 'I found your report on Kernmayr very interesting and I am convinced that your assessment is correct. Not for a moment would I want to be the subject of propaganda à la Rommel and can only reinforce your decision to prevent it.'[72]

Of course, Guderian had never been averse to the idea of a calculated publicity stunt, but only if it portrayed him in a stylish and sophisticated manner. He trusted his reputation far more to Margarete's shrewd judgement than to Kernmayr's journalist flair. It was also instructive that Guderian dubbed Rommel's media 'propaganda' and attempted to draw such a stark distinction between their respective forms of brazen self-promotion. This was not always apparent to Guderian's interlocutors, as one observer noted when, during a heated discussion with Colonel Rudolf Schmundt,[73] Guderian found it necessary to exclaim: 'It's not about my fame, but about the German Reich.'[74] Yet Guderian understood that no press coverage was better than bad press coverage. As he explained to Margarete, 'even the slightest exaggeration can only be damaging. I don't care one bit if the book appears or not. If it's no good, then I'd prefer it not to appear at all. We would only be annoyed or even ashamed, and that's not something I put any value on.'[75] In Kernmayr's long list of lifetime publications there was never a biography of Guderian, so it seems the manuscript was discarded.

While Guderian had given up on the idea of a biography, he had certainly not given up on the idea of achieving fame through the popular press. There was another Austrian war correspondent, Erich Landgrebe, who had been assigned to Panzer Group 2 and appears to have been a long-standing family friend of the Guderians. Although not much is known about their relationship, Guderian mentioned Landgrebe in a letter to Margarete and included photographs of the two in conversation. He also requested that if Margarete wrote to the Landgrebe family, she pass on Heinz's personal regards.[76] Like Kernmayr, Landgrebe was a committed Nazi who had even taken over and 'Aryanised' the Jewish Zsolnay Publishing House in Vienna.[77] Guderian did not discuss the details of their collaboration in his letters to Margarete, but what resulted was a book published in 1942 with the title *Mit den Panzern in Ost und West* (*With the Tanks in East and West*).[78] It was a collection of dramatic war stories from officers and men, including one written by Guderian's son Heinz Günther, and served as an unabashed advertisement for the *Panzertruppe*. Of course, Guderian provided the rousing call to arms in his Foreword:

> In this book, men who saw combat with me in the East and West, and who are drawn from every arm of our tank formations, relate their experiences. [...] Such élan, such boldness,

such readiness for sacrifice! [...] It tells of the heroism of our dead and wounded, of true comradeship and of loyalty to the Reich and the Führer. And so this small book is a contribution to victory![79]

Achieving celebrity was by no means simply a matter of vanity for men like Rommel and Guderian. Their careers tangibly benefited from the exposure because at the highest levels of the National Socialist state as well as the army, the perception of success directly impacted their power and influence. Careers could see meteoric rises, disproportionate to experience or the formal promotion system of the Army Personnel Office (*Heerespersonalamt*). Famous examples typically included panzer generals like Walter Model, who received a promotion or decoration in almost every year of the war, rising four ranks in four years from a Major-General in 1940 to a Field Marshal in 1944. Yet while the reputation of men like Model or Rommel would appear to justify the system and suggest promotion followed performance, this was only superficially true.[80] Only in recent years have much more critical biographies and campaign histories revealed the shortcomings of many celebrated German commanders. This is not to suggest they did not deserve a degree of distinction, but such studies seriously qualify their supposed success and reveal how much their wartime mystique was taken over uncritically into the post-war world.[81] Accounting for the highest-ranking career success in Nazi Germany was not a simple question of military performance, but included high visibility and social connections. This was hardly a uniquely German phenomenon, as research by David Moore and B. Thomas Trout observed a similar pattern of success in the United States military.[82]

Charm Offensives

While leveraging connections certainly played a role in any administrative hierarchy, it was especially important in Hitler's dysfunctional state, where devotion and loyalty often trumped competence and expertise. As Fabrice d'Almeida noted of Germany's high society under the Nazis: 'Personal value and celebrity were indubitably the keys to the society world of the 1920s, and this trend became stronger after 1933. Even participation in parties and politics was professionalised, becoming a full-time job for the political bureaucracy and raising those involved in the social hierarchy by allocating wealth and notoriety to them.'[83] Notions that senior army commanders were somehow too high-minded or proper to debase themselves with social manoeuvring among the Nazi elite can quickly be dismissed. Jockeying for influence, position and status was simply part of the social milieu. D'Almeida suggests there were three tiers of elites in the National Socialist state, the highest consisting of some 200 men and women, who became the familiar faces of official dinners and state receptions. This leading cohort was made up mostly of state ministers, state secretaries, senior party members, SS officers and high-ranking military men, especially those with aristocratic backgrounds. As d'Almeida explained, it was these elites who 'received greetings and gifts on their birthdays from state and party leaders'.[84] With the possible exception of Rommel and Guderian, the panzer generals did not belong in this uppermost tier of Nazi society, but their proximity to it is clear from their personal papers. On 12 May 1941 on the occasion of Schmidt's fifty-fifth birthday, the general received a congratulatory telegram from Hitler. A year earlier, after his promotion to General of Panzer Troops, Schmidt received a congratulatory telegram from Heinrich Himmler.[85] Similarly, while campaigning in the Soviet Union, Hoepner wrote to Irma telling her that he had received a birthday telegram from Hermann Göring, which only reached him on 14 October, exactly one month late.[86] Reinhardt's connections are harder to judge, but in the aftermath of the 1944 July Plot, which in no small part originated in Army Group Centre, where Reinhardt had served continuously since 1941, he was able to call upon and gain the emphatic endorsement of the murderous *SS-Obergruppenführer* Curt von Gottberg, which sufficed to clear him of any suspicion and pave the way for him to be promoted as the new head of the army group.[87] According to d'Almeida's categorisation, Schmidt, Hoepner and Reinhardt most probably belonged to the larger second tier of elites, numbering some 600 to 800 individuals, who were important enough to be acknowledged for their expertise, but perhaps more so for their potential future rise into positions of greater power, responsibility and influence.[88]

Guderian's credentials for admission to the top tier of the Nazi elite are compelling. Most important was Guderian's fervent commitment to National Socialism and the strong mutual admiration he shared with Hitler. Just how committed Guderian was to the Nazi cause is illustrated by Hitler's army adjutant, Major Gerhard Engel, who recorded a meeting in March 1938 with the panzer general in the wake of the Blomberg–Fritsch affair. Guderian told Engel he was 'shocked at what had gone on' in the leadership of the army, but it was his suggested remedy that underlined where Guderian's allegiance lay. According to Engel, Guderian 'blamed everything on the Army High Command, which had not been able to master itself [. . .] and so win the Führer's confidence'. Accordingly, Guderian asserted that trust in the army needed to be restored and suggested new leadership by either Himmler or Göring. Engel was too astonished to make any comment, but it was clear that Guderian valued Hitler's approval over any institutional loyalty to the army's independence.[89]

The Guderians lived in the exclusive Berlin suburb of Dahlem, which was the favoured residence of some of the most prominent members of Nazi society, including Himmler.[90] The Guderians were also fortunate to be related by marriage to General of Infantry Bodewin Keitel, the younger brother of the chief of the OKW (High Command of the Wehrmacht), Field Marshal Wilhelm Keitel. It was through this connection to Bodewin Keitel, who happened to head the Army Personnel Office (until October 1942), that Guderian was able to lay the groundwork for his return to service in 1943.[91] As Guderian knew only too well, exploiting connections was essential to building, or in this case restoring, one's career. Indeed, Guderian cultivated relationships so successfully that it was as though his dismissal from command at the end of 1941 had never happened.

Just how important re-establishing his career in the army was for Guderian is revealed by General of Panzer Troops Wilhelm Ritter von Thoma, who visited Guderian's home in August 1942 before his own departure for service in North Africa. As Thoma revealed in secret recordings conducted during his subsequent British captivity, 'He [Guderian] told me himself: "I am ashamed to go to the barber's because they say: What are you doing here?"'[92] It reflects Guderian's acute sensitivity to his diminished public standing and the shame he associated with inactivity during wartime. Yet despite engaging in the cardinal sin of recurrent unauthorised retreats, which were a sign both of insubordination and of weakness for Hitler, Guderian not only succeeded in restoring himself to active duty, but rose to become the acting chief of the army general staff in July 1944. Bastiaan Willems labels Guderian an 'uncompromising careerist' who 'had taken the time to probe Hitler's attitude towards warfare' and 'had learned not to merely argue his point but to mimic Hitler's rhetoric as well'.[93] Not surprisingly, Guderian came into conflict with his fellow generals, but the sinister extent to which the panzer general had sold his soul was seen in his participation in the new 'court of honour of the Wehrmacht'. As one of a four-man committee, Guderian rubber-stamped the discharge of fellow officers who had conspired against the regime in the July Plot.[94] Such forcible removal from the Wehrmacht was necessary in order for accused officers to be found guilty by the fanatical 'People's Court' and not be subject to the Reich Military Court, which would otherwise have had jurisdiction. One of these victims would be Hoepner, who was thrown out of the army, tortured by the Gestapo, humiliated in his show trial and hanged by wire mounted from a meat hook at Plötzensee Prison in Berlin.[95] Yet Guderian's part in condemning his fellow officers was not too high a price to pay for his new appointment as one of Hitler's senior military advisers.[96] Moreover, with greater access to Hitler, Guderian warranted the attention of other senior Nazis, which he willingly indulged, even to the point of spending Christmas 1944 at an exclusive dinner hosted by Himmler.[97]

As Guderian networked his way to success, Margarete also showed fidelity to the National Socialist cause and the worldview it embraced. Importantly, wives were not just passive onlookers; they shared the celebrity of their husbands and could prove extremely important on the social scene, acting as surrogates for their spouses. As d'Almeida's research makes clear, 'The actions of the wives of male members of this inner sanctum should not be overlooked. In most cases they were surprisingly well informed and used their own celebrity to work in favour of their husbands and friends.'[98] In accordance with the obligatory requirements of National Socialist society, in 1938 Margarete joined the Nazi Party, followed by the National Socialist Women's League (*Nationalsozialistische Frauenschaft*) and the social charity organisation National Socialist People's Welfare (*Nationalsozialistische Volkswohlfahrt*).[99] Just as she unreservedly supported Heinz in personal matters, so too did she offer her backing in the public sphere. In conversations with Guderian's British biographer, Kenneth Macksey, Heinz Günther Guderian explained that his mother became 'absolutely essential' to his father's success, performing as a kind of private 'chief of staff'. Macksey even asserted that she began to exert a degree of control over Guderian's career, writing: 'Of still greater importance were the evolving ambitions of Margarete who, as time went by, came to believe in her husband's great destiny and whose influence upon him, as will be seen, was not only designed to encourage but to guide his footsteps.'[100] Margarete's 1941 letters not only show that Heinz's career manoeuvring was a topic of discussion but also that she clearly had a voice in the conversation. Yet their precise dealings were considered so sensitive that the matter was understood to be beyond discussion even in their private correspondence. Shedding light on the intrigue, Russell Hart suggests Heinz was angling for a leading role in the army as early as 1941.[101] Accordingly, Brauchitsch's dismissal from command of the army was an event of significance for the Guderians and one that Margarete cryptically and guardedly addressed:

> The Christmas surprise with von Brauchitsch getting his marching orders caused quite a stir; there are rumours cir-culating about seven other generals. If they're true, events will have taken the turn that we feared. I don't want to go into any more detail in writing, but you'll understand what I mean. On the telephone recently, I also didn't want to ask; we can speak in more depth at a later date. [...] There will also be changes and consequences for your activities and tasks; I hope with all my heart that it'll turn out for the best. You know how profoundly I experience and share everything with you.[102]

Certainly, Margarete was socially adept and well-connected, maintain-ing a sizeable correspondence that sometimes weighed on her. She rarely included the specifics of who and what she was writing to people about, but among others made reference to Princess Bentheim,[103] the Surgeon General,[104] Mrs Kesselring[105] and Mrs Keitel in relation to the supervi-sion of a military hospital (Margarete was also an active member of the German Red Cross).[106] Clearly, wives could play an influential, if somewhat hidden, role in promoting their husband's career. While there is no information with which to reconstruct the roles played by Irma, Eva and Fridel in furthering their husbands' careers, it is clear Margarete served Heinz's schemes as a confidant, advocate and perhaps even at times a manager of his ambitions.

Given that military success dovetailed so neatly with a high public profile and individual reward, the inducement for panzer com-manders to perform well extended beyond the normative ideas of duty, honour and national obligation. Not only did the celebratory propaganda influence the culture of the panzer leadership, but it also provoked a popular response among elements of German society, especially boys and young men. Military service was transformed from a compulsory stepping-stone mandated by adulthood to a prized experience where glory and adventure culminated into all that was virtuous and noble in manhood. Yet, unlike in other Western countries, whose propaganda targeted youth with fictional characters from comic books,[107] German youth were given real-life heroes whose swashbuckling, death-defying feats were no less dramatic and all the more believable because they were accepted as being true representations of men in war. Leading Germany's successful armies, the generals acquired a degree of stardom and became the object of youthful awe and imagination. As Adelheid von Saldern observed: 'The Nazi system profited from the star cult, because these stars helped to integrate people into the Nazi system. Beyond political propaganda films, the system created an allegedly non-political German media culture which was apparently simply entertainment, radiating modernity and openness to the world.'[108]

Seduced by a fiction of bloodless military conquest led by a cohort of brilliant military leaders, whose own representation became an extension of the mythical *Führerprinzip*, youthful fantasies were indulged at every level. Not only did National Socialism offer a unique brand of military 'stardom' with warfare as the forum for entertainment, but it was not an abstract spectacle removed from the real world of German youth. Unlike modern-day stars, whose worlds are exclusive and not typically open to their myriad of fans, German male youths were destined to join the ranks of the hallowed Wehrmacht, share in their fame and even perhaps become a star in their own right. A guise of infallibility insulated this illusion from its terrifying reality, yet the success of German propaganda was not its ability to respond rationally to the world, but rather its ability to distort responses at an emotional level. As Sebastian Haffner astutely observed in 1940:

> Outside Germany people often wonder at the palpable fraudulence of Nazi propaganda, the stupid, incredible exaggerations, the ludicrous reticence concerning what is generally known. Who can be convinced by it? They ask. The answer is that it is not meant to convince, but to impress. Believe or not, it must not be forgotten. Nazi propaganda disdains to appeal to reason: it addresses emotion and fantasy.[109]

Figure 3.3 Heinz Guderian indulging the adulation of Hitler Youth who were tasked with building defences in 1944

Empowering German youth with such rousing emotion and inspired fantasy was not just a feature of a manipulative propaganda campaign; the panzer generals played an active role in legitimising and amplifying the message.

Among Schmidt's personal papers is an example of the role panzer generals occupied within the imagination of German youth. Although we know that a huge quantity of fan mail was written to German generals serving in the East, almost none of it has been preserved, making surviving examples all the more important. In the first instance the fact that Schmidt was receiving letters at all is itself worthy of some consideration. The letter was dated 5 August 1941, when Schmidt was still a corps commander.[110] At this point in the war there were some forty-four corps commanders on the Eastern Front. Directing them were four panzer group commanders and eight army commanders, who in turn were subordinate to three German Field Marshals at the army group level. It suggests that some German boys possessed a remarkable understanding of the *Ostheer's* principal commanders, perhaps similar to the manner in which subsequent generations of youths prided themselves on knowing the particulars of individual football players and their teams.[111] Further evidence of this is the fact that the young writer knew to address his letter to 'General of Panzer Troops Schmidt', using the correct rank and avoiding a more generic 'General Schmidt'. The boy's writing suggests he is only about ten years old, but in spite of his young age he was clearly following the war in considerable detail and was even able to begin his letter by addressing Schmidt's individual achievements. He first acknowledged Schmidt's recent award of the prestigious Oak Leaves to the Knight's Cross (10 July) and then the capture of Stalin's son (Yakov Dzhugashvili, 18 July), who was seized by elements of the 12th Panzer Division belonging to Schmidt's XXXIX Motorised Army Corps.[112] Given that German propaganda tended to avoid including the names of units or commanders and, as we have seen, Schmidt was not mentioned in any of the Wehrmacht reports in 1941, this boy was clearly doing his homework.[113] Of course, the capture of Stalin's son did receive significant coverage in the German media[114] and even Schmidt's collection of personal papers, as further evidence of the generals' own preoccupation with their media exposure, includes one of these newspaper articles with every reference to 'Schmidt' underlined in red pencil.[115] Indeed, this same publicity may have accounted for the boy's interest in writing to Schmidt.

Beyond the heroic infatuation, there was also a hopeful purpose behind the boy's letter. Underlining National Socialism's obsession with martial concepts, youths pursued their heroes within the Wehrmacht seeking autographed pictures and other military mementos.[116] As one child of the Nazi era recalled: 'Who could command greater respect than a brave general fighting to save the German people from Bolshevism?'[117] For children, the cult of the war hero made celebrities out of simple soldiers, so the generals were viewed as a kind of royalty. A girl named Wolfhilde von König wrote that she followed the war in great detail, keeping a 'war diary' and seeking autographs from generals like Rommel.[118] Ursula Mahlendorf's childhood memoir recalled: 'Ever since Rommel had gone to assist the Italian army in Tunisia in March 1941, I had followed the progress of his tanks through the desert. For my war diaries I cut out illustrations of German tanks and trucks moving over sandy hills.'[119] Another girl remembered: 'We thought of ourselves as soldiers on the home front.'[120] Given the popular fixation with all things military, it is not surprising that revering the generals became a dedicated hobby. As the boy's letter to Schmidt proudly explained, he had already received autographed pictures from Rommel as well as the leading fighter aces of the Luftwaffe in 1941, including Colonel Werner Mölders, Lieutenant-Colonel Adolf Galland and Captain Walter Oesau.[121] 'Maybe you can also send me a picture w[ith] a[utograph] PLEASE!!!'

One wonders how many other personalities in the Wehrmacht the boy wrote letters to, but clearly even senior officers found time for their young fans and readily responded to their requests. The boy signed off his letter as 'the devoted boy' (*der ergebene Pimpf*), which surreptitiously provides a further insight into the boy's world. *Pimpf* does not translate well into English: while the meaning is 'boy' or even something akin to 'little rascal', it also became a short-hand term for members of the German Youth Movement, which was largely co-opted into the *Deutsches Jungvolk*, the first subdivision of the Hitler Youth, for boys aged ten to fourteen. Activities included pseudo-war games and there was even a monthly Nazi magazine called *Der Pimpf*, which contained a mixture of adventure and propaganda stories.[122] After June 1941 many issues described the war in the East, with one issue devoting its lead article to how five German tanks single-handedly defeated half a Soviet division.[123] Another edition paid glowing tribute to Rommel in North Africa, who, its readers were told, 'does not sit far behind the front, rather he directs his army from the front line'.[124] One description of a *Jungvolk* clubhouse included a large inscription on the wall that read 'Be Fighters', while flags hung suspended from chains and a wreath and candles stood before a dented steel helmet commemorating a former Hitler Youth killed in battle.[125] Thus, a 'devoted *Pimpf*' was not devoted to being a boy, but rather to being a certain type of boy, one who learned to idealise Germany's war heroes.

While the above example offers a useful indication of what fan mail to the panzer generals constituted, Guderian's own correspondence offers further insight into its frequency. On 12 August he wrote Margarete: 'I received a huge number of compliments on my Oak Leaves, some of them very nice ones from people unknown to me. [...] Replying to all these letters is a nuisance, in spite of my use of unprinted[126] cards.'[127] Again one observes that Guderian took the time to reply, if somewhat unwillingly, to his well-wishers. Indeed, the reference to 'unprinted cards' probably pertains to his coloured postcards printed in August 1940 featuring a life-like illustration of Guderian in a commanding pose with a bold caption under the image reading 'Colonel-General Guderian'; below this is printed, in smaller type, 'Creator and Leader of our Victorious Tank Arm' (see Figure 3.4). In a third line of text, in even smaller type, Guderian declared: 'All Germans in the world see in our armoured troops a model of the greatest heroism and in their forward charge the beginning of a new era.' For an 'unprinted' card Guderian certainly had a message to communicate. The postcard also featured Guderian's printed signature, in curiously small type, on the right-hand side just above his shoulder.[128] In spite of this printed signature, Guderian reportedly sent these cards to well-wishers with his name signed over the bottom half of the card. The success of Guderian's self-promotion of course meant ever more devotees and admirers seeking contact with him. This in turn generated its own burden for a man who studiously worked to acknowledge his supporters. Writing to Margarete in early November, Guderian listed the family members he had received letters from before adding: 'As for the rest, a huge correspondence of autograph hunters and other people.'[129]

Guderian's 1940 postcard was just another hallmark of his advanced self-marketing, which he further professionalised in 1943 with a new issue of two different postcards featuring contrasting photos. In the first his Oak Leaves to the Knights Cross are clearly visible, underlining an important status symbol that had been absent from the 1940 postcard. In this image Guderian's pose depicts the consummate steely-eyed panzer general, projecting confidence and authority.[130] The second postcard aims for a very different representation, one that aims for a more personal, and even slightly intimate, depiction. Guderian appears capless and is leaning into the camera with his right hand supporting his chin (see Figure 3.5). It is not the traditional military portrait, for although his expression remains solemn, there is an air of warmth and approachability.[131] Both postcards were captioned 'Colonel-General Guderian', but eschewed too much text and

C/0974   Original von Wolf Willrich

Generaloberſt Guderian

Schöpfer und Führer unſerer ſiegreichen Tankwaffe

Alle Deutſchen in der Welt ſehen in unſeren Panzertruppen ein Vorbild größten
Heldentums und in ihrem Vorwärtsſtürmen den Beginn einer neuen Zeit.

Volksdeutsches Kameradschaftsopfer der deutschen Jugend · Volksbund für das Deutschtum im Ausland   Bild 17.   August 1940

Figure 3.4 Heinz Guderian's 1940 postcard

added only his new title 'General Inspector of Panzer Troops'. Clearly,
Guderian was diversifying his image by shrewdly tailoring his representation to either the resolute and decisive panzer general or the sage
father-figure of the German panzer corps.

A rudimentary internet search into the murky world of
Wehrmacht memorabilia revealed similar images of Hoepner, Schmidt
and Reinhardt, all with signatures that matched their wartime documents.
I cannot attest to their authenticity, but it stands to reason that other
panzer generals were engaged in a similar practice. Perhaps attesting to
his own popularity with autograph hunters, my short search located three

Figure 3.5 Heinz Guderian's 1943 postcard, although the image is believed to date from 1941

different signed photographs of Schmidt, each portraying the general in a different posture. The only signed image of Hoepner was a life-like drawing, which appeared to be a postcard, much like Guderian's early example. There was no text or slogan, but Hoepner's name was likewise printed on the card and signed in purple pencil. Nor was this all. The remaining two panzer group commanders from 1941, Kleist and Hoth, each had signed photographs. Indeed, there was also a postcard of Kleist with a familiar sketched image, printed autograph and hand signed in blue ink – suggesting the generals were watching and learning from each other to economise on self-promotion.[132] Finally, the search revealed signed photographs of considerably more junior panzer generals from the Second World War, suggesting the scope and scale of the practice was widespread.[133]

The cult of personality military 'stars' like Guderian built was not just about fostering popular support in Germany; it also fed the status of the men serving in his Panzer Group 2. Indeed, every vehicle belonging to Guderian was distinguished by a large white 'G' on the rear, which differentiated them from all other units. No such person-alised designation was used by Hoepner, Reinhardt or Schmidt, although Kleist's panzer group likewise marked all its vehicles with a large white 'K' and vehicles in Hoth's panzer group used a symbol approximate to 'Hh'.[134] Without question, the stature of a formation's commanding officer was a source of great pride and distinction to the men. Even the personal recognition of an officer in official dispatches or a decoration was taken personally by the men.[135] Thus, Guderian's cultivation of an adoring public image, while at root a product of his ambition, did provide tangible benefits for the morale of his men and esteem of his formations. It also meant that some of Guderian's most ardent admirers were soldiers from his own formations, who also on occasion took the time to write of their appreciation. As Guderian informed Margarete in November: 'Sometimes, I also receive nice letters from subordinates. I'm enclosing two for you, which you can destroy after reading them. They were a treat for me in our truly serious and less than satisfactory current position. I've already answered them.'[136] If Guderian enjoyed the adulation of youthful autograph hunters and admiring subordinates, it should not be sur-prising that during the war both he and Rommel accepted invitations to teach classes at the elite *Kriegsakademie* (War College) in Berlin.[137] According to Dennis Showalter, as a teacher Guderian was 'an acquired taste whose allusive approach and sardonic sense of humour alienated as well as inspired'.[138]

Charting the fame of the panzer generals among the rank and file troops is difficult, but one understudied resource is the myriad of frontline newspapers produced by elements of the propaganda compan-ies for distribution among the soldiers. The recent digitisation of a vast collection held by the Berlin State Library allows advanced database searches giving a quantifiable insight into the degree of exposure each of the panzer generals gained. As one might expect, in the second half of 1941 Guderian enjoyed by far the most references with some sixty-three separate mentions, while, by comparison, Hoepner had twenty-two,[139] Reinhardt nine and Schmidt eight.[140] The tone of these articles could be extremely partisan, not just casting the panzer general in a positive light, but at times acting to build an almost farcical cult of personality. The generals were themselves no doubt aware of what was being published and very probably encouraged the production of such material. Among

Hoepner's private papers was an article he had saved from an unnamed front newspaper dated 14 September 1941:

> Every soldier was filled with pride and confidence when he crossed the border on 22 June as a member of Panzer Group Hoepner; the knowledge of the brilliant successes associated with the name Hoepner enabled him to do new things [...].
>
> All soldiers [...] know the cool daredevil, the unshakeable calm, the coolness, the matter-of-fact deliberation of the commander's leadership, they know that the Colonel-General is always concerned about his soldiers, that every operation is designed in such a way that the greatest success is achieved with the least possible sacrifice. [...]
>
> The commander celebrates his birthday[141] in the midst of new, decisive battles, in the midst of the emerging new, enormous successes. It will be a day like any other, full of work, full of far-reaching decisions, full of black responsibility.
>
> On these days, however, his soldiers feel particularly connected to their commander, all of their experience in these hard battles and proud victories is summed up in the name of their commander.
>
> In retrospect, it is not the number of a division or a corps, not the number of a panzer group that becomes the focal point of memory, but the name of the general under whose leadership, in all the campaigns of this war, the German soldier pinned immortal laurels on his flags.[142]

Status Symbols

Another measure of popularity was evident in the nicknames soldiers gave to their commanding officers, which, as Felix Römer explained, were not just reflections of how the men felt, but part of the Wehrmacht's cultural dynamic that drove the behaviour of officers:

> Among themselves, enlisted men often gave their officers nicknames – depending on the reputation of those concerned, these could naturally be either flattering or malicious. The officers were certainly not always aware of how their subordinates spoke about them, but the fact that they did so must have been clear to every

one of them who knew, from their experiences, how things worked in the world of soldiers. The troop leaders knew that they were under observation. Concern for their own reputation, fear of loss of face, scorn and shame affected them in the same way as it affected everyone else in the Wehrmacht, especially as they possessed particularly pronounced concepts of honours.[143]

Schmidt was popular enough to have earned himself two sobriquets, the most commonly cited being 'Panzer Schmidt', a reference to his energetic, aggressive pursuit of the offensive.[144] Ironically, it was this reckless form of leadership that led to the overextension of his forces, but this was not the conclusion drawn by his men. Being known as 'Panzer Schmidt' was an unambiguously positive reference. The other nickname for Schmidt was cited in a propaganda article by one of the motorised corps' war correspondents, who wrote that 'the soldiers hold onto their "Papa Schmidt" with honest trust'.[145] Indeed, the commander of Panzer Group 3, Schmidt's immediate superior in the summer, was likewise affectionately dubbed 'Papa Hoth'.[146] Exactly how genuine the mutual affection between Schmidt and his men was finds some substantiation in his letters to Fridel. On 1 November Schmidt declared: 'I must say it again: I simply love our people, they're so brave and unassuming.'[147] In return, his men made their own feelings felt when Schmidt was ordered to leave his corps and assume an army command on another section of the front. 'Of course, it's flattering for me when everyone shouts that I mustn't leave now or else everything will collapse. I won't be going to my new deployment before I can, in all good conscience, hand over the corps.' True to his word, 'Papa Schmidt' opted to undertake a four-day tour of his units thanking and encouraging his men. As he noted: 'Everyone here is sad. They'd all like to come with me.'[148]

Hoepner's nickname was more descriptive than affectionate, being 'The old cavalryman' (*Der Alte Reiter*).[149] This probably stems from his first posting as a *Fahnenjunker* in the Schleswig-Holstein 13th Dragoon Regiment.[150] His chief of staff, Chales de Beaulieu, was certainly very fond of him, but other reports suggest Hoepner had a more aloof relationship with his subordinates, which might reflect the more conservative and aristocratic traditions of the cavalry. Herbert von Blanckenhagen, a Russian translator on Hoepner's staff, wrote after the war: 'Colonel-General Hoepner was the brutal and energetic

Bulldog type in his outwardly somewhat heavy appearance and in his facial expression. You didn't have the opportunity to get to know him personally. In complete contrast to Kleist, he had a strange habit of not only separating from his general staff officers, but also eating better.'[151] This was further confirmed by the diary of Captain Hermann Kaiser, who concluded that, unlike Guderian, Hoepner 'had no influence over the young officers'.[152] Of course, the vast majority of men in a panzer group would hardly have had the opportunity to know whether their commanding officer was personable and simply being the 'energetic Bulldog type' was a virtue in the Wehrmacht. Indeed, one of Hoepner's personal photos depicts a bridge renamed in his honour as 'Colonel-General Hoepner Bridge' (*Generaloberst Hoepner-Brücke*), doubtless a sign of appreciation by the engineers who rebuilt or repaired it.[153] One should not attempt to read too much into a nickname, but while it seems that Hoepner was not unpopular among his men, it is probably equally true that he did not enjoy the fervent affection commanded by men like Guderian and Schmidt.

There is no known record of Reinhardt's nickname, if indeed he had one. This is not, however, to assume that the relationship up and down the chain of command was any less important. Reinhardt lamented the conditions under which his men fought, and reflected on this in his letters to Eva. On 8 August he wrote: 'My poor soldiers are not only facing fierce fighting but are also soaked to the skin from the early morning onwards; it's very bad. You will be able to understand how I feel.'[154] Yet in the Wehrmacht feeling any degree of empathy for the men was always in tension with what a commander was expected to achieve. The panzer troops were pushed extremely hard, and those orders were coming as much from the high command as from the corps/group commanders themselves. Reinhardt's correspondence briefly alludes to this as a potential source of dissatisfaction among the men. Writing to Eva on 28 August, he explained:

> In a very precarious situation for one of my divisions, I succeeded during a discussion with the commanders at the front, during which they perhaps regarded me as hard-hearted, in making the correct choice, thank God, so that very difficult hours and heavy losses were transformed into victory and joy. You'll empathise with me as to how difficult such times and such decisions are.[155]

Figure 3.6 Erich Hoepner (right) meeting with an *SS-Brigadeführer* in October 1941

If, by Reinhardt's own admission, success necessitated 'heavy losses', one wonders if all of his men were in fact convinced that the same orders were always fully justified. Even if on this occasion Reinhardt's harsh judgement was considered justified, one wonders how far the men bought into the cult of the offensive, as the relentless orders to attack throughout 1941 continued unabated until the panzer divisions across the Eastern Front were a hollow shell of their former selves. Nevertheless, Reinhardt's letter shows that the mood of subordinates could not be taken for granted and that even senior officers were conscious of having to maintain the respect of their men. To this end, Reinhardt happily told Eva, 'I believe that most of my commanders and troops know me', concluding: 'that divisions etc. that have served under us and are then to be transferred to another corps go only very reluctantly and mourn their departure! This delights us all, because it shows that our work is appreciated and that we are understood on a human level!'[156]

There was scarcely a nonchalant panzer general, but Guderian's nickname 'Quick Heinz' (*Schneller Heinz*)[157] distinguished him from his ambitious contemporaries within the *Panzertruppe*. Kleist had unsuccessfully tried to halt Guderian's drive in May 1940 and, while the drive to the English Channel certainly proved the virtue of rapid forward operations, it disguised the parallel danger of overextension that crystallised in Operation Barbarossa. Guderian's decision to seize Yel'nya in July 1941, as a future jumping off point for a drive on Moscow, came at the expense of linking up with Hoth's panzer group east of Smolensk and closing Army Group Centre's main encirclement.[158] In this instance 'Quick Heinz' was pushing too far, too fast, allowing countless enemy forces to escape the German pocket, while beginning a seven-week battle for Yel'nya that would ultimately be lost.[159] While Hoth and others in the German high command clearly judged Guderian's mistake negatively, it was beyond the grasp of Guderian's rank and file, who were, by and large, emboldened by his well-earned devil-may-care reputation, which they frequently claimed for themselves. This tendency for appropriation was even alluded to in Guderian's letters, when his Panzer Group 2 was 'promoted' to Second Panzer Army in early October. Explaining the designation change to Margarete, Guderian wrote: 'My panzer group is now a panzer army, by the way, and I've therefore been given the title of commander-in-chief. A large number of my colleagues feel elevated by "in-chief" and similar titles.'[160]

While battle honours and designations were the currency of success for formations in the Wehrmacht, the same notion of 'shared prestige' was true of individual awards for senior officers. For this reason, the decoration of high-ranking officers was taken personally by the men and was much more than a simple acknowledgement of the individual. As Felix Römer explained: 'Decorations for superiors were of particular importance, because their standing among their subordinates was dependent on which medals they could boast. Even at the lowest levels, enlisted men sometimes turned up their noses when their military leaders did not fulfil these criteria.'[161] When Reinhardt won the Knight's Cross during the Polish campaign, he wrote in a letter shortly thereafter: 'I cannot tell you how happy and proud I am, not for myself, but for my brave troops, which I was able to lead to particular successes.'[162] Undoubtedly, commanders were aware of how their own awards were collectively valued and this can only have heightened the desire to win them.[163]

The front page of the Vienna edition of the *Völkische Beobachter* often included sidebar headings heralding 'New Knight's Cross Recipients' or 'Awarded with the Knight's Cross'.[164] Decorations were not only a public form of positive recognition, but the absence of acknowledgement was also noted by the men, which speaks to the competition between units and the resulting importance that soldiers derived from belonging to a formation headed by a highly distinguished officer. Not surprisingly, therefore, German front newspapers also included numerous articles detailing awards, with one paper called *Wacht im Osten* running a segment entitled 'Who are the winners of the highest awards?' This feature, published over multiple editions, listed the Wehrmacht's elite according to their medals and among the *Panzertruppe* included Rommel and Guderian, but also Schmidt and Hoth. Notably absent, however, were Hoepner and Kleist and, to a lesser extent, Reinhardt.[165] Just how important this kind of public acknowledgement was is captured by Hoepner's letter of 19 July, as he reflected with indignation on the accolades bestowed upon his fellow panzer group commanders and complained to Irma:

> At present, I'm also somewhat embittered. When it was announced yesterday that the Oak Leaves had been conferred on Guderian, Hoth and Richthofen, my men stared at me, but no one said a word. That was gratifying. You know that I've repeatedly presented the view that my forces are too weak for this task. Now it's the case that those who have many more, are better equipped and, therefore, achieve easier victories, are decorated first. Kleist and I have had the heaviest fighting and the greatest losses, but we're not mentioned. My divisions have suffered twice as many dead and wounded as those of G[uderian] and H[oth], as Lieutenant-General von Thoma told us, who has travelled along the entire front.[166]

Field Marshal Wilhelm Ritter von Leeb, the commander of Army Group North, applied for Hoepner to receive the Oak Leaves on 1 August, but the reply he received would only have added salt to Hoepner's wound. As Leeb paraphrased the reply in his diary: 'The Führer only bestows the

Oak Leaves for outstanding personal bravery.'[167] Such an answer further confirms why ambitious commanders had to risk all at the front or at least be seen to be doing so.

Such was the allure of these coveted decorations that there was even a colloquial term in German for those – like Hoepner – who desperately desired them. Given that the Knight's Cross was hung around the neck, soldiers referred to their officers having a 'sore throat' (*Halsschmerzen*).[168] Thus, the perceived slight to Hoepner was both personal and public. On the one hand, as Römer observed: 'To wear a medal was the ultimate badge of soldierly masculinity.'[169] Yet Hoepner's letter makes clear he was also disturbed by the judgemental gaze of his staff and subordinates, as the unspoken question of why Hoepner had not brought the same distinction to his own panzer group lingered. This only underlines the extent of the shared prestige such awards conferred and the competition among senior commanders to win them. In this sense, analogies between the panzer generals and modern celebrities are not so far-fetched. Not only did both groups enjoy celebrity, the most successful actively cultivated it and measured their fame in awards that their devoted followers cherished almost like their own. When on 1 January 1942 Hoepner's Fourth Panzer Group was given the distinction of being redesignated as the Fourth Panzer Army, Hoepner proudly wrote to Irma: 'Today, we became an army and, as a result, I'm now a commander-in-chief. Everyone is pleased.'[170]

While some 861 men would receive the Oak Leaves during the course of the war, Schmidt and Guderian were only the nineteenth and twenty-fourth recipients respectively, adding further distinction to their achievement.[171] Not surprisingly, for men so conscious of building their reputations, the elation they experienced was in part because their fellow panzer corps and panzer group contemporaries were not receiving the same recognition. As Lisa Pine has observed, an essential stepping-stone to success in the National Socialist state

> was characterised by ambition for promotion or advancement, as well as attempts to displace or discredit peers or competitors. This entitled a condition of perpetual struggle among males not only to acquire power but also to maintain it against all potential rivals. This fitted in very closely with the Nazi idea of struggle and competition from Nietzschean concepts of the *Übermensch* ('superman') and the 'will to power'.[172]

Importantly, the ability to stand out in the highly competitive National Socialist state was an end in itself. It was never an objective assessment of an individual's real achievement – something that Hoepner's complaint to Irma suggests he underestimated. As Guderian wrote to Margarete on 31 July:

> I have now found, as you will have learned, via the bestowal of the Oak Leaves to the Knight's Cross, the appreciation of the Führer for the Russian campaign, which I am of course immensely pleased about. The day before yesterday, Schmundt appeared in order to deliver the little silver cluster, which possesses such high value for the soldiers in this war.[173]

Unlike Hoepner, Guderian did not ruminate on the achievement of his force, but rather reflected with pride on their having won Hitler's approval and appreciation. A similar sentiment was expressed by Schmidt in his July letter to Margarete: 'Now I am doubly glad and proud of the great accolade that your husband has received from the Führer and which he, insofar as I can at present ascertain, has so justifiably earned.'[174] Why were the Oak Leaves so justifiable? Because Hitler had determined it, not because Schmidt knew anything much about Guderian's operations. As Schmidt himself admitted, 'one can only get a real impression [of Guderian's operations] when one has later heard all the circumstances and I look forward to being able to learn all these in person from your husband.'[175] Without stating it, Schmidt is suggesting the published propaganda reports could not be trusted.[176]

The need to impress, rather than achieve, was why the intoxicating allure of military medals and public recognition bred conformity within the military and actively discouraged the timely reporting of the profound problems that were already undermining the German campaign in the East. By the end of July, when Guderian was proudly writing Margarete of his award, the operational strength of his panzer group had been reduced by a staggering 70 per cent,[177] creating an implicit tension between the personal desire to promote one's success and the need to report very real problems at the front. Yet Guderian concluded his letter on 31 July: 'If only the home front knew how much self-sacrifice and heroism is applied here, then it would follow the course of things with the utmost seriousness. The fighting taking place here is much tougher and more difficult than anything previously seen.'[178]

How exactly the home front was supposed to know the extent of the difficulties on the Eastern Front when successful generals, like Guderian, only advertised successes and indulged potential benefactors is left unanswered. Presumably others were expected to report the bad news, but in doing so they would cast themselves as naysayers and pessimists, not sufficiently infused with the 'will' to achieve victory.

While the 'shared prestige' certainly heightened the value of decorations, there was also a tangible individual reward. General of Infantry Rudolf Hofmann, who had served for a time as a department chief in the Army Personnel Office, noted in a post-war report that the award of the Knight's Cross 'automatically led to preferential promotions'.[179] Knight's Cross recipients noted that in addition to favourable publicity, these men were treated to free gifts, invited on tours of civilian industries and offered postcards in their honour.[180] The added prestige of the Oak Leaves can only have furthered this process, as less than 10 per cent of Knight's Cross recipients in the army ever obtain this distinction.[181]

With celebrity and status so inextricably bound to success, Guderian appears to have made the shrewd calculation that name recognition was worth twice as much if there was a familiar face to go with it. Perhaps with an eye to the soaring popularity of Rommel, whose confident image became synonymous with the success of the German Africa Corps, Guderian made sure his propaganda company photographed him in every possible setting. He also had copies made for his own personal archive, which he periodically sent to Margarete along with his letters and other documents.[182] As he informed her on 12 August: 'For safekeeping in my archive, I'm sending you several orders of the day and a very nice newspaper article, along with the newest pictures.'[183] Although evidently much less successful in his self-promotion, Hoepner also leveraged his propaganda company and proved himself anything but camera-shy. He also sent Irma copies of photographs and underlined their value to her: 'Of the things I've sent, the following are valuable: the report of Lieutenant-General [Wilhelm] von Dommes[184] and the thick book with pictures, which the propaganda company presented to me.'[185] Towards the end of the year, as more and more photos were sent, Irma apparently bought a photo album, to which Erich replied: 'Is the photo album for the war pictures? Then it will have to be very big. Fine!'[186] Not surprisingly, therefore, an excellent selection of 1941 campaign photographs exists for Guderian and Hoepner, but the same cannot be said of Reinhardt or Schmidt, who were corps commanders without access to their own propaganda companies (until October and November respectively). Interestingly, Maiken Umbach's extensive study of German photograph albums produced during the Nazi period highlighted two key motivations driving the activity: 'an opportunity structure for furthering their personal ambitions and aspirations or to cope with their own anxieties'.[187]

While photographs served their purpose for the extensive print media, the gold standard for public representation was to appear in the newsreel series released in German cinemas known as the *Deutsche Wochenschau* (German Weekly Review). The initial popularity of these newsreels was so great that they typically generated more interest than the feature films they preceded. In fact, the interest became so great that cinema operators responded by offering special newsreel-only programmes. Although people initially looked upon cinema as a welcome distraction from the war, Germany's string of victorious campaigns transformed the conflict into an extraordinarily popular form of entertainment, made all the more exciting by the fact that the newsreels purported to show 'the real thing'.[188] A public opinion report compiled by the Security Service of the *Reichsführer-SS* in 1940 noted that the newsreels were being greeted by open displays of enthusiasm: 'The riotous applause soon gave way to a gripped silence as pictures followed the Führer walking through the park and at the map table with his generals.'[189] A month after the invasion of the Soviet Union, another report confirmed the newsreels' success at merging news with entertainment:

> According to reports from all over the Reich, the strong interest of the population in the newsreels from the Eastern Front continues undiminished. Numerous reports speak of overflowing cinemas at special newsreel performances. It is often commented that the new kind of newsreel has almost achieved the impossible. [...] It is generally emphasised that the film sequences, despite their length, are not at all tiring, but extremely varied and exciting.[190]

Newsreels averaged about twenty to thirty minutes in length and displayed the real skill of the propaganda companies by time and again capturing the 'action' at the front, which, it goes without saying, exclusively showcased German successes. The reality of course was seldom so one-sided, as was underlined by the fact that nearly 1,000 members of the propaganda companies were killed during the course of the war.[191] While jarringly melodramatic in its theatrical exaggeration, the *Wochenschau*'s sensationalism was accepted in the early years of the war because German forces were clearly advancing and winning victories. Yet, as Jochen Lehnhardt emphasised: 'What was important here was not the reproduction of the real event, but that the viewer was emotionally affected by what was shown.'[192]

This potent new medium was an opportunity the panzer generals looked to turn to their advantage, but once again only Guderian appears to have emerged with any real prominence. On 6 October Hoepner excitedly wrote to Irma, 'my stay on the Duderhof Heights before Petersburg was apparently shown in the newsreel. On 6 October, a man from Tobis Film shot again at my command post. I sent pictures taken by Voigts.'[193] However, digitised records of the *Wochenschau* in 1941 do not reveal a single appearance by Hoepner, which is not too surprising given that only 6 per cent of the film shot was ever used in newsreels.[194] Schmidt and Reinhardt are similarly absent, although the latter featured in later episodes in 1942, 1943 and 1944.[195] For the German public, the panzer general of the Eastern Front in 1941 was unambiguously Guderian. When the encirclement of the Smolensk pocket was announced, Hoth was neither seen nor mentioned in spite of his leading role; rather, it was Guderian whom the narrator singled out as leading the attack and cutting off the Soviet forces. The film showed Guderian discussing operations during the battle scenes and, once the victory had been achieved, for over twenty seconds he was shown beaming at subordinates and shaking hands with his officers as rousing music underscored the victory. The same was true for the battle of Kiev, although at least here Kleist's name was mentioned along with that of Guderian. Once the two panzer groups had met to close the pocket, however, it was Guderian whose face was shown once again beaming in triumph and exchanging words with subordinates. In a December episode of the *Wochenschau*, a smiling Guderian was shown escorting Field Marshal Bock to his car after a meeting, which Margarete read about in the newspaper and immediately wrote Heinz:[196]

> In the newspaper, I read about the reassuring impression made on visitors by the image of coffee between Field Marshal von

Bock and General Guderian in the newsreel. I quickly went there, in order to at least see you on camera, dearest. A tank battle for a village on your front was also shown; a shudder came over me at seeing these pictures.[197]

Clearly, Guderian was judged to be a reassuring face in the unfolding retreat from Moscow, but – as we have seen in Chapter 2 – that too was a staged façade as the panzer general battled his own depression and despair. Ultimately, Guderian's veneer of success in 1941 mimicked that of the Wehrmacht in becoming more and more an illusion for Germans to believe, until reality slowly imposed itself. What is undeniable, however, was Guderian's artful manipulation of the media, in all its forms, allowing him to capture attention and attain a status that propelled his career well beyond his military accomplishments.

While Guderian cunningly exploited the system to his advantage, his celebrated status as the golden child of the *Panzertruppe* in the East inspired some jealousy. Writing to Irma in late November, as his panzer group desperately struggled to maintain its momentum north of Moscow, Hoepner lamented his weakness and somehow decided Guderian was in part to blame. 'The fighting is heavy, because they've taken the best [...] from me. They were taken away by Guderian and Kluge. Now it's they who'll advance more swiftly.'[198] Remarkably, even in late November, the shifting of a few meagre reserves was viewed through the prism of individual achievement and reward. Moreover, when Kluge's right wing did join the attack on 1 December, it stalled almost immediately for lack of strength.[199] Hoepner's claim about Guderian gaining strength at his expense was even more preposterous. The Second Panzer Army was operating almost 200 kilometres further south around Tula, and no one in the German high command was proposing a lateral movement of forces away from Moscow. The fact that Hoepner concerned himself with which of his rivals would advance more swiftly, when by this point in the war the objective of seizing Moscow was well beyond the German army, let alone any individual commander or formation, says everything about the aberrant priorities that clouded German thinking.

The same sense of injustice at being denied public recognition was expressed by Reinhardt, who felt his role in the isolation of Leningrad had passed unacknowledged and unrewarded. More to the point, he cast this as only the latest in a series of setbacks continuing from past campaigns. Writing to Eva on 28 September, Reinhardt stated: 'But we're used to starting off as the poor relation and we've still succeeded in everything developing over time in our favour, in a way that some would never have thought, though it seems to be my fate not to reap the final fruits of victory, as the examples of Warsaw, Paris and Petersburg demonstrate.'[200] Schmidt too had his grievances, but less with his fellow panzer commanders and more with the attention given, as he saw it, to the undeserving role of the infantry. Belonging to Colonel-General Ernst Busch's Sixteenth Army during the fighting around Tikhvin, Schmidt resented his motorised corps sharing any of the spotlight with infantry formations. Writing to Fridel on 15 November, Schmidt was emphatic: 'It's dreadfully difficult. With this army [...] acting as if the infantry is doing everything. Even the special announcement reports "infantry and panzer units". [But] it was one of my panzer divisions and a motorised infantry division, which is counted as a "rapid movement unit". There was no other infantry to be seen within a radius of 150 kilometres.'[201] Once again, given the seriousness of Schmidt's predicament at Tikhvin, it seems remarkable that he fretted over such a trivial matter. On the other hand, one might just as easily argue, given all we have learned about German command culture and its obsession with public prestige, that Schmidt's behaviour was entirely unremarkable. Two weeks before, at the start of November, Schmidt wrote to Fridel: 'We were constantly mentioned in the last army reports [*Heeresberichten*], with the brave actions of our officers, non-commissioned officers, teams and units! The Führer immediately awarded a large number of Knight's Crosses for it by telephone.'[202] In another November letter he stated: 'You will have received enough letters with descriptions of my activities and situation by now, and have heard of the occupation of Tikhvin and of the achievements of my corps from the army reports of the 10th and 11th and from the special announcement.'[203] Clearly, the public representations were studiously followed.

In July, when Schmidt wrote to Margarete, he expressed relief that reports he had been following in the foreign media about Guderian's capture had proven to be untrue. As he wrote to Margarete: 'Today's *Deutschlandsender* report has freed me from the great concern that your husband might have fallen into enemy hands.' Despite his apparent 'great concern', Schmidt then dismissively referred to such reports as 'the hogwash of the English and Russians' and claimed that he viewed them with 'the suspicion that this was all just a "hatched" scheme'.[204] Of course, if enemy propaganda was indeed so untrustworthy, it begs the question why Schmidt bothered to follow it at all. Not surprisingly, his interest was in his own representation, as he wrote to Fridel in December: 'So far, I've been killed twice [and] beaten at Tikhvin, according to English and Russian broadcasting. And yet I'm somewhere completely different – they seem to hold me in particularly high regard over there.'[205] Schmidt was not alone. Guderian also scoured foreign news reports for information about himself and sent the most favourable to Margarete. In response she wrote to him on 27 November: 'The tribute of the English newspaper was very interesting!'[206]

The Power of Privilege

Access to foreign media was no doubt a privilege of high command, but it was by no means the only advantage of rank and position. As we have seen, careerism and individual vanity played a large role in driving behaviour, but there was another very powerful inducement of high command that further compromised a senior commander's objectivity in how he conducted himself and reported information. Colonel-Generals, like Guderian and Hoepner, secretly received a tax-exempt 2,000 *Reichsmarks* payment each month, which each recipient was made aware came personally from Hitler and would continue entirely at his discretion.[207] As Norman Goda observed, such payments came with an explicit 'quasi-contractual relationship in which huge amounts of money would be exchanged for obedience'.[208] Such payments more than doubled the monthly salary of men like Guderian and Hoepner, while also introducing a none-too-subtle conflict of interest. Maintaining such a lucrative income stream meant tempering any negative reporting and, above all, taking care not to contradict or offend Hitler. Indeed, Field Marshals received an extra 4,000 *Reichsmarks* each month, so in addition to maintaining Hitler's already huge supplementary income, there was the added inducement that further promotion would result in even greater financial reward. As Reinhardt and Schmidt were not Colonel-Generals in 1941 (they were both promoted to this rank on 1 January 1942), these payments were not yet available to them, but since Guderian and Hoepner were beneficiaries of the scheme one may look to their correspondence for evidence of its importance.

Shortly after Guderian was awarded the Oak Leaves, he wrote to Margarete that he had decided to reward himself by purchasing an original artwork by Anton von Werner, who had been a favoured painter of the Wilhelmine period, famous for capturing Prussia's landmark political and military events. Guderian, who had a passion for hunting, decided on Werner's 'hunting study', costing 530 *Reichsmarks*.[209] By way of comparison, five years earlier in 1936, with unemployment eliminated, 62 per cent of Germans still earned less than 1,500 *Reichsmarks* annually.[210] Even Guderian acknowledged the sizeable outlay and proceed to justify the purchase to Margarete. 'You'll think me wasteful. But the offer came just at that moment, and as I'm still attached to my old hunting pastime, I was plagued by the desire to buy the little picture. I can pay for it with savings from my time in the field; that makes the matter more bearable.'[211] How such sizeable savings were accrued need not merit too much contemplation. Guderian also encouraged Margarete to indulge herself, even suggesting that she was somehow going without. 'Furthermore', Heinz wrote, 'the thought depresses me that you scrimp and save for my benefit. I won't starve, but you shouldn't go without the little comforts that wartime offers.'[212] If Margarete was more frugal than Heinz, she certainly did not need too much prodding to indulge her own interest in art. During the summer she engaged a portrait artist to paint her, and when in August the work was finally finished, Margarete sent a photograph of the result to Heinz, noting, 'the photograph cannot reproduce the colours of the images; I hope it doesn't disappoint you for that reason.'[213] Suitably impressed, Heinz replied:

> A beautiful, genteel lady looks back at me, with a sweet mouth, a delicate little nose, a clear, somewhat quizzical expression. You look a little bit deridingly in it; apparently, you've often mocked at something during the sittings. But, all in all, a pretty, well-made picture, considerably more accurate than the other one and certainly more gratifying to behold over time. I am extremely pleased about this lovely gift and send you a thousand thanks for it.[214]

Although the cost of commissioning a portrait is not recorded, the expense no doubt reflected a luxury far beyond most Germans.

If the Guderians shared an expensive taste in art, it seems this kind of expenditure was not exceptional. On 1 December Heinz wrote to Margarete promising to send her an undisclosed amount for Christmas presents. 'I don't know what your wishes are and cannot judge what can be bought. But perhaps something will turn up, a pretty work of art or something else that gives you a treat. Then you should get it for yourself and enjoy it.'[215] Clearly, cost was not uppermost in Heinz's mind. Although the correspondence does not disclose what Margarete bought for herself, she did report some of her Christmas shopping. For one person, whose name is illegible, she bought wine, coffee, a book and a Krisling flower bowl. For their eldest son, Heinz Günther, Margarete framed a red-chalk drawing she herself had drawn, and added to this a book, stationery and 150 marks 'for a nice present'.[216] Their younger son Kurt probably received a similar cash gift, making the Christmas outlay well above anything average Germans could afford.

Hoepner's correspondence likewise shows evidence of extravagant expenditure given the prevailing wartime conditions. Not only did the tax-exempt payment enable him to purchase items beyond the reach of workers or soldiers, but it appears money and status sufficed to circumvent strict rationing quotas. On 30 October he wrote to Irma: 'I've now ordered fifty bottles, which, just this once – and confidentially – will be given to me. The money has to be sent in advance to: Nassau Regional Bank, Eltville am Rhein, to the account of the State Wineries Administration. Please arrange for the bank to transfer 260.70 marks! It's certain to include papa's birthday present!'[217] Just six weeks later Hoepner had again placed an order, this time for thirty bottles of French George Goulet sparkling wine. As he encouraged Irma: 'Drink on 24 December and be as jovial as you can!'[218] Hoepner counted himself as something of a connoisseur of French cognacs, the best of which he claimed was *Grand Marnier*.[219] On 9 January 1942, when Hoepner reported to Army Group Centre to be told by Kluge that he would be dismissed from the army on Hitler's order, the general requested two bottles of French burgundy and one bottle each of French cognac and champagne.[220] Some of the officers present speculated whether Hoepner was planning to commit suicide that night, which of course he did not, but it suggests the general had a propensity to acquire whatever he could.[221]

Not only was Hoepner able to procure large quantities of alcohol, but he also appeared to be sending Irma and his daughter Ingrid sizeable shipments of food and other speciality items from the East. Whether Hoepner was paying for these items, appropriating them from army stocks or sharing the spoils of looted businesses and homes remains unclear. What was clear were the quantities. As Hoepner wrote on 26 August: 'I am very pleased that the parcels have finally arrived. As far as I remember, the second crate contained: meat and vegetables, canned goods, tea, pepper, cheese, sweets, a box of soap, tatty tissues and pillowcase and the annual report of the Red Cross. Hopefully, most of these were still there.'[222] No mention was made of the contents of the first crate, but clearly Hoepner was ensuring his family would not go without. In October Hoepner enquired with Irma about receiving his 'deliveries of chocolate bars'[223] and in November he sent a key to a locked suitcase, which he dispatched separately. The contents included his prized hunting weapons along with ammunition, which presumably Hoepner had hoped to find time for after the Soviet defeat or perhaps even during the course of the campaign. The suitcase also contained more canned goods and confectionery as well as two bottles of whisky and another two bottles of the liqueur *Danziger Goldwasser*.[224] One wonders where in occupied Russia Hoepner was acquiring such items if not from the population or army supplies.[225] Indeed, none of the other panzer generals reported sending anything of substance home, while even the soldiers remarked at the absence of things to spend their meagre wages on in the East.[226]

If Hoepner was inclined to profiteer from his position, it only confirms how much more enticing Hitler's monthly inducement would have been for him. Clearly, both Guderian and Hoepner displayed a desire for extravagant expenditure, which, beyond confirming the effectiveness of Hitler's system of payments, also illuminates some of the generals' expensive tastes. It also provides a curious picture of the generals on campaign, that in July 1941, as Guderian was desperately battling south of Smolensk, he was also scouring art catalogues for potential additions to his private collection, or that in October Hoepner was directing the main attack on Moscow while in parallel placing orders for his wine cellar. Perhaps the stresses of command rendered such pastimes important to their mental well-being, but one may also question, given the tremendous responsibility entrusted to them, whether their disposable income allowed a certain indulgence that distracted attention from much more urgent matters. Further evidence to this effect was seen in the summer, when Hoepner engaged in a correspondence with both Irma and the tax office seeking a reduction in his tax burden.[227] Given the enormous tax-free supplement he was already receiving, of which the tax office had no knowledge because Hitler's payments were kept secret, Hoepner was not only prising every last cent out of the state, but making the time to do so during the height of the Soviet campaign.

The wealth of the Colonel-Generals may be further measured by the luxuries they enjoyed at the front. Hoepner was the standout in this regard. On 19 July he wrote to thank his daughter Ingrid for sending him crayfish.[228] On 31 July Hoepner enjoyed red caviar and also noted receiving ten bottles of beer from Riga, courtesy of a pilot in the Luftwaffe. As he told Irma: 'We've had to go without such luxuries for the last six weeks.'[229] Yet relative to almost anyone else serving on the Eastern Front, Hoepner does not appear to have been denied too many luxuries. His income allowed Irma to fulfil a wish list of items. In September he received one package with new braces and sock garters, while another delivered to him a requested medication, some jugs and *Eau de Cologne*, which despite its French name was an upmarket German cologne (also known as *Kölnisch Wasser*).[230] When he celebrated his birthday, in addition to his gifts, Hoepner had four different cakes.[231] Tobacco was in very short supply in Germany with 'enormous queues gathered outside all the tobacco shops',[232] yet on the Eastern Front Hoepner was receiving cigars.[233] Indeed, we only know of the things Hoepner received that he wrote about in his letters to Irma, but a comment at the end of November suggests this may only have been the tip of the iceberg. As Hoepner informed Irma: 'The car is scheduled to leave Berlin again on 14 December, in order to bring us Christmas parcels.'[234] Apparently this was not the first time the car had made this journey and, while there was a well-known unofficial supply line of vehicles circumventing the army's notorious logistical problems, these were overwhelmingly trucks shipping supplies for major formations. Hoepner's dispatch of a car for Christmas presents speaks to the privilege he reserved for himself and his staff officers. It also says something about his wealth, since Berliners in 1941 were struggling to acquire basic foodstuffs, and most consumer products were impossible to find for all but the rich and well-connected.[235]

Guderian's letters also confirm that he was sent special deliveries by Margarete, but both the frequency and the contents of these shipments were much more modest. In August Margarete sent a parcel of pears via 'special courier',[236] to which Heinz expressed his delight and commented, 'there is nothing like that here'.[237] The only other instance of this was in November, when Heinz again reacted to receiving a fruit parcel, suggesting it was indeed an uncommon occurrence. 'It tasted splendid', he noted with gratitude, 'they're very welcome in this country, which is low on fruit and vitamins.'[238] In fact, acquiring fruit and vegetables in Germany was hardly much easier, even for those with an eligible ration card.[239] The ability to gather the fruit for her parcels suggests Margarete had some form of privileged supply, especially since none of her letters ever made mention of difficulties in obtaining food-stuffs, even when she hosted multiple guests. Nor did she ever complain about queuing for anything, which had become a frustrating daily routine for average Berliners. The answer is seemingly revealed at the conclusion to one of Heinz's letters from early December, when he sent his 'warmest regards' to the current house guests, but then added 'and our house personnel'.[240] Clearly, Margarete was not alone in managing her household, which in addition to their spending habits, underlines the wealth and privilege Guderian's position afforded.

By way of comparison, the correspondence of Schmidt and Reinhardt, who were not yet entitled to a 2,000-mark bonus payment each month, presents a contrasting picture. Schmidt does not mention receiving anything from Fridel, although that might be a symptom of his seemingly dysfunctional relationship. Yet there was also no evidence of Schmidt engaging in the excessive spending we observe from Hoepner and Guderian. Reinhardt's letters offer a single reference to Eva sending 'good cigarettes', but otherwise make no mention of money or personal acquisitions.[241] Naturally, we must consider that Reinhardt edited his letters and may well have considered financial matters to be private, but from the picture we gain he does not appear to have indulged in any form of lavish lifestyle. Of course, such comparisons are anecdotal, but given the paucity of information about the private lives of German generals, they remain informative examples.[242]

While letters were the most common form of communication between the generals and their wives, they were not the only option available to them. There existed an occasional possibility for telephone communication, although this was not officially permitted and remained highly dependent upon getting through clogged switchboards and then putting up with often poor-quality lines. Telephone conversa-tions were also anything but private, with other members of the command staff as well as switchboard operators able to listen in on calls. Perhaps surprisingly, the first record of a telephone communication with a spouse is of one undertaken by Schmidt in early July. This, however, was prompted by the four successive nights of British raids on Münster in early July,[243] in which Schmidt noted that the family house 'has been subjected to all sorts of things'. Naturally there was concern for the well-being of Fridel, whom Schmidt was able to reach by telephone and confirm was safe.[244] Fridel then moved to stay with family in Leipzig and there is no further evidence of Schmidt attempting to reach her by telephone. Reinhardt's letters offer no evidence of telephone communications, which may again be a result of his editing, but it could equally be true that he simply respected the army regulations, especially when placing calls was so extraordinarily difficult.

Not surprisingly, Hoepner and Guderian showed no concern for the regulations, but this does not mean that they had an easy time getting connections to Berlin. In mid-July, Hoepner's chief signals officer, Colonel Hans Negendank, attempted to use a recently installed OKH line to Pskov, but without success.[245] Even by the end of the month, all attempts to place a call had failed, as Hoepner dolefully told Irma: 'Hopefully, we'll manage a telephone conversation soon.'[246] His persistence paid off on at least one occasion in August,[247] yet by September the prospect of placing a call had become even more difficult, owing to stricter regulations. As Hoepner explained: 'Unfortunately, it's no longer possible to telephone, because others have overdone it. Now the switchboard in Berlin is forbidden to put calls through to domestic connections.'[248] The conceited claim that 'others' were to blame for having 'overdone' something that Hoepner also abused is only further evidence of the liberties the panzer general reserved for himself. Of course, the new regulations were no reason for Hoepner to stop trying to call Berlin and he wrote Irma of his futile attempts to get through, but on 12 December a letter showed he had succeeded. 'Unfortunately, it no longer works very well,'[249] he lamented. After another successful telephone call on New Year's Eve, Hoepner explained, 'when you're subjected to the type of pressure I'm under here, then you long every hour for the distraction of a kind word or a report about other, pleasant things.'[250]

There is no record of Guderian attempting to telephone Margarete in the summer months, but as the campaign dragged on, he too became indifferent to the injunction against private calls. The first record of his attempt to telephone came on 24 October when he wrote Margarete that his chief signals officer, Colonel Albert Praun, had almost succeeded in making a connection. 'I would have had the joy of hearing your voice for a few minutes, but unfortunately the connection didn't materialise. Praun will repeatedly try to get through; perhaps it'll work sometime. It would be a pleasure in the desolation of this country and the attendant circumstances that prevail.'[251] Margarete too despaired at the missed opportunity. She waited on the telephone for half an hour until the operator said the connection would have to be re-established. 'I lay awake for a long time, waiting, before I sadly had to abandon my hope.'[252] It would not be until the final week of November that they finally succeeded in making a connection, a result which elated Margarete. 'It is exhilarating to hear your beloved voice and to be joined in thought at the same time.' Yet she also alluded to the sinister realities of such communication in Nazi Germany: 'It's only tricky to find the right words that one would like to say, because all kinds of agencies are listening in. As a result, everything sounds so commonplace and mundane; one cannot speak from the heart.'[253] Just as Hoepner took solace from hearing Irma's voice, Guderian in his much more fragile mental state appears to have desperately sought further telephone contact. There were at least two more successful telephone calls made in December, including one on Christmas Day, just twenty-four hours before Guderian was dismissed from his command and sent home.[254] Indicative of Guderian's frame of mind and perhaps anticipating his fate, Margarete reflected on their call:

> The thought of being together with you in the beautiful countryside, away from all the commotion of the war, is so heavenly that it already gives me pleasure just to dream a little. A shimmer of hope like that revitalises me time and again; after our telephone conversation, I lay awake for a while and felt you close to me by virtue of the sweet voice I'd heard.[255]

The extent to which entitlement and privilege motivated the German generals is a useful indicator of their susceptibility to the system of rewards in Nazi Germany, not only from Hitler's payments, but the glamour of celebrity and official prominence. Hoepner and Guderian clearly sought this reward and indulged in its benefits even while on campaign. When Hoepner was searching for what he believed would be a stable winter quarters he fixated upon an old Boyar castle, which had been converted by the Soviets into a museum. As he informed Irma, 'it looks very beautiful on aerial photographs'.[256] There was also an attendant cathedral, which, Hoepner noted, 'was a very impressive building with highly valuable pieces'. Unfortunately, two days later, on 29 November when Hoepner arrived to inspect his prized headquarters, he found a ruin with the buildings having 'suffered greatly as a result of the fighting'. The castle was then 'out of the question for our quarters', but Hoepner consoled himself with 'the great pleasure of visiting the sauna here'.[257] Given the timing of these events, as his troops desperately fought north of Moscow in appalling conditions, one wonders whether Hoepner's priorities were again misplaced.

If a weakness for certain luxuries can be said to have clouded the judgement of the generals, then the promise of ostentatious wealth and extravagance exploded whatever convergence might still have remained between professional and political loyalties. Hoepner never had such an opportunity after his military career ended in ignominy in January 1942. Guderian had, of course, also been unceremoniously sacked at the end of December, yet here again we see the panzer general's proficiency at marketing himself and rebranding his tainted image into something palatable enough for Hitler not just to re-employ him, but to be persuaded to provide Guderian with a wholly new role (as Inspector General of Armoured Troops) with wide-ranging autonomous powers.[258] Just how well Guderian succeed at ingratiating himself with the establishment may be gauged by the unprecedented generosity of Hitler's lavish personal bequest, which, some have suggested, was less a vote of confidence than a shrewd (and as it would turn out highly successful) method of tying Guderian ever closer to the regime.[259] Unlike Hoepner, Guderian's dismissal from command did not result in the loss of his monthly bonuses from the Reich Chancellery, so he still profited handsomely from the entitlements of his rank, but this was nothing by comparison with what was to come. Even before taking up his new appointment, Guderian was informed in late 1942 that he would be provided with a family estate in the newly annexed Warthegau region of West Prussia. A list of prospective estates was prepared, all of about 4,000 acres in size.[260] It was Guderian's opportunity to join the truly wealthy aristocratic class of landed Prussian Junkers, which, beyond giving him greatly increased status, reclaimed a family heritage that had once included lands in Kulm, east of the Vistula. Yet, if there was any doubt about Guderian's ambition and lust for prestige, Hitler's lavish offer revealed just how far greed trumped gratitude.

Having toured the listed estates, Guderian and Margarete moved on to even larger properties and settled upon a 7,000-acre estate called Schöngarten, which had never been on offer. The local *Gauleiter*, *SS-Oberführer* Dr Arthur Greiser, reported that this property 'was particularly popular with Mrs Guderian because of the residential building, which is in a good cultural and structural condition and is located in a particularly beautiful park'.[261] The request to obtain Schöngarten was, however, promptly rejected and the Guderians settled upon an estate named Deipenhof – a well-kept property that contained a mixture of meadows, pastures, gardens, parks, forests, water and homesteads.[262] It was well kept because it was still occupied by its Polish owner, himself a former officer. This was a problem Greiser would solve, thanks to his ruthless reputation for evicting, and sometimes murdering, Polish landowners.[263] Later in the war, Field Marshal Erich von Manstein's adjutant noted a conversation between the two senior commanders concerning Deipenhof:

> 'Tell me, Guderian, I hear you've got yourself an estate in Posen province. How did you do it?' And Guderian told him quite uninhibitedly that he had been given a list of fine Polish estates which he had viewed over a few days, before deciding on the most suitable property. Manstein was taken aback and asked if the Polish owners had still been living there. When Guderian said they had, he asked what had become of them. Guderian said he did not know, when he had taken over his estate the Poles had gone and he had no idea what had become of them. Manstein was speechless. His face twitched once or twice, and I knew him too well to be unaware what it meant: that method of coming by an estate was not his style.[264]

Whatever the truth of Manstein's supposed indignation,[265] Heinz and Margarete remained unperturbed by their part in the theft of Deipenhof. Indeed, as a commercial enterprise the estate was estimated to have a potential income of 1.24 million *Reichsmarks* per year,[266] offering a powerful inducement to weigh up against any moral reservations about his own personal enrichment. It was the same calculation that allowed Guderian to sacrifice his professional independence for political expedience. Nor was this unknown during the war. As General of

Panzer Troops Thoma told his fellow captives at Trent Park in 1944: 'That's the man who later emerges and lets that sloppy job be foisted on him, [...] who lets Hitler present him with an estate in the Warthegau, in spite of the way in which he has been treated!' Thoma then declared that Guderian 'lets himself be bought, and isn't ashamed'.[267]

If the acquisition of Deipenhof was revealing from an ethical point of view, Guderian's subsequent behaviour sheds even more light on his character and priorities. One could assume that the princely gift of Deipenhof, which would prove to be the most expensive gift Hitler ever gave to one of his field commanders, might elicit an outpouring of appreciation, but nothing could be further from the truth. As Gerhard Weinberg noted, Guderian's gratitude may be measured by a sizeable file of correspondence that the panzer general subsequently wrote lobbying authorities for an even larger and more elegant estate.[268]

In April 1943 the former German diplomat and anti-Hitler conspirator Ulrich von Hassell wrote in his diary:

> The longer the war lasts the lesser my opinion of the generals. They have undoubted technical ability and physical courage, but little moral courage, absolutely no broad world vision, no inner spiritual independence or that strength of resistance which rests on a genuine cultural basis. For this reason, Hitler was able to make them subservient and bind them hand and foot. The majority, moreover, are out to make careers in the basest sense. Gifts and field marshals' batons are more important to them than the great historical issues and moral values at stake.[269]

Such an astute insight demonstrates why our picture of the German generals needs to be informed, wherever possible, by a perspective that takes us beyond the battlefield. The view gained by their private corres-pondence reveals just how much they understood a successful career to be built on perception, patronage and popularity over strictly military performance. Even Hitler's chief military adjutant, Rudolf Schmundt, was said to have remarked at an adjutants' conference: 'The worst people are the generals; if they are not promoted or given accelerated promotion and awarded the Knight's Cross, they are discontented.'[270] To no small extent, this informed the command culture of the army, especially among the more aggressive-minded panzer generals, whose leading personalities unashamedly marketed themselves as well as their victories for personal gain. Guderian was undoubtedly the most skilful and ruthless at this, which unsurprisingly correlates to his success in the National Socialist state.

As will be explored in Chapter 5, Hoepner was in fact much more critical of Hitler's military direction in 1941, but there was not yet any hint of the resistance activities in which he would later engage. Indeed, Hoepner was an excellent example of the 'resistance' in 1941 – a movement within the army that scarcely engaged in any activity at all, despite their full knowledge of the mass murder being perpetrated in the East. At this point, Hoepner was much more interested in the career he wanted to build within the Nazi system rather than anything he might achieve by its downfall. Only after his failure to enrich himself within the system of reward, when he had been dismissed from his post, publicly shamed and cut off from financial bonuses, did Hoepner eventually become a conspirator – a circumstance that reflected his own sense of injustice rather than anything inflicted upon others.

At the beginning of Barbarossa, Schmidt and Reinhardt had less visibility by virtue of their lower rank and command and, therefore, less opportunity to capture attention and make names for themselves. As corps commanders until the autumn, they did not have the same access to the propaganda companies, were much less likely to be named in special announcements and were not yet entitled to the privilege of special payments. This, however, did not mean they shied away from promoting themselves whenever the occasion arose, something at which Schmidt in particular excelled. Indeed, their respective rise to panzer group and army command reflects their success, both on and off the battlefield, in managing their political, public and professional profiles towards advancement.

Becoming a member of Hitler's military elite did not result from a selfless act of service; it was a conscious and purposeful pursuit touted at every opportunity to emphasise professional standing and win official endorsement. As d'Almeida's research discovered:

> under Nazism, getting rich and rising in society were not a matter of chance. Nazi court life was based on an opacity that favoured obedience. It masked interactions and mutual influences to present the ideal form of a pyramid of vassalage and obligations. In reality, power relationships and *de facto* situations left room for individual initiative and rapid promotions obtained by means of demonstrated favour, servility, activity and efficiency.[271]

Crafted public profiles, steadfast political reliability, unflinching bravery in command and absolute conviction in victory were the hallmarks of successful panzer generals. Yet the contrast between the private generals, wallowing in ever increasing doubt and depression, and the public generals, beaming with confidence and clamouring for recognition and acclaim, could not be greater, nor more representative of the disfunction and duplicity inherent within the Nazi state.

4 THE CRIMINAL GENERALS

We should not be surprised that the private correspondence of the panzer generals does not directly allude to their role in Nazi Germany's criminal activity. This is not to say their letters do not provide some compelling evidence of their complicity, but their silence on many subjects is noteworthy in itself. If we can prove their role in war crimes, but none of their letters refer to this, it becomes what David A. Gerber refers to as the 'strategy of silence' when a writer refuses to address certain subjects in order to spare or protect the addressee and maybe also himself.[1] Yet before we even consider this, we must recall (from Chapter 1) that the individual collections almost certainly contain gaps in the correspondence. This can only be definitively confirmed for Guderian and Hoepner, but the other collections also have inexplicable gaps in the correspondence, which strongly suggests letters are missing. Whether the absent letters were purposefully withheld or simply lost can only be a matter of speculation. If letters were destroyed or withheld from what was made publicly available, this would suggest that communication was in fact more open on supposed taboo subjects. Even among the letters that were donated there are some curious anomalies. A section of Guderian's letter from 1 December has been cut away from the page, with writing disappearing into the cut, so we can be sure the section was removed at some point after the letter was written.[2] Speculating that any self-censorship pertained to subjects of a criminal or pro-Nazi nature is of course just that – speculation – but the absence of any of these statements among men who are known (from other source material) to have identified and engaged with these views and policies makes the 'strategy of silence' hypothesis a plausible one.

There is also a question about what other subjects the generals might have felt the need to censor. As will be discussed in Chapter 5, their highly sensitive military operations were freely committed to paper, which could have posed serious security risks, but these were liberties the generals felt entitled to take and seemingly felt no shame about even after the war. So, if they were not concerned about military secrets, what might they have felt compelled to expunge from the record? In a post-war world, in which the generals furiously insisted upon their apolitical status and honourable service records, any evidence that contradicted this narrative risked not only their personal reputations, but also the burgeoning myth of a 'clean' Wehrmacht.

Enemy in the East

Establishing what the panzer generals thought about their Soviet enemy necessitates taking a somewhat broader perspective than simply the year 1941. Although there was an Eastern Front against Russia throughout much of the First World War, it was the Western Front that shaped the experience of the panzer generals. Guderian and Hoepner served exclusively in the West, while Reinhardt and Schmidt spent most of the war in France with only a period each on the Eastern Front (Schmidt 1914–1915 and Reinhardt a period in 1917). Of course, it must be remembered that in these periods German lines did not extend into Russia proper and therefore officers who experienced 'the East' were actually fighting in present-day Poland or later Lithuania, Latvia and western Belarus. In fact, the formative experience of fighting in the East came after the First World War, when in 1919 Guderian, Hoepner and Reinhardt were deployed to command free-booting paramilitaries to help secure the German eastern border as part of the infamous *Freikorps*.[3] These campaigns were typified by brutality and violence against both combatants and civilians; as Michael Mann observed:

> Though the *Freikorps* killed and raped with abandon, they had no developed theory of political or ethnic cleansing. The 'enemy' was to be scared off, some killed, but his identity was straightforwardly geopolitical: He was usually a Pole or a Balt allowed by the 1918 Peace Treaties to seize German lands. There was anti-Slav racism, but the 'Judeo-Bolshevik', later central to Nazi demonology, was rare.[4]

By contrast, Johannes Hürter sees the massacres of the *Freikorps* less as a consequence of national divisions than of a real or imagined association with communism, which, he states, made the killings much easier.[5] Erich von Manstein, Hoepner's second corps commander in the summer of 1941, wrote with regard to 1919 of a 'Bolshevik threat from the East'.[6] Likewise, Guderian's letters to Margarete from this period make reference to his 'Bolshevik' enemies, who he claimed were responsible for thousands of murders.[7] He also made explicit references to the resident national groups, casting them in the most derogatory terms. Writing to Margarete on 24 May 1919, Guderian stated: 'There one wants to deliver parts of our country to the barbarians! These are the half savages like the Poles, Lithuanians and Latvians. Poor, dirty, incompetent, stupid and mean, degenerate and insidious.'[8] Revealingly, Guderian's letters from this period not only foreshadow his hatred of Bolshevism and Eastern nationalities, but also his view of the new German government. Complaining that men were not being pressed into service, Guderian fantasised to Margarete about a time in Germany when 'the dictator forces these hordes of pigs to the front with brutal violence'.[9]

There are no known sources from Hoepner or Reinhardt relating to their time in the East in 1919, but the prevailing culture within the army and their subsequent career advancement would suggest they were not repelled by the brutality of the *Freikorps*. Indeed, twenty years later, when Hitler's campaign against Poland was being set in motion, their respective writings depicted a devious enemy who had to be countered with the harshest of methods. At the end of August 1939 Hoepner told his officers that the troops must 'Be informed in detail about the Polish national character', which he determined was exemplified by 'underhandedness', and warned against a 'misunderstanding of mildness'. Attacks in the German rear, Hoepner claimed, were to be expected and 'the strictest measures must be taken by all leaders'.[10] Not only was the character of the Polish campaign to echo his previous experiences in the East, but Hoepner showed no reluctance about Germany again embarking upon a major war. On 1 September 1939 he proudly wrote to Irma: 'The Poland question has to be resolved at last.'[11] Even a week into the Polish campaign, when Britain and France had declared war on Germany, Hoepner remained emboldened by his successes and he wrote of the 'wonderful situation', declaring: 'Now I hope that this time we will see a victorious war.'[12]

Reinhardt wrote about the war against Poland while awaiting trial at Nuremberg in 1948, but even as he languished in prison, the panzer general remained utterly unrepentant. Reinhardt pointed to the 'danger coming from Poland' and wrote of Germany's hope for resolution 'in a peaceful way through Hitler's diplomatic skill, which had now been proven several times'.[13] Casting Hitler as the peacemaker towards Poland shows the extent of Reinhardt's devotion to his Führer even years after the war had ended. Indeed, as many German generals prepared to denounce Hitler to save themselves from prosecution, Reinhardt was not one of them. Having brazenly blamed Poland for the war, the panzer general admitted that in retrospect Germany's campaign of conquest and subjugation had been 'criminal', but then shamelessly added that this fact made no difference to him: 'Even if I had known at the time that this war was criminal, I would not have let my soldiers down. Their fate was my fate too.'[14] In other words, Reinhardt remained unmoved by the devastation and mass murder that became synonymous with the German conquest of Poland and even more so with the subsequent years of Nazi occupation.[15]

Given Hitler's expansionist war aims for the East, we should not be surprised at the congruence between the panzer generals and

Figure 4.1 Georg-Hans Reinhardt (third from left) during a visit to Hitler's Ukrainian Vinnytsia headquarters in March 1943. From left: Field Marshal Günther von Kluge, Hitler, Reinhardt, Colonel-General Walter Model, Colonel-General Gotthard Heinrici, General of Infantry Walther Weiss, Major-General Hans Krebs

National Socialism. After his days in the *Freikorps*, Guderian showed an utter disdain for the Weimar Republic and fantasised about a nationalistic, authoritarian government taking power in Germany. Guderian's letters spoke of 'the disgusting democracy of the centre parties', as well as the 'cowardice, stupidity and weakness of this wretched government'. Alternatively, he claimed: 'The great energy stands on the extreme right and left.' Indeed, Guderian made no secret of his desire for a dictatorship: 'The sooner we get to the dictatorship, the better [...] When will the saviour finally come to this country? It's enough to make you weep.'[16] In spite of expressing such views, Thoma maintained that Guderian did not embrace National Socialism until 1933. Thoma was recorded telling his fellow prisoners of war while in British captivity: 'Guderian is a decent fellow in himself. I have known him since he was a *Hauptmann* [Captain]. He was very keenly opposed to the Nazis and always spoke of them as "stupid sheep". Then the Nazis came into power and he suddenly swung over.'[17] This view was further confirmed after the war by Colonel-General Gotthard Heinrici, who declared in a letter that Guderian 'welcomed the seizure of power by National Socialism'.[18] Such overtly political views were by no means exceptional within the army and stand in stark contrast to post-war claims of senior officers being 'only soldiers'.

On the surface, Hoepner is a more complex figure. He is often framed by his most famous role in the history of Nazi Germany, which has nothing to do with the campaigns he fought from 1939 to 1942, but rather his projected appointment as the commander of the Home Army and later commander-in-chief of the whole German army as a consequence of the July 1944 plot.[19] Hoepner certainly did show a personal distaste for Hitler, occasionally referring to him in letters from 1939 as 'Adolf', which displayed an overly familiar tone and shunned the long established convention of referring to him only as 'the Führer'.[20] More substantively, in this early period Hoepner had planned to take part in the army's 1938 coup,[21] but like so much of the resistance, it was much ado about nothing. Discussion trumped action and nothing came of these plans. The tangible actions by 'military resisters' functioned time and again as enablers of the Nazi regime, not opponents to it.[22] Hoepner's example is characteristic. His substantive role in the history of the Nazi state was very much concentrated in the early part of the war when he commanded major formations, contributed to Germany's offensive successes and facilitated Nazi policy in his area of command.

Figure 4.2 Heinz Guderian being awarded the Knight's Cross
of the Iron Cross by Hitler in October 1939. From left: Guderian,
General of Infantry Hermann Hoth, General of Infantry Adolf Strauss,
Hoepner, Lieutenant-General Friedrich Olbricht and Hitler

In fact, the German military resistance before 1943 was a lot of
smoke with very little fire and even when tangible actions began to be
taken, the motives of most senior army participants were dominated by
Germany's prospects of winning the war, not any moral stance on
Germany's genocidal policies.[23] After the war, Lieutenant-General
Moriz von Faber du Faur admitted in his memoir: 'There is nothing
better than winning, and we won for a while – and we all enjoyed it,
there is no doubt about that. [...] We must not forget that. [...] Also
some of today's heroes of the resistance, Canaris, Witzleben, Rommel,
Höpner [sic], Halder, Kluge and many others enthusiastically
participated.'[24] Indeed, it was resistance members, like Hoepner, who
in the early years helped establish Hitler's empire and implement his
policies. There is no question Hoepner was also a more clear-eyed
sceptic of the Nazi regime, but that only makes his dutiful service
more dubious because he was clearly not as naïve as many of his
comrades. Perhaps there was a degree of fatalism about his support,

Figure 4.3 Erich Hoepner meeting Hitler in late September 1939 towards the end of the Polish campaign. From left: General of Infantry Walter von Reichenau, Colonel-General Wilhelm List, Hitler, General of Infantry Gustav von Wietersheim, General of Infantry Johannes Blaskowitz, Lieutenant-General Erich von Manstein, Hoepner, Heinrich Himmler

but as we will see, there was also a genuine conviction in the most extreme aspects of Nazi policy in the East, rendering Hoepner's discourteous references to 'Adolf' little more than cheap talk.

Schmidt's role is similarly contested. Fabian von Schlabrendorff, a lawyer and reserve lieutenant at the heart of the resistance movement, claimed that Schmidt rebuked Hitler to his face when claiming 'that an aggressive war was not justified'.[25] Later, in March 1943, Schlabrendorff insisted that during Hitler's visit to Army Group Centre the dictator let his contempt for the generals run free until Schmidt supposedly intervened and stopped the tirade.[26] No other sources attest to these events. The fact that Schmidt's career advanced so rapidly, with decorations, elevation to army command and promotion to Colonel-General, suggests his interactions with Hitler were far from confrontational. Indeed, when Schmidt was interrogated after the war by Soviet intelligence, he was asked about his relationship to Hitler and, in response, listed each of his individual meetings with the dictator. In reference to the March 1943 meeting, which was to be Schmidt's last, he made no mention of

Figure 4.4 Rudolf Schmidt (left) in conversation with Hitler (right) at the Ukrainian Vinnytsia headquarters in July 1942, with *Obergruppenführer* Max Jüttner (centre)

a confrontation, nor did he offer any hint of an antagonistic relationship.[27] Given the circumstances Schmidt found himself in, facing a Soviet trial for war crimes, one would think Schmidt would be motivated to emphasise any instance of opposition to Hitler.

We know Schmidt did, in fact, become more critical of the regime by early 1943, but there is no evidence of this in his letters to Fridel. This might be another indication of their distant marital relationship, because Schmidt was apparently much more honest and open in letters to his younger brother Hans-Thilo.[28] However, Hans-Thilo was working as a spy for the French intelligence service and, when his home was raided by the Gestapo in April 1943, they discovered Rudolf Schmidt's letters, which blamed Germany's leadership for the mistakes and setbacks of recent times.[29] 'Otherwise, things are not looking very good at Stalingrad,' Rudolf Schmidt wrote his brother, before adding: 'There is no righteousness, least of all among those who think they have a monopoly on it.'[30] Schmidt was immediately relieved of his command and Goebbels noted in his diary on 10 May 1943: 'This is now one of the Colonel-Generals in whom the Führer had invested a lot. So he [Hitler] has once again experienced a serious disappointment.'[31] Hitler had indeed invested in Schmidt and any sense of betrayal or disappointment only further serves to cast doubt on Schlabrendorff's claims that Schmidt had previously clashed with Hitler. In fact, Schmidt had worked studiously to build his career and the scandal threatened to undermine everything. Among his most recent achievements was the draft plan for the renewed German summer offensive around Kursk, which originated with Schmidt and was subsequently adopted by the rest of the high command.[32] Transported back to Germany under guard, Schmidt was imprisoned until July and then, on Hitler's order, transferred to the Führer reserve (a pool of temporarily unoccupied high-ranking military officers). On 30 September 1943 he was formally dismissed from the army.[33]

Schmidt's military career was over, but this was not yet a reality he was prepared to accept. In spite of his apparent doubts about Germany's leadership, Schmidt did not follow Hoepner's example and seek the restoration of his career in a new post-Nazi government. When Colonel Henning von Tresckow approached Schmidt in early April 1943 on behalf of the conspirators, he was firmly rebuffed.[34] Schmidt wanted nothing to do with the resistance before or even after his arrest, which, for a man tainted by disloyalty but hopeful of redemption under the Nazis, made perfect sense. It also reveals where Schmidt's ultimate loyalties lay. Even with the likely execution of his brother by the Nazi state, which was pre-empted only by Hans-Thilo's suicide in September 1943,[35] Schmidt, like Guderian before him, made representations towards influential advocates with the goal of restoring his career. Revealingly, Schmidt was able to call upon Heinrich Himmler, with whom he maintained a friendly relationship and, as we have seen, from whom he had previously received congratulatory telegrams upon his successes.[36] As a testament to the strength of their association, especially given that the damning evidence against Schmidt came from his own hand, Himmler nevertheless promised to intercede with Hitler on his behalf. Himmler assured Schmidt that he would offer 'urgent advice to prove his trust in the Führer' and sounded an optimistic tone by claiming: 'The war still gives such opportunities that reinstatement cannot be ruled out.'[37] Himmler's first approach failed to move Hitler and he unsuccessfully tried again in early September. A third attempt was likewise conclusively rejected by Hitler, which is noteworthy for the fact that Himmler was prepared to risk his own prestige on what was seemingly a lost cause.[38]

It all underscores the basic conclusion that Schmidt, whatever he might have privately written to his disaffected brother, was not himself prepared to cut ties with the regime, to say nothing of embracing the resistance. Schlabrendorff maintained that Schmidt was 'one of the most talented of the German military leaders', but if so, what was he thinking might be achieved in the aftermath of defeats at Stalingrad, Kursk and the Allied landings in Italy? Importantly, Schlabrendorff also pointed to Schmidt's 'invincible optimism', which he stated 'was invaluable to us because he was always able to find a silver lining no matter how bleak the situation'.[39] Given the primacy of 'will' in the National Socialist state, such a die-hard attitude no doubt impressed Hitler as much as it did the resistance, which helps explain both his career success and his delusional belief that all was not lost for himself or Germany in the second half of 1943. Even if the strategic and military realities of Germany's position were not able to disassociate Schmidt from the regime, one might have thought that his brother's example as someone working against the Nazis, which caused his brother's death – to say nothing of the countless murders perpetrated by the regime – might have evoked another response. The fact that they did not, and that Schmidt's only desire was to regain Hitler's favour through his friend Himmler, is a conclusive indictment of a man that some have presented as being an opponent, and even a victim, of the regime.[40]

With his military career over, Schmidt eventually took a job in a chemical business then switched to working for a building firm, before finally starting his own company Rhein-Beton (Rhine Concrete) in November 1944. Curiously, as Schmidt related his late-war and post-war activities to his Soviet captors, he made no reference to Fridel having been involved in any of his activities or deliberations. Moreover, during this period, Schmidt relocated a number of times, but always referred to these in the singular, not the plural: 'Then I moved to another apartment at Pestalozzi Street No. 8.'[41] This may suggest he and Fridel were no longer living together.[42]

Reinhardt's political outlook presented no ambiguities about his enthusiastic embrace of National Socialism and even in court at Nuremberg he openly questioned how many of his fellow officers were really any different. Speaking on 22 June 1946 Reinhardt declared: 'I believe there was no officer who did not stand behind the Führer and his extraordinary successes. Because out of necessity, out of a huge need that consumed Germany, Hitler brought Germany up again, domestically, economically and externally, and every officer had to feel that and stand behind the Führer as a matter of patriotism.'[43] While Reinhardt never admitted to any guilt in his own conduct of the war, and saw his prosecution in the High Command Trial as simply 'victor's justice', he did not shy away from his Nazi sympathies, in part because he struggled to find fault in anything he had believed. Both during and even after the war Reinhardt held Hitler in the highest regard, seeing him not only as a saviour of Germany, but also as a man of extraordinary talent. After receiving the Knight's Cross from Hitler, Reinhardt wrote on 30 October 1939: 'We discussed a lot and were always amazed at how exactly the Führer actually knew everything, including some of the wishes and worries that we have. Only a genius, which the Führer is, can have such extensive knowledge.'[44] With such pro-Nazi views it is not surprising that Reinhardt never had any role in the resistance in spite of knowing key members within Army Group Centre. When the July Plot finally took place, Reinhardt's diary captured his sense of shock and dismay at what had happened. On the day of the bombing, he wrote: 'Assassination attempt on Führer, thank God he is saved. His speech at night. Incredible act. Why now also this?'[45] The next day, as the participation of his fellow officers was revealed, Reinhardt reacted with utter incredulity: 'Completely broken. Incomprehensible! What did our officer class have to do with this act? We can only be deeply ashamed.'[46]

It was also in July 1944 that a new chief of the army general staff was to be appointed, a position that, as we have seen, would ultimately go to Guderian, but Reinhardt was seen as a serious candidate. In fact, one of Hitler's most trusted military advisers, Rudolf Schmundt, proposed two names. The first was Field Marshal Manstein and, failing that option, his second proposal was not Reinhardt, but rather Schmidt. Schmidt remained undeterred by Himmler's failure to secure his reinstatement in 1943 and continued lobbying behind the scenes. The fact that Hitler was unwilling to reappoint him in even a local command made any thought of him becoming the new chief of the army general staff preposterous, but then Schmidt was apparently known for his 'invincible optimism'.[47] Knowing Hitler as well as he did, Goebbels considered both Manstein and Schmidt 'totally unsuitable' and was not surprised when both were rejected. At this point, Reinhardt's name came into play as Goebbels recorded in his diary: 'Colonel-General Reinhardt is proposed to him [Hitler], who is said to be cut from better wood.'[48] Of course, Reinhardt was unsuccessful, but it shows his perceived reliability among the Nazi elite; he was rewarded in August 1944 with the command of Army Group Centre.

Having believed unquestioningly in Hitler throughout the war, the realisation that the dictator was a criminal only began to dawn on Reinhardt in his post-war incarceration. Reinhardt's diary from early June 1945 charts his battle with the truth, as well as his own complicity in the failed experiment of National Socialism: 'Through stories and so on, my belief in the person of Hitler begins to waver. Or was it, as we previously believed, actually only his inner circle [who were] guilty? Terrible if one is supposed to be mad at everything that one has previously believed and served.'[49] A month later Reinhardt was in despair over his loss of perspective: 'Does life still have meaning? All ideals, all the good things we have lived and worked for have been destroyed.'[50] Such woeful self-pity, of course, took no account of the full horrors Nazi Germany had perpetrated, but as one of the privileged elite, Reinhardt experienced only 'the good things' of acquiescence in Hitler's New Order.

While it cannot be said that Guderian, Hoepner, Schmidt and Reinhardt were of entirely the same mind on Hitler, the spectrum spanned total adherence to broad agreement. Without question they each recognised that their individual success was tied to the National Socialist agenda, so even if a man like Hoepner was not convinced of Hitler's genius, he was far too career-minded to do anything but privately scoff and jeer. Substantively, there was a great deal that united the generals with National Socialism, especially in perceptions of 'the East' and the Communist Soviet state. It was this uniformity and shared world view that drove their complicity in Nazi criminality.[51] Klaus Latzel's extensive work on German soldiers' letters from the Second World War cautions against identifying National Socialist ideology as shaping German views of 'the East'. Instead, his research shows how racist and culturally superior attitudes towards countries and peoples in the East had much longer and deeper roots in German society, and were radicalised by National Socialism rather than instigated by it.[52] Michaela Kipp's later study of soldiers' letters confirmed many of Latzel's conclusions and showed how the war was represented in terms of German 'cleanliness' and 'purity' against the 'filth' of the East both figuratively and literally.[53] Finally, Felix Römer's study of secretly recorded conversations between German soldiers in American captivity at Fort Hunt revealed a 'practically unanimous' set of opinions about the Soviet enemy. From almost 600 soldiers questioned, almost 500 expressed 'a thoroughly negative opinion'.[54]

The sentiments expressed by German soldiers are also identified in the letters of the generals. Writing to Margarete on 1 July, Guderian noted: 'The first Russian[55] localities – so far, we were in Poland! – create a rather bleak impression.' The stiff resistance by the Red Army was presented to Margarete as being conducted by 'fanatical people of another mindset'.[56] Just one month into the campaign, Guderian was already longing for Margarete and he dreamed of their reunion, 'after this campaign in this apathetic and barren land, after all the unpleasantness I've encountered here'.[57] The fact that Germany's invasion was the cause of all Guderian's 'unpleasantness' was of course entirely lost on him, but derogatory references to Russia, blaming the country for his own grief and hardship, were not uncommon. On 15 October Guderian was again thinking of Margarete when he wrote that his experiences 'aroused many emotions in me, which in some cases trigger here in this disgusting country somewhat wistful feelings regarding lovelier and generally carefree times'.[58] In another letter Guderian contrasted 'this wretched country'[59] with Margarete, continuing: 'in the atmosphere of purity, which radiates from you all the way over here into the most boring of all countries'.[60] For her own part, Margarete took her cue from Heinz and wrote: 'The Russian campaign must now be endured with all its hardships in this terrible country.'[61]

When Hoepner's panzer group exited the Baltic states into Russia, he recorded his impressions for Irma: 'Now, for the first time, I'm in old Russia. It's rather bleak. We're on a former estate, where the Bolsheviks once set up a technical school. The former residential buildings are awfully squalid, dirty, unusable.'[62] Schmidt took a similar view when he moved to his new command at Second Army and took up residence in the city of Orel. Writing to Fridel, Schmidt observed: 'Our living quarters are very primitive. No notion of the organisation and living culture of the people here, or [they] were too obtuse for it.'[63] Schmidt also bemoaned the general condition of the Russian population, which, he noted, 'lives and exists extremely primitively'.[64] Reinhardt described Russia to Eva as a 'dreadful country' in which 'everything is abnormal', the implication being that Germany represented the example of a virtuous and 'normal' nation.[65] As for the people, Reinhardt's letters contain the only example of outright anti-semitism, which, even as he edited his correspondence after the war, he clearly did not feel it necessary to expunge. The single reference comes five days before the German invasion, when Reinhardt attempts to explain to Eva why the coming war with the Soviet Union was necessary: 'As soon as they are armed, they – whose leaders are very Jewified, after all – will start a war against us with England or on behalf of England.'[66] Antisemitism was not Reinhardt's only prejudice. After the campaign had begun he reported to Eva on the capture of female soldiers, remarking 'I hear they're awful women!'[67] Such comments might disguise more brutal realities given that other commanders, such as Field Marshal Kluge, issued specific orders that instructed: 'women in uniform are to be shot'.[68] In fact, at this time Kluge was the commander of the short-lived Fourth Panzer Army[69] to which the panzer groups of Guderian and Hoth were nominally subordinated.

The views of the panzer generals conformed not only to wider trends seen in the German soldiers' letters, but also to those among their fellow generals. One method of assessing this comes from the Trent Park internment camp for senior German officers, which was operated by British intelligence from August 1942 until October 1945 and secretly recorded their private conversations. In total some eighty-four German generals stayed at Trent Park and detailed profiles were developed on all of them.[70] Ultimately, only one man, Lieutenant-General Georg Neuffer, who belonged to the Luftwaffe and had served in the Soviet Union, was determined to be 'the only long-term officer at Trent Park ever to have a good word for the Russians'.[71] Surviving letters from other senior commanders who served on the Eastern Front in 1941 reflect, if anything, even more virulent opinions than those of the panzer generals. In just the month of July, Field Marshal Gerd von Rundstedt, commanding Army Group South, described the people to his wife Luise in various letters as 'Dirty Jewish nest', 'bottomless degenerate and dirty', 'unimaginable filth and neglect' and 'legendary filthy nest'.[72] Kluge's only known letter from the 1941 campaign to his wife Mathilde makes references to the poor quality of food available in the East and then continues: 'But these Asians may live on sand and earth for days.'[73] Manstein, Hoepner's second corps commander, summed up his experiences in the East to his wife Jutta-Sybille on 9 July: 'Infinite vastness, miserable order, wretched villages, horrible roads, unspeakable dust and water, which at best suffices for washing.'[74]

Beyond the influence of long-standing German attitudes towards the East, many of the generals' negative attitudes towards the

Soviet Union were tangibly impacted by their individual experiences of visiting the Soviet Union during the period of cooperation between the Reichswehr and the Red Army.[75] Among the panzer generals to have visited the Soviet Union were Guderian (1932), Hoth (1927), Manstein (1931–1932) and Model (1931), while Reinhardt conducted classes for high-ranking Soviet officers on exchange to Berlin. Although Guderian left no account of his time in the Soviet Union, the general impression of German officers appears to have been positively influenced at the time by the hospitality they received as well as the relationships they built with Soviet officers, but this was later forgotten when almost all of these men were murdered in Stalin's purge of the Red Army. Even at the time, German officers formed deeply negative views of the Soviet government with its much-feared commissars and mandated political obedience.[76] Manstein left one of the few available accounts, with a perspective that it may be assumed was generally shared: 'Because, no matter how much the Soviet regime invoked the Western ideas of Marxism, no matter how eagerly it took up the technical achievements of the Western world, the Soviet Union was no longer Europe! The shadow of Asian despotism lay over the country, the people and everything that was going on.'[77] Three weeks into Operation Barbarossa Reinhardt was forced to reflect on his time teaching Soviet officers and the knowledge he had imparted. Writing to Eva on 16 July he noted: 'Sometimes, I'm almost afraid that the fellows in my lessons learned too much. Because even if almost all my students are now dead, they've been able to pass on for almost ten years what I taught them in Berlin.'[78] While such a statement might almost be dismissed as boastful arrogance, one Soviet account of Reinhardt's classes left no doubt about their value: 'If the German army has no more room for P[aulus] and R[einhardt], we will take them in with open arms; they are irreplaceable teachers that we can especially use.'[79] Clearly, German technical and command skills were apparent, but their cultural and racial conceptions fed a conceited over-confidence that undermined their advantages and helped pave the way to barbarism.

Criminal Orders

On 30 March 1941 Hitler spoke to an assembly of roughly 100 senior Wehrmacht officers, including Guderian, Hoepner, Reinhardt and Schmidt, for two and half hours on the nature of the forthcoming war against the Soviet Union. The address was to be a watershed moment, not only in the history of the Second World War, but for the German army. Hitler made clear that the war he intended to fight against the Soviet Union was to be very different from those that preceded it.[80] As the chief of the army general staff Colonel-General Franz Halder noted in his diary, Operation Barbarossa was to be a 'Clash of two ideologies'. Hitler then took aim at the nature of the Soviet state: 'Crushing denunciation of Bolshevism, identified with social criminality. Communism is an enormous danger for our future. We must forget the concept of comradeship between soldiers. A communist is no comrade before or after the battle. This is a war of annihilation. [...] We do not wage war to preserve the enemy.' Halder then recorded how Hitler foresaw the role of the army in his new 'war of annihilation'. In order to achieve the 'extermination of the Bolshevist commissars and of the communist foe' Hitler made clear there would be 'no job for military courts. The individual troop commander must know the issues at stake. They must be the leaders in this fight [...] Commissars and GPU men[81] are criminals and must be treated as such.'[82] There could be no doubt about the methods to which Hitler was referring. Hoth, who attended the same meeting, noted: 'Crimes of Russian commissars [...] deserve no quarter. To be removed not by court martial, but by the troops. Not to be sent to the rear.'[83] Halder's account concludes with Hitler insisting: 'Commanders must make the sacrifice of overcoming their personal scruples.'[84] Hitler need not have worried. Not only was the army leadership prepared to back such policies, but individual commanders took the initiative in drafting similar orders for their men. On 2 May Hoepner issued an order to his Panzer Group 4 justifying the need for 'unheard-of severity' in the forthcoming war against the Soviet Union:

> The war against Russia is an essential component in the German people's struggle for existence. It is the old struggle of the German against the Slavs, the defence of European culture against the Muscovite-Asiatic flood, the resistance to Jewish Bolshevism. This struggle must aim at the destruction of today's Russia and therefore be waged with unheard-of severity. In design and execution every engagement must be guided by the iron will to completely and mercilessly annihilate the enemy. In particular, there is to be no sparing the upholders of the current Russian-Bolshevik system.[85]

Given the ruthless nature of the Polish campaign, the fact that Barbarossa required such special instruction says everything about the projected escalation in violence. Even the French campaign had been a needlessly violent affair. At least 1,000 captured African soldiers from French colonies had been murdered by German forces and these atrocities included the involvement of numerous panzer divisions (1st, 5th, 6th, 7th, 9th and 10th).[86] One might also point out the terrible suffering among the droves of French refugees.[87] Observing the scenes of misery pervading the French populace, Guderian wrote to Margarete in June 1940: 'The Middle Ages were humane compared with the present.'[88] Reinhardt was also disturbed by what he observed in France, describing dead civilians on the sides of the road and families begging for food.[89] While these events resulted from the war, the culpability of the German generals was indirect. Hoepner, on the other hand, found himself involved in a well-documented atrocity. Under his command, but without his knowledge or consent, the *SS Totenkopf* Division massacred ninety-seven British prisoners of war in the village of Le Paradis.[90] The killers had acted independently and Hoepner, incensed at their behaviour, lodged protests, but ultimately allowed the matter to pass without consequence.[91] If Hoepner's moral outrage was short-lived in 1940, the order he issued for Barbarossa showed a willingness to not only tolerate excess under his command, but even to encourage it.

Hoepner was not alone. Reinhardt reissued most of Hoepner's order from 2 May to his own corps, but finessed the colonial aspect and added that the struggle for existence was 'especially about the economic independence of Greater Germany and the European area it ruled'.[92] Whatever orders individual commanders issued in their own examples of 'working towards the Führer',[93] the army high command took the initiative and drafted orders to ensure Barbarossa was uniformly conducted with the requisite ruthlessness demanded by Hitler's instructions of 30 March. These became known as the notorious 'criminal orders', two of the most important being issued on 13 May and 6 June 1941. The first of these was known as the 'Decree on the Exercise of Martial Jurisdiction in the Area "Barbarossa" and Special Measures of the Troops'.[94] This order freed German soldiers from any form of prosecution for war crimes committed in the Soviet Union (except for sexual misdeeds with what were judged to be racially inferior Slavs),[95] while at the same time opening the way to collective reprisals against 'suspects' deemed to have engaged in 'criminal action'. The second criminal order was titled the 'Guidelines for the Treatment of Political Commissars'[96] and required that upon capture these men be separated from other prisoners of war and promptly shot. Importantly, these orders were specifically directed towards the officers of the army, who were then required to carry out the executions independently of the SS or SD.[97]

While criminal behaviour had certainly been a feature of the army's earlier campaigns, the Commissar Order and the Martial Jurisdiction Decree effectively transformed atrocities from being an exception to a purposeful policy. Even more revealingly, these new orders were greeted by the panzer generals without a word of dissent, including by Guderian, whose post-war memoir emphatically claimed he had rejected the order and refused to pass it on.[98] While serious readers of German military history will long have been disabused of such falsehoods, the director of the German Tank Museum in Münster, Ralf Raths, explained that everyday visitors often entertain romantic – and utterly false – ideas about the criminal culpability of the *Panzertruppe*:

> While the crimes of the [non-panzer elements within the] Wehrmacht are recognised by almost all visitors as an historical fact, albeit occasionally reluctantly and through gritted teeth: the panzer, according to a calming logic, constituted an offensive weapon at the head of the army, which did not have any time to commit war crimes. [...] This results in the panzers having been a part of the Wehrmacht, which is unburdened and can still be 'enjoyed' today. [...] The fact that research has long ago clearly addressed the involvement of the panzer army in criminality has not yet penetrated the popular image of the tank.[99]

So how were the fast-moving panzer troops complicit in war crimes? Felix Römer, who has written the seminal work on the Commissar Order, singled out the panzer troops in his study: 'The focal points of the extermination policy were mainly in the frontal sections of the Panzer Corps, the fast, armoured troops that spearheaded the German offensive.'[100] Overall, there were forty-four German corps in Operation Barbarossa, with the clear majority belonging to infantry armies, yet recorded executions of commissars occurred disproportionately in corps from the panzer groups. For example, of the ten corps with the highest number of executed commissars, six belonged to the panzer groups. The overall average of executions per corps type also disproportionately favoured panzer corps and not by an incremental number – they registered seventy-three executions as against forty-two for the remaining corps.[101] It goes without saying, therefore, that Hoepner and Guderian passed on the Commissar Order and that their constituent corps and divisions implemented it.[102]

Guderian's Panzer Group 2 reported shooting 196 commissars in the time between 22 June and 31 October 1941.[103] Two of his leading corps (XXXXVII Army Corps [motorised] and XXIV Army Corps) reported killing eighty and seventy-five commissars respectively.[104] Jacob Capell, a corporal in the 3rd Panzer Division (belonging to XXIV Army Corps), was recorded telling another POW at Fort Hunt: 'When we took prisoners in Russia, we shot the commissars straight away.'[105] Such a statement raises a question about whether the available figures on commissar executions under-represent the true scale of the killings, given that researchers can only count executions that were officially recorded. Even Guderian's correspondence provides a reference to his true feelings on the preferred fate of Soviet commissars. Writing to Margarete after the fall of Roslavl in early August 1941, Guderian added: 'The Pol.[itical army] leader was killed in action. A nice success.'[106]

While Guderian's panzer group managed to kill almost 200 commissars in the first four months of the campaign, Hoepner's panzer group either proved much more proficient at rooting out and killing commissars or was simply more inclined to record their deaths because in only the first four weeks of the campaign they reached nearly the same figure. In a radio report sent to Army Group North, Hoepner's panzer group reported 172 executions between 22 June and 19 July 1941.[107] That the senior commanders recognised what they were doing to be criminal is proven by a communication from the chief of staff at Army Group North, Lieutenant-General Kurt Brennecke, to Chales de Beaulieu, his counterpart in Hoepner's panzer group. Writing on 2 July 1941, Brennecke recommended: 'I consider it necessary to destroy the OKH's decree on the treatment of political commissars, so that it does not fall into enemy hands and can be exploited for propaganda purposes.'[108]

As part of Hoepner's panzer group, Reinhardt was not only complicit in passing on the Commissar Order to his XXXXI Panzer Corps, but ensured that it was ruthlessly implemented. Of the forty-four corps taking part in Operation Barbarossa, Reinhardt's corps registered the third-highest number of killings, with 145 separate instances of confirmed executions.[109] His loathing of the commissars is even briefly referenced in his letters to Eva, when he wrote about the myriad of Soviet defences being built by press-gangs of men, women and children 'under the yoke of the commissars'.[110] When the prosecution confronted Reinhardt at his post-war trial with the evidence showing he had implemented the Commissar Order, he emphatically denied all responsibility. Instead, Reinhardt claimed, 'These reports are not commissars who were shot pursuant to the Commissar Order, they were not liquidated, that is, killed after capture, they are fictitious figures.' According to his defence it was all an elaborate numbers game, 'in order to deceive higher headquarters'.[111] Unsurprisingly, the court was not convinced.

At the beginning of Operation Barbarossa, Schmidt's XXXIX Motorised Army Corps came under the command of Hoth's Panzer Group 3. Unlike the other panzer group commanders, Hoth was one of the few generals after the war to admit issuing the Commissar Order and Schmidt proved to be both dutiful and highly proficient in its implementation.[112] In fact, Schmidt's corps murdered at least 186 commissars, giving it the notorious distinction of registering more killings than any of the other forty-four corps serving on the Eastern Front.[113] This fact belies Schmidt's representation as 'a "different" commander'[114] based upon his September 1941 'Memorandum on the possibilities of shaking the Bolshevik resistance from within'. Here, Schmidt argued for revoking the Commissar Order on the basis that it only stiffened resistance and encouraged fighting to the last. Schmidt's memorandum went even further, arguing for 'the formation of a Russian government' in the hope that the Soviet people would 'turn away from Bolshevism'.[115] The memorandum was sent to the Sixteenth Army with the request that it be forwarded to Hitler, but another copy was dispatched to Hitler through private channels.[116] Importantly, Schmidt's reasoning was entirely based upon pragmatic benefits for Germany; there were no ethical, moral or legal issues raised. In fact, Schmidt's corps did not stop executing commissars as it awaited an answer that never came.[117] Moreover, the intelligence officer for Hoth's panzer group, which by the beginning of the month had killed 170 commissars, reported in mid-August that the 'special treatment' reserved for the commissars constituted 'no problem for the troops'.[118]

By no means was the army's murder limited to commissars. In fact, the Martial Jurisdiction Decree granted officers *carte blanche* to enact their own forms of 'justice' and these could be directed indiscriminately at the civilian population. As the order read, 'elements suspected of criminal action' were to be taken to the nearest officer who, without recourse to military courts, would decide 'whether they are to be shot'. In the event that no perpetrators could be identified following an attack, the order empowered battalion commanders and above with the right to initiate 'collective violent measures', which the OKH recommended to be 'shoot thirty men'.[119] In practice, records from Army Group North between July 1941 and February 1942 tell of Soviet civilians being shot or hanged because 'they made anti-German remarks during a village meeting'; 'the man could not disprove that he had been employed as a spy'; two men had 'anti-German tendencies'; a man had 'a stubborn character'; a man 'gave an impression of cunning'; five civilians 'listened to Radio Moscow'; a woman had 'communist tendencies'; a distiller, his wife and two children were suspected of 'making preparations for distributing Schnapps to partisans'.[120]

Given the open-ended scope for identifying 'crimes' against the Wehrmacht, it is hardly surprising that the Martial Jurisdiction Decree was implemented by Hoepner, Guderian, Reinhardt and Schmidt. Indeed, every corps participating in Operation Barbarossa showed evidence of its implementation.[121] After the war, on 5 November 1945, Guderian was subjected to Allied interrogation and asked about the Martial Jurisdiction Decree. Already at this point, the panzer general had formulated his defence: 'I did not take the order with me into the field and did not distribute it. Therefore, Panzer Group No. 2 treated the civilian population in conformance with the Geneva Convention and International Law.' Guderian clearly understood the criminal nature of the order and even explained this to his interrogators: 'The order was formulated in such a manner that excesses on the part of our troops could not have been prevented.' Having been so categorical on this point, when the interrogator switched his questioning to the rest of the German army, Guderian's desire to protect the army's good name against such a clear violation required a strained logic:

[GUDERIAN:]   I could not imagine that any army chief with a sense of dignity would execute any such orders unless there were compelling reasons for his doing so, and I have never learned in conversations with my colleagues that any reprisals of this nature were ever applied.

[INTERROGATOR:] There were a number of commanders who not only
                   complied with these orders but went even further.
[GUDERIAN:]   I didn't hear of any such thing.[122]

If none of the army commanders were complicit in acting against the
Soviet population, aside from the inexplicable exception of those with
'compelling reasons for his doing so', at the very least the interrogator
wanted to know how Guderian justified so many atrocities on Soviet
soil. Guderian had no answer for this and instead attempted to shift all
the blame to the most convenient scapegoat: 'As I have said', he insisted,
'I have not heard that any criminal actions on the part of the armed
forces were committed. I did hear rumours about very undesirable
activities on the part of police forces in the rear areas.' Yet the interrogator did not allow Guderian to deflect from the army's own responsibility and confronted him with the fact that there were senior
commanders 'who did not think it was their duty to ignore these orders'.
Guderian had painted himself into a corner and then had to walk back
his earlier comments to explain why otherwise honourable men, including supposedly Wilhelm Keitel whom he defended as 'basically a decent
character', had issued such an ostensibly criminal order. As Guderian
unconvincingly explained: 'I think that these orders were issued because
people did not have sufficient sense to realise what they would lead to. It
was not meanness but lack of judgement.'[123]

    The problem with anything Guderian said or wrote after the
war was not his lying. This would only have been an issue if anybody
had had the ability to review the military files, which would not be
possible until a decade after his death. As a result, Guderian did not have
to account for his wartime record because he simply refused to disclose
it. Instead, Guderian expertly applied himself to reconstructing a career
that maximised his military reputation, while minimising his political
(and criminal) liability. In this sense, the post-war Guderian was not so
much a changed man as he was a continuation of the same self-
promoting careerist, who was simply playing to a new audience.
Candid observations about Guderian's true character were made during
the war by the anti-Hitler conspirators, who in early 1943 tried to
recruit him to their cause, but quickly discovered who they were dealing
with.[124] According to the diary of Hermann Kaiser: 'He [Guderian] is
vain, impertinent, never sees the big picture, talks a lot, [is] easily
influenced, changes his mind and can never be brought to action.'[125]

Their engagement confirms that Guderian had knowledge of the resistance movement, but, having recently been installed as Hitler's new Inspector General of Armoured Troops (1 March 1943), showed no further interest in the plot. Even Guderian's loyal adjutant, Major Bernd Freytag von Loringhoven, admitted after the war: 'Guderian had an ambivalent attitude towards the July Plot.'[126] Having been rebuffed, the conspirators denounced Guderian as an 'unlimited opportunist' and considered him to be 'dangerous' as a result of his 'double nature'.[127] Guderian was indeed loyal to his own best interests. General of Panzer Troops Heinrich Eberbach was recorded privately telling his son in British captivity in 1944: 'Guderian said to me long ago: "The Führer is mad!" I shared the idea he had at the time: to get hold of the Führer, let's say imprison him, but at any rate keep him alive and to liquidate his entire entourage.' Eberbach's son questioned his father's portrayal: 'Well, I don't think that Guderian would have been given the job of chief of staff if he hadn't been considered very reliable.' To which his father, who had served under Guderian in 1941, answered: 'That man, whom they held to be so reliable, told me that. I'm just waiting for the moment when Guderian shoots the Führer and all the others at the top.'[128] Such seditious thoughts contrast with Guderian's fulsome public fidelity to the regime in the aftermath of the July Plot. Writing in the *Völkischer Beobachter* in July 1944, Guderian lamented the attempt on Hitler's life as the 'darkest day in the history of the German general staff', and concluded: 'There is no future for the Reich without National Socialism.'[129] Not surprisingly, therefore, in the post-war world, where Guderian was once again seeking to advance his own interests, he reinvented himself to his American captors as an anti-Nazi and shamelessly denied all knowledge of the army's wartime criminality.

Given Guderian's notorious unreliability it is perhaps not surprising that his tenure as chief of staff includes evidence that he may have inadvertently encouraged the Hungarian decision to seek terms with the Soviets. According to Vilmos Nagy, a confidant of the Hungarian leader Miklós Horthy who had previously served as his Minister of Defence, a visit by Guderian in late August 1944 'significantly strengthened the regent's resolve' to request a ceasefire. As Nagy wrote in his 1947 memoir:

> Guderian was unable to provide any news that would have offered the regent reassurance concerning the successful

continuance of the war. Guderian openly declared that the rumors that had been spread concerning miracle weapons were completely baseless. He said quite sincerely that yes, the weapons industry in Germany was working on first-rate inventions, but it was not producing any weapons that would decide the outcome of the war.[130]

While Guderian's claims were unquestionably true, they hardly served Germany's purposes and suggest that his naïve candour was a symptom of his inexperience with international relations and coalition warfare. Yet, whatever Guderian said about the war during his visit to Budapest, his thinly disguised rejection of the Hungarian state on the basis that it lacked 'purity' must have confirmed every condescending stereotype the Hungarians had formed about their German allies. Evidence for this comes directly from Guderian's memoir, in which the panzer general alluded to a conversation with Horthy that included 'the problems of nationality in Hungary', explained by Guderian as 'for hundreds of years racial groups of many sorts had lived in close proximity to one another'.[131] Given that the Germans in combination with the fascist Arrow Cross were shortly to overthrow Horthy and begin the mass murder of Hungarian Jews in the name of national purity, a fact Guderian must have known when writing his account, this only confirms his enduring post-war antisemitism.

While the 1941 Martial Jurisdiction Decree authorised all manner of excesses, individual commanders taking part in the invasion of the Soviet Union issued further orders or reported actions of a blatantly criminal nature against specific groups. Hoepner's panzer group reported capturing 'young communists', a political youth organisation in the Soviet Union whose members could include teenagers as young as fifteen, fighting alongside the Red Army. The report read: 'Young communists. Organised gang, some in uniform, some in civilian clothes. Uniformed to be treated like soldiers, the civilians, according to reports so far, shot dead.'[132] The fact that these youths may not have had any choice about fighting with the Red Army and simply lacked uniforms did not alter their fate. The treatment of wounded Soviet POWs by the panzer group was also addressed in a report: 'It goes without saying that German medical officers only care for wounded prisoners of war when the last German wounded man has been treated.'[133] In another instance the chief of staff at Army Group North, Brennecke, had to request Hoepner's panzer group not to deploy its troops in areas where Soviet POWs were being made to work because they tended to intervene and shoot them.[134] Hoepner may not have been individually responsible for these actions and orders, but, given his instructions from 2 May 1941 insisting that 'every engagement must be guided by the iron will to completely and mercilessly annihilate the enemy', a degree of culpability cannot be avoided.

If Hoepner bears a degree of responsibility for orders issued within his panzer group, Reinhardt went further by taking the initiative in issuing his own criminal orders. When in December 1941 Panzer Group 3 was preparing defensive positions, Reinhardt himself ordered that all military-age men in the combat zone be interned in German POW camps, while Soviet civilians were to be forced 'to the East' – that is, across the front line.[135] The following year Reinhardt also passed on the notorious Commando Order, requiring that captured Allied commandos be killed without trial, even if in proper uniforms. Although most known executions from this order are of men fighting with the Western Allies (American, British, Canadian and Greek), Reinhardt was one of the select German commanders on the Eastern Front known to have issued the order to his own troops.[136]

Although the execution of German soldiers is typically associated with brutal generals like Ferdinand Schörner in later years of the war, in 1941 Schmidt foreshadowed this practice by offering one of the most frivolous pretexts for execution. Having overheard a report about poor morale among his forces defending the town of Livny in early December 1941, Schmidt instructed that 'individual people, who engage in defeatist talk' be shot as examples to wavering units.[137] Schmidt, like so many of the panzer generals, liked to style himself as being extremely close to, and supportive of, his troops, but in line with the National Socialist ethos, reward was always conditional on unquestioning obedience, with anything less often followed by harsh retribution. Nor was Schmidt alone among the panzer generals for issuing the death penalty in 1941. During Guderian's post-war interrogation he claimed to have learned about two soldiers from his panzer group who had 'violated provisions of international law'. They were tried for their actions and received sentences that Guderian considered 'rather mild', so he intervened and told his interrogators: 'I ordered capital punishment against them.'[138] Of course, Guderian's record in 1941 pales by comparison with the rampant execution of thousands of German soldiers that took place under his tenure as acting chief of the army general staff in 1944–1945.[139]

The War behind the Front

While it is clear that the panzer generals supported and even initiated their own criminal orders, there is very little evidence of these activities in their letters home. Nor should we be surprised at this. As Nicholas Stargardt has observed:

> Indeed, one of the longest lasting illusions sustained by couples was the hope that the war could be treated as lost time to be bracketed out of the married life as a wasted interlude. These oft repeated sentiments of course also underlined one of the primary purposes in writing – to reassure their spouses that the relationship was intact, that the war had changed nothing that was fundamental to their relationship – and this emotional imperative often cramped what could be said in war letters.[140]

Stargardt was writing about the rank and file of the German army, but the point stands for the generals too. From the available letters, the panzer generals studiously ignored the harsh reality of the war in the East and how that manifested itself in orders and behaviour. If this is in fact representative of all the letters they wrote, which it may not be (explaining why some letters 'disappeared' or were excluded), it suggests the generals were consciously preserving an image of themselves free from any suggestion of guilt or overtly violent associations. Writing to their wives and being connected with their non-military world was a reminder of familiar societal norms where civilians, unlike in the East, were respected and accorded protected status. Observing these rules in their letters validated the moral and emotional sense of a 'righteous self', which social psychologists tell us is an almost incontrovertible core belief.[141] Not only did letters substantiating such norms reinforce the positive self-image of the generals, but also the exclusion of contradictory information indirectly acknowledges that the generals were aware that their transgressions contravened an accepted legal and moral order.

Social psychologists have also identified the important concept of 'self-licensing', by which an individual's immoral actions are minimised by acting in an altruistic and morally acceptable manner.[142] When viewed in this light, the oft repeated concerns for the well-being of the troops or the love expressed for family can be seen as reaffirming positive self-conceptions of compassion and benevolence, tempering the need to be 'hard' and uncompromising in other areas of policy.[143]

In one letter from early November, Guderian consoled Margarete on the second anniversary of her mother's death, ruminating on the importance of family:

> On 4 November, two years had passed since your dear mother closed her eyes for the last time.
>
> On this day of painful memories, I thought of you and particularly regretted not being able to spend this day at your side.
>
> You know the veneration and love with which I was attached to your mother and I know how uncommonly deep your bond with her was. But it is general human destiny to become increasingly lonely in old age. We must now reconcile ourselves to this and seek comfort in the hope that at least we both will be once more brought together by fate and that a few more years of happy and healthy life together may be granted to us, and with both our boys.[144]

Along the same lines, David Harrisville's research into the moral world of the German soldier on the Eastern Front demonstrated that 'perpetrators are rarely sadists, but ordinary people who consistently see themselves in a positive light and regard their actions as morally defensible. [...] in the case of German soldiers on the Eastern Front, soldiers often insisted on their inherent decency by reflecting on acts of kindness towards family members, comrades or Soviet civilians'.[145] Writing to Irma, Hoepner included very little about his interactions with Soviet civilians, but at one point he implied a familiar, and even playful, form of contact with them. Referring to a nickname he had apparently been given, he told his wife that he was known as 'bear Goepner', adding that the Russians could not pronounce the 'H' in his name.[146] In fact, the exposure of senior German officers to the Soviet civilian population was minimal and often only occurred for propaganda purposes. In the early days of the invasion, Guderian wrote of the people's euphoria at regaining their religious services and noted in consequence: 'The people are very friendly so far [...] we are regarded as liberators.' Yet, perhaps with a view to German plans for the East, Guderian then added: 'Hopefully, the people will not be disappointed.'[147] By the early autumn, Guderian's characterisation of army–civilian relations suggested a less enthusiastic mood: 'We're getting along tolerably with the populace. However, we hardly touched any industrial regions. It might be very different there.'[148] Schmidt's letter to Fridel, after arriving in the city of Orel, confirmed that conditions in the urban areas were indeed very much worse for civilians, which can only have negatively influenced their view of occupation. Observing the desperate poverty within the city, Schmidt wrote: 'How it's all supposed to go with the population, I don't know. I think there'll be a dreadful famine with an appalling amount of death.'[149] In fact, by this time a city-wide famine had already begun in Orel, with instances of cannibalism being reported in December,[150] but none of this prompted words of regret or concern – to say nothing of action – from Schmidt. In the battle for hearts and minds, such indifference proved decisive. Karel Berkhoff's excellent study of Soviet propaganda concluded: 'What saved Stalin's day, was less his propaganda than the reality: Hitler's regime offered no liveable alternative to Stalin's.'[151]

Given the dire poverty of the Soviet people, which was compounded by the privations imposed by the war, the generals displayed little understanding or sympathy for the plight of the population. In the opening weeks of the war, Reinhardt observed with disgust how peasants scrambled to loot despite an artillery bombardment. He related the event to Eva, concluding, 'terrible, I hate that!'[152] Of course, looting under fire speaks more of desperation than greed, but if theft upset Reinhardt, then the German army was, without question, the principal offender. From the army level down to the individual soldier, the *Ostheer* perpetrated an organised plunder of cities, towns, villages, farms and individual peasant houses on an industrial scale.[153] Indeed, the starvation in Orel and throughout the occupied regions of the Soviet Union was often a result of the army's forced requisitioning.[154]

We have already seen how Hoepner shipped whole crates of foodstuffs home, but a subsequent letter shows that, in addition, he also dispatched 'parcels and suitcases' with even more items. As his letter from 14 December made clear: 'I'm sending you a Christmas parcel, which is merely meant to demonstrate that I'm thinking about you. Aside from the things that have already been sent in parcels and suitcases, there is nothing. Two wooden spoons that are typical here are the only particular items.'[155] Clearly, Hoepner was keeping a sharp eye out for anything of interest for his family. While plunder for personal gain was frowned upon, there was no serious attempt to prevent it, especially by senior commanders. On the other hand, 'living off the land' for the purposes of the army was part of Barbarossa's planning and considered not only acceptable, but wholly necessary to feed the troops. As Guderian reported to Margarete: 'We're helping ourselves in a makeshift way.'[156]

While Barbarossa began with the theft of household food and livestock, by the autumn cold nights were pushing more and more soldiers into peasant houses. Sometimes cohabitation was permitted, but more often than not the inadequacy of housing forced the eviction of the civilian population, which under the conditions resulted in untold deaths, especially from November and December. As early as 5 September Schmidt wrote: 'The towns are dreadfully desolated. Nevertheless, our people now have to go into the houses in the cold and wet, despite the filth and vermin in the buildings, insofar as they are not burned down. I'm still living in my little trailer, cold and primitive. You can't imagine the wretchedness everywhere in Russia.'[157]

Once again, Schmidt spared no thought for the civilian population and, like so many of the soldiers' letters, the dreadful implications of this practice were left conspicuously unaddressed. Similarly, a letter from Hoepner on 21 September left Irma in no doubt about the practice of eviction and was even suggestive of the pitiless method employed. As Hoepner casually reported: 'All localities have been burned down. Smolensk is in ruins; Roslavl likewise. [...] Our accommodation is not yet ready. Aside from cleaning and throwing people out, we're still without our vehicles, which won't be here before this evening, at the earliest.'[158] Such indifference to the fate of the civilian population was the true face of German occupation. At his post-war trial for war crimes, Reinhardt attempted to make a virtue of his supposedly modest needs by insisting that he only ever took two rooms for himself in a peasant's house.[159] The fact that most peasant houses consisted of a single large room, sometimes partitioned by makeshift curtains, but were certainly not multi-roomed houses, seems to have been lost on Reinhardt. Indeed, there is no evidence in the correspondence by the panzer generals that any of them shared their dwellings with civilians.[160] Reinhardt, however, insisted to the court that his 'modest requirements' were governed by the desire that no one be forced to abandon their home on his account.[161]

Reinhardt's purported concern for the civilian population contrasted with his record. At his post-war trial the judges singled out his approach to the forced use of civilian labour. Citing his own personal directives, the evidence showed that Reinhardt denied food, wages and liberty in order to compel people to work in his area of command.[162] Reinhardt also issued an order for the shooting of civilians who attempted escape, but, when confronted by this, the general tried to argue that the order intended only that they be fired upon, not shot dead. Such reinterpretation of Reinhardt's orders was a constant feature of the defence. At one point, defence attorneys even sought to challenge the interpretation of the term 'special treatment', a well-established euphemism for murder, contending it was merely intended to denote the segregation of people.[163] Yet Reinhardt's panzer group not only murdered people who attempted to escape, it also targeted the innocent and vulnerable. After the occupation of Kalinin in October 1941, the inmates of a city asylum were murdered on the pretext that they 'posed a danger' and constituted an unacceptable burden.[164]

If the civilian population could be wantonly mistreated and even murdered by the army, the emergent threat from the nascent Soviet partisan movement in 1941 elicited a uniquely savage response. Even in the summer months when the occupied territories were somewhat smaller and organised resistance had hardly had the chance to coalesce, Hoepner complained of a constant threat. On 1 August he wrote to Irma: 'There are still many Russian soldiers and partisans hanging around in the woods; at night, they lay mines on the railway tracks and attack baggage trains. My sentries open fire every night.'[165] Initially, the hope of a quick victory negated a comprehensive focus on the rear areas, but by the autumn army commanders across the Eastern Front were grappling with the scale of the problem. Although there had been a steady process of radicalisation in the *Ostheer's* brutal approach to security issues, a formula for the army's response was encapsulated by an order issued on 10 October by Reichenau, the commander of Sixth Army, which called for the killing of all those suspected of partisan involvement, including Soviet soldiers captured behind the lines.[166] Senior commanders across the Eastern Front subsequently reissued the order to their own forces, including Guderian and Hoepner. Guderian prefaced the order by writing: 'I adopt this order of the 6th Army as my own. It also applies to the Panzer Army.'[167] On the same day the order was issued (6 November), Guderian's subordinate XXXXVII Army Corps (mot.) reported overrunning a partisan camp and capturing fifty men, all of whom were shot.[168] Yet this was only a tiny fraction of the murders taking place behind German lines. In the course of November, records indicate some 14,037 Soviet prisoners were captured in Army

Group Centre's rear area (not including those taken in the drive on Moscow at the front), which attests, first, to the scale of the problem behind the front and, secondly, to the magnitude of the killing if orders like Reichenau's were being implemented.[169] It was also in November that Guderian, Hoepner, Reinhardt and Schmidt commanded four of the army group's six largest formations.

References to a 'partisan war' imply some form of combat, but this belies the murderous reality of German anti-partisan operations. Reichenau's order stated: 'Fear of German counter-measures must be greater than the threat posed by the Bolshevik remnants roaming about.'[170] Reprisals for partisan attacks or sabotage were often targeted against the nearest town or village and, in keeping with Reichenau's order, exacted a vastly disproportionate response in blood and destruction. Importantly, the extreme violence of these operations was not only understood by the German generals, it was considered a mark of distinction. The problem was supposedly half-measures driven by a 'misguided humanity', which endangered the pacification programme and potentially cost German lives. In the National Socialist military ethos, a commander not only had the right to kill in order to protect his men; it was an obligation to be conducted without pity or hesitation. Leniency in the eyes of the Wehrmacht was not only taboo, but dangerous. It suggested individual weakness as well as a wholly misplaced sympathy for the enemy, which compromised the German national community.[171] Even prior to Nazi rule, the German military leadership fostered a culture of violence towards its enemies that often contradicted existing international law. As Isabel Hull has convincingly argued, the most senior German commanders believed that 'the exceptionality of war raises it above law'.[172] The pursuit of victory, no matter the cost, was seen as paramount, which is why Hitler's generals were so amenable to the radicalisation of military policy under his rule.

Interestingly, the violence called for by the generals did not cause them to choose between moral and professional duties. Although it may appear counter-intuitive, the violence may even have served to reaffirm their sense of morality. André Mineau's study of Operation Barbarossa highlighted 'survival, necessity and self-defence' as key drivers of German behaviour. As he explained:

> Nobody could be against that or issue any blame for any attitude or behaviour motivated in this manner. At this point, the

German mind had come to closely intertwine ideology and ethics. Ideology had penetrated military morality to found and, consequently, to orient values, virtues and rules. But morality could lend its traditional notions in such a way that the requirements of ideology could be termed 'good', 'necessary', or 'acceptable'.[173]

Writing in 1941, a similar conclusion was reached by Ernst Fraenkel, who observed that 'the identification of law and morality in the Third Reich has resulted in the assimilation of morality to National Socialist law'.[174] Likewise, Mark Mazower has argued: 'There was no contradiction between the brutality of the Nazi regime and its reputation as the "guarantor of public decency and of law and order"': on the contrary, that very image permitted its troops to justify many of their most brutal actions.'[175]

With an affirmed sense of righteousness, and even entitlement, to perpetrate violence against real and suspected enemies within the civilian population, the panzer generals not only took part in the anti-partisan war, but also embraced it as well as its ruthless methods. When a truck belonging to Hoepner's command staff was attacked by alleged partisans in early August, the nearby village of Straševo was burned to the ground, with the panzer group reporting that 'some suspected partisan [sic] residents were shot'.[176] The panzer group then made a public declaration in German and Russian that read: 'In the future the same will happen with every village in the vicinity of which partisans or other criminals operate and whose population is in any way connected with them, without being immediately reported to the next German military authority.'[177] Hoepner's panzer group was true to its word. The subordination of the 285th Security Division to his command gave Hoepner a dedicated formation for the conduct of anti-partisan operations, which, while under his command from early August to mid-September, killed several hundred suspected partisans and burned dozens of villages. The records of these operations also include a guide to the alleged composition of partisan groups, which were supposed to consist of 'armaments workers, convicts, young people, Jews and party functionaries'.[178] All of these actions preceded Hoepner's decision to issue Reichenau's notorious order. In fact, as an indication of the lengths to which Hoepner's panzer group was prepared to go in their anti-partisan operations, in August a submission was made to Army Group

North requesting the use of Blue Cross – a gas chemical agent used in the First World War.[179] Such an escalation in the already bitter partisan struggle was rejected by the high command. Not even Hitler wanted to enter into gas warfare, revealing just how ruthless and reckless Hoepner was prepared to be.[180]

Guderian's formations were also clearly engaged in brutal anti-partisan operations in 1941, but he undertook an even more senior role in 1943 when he became involved in discussions with the SS regarding anti-partisan operations. Testifying at Nuremberg, *SS-Brigadeführer* Ernst Rode, who served as a member of Himmler's personal command staff from 1943 to 1945, told the court: 'My function was to furnish the forces necessary for anti-partisan warfare to the Higher SS and Police Leaders and to guarantee the support of army forces. This took place through personal discussions with the leading officers of the Operations Staff of the OKW and OKH, namely [. . .] Colonel-General Guderian.' In addition to Guderian, Rode listed seven other army commanders with whom he coordinated policy, but also pointed to the centrality of the army in these operations. As Rode continued his testimony, 'since police troops for the most part could not be spared from the *Reichskommissariate*, the direction of this warfare lay practically always entirely in the hands of the army.'[181]

During his post-war interrogations Guderian emphatically maintained his innocence and rejected any wrongdoing on the part of his men for their treatment of Soviet civilians. 'As far as I know', the panzer general claimed, 'my troops were never guilty of any senseless punishment. As far as I know, my troops were never guilty of any senseless destruction.'[182] This was of course untrue even in 1941, but given Guderian's role from 1944 it was an absurd claim. Captain Wilhelm Scheidt, who served in the War History Section of the OKW from 1941 to 1945, testified at Nuremberg: 'I remember that, at the time of the Polish revolt in Warsaw, *SS-Gruppenführer* [Hermann] Fegelein reported to Colonel-General Guderian and Jodl about the atrocities.'[183] Not only did Guderian know about the murders perpetrated against civilians; he offered no objection to the increasingly murderous orders Hitler and Himmler issued to suppress the uprising.[184] The same was true of Reinhardt, who had recently become the new commander of Army Group Centre (16 August) with insight into the brutally repressive measures employed in Warsaw.[185] Although after the war many generals sought to point out that civilians taking up arms were subject to the

death penalty as irregular combatants under international law at the
time, at the very least court martial proceedings were required to establish any guilt. Moreover, indignation at the concept of 'armed civilians'
was shown to be a farce when Guderian himself proposed the formation
of the *Volkssturm*, an armed national militia mobilising civilians – often
without adequate training or even uniforms – for the defence of
Germany.[186]

Reinhardt was one of the few senior German commanders to
serve continuously from the day German troops crossed the border into
the Soviet Union to the day they were ejected. For most of this time
Reinhardt commanded the Third Panzer Army, which fought a constant
battle against Soviet partisans and became a major focus of his post-war
trial. While acknowledging the bloody nature of this warfare,
Reinhardt, however, insisted all of the blame lay with the Soviets themselves. As he testified in May 1948:

> My troops were compelled to conduct anti-partisan warfare in
> order to defend themselves against the bandit war that was
> forced upon us [and] from which we suffered badly [...]. And
> if this bandit war has cost victims, I expressly state heavy sacri-
> fices on both sides, then the guilt lies with those who organised
> it, but not with my soldiers, who resisted it.[187]

It is perhaps not too surprising that Reinhardt sought to shift
responsibility as part of his defence, but, as his testimony continued,
he went so far as to justify policies of wholesale murder in the rear
areas:

> At that time there was a general announcement in the country,
> which was posted everywhere, that prisoners of war behind the
> front had to report themselves by a certain time, otherwise
> they would be punished with death. This account may sound
> harsh today. Under the situation then, this provision was
> a military necessity. We were under attack at the time. The
> bandit war began behind our front. With the speed of action it
> was not possible to take all Russian prisoners captive. Those
> who wanted fled to the woods. Searching the forests was not
> possible because we had no strength. So the prisoners had to be
> forced to give themselves up in this way, under penalty of
> death.[188]

Reinhardt's proclamation was no idle threat. In fact, the prosecution presented evidence showing that Third Panzer Army targeted far more than just defiant Red Army men who had refused to give themselves up. A February 1943 report from one of Reinhardt's formations read: 'in order to keep bands from resettling in this territory the population of villages and farms in this area were killed without exception to the last baby. All homes were burned down.'[189] Even such murderous policies did not ensure the Third Panzer Army's security. When another local population near Vitebsk was identified as helping the partisans, Reinhardt negotiated with the SD to remove all 3,808 people to the Auschwitz concentration camp. There they lived for a time in a separate section of the Birkenau complex, referred to as the 'Russian family camp', but they were eventually all gassed. Summing up Reinhardt's responsibility, the prosecution at his trial declared:

> It is entirely immaterial, for the determination of Reinhardt's guilt, whether the Vitebsk deportees were driven to the gas chambers at Auschwitz one day or one year after he had deported them there; the children were exterminated shortly after their arrival, their parents sometime later. One must expect any human being of mediocre decency and standards of morality to consider it a crime to deport children to a concentration camp. General Reinhardt's intimate knowledge of the practices of the SD put him in a position to judge better than anybody else what an enormous risk threatened every human life against whom the SD murderers were turned loose.[190]

Reinhardt was not the only one of the panzer generals to be tried for his crimes after the war. Although Schmidt escaped the attention of the courts at Nuremberg and lived freely in the British zone of occupation, in 1947 he foolishly crossed into the Soviet zone to retrieve possessions from his former residence in Weimar.[191] Arrested after a pistol was found in his luggage, Schmidt was sent to Moscow for interrogation. The Soviet authorities were primarily interested in his wartime role at the head of the Second Panzer Army and its occupation methods. Ominously for Schmidt, his subordinate in command of the rear army area (*Korück 532*), Lieutenant-General Friedrich-Gustav Bernhard, had already been convicted and executed for war crimes by the Soviet authorities in 1945. Although one can

Figure 4.5 Georg-Hans Reinhardt's registration photo taken at Nuremberg in February 1948

reasonably question anything obtained by Soviet interrogation methods, Schmidt admitted to the burning of villages and 'numerous atrocities against the civilian population'.[192] He also admitted that Bernhard had acted on the basis of his (Schmidt's) orders. For these and other crimes, including the deportation of civilians to Germany for forced labour and the mistreatment of Soviet POWs in local camps, Schmidt was sentenced in 1952 to twenty-five years in prison.[193] Two days after the sentence was pronounced, a distraught Schmidt penned a letter to Stalin himself, pleading for leniency:

> I have always been on friendly terms with the Russians [. . .] As far as dealing with the partisans from the beginning of 1942, I gave my commanders the order to act in accordance with the Hague Convention. Hitler's brutal order on how to deal with the partisans, which contradicted my instructions, led to a great deal of uncertainty among the troops about how to behave. My verbal orders, which I had given the commanders of the corps, and the contradicting orders of Hitler, did not always reach the

lower units because of the partial exchange of troops. In doing so, my troops committed these crimes that I did not know about at the time. [...]

I also gave orders to take hostages, but I never gave orders to shoot these hostages.

I gave the order to transport workers to Germany. [...] At first there were a lot of volunteers. Later on, their numbers decreased noticeably. From the high command, which is to say from Hitler, orders had been coming since the beginning of November to press ahead with the mobilisation of workers by all means, including coercive measures. [...]

I did everything I could to help the prisoners of war. But it was still some time before this aid had an effect, because the [German] army itself needed everything as a result of its defeat. [...]

I should plead guilty to all other violations and crimes committed against the civilian population and prisoners of war, because I failed to control and intervene vigorously, as well as because I was responsible for everything that was done by my troops in my area of responsibility. [...]

Great Generalissimo Stalin!

I apologise for these long explanations. I intended to convey an understanding of myself as a person in order to show that I am neither a cruel and uncouth person, nor am I an enemy of the Soviet Union, but on the contrary highly value its ingenious leadership and am inspired by it. Because I was responsible for the actions of my subordinates, I ended up in the position of a criminal. I deserve a conviction, but I ask that my sentence be lessened with a pardon so that I can see the light of freedom again.[194]

Clearly, the records surrounding Schmidt's conviction in the Soviet Union are problematic. It is true that from 1942 Schmidt pursued more calculated policies towards the partisan problem, rejecting collective reprisals and the indiscriminate murder of the civilian population.[195] Some have suggested that these policies placed him apart from many of the other generals in the East,[196] yet Schmidt was above all a pragmatist who recognised the many benefits of local support for the German occupation and wider war effort.[197] Schmidt was no less ruthless towards those who could be identified as partisans; his objections to arbitrary violence were not motivated by any altruistic or humanitarian considerations. Indeed, Schmidt's challenge to German occupation policies came only after the failure of Operation Barbarossa and the realisation that a long war, and consequently a long-term occupation, had become inevitable. Thus, his motivation was entirely self-serving. Because Schmidt's new policies made a lot of sense and measurably advanced the German cause, from a Soviet perspective, that made the commander of the Second Panzer Army a much more dangerous enemy. Ultimately, however, Schmidt's occupation policies were calculated to serve the wider German project in the East, which unambiguously aimed to destroy the Soviet state and usher in Hitler's frightful New Order.[198] While there can be no debate that the Soviet legal process failed to meet any standard of evidence necessary for a conviction, it does not change the fact that Schmidt was criminally liable.

While Schmidt and Reinhardt were held to some form of account after the war, in each case only a fraction of their sentence was served before they were released back to civilian life. Schmidt was freed in 1956 and sent back to Germany; Reinhardt's conviction in 1948 led to a fifteen-year sentence, but he was released in 1953. Hoepner, of course, was executed in the aftermath of the July Plot, but the Nazis also took revenge on his family. Irma, his daughter Ingrid, his one-year-old grandchild and his sister were all sent to Ravensbrück concentration camp, where they were sentenced to hard labour shovelling sand and loading bags of coal and stone.[199] Hoepner's younger brother was sent to Buchenwald concentration camp,[200] while his son Joachim was arrested at the front on 25 July and held first in Moabit Prison in Berlin before being moved to the fortress at Küstrin in December 1944.[201] Only Guderian, whose career progressed the furthest under National Socialism and who was an intimate of the Nazi elite, faced no form of justice at all.

War of Annihilation

On the strength of the crimes discussed thus far, the panzer generals in Allied hands were certainly afforded a remarkable degree of leniency. This may be said even before one considers their role in facilitating and enabling the Holocaust in the Soviet Union. Of course, one may observe that we have already been discussing these crimes since

Figure 4.6 Erich Hoepner at his trial in Berlin for participation in the July Plot to assassinate Hitler (August 1944)

the delineation between the targeting of Jews and partisans was never so clear-cut.[202] As one characteristic German report stated: 'Where there is a partisan there is a Jew and where there is a Jew there is a partisan.'[203] When Guderian and Hoepner passed on Reichenau's infamous order, they were no doubt aware of the passage that read:

> The soldier in the East is not just a fighter according to the rules of the art of war, but also the bearer of an implacable national idea, and the avenger of all the bestialities inflicted on the German and related peoples. For that reason, the soldier must

have full understanding of the need for a harsh but just punishment of Jewish sub-humanity.[204]

Unsurprisingly, the private letters of the panzer generals provide no evidence of what was happening to the Jews in the Soviet Union. Even studies of soldiers' letter collections suggest that the topic of Jewish persecution and murder, while not entirely absent, was largely taboo.[205] Presumably, only in the most antisemitic families could the horrific actions against Soviet Jews be discussed openly without compromising the assumed virtue of the German cause.[206] For the majority of men who avoided direct engagement with the subject of Jews or racial inferiority, Felix Römer's study of recorded conversations by German soldiers suggested prejudiced views may have been so self-evident as to be passed over:

> The views of other nations or 'races' were among those background convictions that were too abstract and, in part, also appeared all too self-evident for much to be said about them. One thing proved to be the case every time: the fundamental idea of difference and superiority vis-à-vis other nations was deeply entrenched in the mentality of the Germans; it was the unavoidable flip side of nationalism and a legacy of the nineteenth century.[207]

Importantly, the absence of discussion in the letters of the panzer generals is not a reflection of what they knew about Jewish persecution in the East. The *Einsatzgruppen* were ordered to press forward with every new advance, seizing their victims almost as soon as the mobile divisions had captured their villages and towns. In isolated instances the individual killing squads were even caught up in the fighting.[208] Not surprisingly, therefore, the panzer generals were fully aware of the murder programme as well as complicit in their support, because the killing units were in their zone of operations and drew their supplies from the panzer group's logistics chain. The favourable interaction was highlighted by the murderers themselves. Arthur Nebe, the leader of *Einsatzgruppe B*, reported that cooperation with the army was 'excellent' and that Army Group Centre 'has proven to be successful, especially in the liquidation actions in Białystok and Minsk, and has not failed to affect other commandos'.[209] In Army Group North, where Hoepner and Reinhardt began the campaign, Franz Stahlecker, the head of *Einsatzgruppe A*, reported: 'From the outset, it can be emphasised that cooperation with the Wehrmacht is generally good, in individual cases, for example with Panzer Group 4 under Colonel-General Höppner [sic], it was very close, almost cordial.'[210] Such a report highlights the fallacy of framing Hoepner as an anti-Nazi general simply because he joined the July Plot in 1944. Indeed, on that basis it may be pointed out that a man like Nebe, who was directly responsible for tens of thousands of Jewish murders in 1941, also became a conspirator in the plot.[211]

The panzer generals understood that Barbarossa was not simply a conventional war against a conventional enemy. Nor was this type of warfare especially new to them. With the exception of Schmidt, they had already experienced the excesses committed by the *Freikorps* against 'Bolshevik' enemies in 1919. Twenty years later in 1939, the Polish campaign was marked by similar atrocities. The panzer generals did not shy away from these kinds of conflicts in spite of their well-earned reputations as forceful, and even uncompromising, personalities.[212] Their identification with National Socialist conceptions of warfare forestalled any prospect of opposition and they shared a racialised view of the world. As Nicholas Stargardt's study of wartime letters argued, 'the moral demands of the Third Reich were sustained by cultural values – especially when it came to wartime patriotism – which were older than the regime and which became increasingly deeply contaminated by the most extreme characteristic of Nazism, namely the genocidal war Germans were waging.'[213] At a military conference in 1944 Guderian emphatically told Hitler, 'I'm for racial purity.'[214] At another point Guderian complained about officer attendance at lectures organised by the army high command, writing: 'It is [...] wrong to stay away from a lecture because at some point you have heard something about the same topic. For example, "Racial Biology" is such a comprehensive field that every new lecture always brings something new.'[215] Even after the war, Guderian revealed his unreconciled antipathy towards Jews, referring to the 'immigration of undesirable Jewish elements from Central and Eastern Europe'.[216]

Hoepner's reports from 1941 not only took aim at Jews for being communists and saboteurs;[217] he wrote an order in early July that showed awareness Jews were being targeted by Latvians for mass murder in his area of operations. In fact, his order acknowledged the participation of his soldiers, which he wanted stopped, given that, at this point, not even the *Einsatzgruppen* had explicit orders to murder everyday Soviet Jews. As Hoepner wrote: 'I ask that you do everything possible to ensure that the troops stay away from these internal political disputes.'[218] While Hoepner was not yet prepared to support these mass killings directly, he clearly knew what was happening and took no steps to prevent such pogroms, which functioned to condone and enable the process.

At his war crimes trial in 1947–1948 Reinhardt was convicted on the second and third counts,[219] receiving a fifteen-year jail term. Among his more egregious crimes, Reinhardt's sentencing noted that he 'cooperated with the S.D., especially by handing over partisans' supporters and partisan suspects to the S.D., including men, women, and children, knowing that organisation's function'.[220] Documents from the Secret Field Police (*Geheime Feldpolizei*) reflect the nebulous category that 'partisans' supporters' constituted and show that Jews were being arrested in Reinhardt's area of responsibility simply because they were Jews.[221] Reinhardt's legal team attempted to argue that there was no deliberate targeting of innocent Jews, but orders issued within Third Panzer Army showed that fervent antisemitism was actively cultivated among certain units:

> It appears a propitious moment to again recall to our troops the crimes which the Jews at one time committed in Germany against the German people with the help of their devilish and insidiously treacherous intellectuals who now again appear with their propaganda material and the same aims. It is [an] eternal tribe of parasites which has been gnawing at the strength of the Western peoples for over 1,000 years and which now, through Bolshevist evil, is probably committing its last work of decomposition. The brave German Western individual still is not energetic enough with these hellish monsters. He still treats the Jewish monster too much in accordance with decent concepts, instead of releasing his entire hatred and will of destruction against the breed of a 1,000-year-old infernal world.[222]

Schmidt's record on Jewish persecution in the East yields no evidence of his direct support, which is only to say that the paper trail – that was in any case thin, thanks to a conscious effort not to commit details of the Holocaust to paper – simply does not exist to indict Schmidt personally. For those who have sought to present Schmidt as a different kind of German commander,[223] one could equally point to the fact that there is no paper trail showcasing his objection to the colossal scope of the crime taking place. Indeed, like every other senior German general, the role in which Schmidt served month after month netted ever more Jewish victims for the SD.[224] Schmidt's past also offers evidence of his National Socialist allegiance. In 1937, when speaking to new recruits after taking over as commander of the 1st Panzer Division, Schmidt was unambiguous:

> We have once again become a powerful, respected people that plays a crucial role in the world. This tremendous change took place without major disturbances thanks to the genius of our Führer, an unprecedented phenomenon in history. As a strong haven of peace, for the safety of the German people, the German Wehrmacht stands behind the Führer [...].[225]

The record of criminal culpability among the panzer generals is both ubiquitous and incontestable, yet the fact that their correspondence reflects very little of this is unsurprising. In the first instance, social psychologists would posit that the imperative of a positive self-narrative mitigates against a realisation or acceptance of any moral responsibility. Actions in defence of Christian, cultured Europe, even if these included a programme of systematic murder, could be justified as a necessary evil. The fact that what was happening in the East was also a result of state policy further allowed individuals to devolve accountability and see their role simply as that of a functionary, a perspective reminiscent of Hannah Arendt's ground-breaking work on the banality of evil.[226] Yet the fact that the panzer generals recognised the extraordinary violence perpetrated against non-combatants to be wrong and did not wish to share their knowledge of such events, to say nothing of their own participation in them, suggests an admission of guilt as well as a desire to avoid any anticipated shame. Of course, this is supposition – some of the generals may have discussed these events and simply destroyed those letters, which would suggest there was no sense of shame or guilt about these actions and perhaps even a degree of satisfaction about what was happening. For die-hard defenders of the German generals, who will hold fast to an absence of criminal evidence in their letters, the real absence to be confronted is the total lack of moral outrage by the generals. Six hundred thousand Jews were being gradually shot at sites across the occupied Soviet Union in 1941 and none of the panzer generals found a single occasion in over 120 letters to express a word of dismay about it, even in private. The more likely answer, of course, is simple – the panzer generals simply did not have any such moral indignation over the genocide of Soviet Jews.

While there is no scenario that exculpates the panzer generals from their criminal liability, there is a question about the role of their wives, and more particularly Margarete, in how we understand the duality of correspondence and its behavioural implications. Social historians researching gender identity within the Nazi state have considered the role played by perpetrators' wives in helping to maintain a façade of normalcy, while easing the psychological burden of command. As Claudia Koonz concluded, men, such as the panzer generals, 'rationalized their participation in schemes for Nazi genocide and repression by divorcing what they did from who they were'.[227] Koonz's research also explained how a prominent male in the Nazi world could '"split" his identity as a public man from his warm and loving feelings for his family. Nazi wives did not offer a beacon of strength for a moral cause, but rather created a buffer zone from the husband's job. Far from wanting to share their husband's concerns, they actively cultivated their own ignorance and facilitated his escape.'[228] Koonz poses an important question. How are we to view Margarete's role? Was she an innocent bystander oblivious to everything happening in the East or did she serve as an enabler of violence, functioning as a 'buffer' from Heinz's reality, while embracing a 'cultivated ignorance'?

Importantly, Margarete's letters contain almost no political commentary. There is no discussion of Germany's drive for *Lebensraum* in the East, no judgement of communism or its supposed Jewish-Bolshevik leadership. Yet we know Margarete was a devout Christian and a member of three National Socialist organisations, including the Nazi Party. Her available letters also begin more than two months into the campaign, after the act of war and any commentary about it had presumably already been communicated. Of course, this again poses the question of whether the available letters were purposely chosen for their apolitical content, especially when Heinz was clearly receiving and saving the correspondence. We know she wrote many more than the thirteen surviving letters dating from 1941, so what happened to the others? Political support for Germany's war against the Soviet Union was widespread among elites in the Nazi state, bolstered by the hostile representation of the Soviet Union in Nazi propaganda and, more importantly, *Lebensraum*'s promise of vast new lands, titles and career opportunities. Perhaps these were beyond Margarete's concern or interest, but we have seen that she took an active interest in her husband's career and cannot have been unaware of the accolades that flowed to senior army officers after the campaign against France.

While German women are often absent from the military histories of 1939–1945, that was not the view even within the excessively patriarchal Nazi state. Women were essential to the war effort even before they were drafted into the factories and civil service. Gudrun Schwarz summed up the vital role of the National Socialist woman in preparation for war. According to Schwarz, 'hero mothers' raised their offspring for the national struggle, strengthened their husbands and sons in their enthusiasm for war, sent them proudly on campaign, cared for wounded fighters and, if necessary, celebrated the heroic death of their kin as a gift to the fatherland.[229] Such a description certainly correlates with Margarete's example. As early as 1934, Hitler's speech to the National Socialist Women's League made clear the indispensable role of women in sustaining the fighting power of the German man:

> If the man's world is said to be the state, his struggle, his readiness to devote his powers to the service of the community, then it may perhaps be said that the woman's is a smaller world. For her world is her husband, her family, her children and her home. But what would become of the greater world if there were no one to tend and care for the smaller one? How could the greater world survive if there were no one to make the cares of the smaller world the content of their lives? No, the greater world is built on the foundation of this smaller world. This great world cannot survive if the smaller world is not stable. Providence has entrusted to the woman the cares of that world which is her very own, and only on the basis of this smaller world can the man's world be formed and built up. The two worlds are not antagonistic. They complement each other, they belong together just as man and woman belong together. [...] So, our women's movement is for us not something which inscribes on its banner as its programme the fight against men,

but something which has as its programme the common fight together with men.[230]

Such a view was repeated in the official Nazi women's magazine, which declared: 'We see the woman as the eternal mother of our people, but also as the working and fighting comrade of the man!'[231] Thus, the separation between front and *Heimat* was only geographically apparent in the minds of true National Socialist women. Lamenting the comforts of her privileged removal from the deprivations of the campaign, Margarete even wrote Heinz in November 1941: 'With the greatest sympathy, we are thinking of you in terrible, wintry Russia and we are grateful and ashamed that we are permitted to have a nice, warm, well-kept home here.'[232]

Such expressions of solidarity personified the *Volksgemeinschaft* (people's community) popularised by Nazi propaganda. Indeed, far from a separation into mutually exclusive worlds, husbands and wives often bonded through their suffering and loneliness. This was also reflected by Margarete's letters to Heinz and his in return. As Gaby Zipfel observed more generally:

> The couple, temporarily separated from one another between the war front and the home front, act in a gender-specific manner, but not independently of one another. By supporting the man and knowing that he needs her support, the woman assures herself of her own importance [...] she listens, suppresses, excuses in the endeavour to preserve her idea of an ideal world.[233]

This endeavour also allowed men like Guderian to indulge notions of domestic bliss, while he sought strength to prosecute an aggressive war of conquest and annihilation. Gudrun Schwarz dubbed the same phenomenon 'normality in horror' (*Normalität im Grauen*) and then continued: 'By creating a stable domestic framework, she [a wife] should ensure his [the husband's] emotional balance, be his source of strength and give him emotional support.'[234] Margarete certainly played this role, writing to Heinz in December 1941, when he was clearly struggling with depression: 'God allowing, this terrible war will not last too long, will end happily and [be] overcome in good health, so that we can continue our common life together, which was already interrupted early on by the unfortunate World War.'[235] Margarete's loving sentiment is in itself understandable, but one cannot ignore that it also had real-world implications. As we have seen in Chapter 1, no other person reassured and bolstered Heinz like Margarete.

Women like Margarete are easily confused with innocent bystanders, especially if their 'guilt' relies on loving and supporting their husbands. Yet Margarete made no pretence about being a bystander in the war; she longed for Germany's victory and spared no thought for the countless foreign victims of her nation's repeated invasions and occupation. Reflecting upon the Japanese attack against Anglo-American possessions in December 1941 Margarete rejoiced. She did not lament the growing conflict or its many new victims. In fact, she had blunt words for the English and Americans:

> Japan's entry into the war seems to me to constitute a favourable development, however. The first successes are fantastic and will inflict great pain on the English and the Americans, as it strikes at their precious fleet and possessions overseas. Hopefully, Japan will succeed in conquering Hong Kong, Singapore and the Dutch Indies, so that they will be able to continue the war and win it.[236]

Clearly, Margarete was not a simple bystander innocently observing the war. She delighted at Japanese successes, just as she did at German successes, which placed her in the conflict with a voice and an opinion about who should win it. Her words had implications, not just for Heinz, but for anyone she engaged with on such matters. Margarete supported the party line, the war effort and her influential husband: whatever she was, she was not a bystander.

If one can conclude Margarete held a degree of complicity for the events in which she was engaging, how far might that have extended, especially in enabling the criminal side of the Nazi enterprise? In the first instance, one needs to disassociate the evil act from the evil intent of most perpetrators or enablers. Stanley Milgram's famous 1961 experiment on obedience to authority to explain the psychology of genocide was itself a response to the trial of the Nazi war criminal Adolf Eichmann in Jerusalem. Milgram's findings unexpectedly revealed that a very high proportion of subjects would obey instructions to harm people, albeit reluctantly, if told to do so.[237] Such evidence had allowed researchers to '"humanize genocide", to recognize that such horrific actions are in fact within the capability of ordinary human beings and not only deviant, pathological monsters or sadists.'[238] While this helps explain the functional role of the panzer generals themselves, Margarete was removed from the process itself, except for the fact that she, like many women, must have known that the German state was engaged in mass repression through violent means. Adelheid von Saldern's study of everyday women in the Nazi state – not privileged members of the elite like Margarete – concluded: 'women were commonly co-observers, co-listeners and co-possessors of "guilty" knowledge, rather than co-perpetrators; their "complicity" consisted of passivity and toleration in the face of action, but not the action itself'.[239] If average German women possessed 'guilty knowledge', Margarete's access to senior officers and their wives, the exclusive community of her Dahlem suburb and everything Heinz shared must have rendered her immeasurably better informed. Yet Margarete's letters would suggest that Koonz was correct and that she 'cultivated ignorance' by avoiding or dismissing uncomfortable subjects. Instead, she projected herself as a dignified, Christian woman and a proud mother and wife. She indulged Heinz's much-needed domestic bliss and expressed the desire, not for peace, but for victory, which, with knowledge of what that entailed for the subject peoples and especially Jews, seemingly caused her not a moment's pause. If Margarete Guderian was in any way representative of the other generals' wives, they were neither bystanders, nor innocent. As Koonz astutely observed:

> Looking back at Nazi Germany, it seems that decency vanished; but when we listen to feminine voices from the period, we realize instead that it was cordoned off. Loyal Nazis fashioned an image for themselves, a fake domestic realm where they felt virtuous. Nazi women facilitated that mirage by doing what women have done in other societies – they made the world a more pleasant place in which to live for the members of their community. And they simultaneously made life first unbearable and later impossible for 'racially unworthy' citizens. As fanatical Nazis or lukewarm tag-alongs, they resolutely turned their heads away from assaults against socialists, Jews, religious dissenters, the handicapped, and 'degenerates'. They gazed instead at their own cradles, children, and 'Aryan' families. Mothers and wives [...] made a vital contribution to Nazi power by preserving the illusion of love in an environment of hatred, just as men sustained the image of order in the utter disarray of conflicting bureaucratic and military priorities and commands.[240]

Figure 4.7 Heinz and Margarete Guderian in Schwangau bei Füssen in 1953

Whatever some might wish to believe about the strictly professional contributions of the German panzer generals, the fact remains that they engaged in two parallel wars, one against a conventional enemy and one against defenceless civilians. These wars cannot be separated in our judgement of these men because they were fundamental to who they were and how they understood warfare. As Johannes Hürter has concluded:

> In spite of all limitations in executive authority, it was especially the commanders of the army groups and the armies who fundamentally possessed enough in the way of formal competence and informal options to consent or preclude, impede or promote, protest or remain silent. The fact that they did not use the scope of action remaining open to them in favour of the helpless victims, indeed as a rule did not even make any attempt to do so,

provides a measure of the responsibility of the military elite for this first, so important and ground-breaking stage in the genocide.[241]

What we see in the panzer generals' private letters is that their public silence was replicated even in the unregulated private sphere. There was no inner conflict or concern about what was happening; they did not rage against the injustice or lament the stain on their noble profession. None of this is surprising because the generals were actively engaged in the German army's criminality, including the Holocaust. Their long military service and many campaigns had erased any moral or intellectual objections to the application of force in the achievement of their objectives and the fact that National Socialism wholeheartedly embraced this philosophy made them supporters, not opponents, of the regime.[242] To the extent that Margarete's example is generalisable, we also learn that there was no moral corrective even by those closest to them who theoretically remained uncorrupted by the demands of war. Indeed, wives served as invaluable sources of emotional comfort and support, even when they must have known that the war their husbands were waging exposed civilians to repression, suffering and death.

After the war had ended, when the death camps were public knowledge and Europe lay in ruins, the unreconciled views of senior generals were secretly recorded by American intelligence. Heinz Guderian was talking with Field Marshal Wilhelm Ritter von Leeb about the merits and drawbacks of National Socialism. The exchange of views ended with Guderian stating: 'The fundamental principles were fine.' To which Leeb replied: 'That is true.'[243]

5 THE MILITARY GENERALS

Three days before Operation Barbarossa, in his final letter to Eva before the campaign began, Reinhardt dared to share his own doubts about what was being planned:

> Sometimes, one almost has the impression that we have so far indulged the supreme authorities to such an extent that they think we are capable of anything. I hope that we are capable of anything; we'll certainly make every effort and set out with the same faith in our Führer and in our own strength with the tried and tested slogan 'Panzer onward!'[1]

Clearly, the requisite optimism that built high-flying careers in the army, but corrupted an objective military culture (as discussed in Chapter 2), was apparent to Reinhardt on some level. He seemed to sense that the invasion of the Soviet Union might be biting off more than the Wehrmacht could chew. Indeed, his letter to Eva went on to become a justification for the coming war, and it is tempting to wonder if, in convincing her, Reinhardt was at the same time convincing himself. Notably, Reinhardt's justification was entirely political, avoiding the more pertinent military questions that underscored his scepticism about what could be achieved. As he wrote to Eva:

> We must attack and destroy them, the quicker, the better. I don't yet know the precise context of our reasons for war. But I think that the Russians have also been playing fast and loose for a long time now. The fact that they are not yet ready is

the only reason why they are friendly towards us. [...] Already in Yugoslavia, we discovered the activities of Bolshevik-Russian agitators against us. That is why we must fight Bolshevism in Russia and hopefully achieve a swift victory! We are ready.[2]

Unlike the grave doubts about Operation Barbarossa that Guderian claimed to have had in his memoir,[3] his last letter to Margarete before the invasion, written on 16 June, expressed only a 'general fear of the mosquito plague' in the East, but otherwise continued: 'Aside from that, however, the mood is good everywhere and full of hope, and I think that we'll make it.'[4] The early weeks of the campaign seemed only to confirm Guderian's optimism, as he reported to Margarete on 29 June: 'our undertaking has measured up to the high expectations. [...] the first hostilities were so successful and our superiority was so apparent that the enemy has shown signs of exhaustion and moral despondency since yesterday.'[5] Two days later Guderian was even more unequivocal: 'we're approaching the last major section of the [Soviet] front. If we succeed in passing it, then the route to the interior of the empire is open and the campaign, in my view, can no longer be lost.'[6] By 12 July Guderian believed an end to Soviet resistance was at hand. Having seized crossings over the Dnieper River, which Guderian held to be the last line of defence, Panzer Group 2 was engaging the remnants of the Red Army. 'I hope to defeat them in the coming days', he told Margarete, 'and achieve in the process a success that will decide the campaign in our favour.'[7] There was no ambiguity about how Guderian saw the campaign continuing. Not only was the war being won, but he was the one winning it. Such initial optimism, excitement and anticipation go a long way towards explaining Guderian's psychological decline over the course of the year as the campaign transformed from an impending victory to exhaustion, stagnation and ultimately forced retreat in winter.

Hoepner was more circumspect in his approach to Barbarossa. His letters offer none of the casual predictions about a quick victory and his former aide-de-camp claimed the same after the war: 'Hoepner considered a war against the Soviet Union to be out of the question and the whole deployment a bluff.'[8] Yet when it became clear that German forces were indeed going to invade, Hoepner appears to have looked favourably on the outcome. At the end of August, when the anticipated victory had failed to eventuate, Hoepner admitted to Irma his own underestimation of the Soviet enemy: 'I don't have any ideas other than the hope that this campaign will soon be over. Unfortunately, I considerably miscalculated, though everyone else did, too.'[9] Hoepner's hopes then rested on one last month of campaigning because, as he told Irma, 'The campaign has to be over by late September due to the whole supply situation and the cold.'[10] Yet, here again, Hoepner evinced a healthy objectivity in assessing Germany's prospects, refusing to insist blindly that, just because the campaign had to be ended, it would be. As Hoepner explained: 'The Russians have formed several reserve armies, which are deployed on the general Lake Ilmen–Bryansk (southwest of Moscow) line. These, though, are weak and poorly equipped. Of 250 divisions that could be deployed, however, around 140 have been defeated. I don't yet know if we'll succeed in finishing off the Russians. If not, we'll have to halt before the winter.'[11]

Such objective honesty was, however, rare among the panzer generals. It took Guderian until December to admit mistakes had been made; even at that point, he preferred to attribute failure to geographic and environmental factors. 'We considerably underestimated the enemy, the vastness of the country and the pitfalls of the climate, and now it's come back to roost.'[12] Schmidt also identified geographic and environmental factors, but more as a source of Soviet good fortune rather than any German miscalculation. Even before Barbarossa's failure was attributed to bogus scapegoats like October mud and an unusually harsh winter, Schmidt pinned Germany's failure squarely on the summer rains: 'If we had the good weather of July, the war would be over. But now the heavens have become the Bolsheviks' saviour.'[13] If Schmidt was seriously prepared to blame Germany's lack of success on rain, then it is hardly surprising that he also felt no shame in pointing to the vast size of the Soviet Union as late as December 1941: 'Russia is simply very large. It's this spatial expanse that presents the problem. That's why it will now take considerably longer than was assumed.'[14] Only after the war, when Schmidt was being interrogated by Soviet intelligence officers, did he claim to have objected to a Soviet invasion from the very beginning.[15] When he wrote to Stalin after his conviction for war crimes, Schmidt even claimed: 'In 1941 I was distressed and unhappy when Hitler broke his word and invaded the Soviet Union. I understood the consequences that would have for Germany.'[16] Yet when Schmidt wrote to Paulus in July 1941, relating his experiences of the campaign, he concluded the letter: 'Otherwise, we are in a good mood and look forward to the future.'[17]

Delusion and Disclosure

As the winter crisis engulfed Army Group Centre, all four of the panzer generals grappled with its dire implications. Unlike Hoepner, Guderian was never prepared to admit any personal liability for underestimation or miscalculation; in his conception it was the senior army leadership who bore all the responsibility. Guderian channelled his anger and frustration on 8 December:

> We are facing the sad fact that the senior leadership has overdone things, did not want to believe the reports of the troops' declining combat strength, only made demands, did not make provisions for the harsh winter and was now surprised by the Russian cold of minus 35 degrees. The strength of the troops was no longer sufficient to carry out the attack on Moscow, so that, with a heavy heart, I had to resolve on the evening of 5 December to break off the unwinnable battle.[18]

The gall of Guderian's accusation is remarkable, given that he had advocated for the offensive at every stage, knowing full well – and choosing to disregard – the exhaustion within his ranks, the lack of supplies and the freezing conditions. In his post-war memoir he even credited himself with saving the situation because he ordered his Second Panzer Army to halt its attack on 5 December, just hours before Bock's general order; 'had I not done so', Guderian insisted, 'a catastrophe could not have been avoided'.[19] After five and a half months of relentless attacking, one wonders what difference a few hours made, but the real point was that once again Guderian had removed himself from any responsibility for the events impacting his panzer army.

On 16 December Guderian wrote his last known letter to Margarete for 1941, in which he continued his attack on the senior leadership for everything that had gone wrong, but, revealingly, excluded Hitler from any blame and in fact cast the dictator as the solution to Germany's problems:

> The complete underestimation of the enemy and the resulting recklessness with regard to preparations for the winter

campaign in Russia have placed us in a very difficult position. How we are supposed to come out of this again, I don't yet know myself. In any case, we must act quickly and energetically, and at present there is no hint of this.

I am only happy that the Führer is now at least in the picture and will hopefully intervene with his usual vigour in the bureaucratised gears of the army, the railways and other machinery.[20]

Not only does this reflect Guderian's slavish devotion to Hitler, who had without question been inextricably involved in the day-to-day decisions of the high command, but more importantly, it underlines the panzer general's fundamental misunderstanding of Germany's predicament. Apart from the fact that Hitler was not a good crisis manager, even if he had been, the systemic nature of the crisis unfolding on the Eastern Front had progressed well beyond any decisions Hitler might or might not make – a fact that Guderian's blind devotion could not grasp. There was simply no quick fix to the lack of trains arriving on the Eastern Front or the absence of winter equipment for three million men. Yet here again the primacy of National Socialist 'will' as a catch-all solution to any problem allowed circles to be squared. In Guderian's mind, Hitler's iron conviction and indomitable will could deliver the impossible, a conclusion that should have been completely anathema to his general staff training.[21]

Margarete consoled Heinz by insisting on her own 'unshakeable faith' in the outcome of events and reminding him of his 'old wartime luck'.[22] Such words were intended to soothe and support her husband, but if such platitudes comforted Guderian they only underlined the problem. Faith and luck did not change the concrete realities of war. It was the artificial acceptance of such intangible elements – the 'spiritual', 'chance' or 'destiny' – that muddied the water in what was, and was not, possible for the panzer generals. Nor was Guderian alone in struggling to reconcile political and ideological views with everyday realities. Reinhardt's letter to his wife on 17 December portrayed an optimism bordering on denial, but in doing so he also betrayed an unmistakably National Socialist view of the war and its consequences for Germany:

Even if the end of the year brings some setbacks for us with it, and as painful as they are for us, something good might still come out of it, namely that we sense that there are limits to what we can achieve and learn from adversity to become even tougher and that everyone in the whole nation must contribute in order that we are victorious, because for us there can only be complete victory or the end of Germany!²³

If the silver lining in Barbarossa's miscarriage was that Germany had learned 'that there are limits to what we can achieve', one identifies not only the preceding hubris in thinking, but an enduring lack of understanding for the consequences of military failure in 1941. Even after reaching this conclusion, Reinhardt did not advocate for political solutions or reduced war aims, but rather saw only the imposition of ever greater demands on the nation, casting the war as a choice between victory or death. Such a National Socialist view of the conflict explains why men like Reinhardt served so loyally on the Eastern Front until 1945.

If it took Reinhardt until December to grasp that there were limits to what Germany might achieve, Schmidt's letter from 26 December reveals that he was coming to a similar realisation, but it manifested itself in shock and indignation: 'That was an awful Christmas celebration! Battle crises, Russian breakthroughs, alerts everywhere. It was and still is just awful! [...] It is simply astounding that the victorious German army, harried from victory to victory, finds itself all at once now in such dire straits by the power of the winter and the Russians, who cleverly calculated with it setting in.'²⁴ Only someone who had been convinced of Germany's absolute superiority could be 'all at once' surprised by Soviet endurance and tenacity. Even Schmidt's characterisation of 'the victorious German army' reflects his narrow operational conception of warfare. Progressing 'from victory to victory' had not produced a strategic result, something which Hoepner had already feared back in August. Yet Schmidt, who took over command of a second German army as of 26 December (after Guderian's dismissal), was unable to see the bigger picture – an all-too-common limitation among senior generals within the army.

Any discussion of military events within the generals' letters must acknowledge the degree of entitlement they demonstrated in providing their wives with such a rich stream of highly classified information. As noted in Chapter 1, letters were bound by the 'Ordinance on Communication', stipulating that information was subject to secrecy regulations, the most important being the distribution of information related to army matters.[25] Even the lowest-ranked soldier was forbidden from writing details about the place, time or background to their combat operations. They were also instructed not to provide the names of officers or even their comrades.[26] Unit designations, size and composition – including reports of losses – arms and equipment and future military intentions were all strictly prohibited.[27] Of course, not all soldiers adhered to every regulation because they precluded discussing anything substantive about their military service, but most adhered to the general obligation not to pass on information of value to the enemy. As William Lubbeck wrote after the war: 'Because of military censorship, we could not write about our units, where we were or our battles at the front.'[28] Similarly, Johannes Hamm wrote home in November 1941:

> There will be an attack tomorrow for sure, but we are not part of it. It's a certain comfort to me that we are part of an armoured command here. Of course, I cannot name names, I am not even allowed to say the sea, the coast of which we are currently safeguarding, but it does not take much to guess its name.[29]

Even if Hamm thought the information was obvious, the fact that he still did not mention the details reflects his general acceptance of the censorship rules. The contrast this makes with the letters of the panzer generals could not be starker.

Just because the letters of the generals were not subject to censorship does not mean that they were free from the requirements of the Ordinance on Communication. There is also evidence from their letters that they knew they were not supposed to be sharing operational details. On 30 June Hoepner wrote to Irma about his 'tank battles on the Dubysa [River] north of Kovno and the capture of Daugavpils'. Yet despite having already flouted the secrecy regulations, Hoepner added: 'I cannot yet inform you of my further actions by letter. Perhaps you will learn about it before this letter arrives.'[30] At times, Hoepner attempted not to mention place names, but these were the exception – typically he simply forgot or ignored the regulation. In a letter from 13 July, he referred to a place name only as 'A.'.[31] In a letter written three days later, however, he named the town as 'Allenstein' in Prussia.[32] Even using the first letter of a location was hardly a convincing attempt at concealment, especially when Hoepner inconsistently applied such an elementary security protocol. In some instances, he specifically discussed his location. In his letter from 13 July, Hoepner informed Irma: 'You're surprised that I was still near Daugavpils on 4 July. I cannot change quarters with my large staff so frequently [...] Now, for the first time, I'm in old Russia.'[33] Moreover, from 13 July Hoepner started headlining his letters with his current location 'Near Pskov'; 19 July 'Anisimovo, near Pskov'; 1 August 'Strugi Krasnye'; 18 August 'Lake Samra'; and 5 September 'Meskno (60 km south of Petersburg)'.[34] Such brazen breaches of security were by no means limited to Hoepner. Reinhardt's letter from 12 July offers an especially absurd example, which demonstrates the general contempt for security regulations. As he wrote to Eva, 'it might be the case that we're involved in the conquest of a major city (it begins with P; postscript: I'm talking about Pleskau) worthy of mention'.[35] Sometimes the liberties taken potentially compromised the security of the panzer group's command, as Guderian's letter of 15 July told Margarete: 'I'm enclosing a few pictures from a visit by the fighter pilot Mölders to our forest camp near Borisov a little while ago.'[36] On 24 October Schmidt wrote Fridel a note with a single sentence specifically informing her of his location: 'Right now, we are in the midst of decisive battles in the region of Tikhvin, high in the north, eastward of Lake Ladoga.'[37]

The regular inclusion of location markers was similar to the naming of leading army commanders. Half-hearted efforts were sometimes made to avoid the use of names, but more often than not this regulation was likewise disregarded. Ignoring for a moment the actual substance of the discussion, Guderian's letter of 4 July initially sought to withhold or disguise the names of prominent army commanders:

> To effectively curb our zest for action, one has established a 'panzer army' and naturally entrusts it to someone who hasn't previously had anything to do with the affair. He immediately proved himself to be an extremely effective brakeman. It was the idea of Mr von B., who will also appear here tomorrow in the vicinity. The Führer apparently agreed to it.[38]

Field Marshal von Brauchitsch was clearly 'Mr von B.', but the other commander, Field Marshal Günther von Kluge, was left unnamed. Of course, crediting Guderian for such an omission would neglect the fact that he was sharing far more sensitive information about the debates and changing structure of Army Group Centre's command. Yet later in the same letter Guderian gave up all pretence of adhering to the regulations and named three of his subordinate divisional commanders.

'Yesterday, I visited [Major-General Walther] Nehring,[39] who has to overcome very heavy fighting, and today [Lieutenant-General Ferdinand] Schaal[40] and [SS-*Gruppenführer* Paul] Hausser,[41] for whom it was somewhat easier.'[42] Hoepner also freely discussed changes in command, naming everyone involved. On 20 December he wrote to Irma: 'Brauchitsch has had himself discharged. A[dolf] H[itler] has assumed command of the OKH himself.[43] Rundstedt[44] has been replaced by Reichenau and Bock[45] by Kluge.'[46] Of course, this was hardly news that Soviet intelligence would not soon learn, but it illustrates the liberty German generals took in regard to security matters.

The letters also reveal other deliberate security violations. One of the six specific prohibitions cited in the Ordinance on Communication was a ban on sending any form of enemy propaganda, specifically pamphlets dropped by the enemy planes. Hoepner, however, not only included one for Irma, but also specifically drew attention to it as well as the veracity of its content. On 21 December he wrote: 'You'll already be aware of the situation here. I'm enclosing a Russian flyer, which describes matters more or less accurately.'[47] The fact that Irma was indeed well informed about the military situation in the East was precisely the problem. Yet Hoepner seems to have had second thoughts about the inclusion of the Soviet propaganda pamphlet and two days after sending it wrote again to Irma asking her to: 'Please hide the Russian flyer that I recently sent you!'[48] The irony here is that beyond the incriminating flyer itself there were now two letters referring to it. It underlines the false sense of security generals attributed to their private letters. At the top of another letter from 14 December Hoepner wrote in red pencil: 'Please do not discuss this matter!'[49] The letter certainly contained highly sensitive information, but just about all the letters from the panzer generals did this on some level. In fact, Hoepner's instruction not to 'discuss' the contents underlines that he saw no risk whatsoever in the letter itself. Whether Irma could be trusted not to divulge the information was irrelevant if the letters themselves, which were clearly being saved, could be read by a third party. The fact that all four panzer generals were writing about highly sensitive operational and strategic matters in letter after letter, completely in violation of regulations, suggests that many other senior commanders were as well.[50] The potential for security breaches, while not known to have occurred, was significant and one may add that the vulnerability of their wives, had they been targeted for such information, could have been considerable.

The above cited infractions by the panzer generals were only violations of a statute written for soldiers and junior to middle-ranking officers, who were never in possession of anything other than local intelligence. What the panzer generals were openly writing about was inconceivable to the framers of the Ordinance on Communication and was not just unprofessional, but criminally negligent. As the German security protocol for classified military information unambiguously stated: 'Every document which contains classified information must be constantly under control from its origin to its destruction.'[51] As Major-General Rudolf Langhaeuser noted in a post-war study: 'All correspondence and business communication were also governed by this regulation whether the subject-matter left the place of origin or not.'[52] Of course, not only did the letters of the generals leave their place of origin, but also there was no mechanism for their subsequent control or destruction.

The best illustration of the heedless privilege the generals reserved for themselves was their shared knowledge of Operation Barbarossa before its commencement. On 26 May 1941 Hoepner told Irma: 'Nothing will happen here before 20 June. The question is constantly asked here as to whether it will happen at all. There is even talk of a 99-year-lease of Ukraine. On the one hand, I cannot imagine that the USSR would risk this loss of prestige. On the other hand, this would not satisfy our demands.'[53] Guderian was more careful in his language,[54] but the subtext of what was coming did not take much imagination. Writing to Margarete on 16 June, Guderian explained:

> Tomorrow, in order to avoid unimportant ovations, I want to take a long drive to the area that particularly interests me, in order to check the water level of the large stream and subject the opposite bank to a detailed examination. [...] My accommodation here is, as I already mentioned, rather nice; the office and officers' mess are also good and, taken together, we surely won't manage something so comfortable and clean so soon again.[55]

Three days before the invasion began, Reinhardt not only revealed Germany's intention to attack, but alluded to the difficulties resulting from Hitler's plans for the Soviet East. On 19 June Reinhardt explained:

> I am once more writing a serious letter, for when you receive this letter, we will be at war again. A war not only for parts of the

great German Wehrmacht but the whole of it and for the entire German homeland. This new phase in the war will be difficult, perhaps the most difficult, because the Russians know what is at stake for them, and they'll fight accordingly.[56]

Whether Schmidt also revealed knowledge of Operation Barbarossa in advance of the invasion is unknown because we have no letters from him in the period before 22 June 1941.

As we have seen, letters were typically sent by courier as officers shuttled back and forth between their headquarters and Berlin or the OKH headquarters at Mauerwald in East Prussia.[57] This suited Guderian and Hoepner since their wives lived in Berlin, but Fridel was in Leipzig[58] and it is unknown where Eva resided in 1941.[59] It is less clear how much of this correspondence was, at least in part, trusted to the German postal service. Field Marshal Rundstedt, for example, frequently asked his wife to send him six-*Pfennig* stamps, so that he could dispatch his letters with a courier as far as Germany and then they would reach her in Kassel through the standard postal service.[60] Perhaps Schmidt and Reinhardt were using a similar system. It is evident from Margarete's letters that while she was able to access a reverse courier system through her privileged contacts in Berlin,[61] she was also on occasion sending some letters as standard field post, entailing weeks of delay.[62] Margarete's letters were of less intelligence value, but she still possessed a remarkable knowledge of events, which other wives likewise shared, making letters in both directions a potential, if unexploited, security risk.[63] The abrogation of responsibility that the panzer generals assumed for the sake of their private correspondence endangered not only Germany's most important operations in the East, but the lives of countless soldiers.

In an age of incredibly sophisticated code breaking, a softer target with such potentially rich information could scarcely have been conceived by Allied intelligence. Moreover, the short transmission time between the front and the home residence meant that the information would still have been operationally active if it could be accessed by an efficient spy network. Domestic workers were in short supply – Rundstedt's letters cite this as a problem[64] – so home access, whether existing or 'manufactured', was likely possible. If indeed targeting women like Margarete, Irma, Eva and Fridel was a missed Allied intelligence opportunity, it only existed because of their husbands' flagrant disregard for basic security protocols.

Discord and Dysfunction

While the letters under consideration here represent the Eastern Front from the perspective of the panzer generals, it is important to note that the *Ostheer* was made up of a far bigger proportion of infantry formations organised into nine armies, which provided the bulk of the men for the three army groups. It was to these armies that the panzer groups were periodically subordinated in the early months of the war, although in practice, even before they themselves achieved the equal status of 'panzer armies', the panzer groups operated with a large degree of autonomy and independence. The fiercely individualistic culture of the *Panzertruppe* combined with the headstrong personalities of the men who commanded them led to a degree of independence that a formal chain of command disguises. While this self-determined freedom of action is often celebrated within Anglo-American military histories as one of the hallmarks of German success, Marco Sigg's study points to a different conclusion. Such freedom of action is often incorrectly identified as resulting from the command system known as *Auftragstaktik*,[65] but what the panzer generals granted themselves often well exceeded their nominal orders or even disregarded them entirely. Sigg singles out Rommel and Guderian in May 1940 for their impulsive style of leadership that, while justified by events in this instance, did not just amount to autonomous decision-making, but constituted an outright revolt against their superiors.[66] Even where the actions of the panzer generals adhered to the entitlements of the *Auftragstaktik* concept, Sigg shows that from 1870 to 1940 there are many instances where German operations came close to descending into chaos due to the 'high-handedness' (*Eigenmächtigkeit*) instead of 'independence' (*Selbständigkeit*) of subordinate leaders.[67]

While the panzer generals are well known for their often brash insistence upon autonomy, the army commanders are contrastingly portrayed as more passive figures. Yet, by any objective measure, these men were still aggressive commanders in their own right, especially given their much-reduced mobility and offensive firepower.[68] They did not always accept the same level of risk as the panzer generals, but one must recognise the dangerous cult of the offensive that pervaded the *Panzertruppe* and routinely led to costly overextension. This is not to suggest that the army commanders were always correct in their more conservative assessments, but more often than not their concerns during the 1941 Soviet campaign were well justified.

The first major dispute to exemplify the strategic debate between consolidation and exploitation took place in late June as the first major encirclement, focused on Minsk, was being closed. Guderian was already preparing his next push to the East and utterly rejected any authority that questioned his intentions. Panzer Group 2 was grappling with serious problems in the rear, Guderian's encirclement front was extremely weak and he had long and vulnerable lines of supply. Yet this is not how Guderian presented the situation to Margarete in his letter of 4 July: 'Resistance has increasingly stiffened in the past days and our advance has become correspondingly slower, unfortunately caused in substantial part by interference from above, as in France. All the big shots are chasing shadows near Białystok, instead of looking to the front, where the new enemy is.'[69] Suggesting the problems in the rear were the equivalent of 'chasing shadows' showed a staggering ignorance of the problem, which was being reported by Guderian's own men. As the 18th Panzer Division swept eastwards forming the southern arm of the Minsk encirclement, General of Panzer Troops Joachim Lemelsen's XXXXVII Army Corps (mot.) was inundated with radio messages from the division reading: '"Alarm", "Help", "enemy panzer breakthrough"'.[70] As the division continued to battle through the gauntlet of escaping Soviet units, instances of panic occurred among the supply columns to the rear. Even by 30 June. when Guderian and Hoth had 'closed' the ring at Minsk, Lemelsen wrote in his private diary that Guderian's southern flank was 'damn weak and has many holes'.[71]

Guderian's determination to continue his advance proceeded against the explicit instructions of Kluge and came to a head when Guderian was threatened with dismissal. That Guderian took this seriously is seen from a comment to Margarete: 'I will do my duty, and when it's no longer possible, I myself will go. Anyway, I'm now fully objective and would breathe a sigh of relief if I could leave.'[72] Once again, in Guderian's skewed representation he was only doing his duty and for that he might have to go. Yet the clash was more serious than Guderian acknowledged. Lemelsen was with Guderian on the night of 5 July and wrote in his diary that the panzer general was 'still very depressed' because Kluge was threatening him with a court martial for disobedience.[73]

The bitterness and inflexibility on both sides represented much more than the personal animosity of two commanding officers: the dispute represented a fundamental division over German strategy and

Figure 5.1 Heinz Guderian posing for the camera on 1 July 1941 as he watches his men drive into the distance

how the war was to be waged. Kluge was backed by Hitler, and Guderian by Bock and Halder.[74] Kluge was fixed on sealing the pocket as tightly as possible, netting the greatest bag of prisoners, securing the tenuous routes of advance and bringing up as much infantry support as possible. He was not in principle opposed to Guderian's desire to continue the advance, but a long reckless thrust posed very real dangers, while undermining the accomplishment at Minsk. Guderian, by contrast, saw little point in expending precious time and strength on forces he regarded as beaten and of only modest threat to his rear area. In his opinion, rather than fretting about rounding up every last prisoner, it was better to maintain the momentum of the advance, keeping the enemy off balance, and seize the next objective. The two views proved irreconcilable, but soon became lightning rods for each side to explain the delays in the campaign.

The compromise between the competing extremes soured Kluge's triumph and left Guderian's continued drive conspicuously under-resourced. Yet it would be incorrect to suggest that an obvious choice existed or an opportunity was somehow missed. The fact remained that German forces were simply attempting too much for the space, time and resources available. Guderian was right to seek a rapid solution through the deepest possible penetration, but he underestimated the threat to his rear between Slonim and Minsk, as well as the strength of opposition further to the east, for which he would desperately need more supplies and Kluge's infantry. The same dilemma confronted Hoth but, for the panzer generals, bold action in the face of danger was the hallmark of previously victorious campaigns. Neither man was about to shy away from the perils of forward operations, or give in to the supposedly weak-willed reservations of army commanders. Of course, the distinction between infantry and armoured commanders was hardly indicative of their position, as even many hardened panzer generals recognised the problem of an unrelenting advance. When Lemelsen met with Guderian before the campaign, the planning devolved into a 'very excited argument'.[75] A week later when they met again for Guderian's birthday, Lemelsen alluded to Guderian's impetuous nature, observing, 'when he is in a good mood, he can be awfully pleasant and nice, but when the blood rushes to his head, it's over! You have to know him.'[76]

At Panzer Group 4, Reinhardt was also confronting the insatiable demands of his commanders, telling Eva on 12 July:

> If the higher-ups convince themselves that we can continue to advance just as swiftly as we have done so far, then things could get dangerous. Then I'll have to stand before my troops and tell them in a timely fashion that the impossible cannot be asked of them. I've therefore demanded that the 'higher-ups' come here for once. They won't be put in any danger (that would be a pity!) but just accompany us on a drive along our so-called roads. [...] The 'higher-ups' haven't a clue about any of this, not to mention the daily fighting at the front, the uncertainty of being shot at from behind as well as from the side from bushes and woods, etc.[77]

If Reinhardt was exasperated by the incessant pace of the advance in the first half of July, Army Group North soon intervened to halt Hoepner's panzer group and reorganise the advance. Hoepner immediately expressed his frustration, but unlike Guderian he accepted Leeb's order and correctly identified the main cause of the problem. Writing to Irma on 16 July, he noted: 'I'm still near Pskov and I'm rather ill-tempered, because the breakthrough to Leningrad is currently on hold.

There are several reasons for this. The decisive cause, however, is our weakness.'[78] Reinhardt, on the other hand, having recently chastised his superiors for asking too much of him, now rebuked them for holding him back. On 23 July he told Eva:

> Everyone is waiting and hoping that we can soon advance again, and I'm annoyed at the 'higher-ups' for not letting us loose. As none of the 'higher-ups' come to us, I held forth about it again in a letter today; I'm keen to see how they will decide in response to my stinging letter, which is now on its way by aircraft.[79]

Reinhardt did not get the answer he was looking for and, as the days passed idly by, his fury grew. What is surprising is that men like Reinhardt were utterly unable to recognise that Army Group North was hampered by insufficient forces for a simultaneous advance on Leningrad as well as the necessity of maintaining contact with Army Group Centre's northern flank. The two objectives were pulling apart as the German advance deepened, forcing Leeb to stretch his limited formations accordingly. There was also a need to allow infantry support to catch up to the panzer group and the soldiers simply could not march any faster.[80] Yet Reinhardt, like so many of the panzer generals, was oblivious to the wider strategic realities and focused only on his narrow task at hand – in this case reaching Leningrad. He routinely reduced complex issues to the baneful decisions of those acting above. Accordingly, Reinhardt wrote to Eva on 26 July:

> At present, our existence is unfortunately monotonous and bor-ing, [...] we're still very annoyed about the superior authorities, who cannot, or rather, do not want to acknowledge that it is wrong for us to wait and now, more than ever, make life difficult for us with stupid telephone conversations, orders, etc. This is exasperating and stretches our nerves, though mine are still in good condition. Yesterday evening, I personally talked to them on the phone, as [Colonel Hans] Röttiger [XXXXI Army Corps chief of staff] has lost all desire to do so, but so severely that there can now be no doubt about my views and intentions. They'll 'wait' so long that it is then too late and the Russians will have countered with defensive measures that are too strong for us![81]

By the start of August, Hoepner, who had previously shown a degree of understanding for being halted, having assumed it would only be a matter of days,[82] was growing increasingly exasperated at the continued inactivity. There was a flurry of meetings and discussions between the representatives of the OKW, OKH, army group and his panzer group, which Hoepner characterised as 'constant bother with senior authorities'. He lamented the loss of time and the costly defensive battles his panzer group had been forced to fight and, like Reinhardt, predicted the renewed advance 'will be harder now'.[83]

On the evening of 7 August, only hours before Reinhardt could finally restart his offensive on the lower Luga River, the planned addition of Manstein's LVI Army Corps was withdrawn by the army group. After three weeks of delay there could be no illusions about the strength of Soviet forces or the dug-in field fortifications that Reinhardt's unsupported attack would have to confront. Reinhardt was given the option to stand down his own forces, but after all his bluster and harsh language directed at the lack of resolve among the senior leadership, he rejected this.[84] On 8 August his attack drove forward, but made little early progress, which soon caused him to regret his decision and inform the panzer group that he was ending the offensive. This was out of the question for Hoepner and, in spite of it being after midnight on 9 August when he received this news, he immediately called Reinhardt, who had only just managed to get to sleep. The strain, fatigue and divergence of opinion proved explosive. Reinhardt wrote to Eva about the exchange on 10 August, but tellingly neglected to make any mention of his decision to call off his offensive:

> A fierce quarrel with Hoepner, who was blaming us for things not going as hoped. Because he did not first ask why we wanted to act differently but instead blustered in and issued contrary orders, etc., I became very angry after all the nervous tension that the day had cost us – incidentally at 1 o'clock in the morning, after I'd just managed to get to sleep with aspirin – and we gave each other a piece of our minds. Some thanks for being held back for almost four weeks against my will and contrary to my warning that conditions for our new operation were deteriorating day by day. Angry and agitated, it took me a long time to get back to sleep, though I had been quite severe before the conversation then calmed down.[85]

The arguments for and against continuing German offensives are in many respects captured by Reinhardt's letters. He wanted to attack when not permitted, but then blamed the higher command for forcing him onto the offensive, even when he was given the choice. The insoluble dilemma for the panzer generals was that, on the one hand, there was always the pressure for constant gains, the need to stay on the front foot, requiring panzer generals to force the issue even under less than perfect circumstances. On the other hand, attacking into the teeth of Soviet defences without sufficient support clearly resulted in heavy losses. The 6th Panzer Division, for example, had already lost up to one-third of its forces by the end of 8 August.[86] Yet at the end of the day, for panzer group commanders like Hoepner and Guderian, there could be no dilemma. There could be no doubt about what the priorities were. This is not to suggest the generals were cynically indifferent to the cost of their operations, nor that they were disingenuous in their concern for their men. There could be no dilemma, because in their minds the problem and the solution were one and the same thing. The faster the attack proceeded, before enemy defences coalesced into something greater than the power of the offensive, the better for the attacking forces, saving men from harder fighting and ultimately more losses. As a result, the attack became a dogmatic response, confirming the Wehrmacht's cult of the offensive, which the *Panzertruppe* embodied. As a rhetorical device, emblematic of National Socialism, the danger of such reasoning was the absence of an end state. The logic for the attack could be incessantly applied until it reached inevitable self-destruction. It was an insidious logic, but became a pillar of National Socialist military thinking because it always appeared to be the lesser evil. On the lower Luga River, such reasoning proved itself one more time as Reinhardt was ordered (and shamed) into continuing his attack, which eventually unhinged Soviet defences and allowed for a new phase of exploitation.[87]

In the centre of the Eastern Front, Guderian and Hoth were also pushing further to the East throughout early July, attempting to close a second encirclement at Smolensk. Yet before making contact in the newly emerging pocket, Guderian charged off further to the East, seizing the town of Yel'nya instead of linking up with Hoth near Yartsevo as Army Group Centre had ordered. Bock and Kluge had tried to assert their authority, but Guderian simply ignored their orders.[88] After the war even Hoth looked upon Guderian's decision with embittered resignation: 'To Panzer Group 2 the taking of the heights at Yel'nya, for the later continuance of the advance eastward, appeared more important than the completion of the [Smolensk] encirclement.'[89] Not surprisingly, Guderian's obstinate defiance of his superiors was selectively explained to Margarete. On 24 July he wrote: 'There was more friction with my superiors, which is always provisionally pasted over. It's not pretty.'[90]

Unlike the letters of Guderian, Hoepner and Reinhardt, Schmidt's letters offer almost no comment on the senior leadership or on their direction of the campaign. Judging only by his letters to Fridel, Schmidt seems to have given such matters no consideration and concentrated mainly on the tasks at hand. Hoth, Schmidt's immediate commander at the start of the war, was by many accounts an amiable commander, which no doubt counted towards Schmidt's apparent satisfaction.[91] Yet further evidence would suggest that Schmidt did not commit all his thoughts to paper when writing to Fridel. Schmidt's known correspondence also includes his July letters to Margarete Guderian and Friedrich Paulus. To Margarete, Schmidt presented himself as a dutiful family friend, politely enquiring after Guderian's well-being and requesting his field post number to undertake his own correspondence. He ended the letter: 'In the hope that you, your relatives in Krefeld and your husband continue well, I kiss your hand and am your very obedient servant.'[92] Yet in his letter to Paulus, Schmidt struck a rather different tone – and one which accords with the resentment Guderian tended to attract. Recounting for Paulus his corps' success, Schmidt wrote: 'I am happy for the corps, which has done very well and has always been at the head of the army. (Perhaps to the grief of Guderian.)'[93] Such a comment suggests that friendship did not preclude rivalry, but one might also question whether Schmidt's friendship was, at least in part, a steppingstone to his own success, given Guderian's status and seniority. Such a hypothesis is strengthened by an account from the French campaign in which the two panzer generals were said to have clashed so fiercely that Schmidt asked to be relieved of his command.[94]

We have already seen in Chapter 2 how much more candid and open Schmidt was to Paulus, over anything he wrote to Fridel, and his frankness extended to criticism of command arrangements. The establishment of Kluge's Fourth Panzer Army had clearly failed to rein in the recalcitrant Guderian, while Hoth was not in need of such close direction. Bock had also become frustrated with Kluge's own complaints, which had at times been directed over his head to the OKH.[95] The result was that Kluge's Fourth Panzer Army was dissolved, evoking firm approval from Schmidt and confirming that the strategic machinations at the top of the army were not unknown to him, and that he did not lack an opinion on them. 'It's good that Kluge is gone again,' Schmidt told Paulus. 'These intermediate positions only inhibit and do not benefit.'[96]

If Schmidt was happy to see the end of Kluge's command, Guderian was positively elated and took the new development as confirmation of his own divergent strategic approach. Sharing the news with Margarete, Guderian did not hide his satisfaction, 'after it [the Fourth Panzer Army] had made my life unduly difficult and provided little in the way of a positive contribution'. As for Kluge himself, Guderian did not mince words, telling his wife that he 'constantly interfered in the details and was also very vain. Ultimately, in the interest of the cause I had to defend myself, which led to acerbities, though I would gladly have avoided it.'[97] Guderian then proudly declared: 'I'm again directly subordinated to the army group and we get along very well.' Of course, Kluge was not the one acting on his own initiative, but rather was following Bock's orders, which, the panzer general was about to discover, had not changed simply because the Fourth Panzer Army had been dissolved. Thus, Guderian was shocked to find himself in the same position as before and a week later wrote to Margarete of his despair:

> Your loving compliments [...] did me good, especially as the gruelling irritations are not yet over, despite my release from being subordinated to Mr von Kl[uge]. They've now just shifted. I don't know how long my heart and nerves will be able to endure it. [...] It's enough to drive one to despair. How I'm supposed to escape this devilry, I don't know. No one is helping me in this situation.[98]

Nor was it just Army Group Centre that did not meet with Guderian's expectations. At a meeting with Hitler on 4 August the dictator failed to support a continued drive towards Moscow, although, as Guderian noted, 'the Führer himself was exceedingly sympathetic. What a pity! What a pity!'[99] Even with the conclusion of the battle of Smolensk, Guderian's propensity to butt heads with his superiors immediately complicated his next operation and this time he took aim at the army's high command. On 12 August he wrote: 'At present I'm preparing a new attack, but the OKH is making problems and has reservations. There's not much in the way of autonomy in the conduct of the war and one has to search for such opportunities with a lantern.'[100] Clearly,

Guderian's search for independent 'opportunities' essentially meant finding a way of proceeding in spite of his superiors. Even Loringhoven, Guderian's adjutant, wrote after the war that Guderian was known as *Brausewetter* (Roaring Weather) by his immediate subordinates for the manner in which he raged against his superiors, including eventually even Hitler (in 1945).[101]

Guderian's obstinacy stood out even among his fellow panzer commanders, which was no doubt a result of his own incorrigible character, but appears also to have been fed by the mythos of infallibility and acclamation within his own command. Colonel Barsewisch, the senior Luftwaffe officer at Panzer Group 2, noted in his diary in early July: 'When Guderian decides, it is as if the God of war himself is riding across the valley; when his eyes light up, Wotan seems to hurl lightning bolts or Thor seems to swing the hammer. The spark immediately jumped between us and I was fascinated by this incredible personality.'[102] In other entries, Barsewisch refers to Guderian as being 'A bull of energy'[103] and 'A fantastic man!'[104] Lemelsen, one of Guderian's hard-pressed corps commanders with whom there had been some bitter disagreements even before Barbarossa began, nevertheless remarked in his diary: 'I especially adore him because he is a complete soldier.'[105] Likewise, Guderian's aide-de-camp, Lieutenant Joachim von Lehsten, noted: 'Everyone respected and admired this man; a remarkable leader of outstanding ability.'[106] There can be no question Guderian brought a natural ability to the aggressive operational style of warfare practised by the Wehrmacht, but command also has a collaborative ethos that benefits from open opinion and shared expertise. If Guderian could not accept the authority and directions of those in the chain of command superior to himself, how much attention would he pay to the advice of those serving beneath him? More to the point, if the men on his staff were drawing comparisons with the god of war firing lightning bolts, one wonders how far Guderian's mystique of infallibility compromised their own ability to critique or provide counterweights to his actions and decisions.

From Guderian's point of view, the problem of command was a simple one, as he explained to Margarete: 'the root of the evil lies in the discrepancy in opinions at the top. [...] This results in unclear orders, frequent counter-orders, an absence of directives, sometimes for weeks on end. That is very unfortunate and leads us to miss many an opportunity.'[107] Although Guderian does not make any reference to

Hitler, the quintessential missed opportunity angering the generals of the OKH and Army Group Centre, as well as individual commanders such as Hoth and Guderian, was the dictator's refusal to continue the offensive towards Moscow and instead to divert the panzer groups north to support Leeb and south to seize Ukraine. The unresolved issue embittered the strategic direction of the campaign for weeks, but the final act in the resolution of the command crisis would see Guderian playing the principal role. It was both Guderian's headstrong and uncompromising attitude and his renowned status as a dynamic battlefield commander that the army high command wanted to leverage in its last-ditch attempt to influence Hitler in favour of the Moscow alternative. Guderian agreed to fly to Hitler's Wolf's Lair headquarters and repeat his view that a southern operation was 'completely impossible'.[108]

According to Guderian's account, Hitler remained utterly unconvinced and proceeded to instruct his visitor about why 'generals know nothing about the economic aspects of war'.[109] Guderian claimed all those present nodded in agreement with everything that Hitler said and that was the end of the matter. 'I did not think it right to make an angry scene with the head of the German state when he was surrounded by his advisers.'[110] Of course, Guderian had previously felt no aversion to bitterly contesting the orders of his superiors over decidedly lesser matters. For a man who was extremely reluctant to compromise and at the same time exceedingly ambitious, such an accommodating attitude almost certainly had an ulterior motive. Kenneth Macksey suggested that Guderian's unofficial consideration as a replacement for Brauchitsch may have accounted for his uncharacteristic backdown.[111] In any case, Guderian returned to Army Group Centre explaining that he was duty bound to 'make the impossible possible'.[112] Such a rhetorical backflip disgusted Halder, who unloaded on Guderian with a tirade of accusations.[113] Likewise, Bock could not understand how Guderian had presented such a scathingly dismissive critique of Hitler's plan only to propose carrying it out with the same forces that yesterday were regarded as incapable of doing so. 'Oh, what a rubber lion!'[114] he contemptuously remarked to his staff.

While Guderian could not hide his duplicitous behaviour from the army commanders, he certainly was not about to appear inconsistent or contradictory to Margarete and, accordingly, his next letter to her completely whitewashed his past opposition to Hitler's alternative. As he disingenuously explained:

> During the night of 23rd to 24th, I was received by the Führer; he was, as always, very nice and objectively clear and unambiguously in favour of the direction in which I strive. His next-representatives in the army [the men in the OKH], however, have very different ideas and this resulted in grave differences of opinion, which have a most negative impact, even reaching my sphere.[115]

Guderian believed that Halder and Bock were deliberately withholding resources from his southern offensive, slowing his progress and endangering his success.[116] Of course, none of his previous reservations about the feasibility of the Ukrainian operation were considered and the fact that Army Group Centre had an extremely long – and lengthening – front, which was under sustained Soviet attack, did not factor in Guderian's analysis.[117] Instead, everything was the result of a malicious plot by his vindictive superiors. As he complained to Margarete on 2 September:

> Since the 27th, I have been struggling to get reinforcements, which are granted to me drop by drop and too late. Only God now knows whether our task can be achieved. It would be my first failure, but I feel completely guilt-free. [...] We have all made every effort and are still doing so, but it becomes more difficult day by day, because irresolution and timidity from above prevent enough forces being deployed simultaneously, and instead they want to do everything 'piecemeal'.[118]

Six days later, even as Guderian's advance was threatening the rear of the entire Soviet South-Western Front, he was still fixated on his lack of support from Bock:

> There has been more hassle from above than ever before; unfortunately, there is still an almost complete lack of understanding for the demands of our situation and my military branch. Delays, setbacks, losses and other avoidable things result from this. [...] My discussion with Mr von Bo[ck] is today. Even there, however, I have little hope of understanding, especially as this man has even managed to turn the leadership against me. The latter is particularly painful, but I must endure it.[119]

It seems almost remarkable that Guderian focused so much on being actively hindered by his own command, especially when any objective assessment of the problems he faced could list numerous other factors – not least of which the Red Army – more prominently. That Reinhardt and, to a lesser extent, Hoepner did the same might suggest another answer. According to Felix Römer's analysis of private conversations by German soldiers: 'The focus of such battle-hardened combat soldiers was [...] first and foremost their own military performance. As in this example, they delighted in incorporating foils into their stories from whom they could all the more clearly set themselves apart.'[120] Perhaps in emphasising the inadequacies of their superiors the panzer generals were surreptitiously underlining their own achievements? They certainly tended towards being exhibitionists, whose egos naturally sought to impress, which is not to suggest the command conflicts were contrived, but they may have been somewhat deployed for effect. Knowing better than the flailing Red Army command was one thing, but knowing better than the German command suggested some measure of exceptionalism. In Schmidt's case, the fact that his letters seldom sought to impress, which could be a further symptom of his somewhat estranged relationship to Fridel, may also account for why he never bothered to contrast himself with anyone. The evidence does not suggest, however, that Schmidt was a particularly pugnacious personality or had fractious relationships with his superiors.

In spite of Hitler insisting upon the diversion of Army Group Centre's armour to assist the German advance on the flanks, Hoepner's panzer group was still forced to give up formations to reinforce Leeb's struggling armies. This constant dispersal detracted from the drive to Leningrad and infuriated Hoepner, who felt he was being denied his own moment of glory and the due recognition such an achievement would entail. As he complained to Irma on 18 August:

> My friend [Colonel-General Ernst] Busch [commanding the Sixteenth Army] suffered a strong Russian breach (south of Staraya Russa). Neither he nor Leeb had reserves. Now, mine have been taken away from me (for the third time), in order to iron things out. I'm therefore lacking the forces needed for my thrust towards Leningrad. [...] Thus, I suddenly have tasks that I have to fulfil with insufficient forces, are never fully realised, and, therefore, receive no recognition.[121]

Unlike Guderian, Hoepner at least understood the reason for his forces being removed and he did not oppose their reassignment. Yet his letters to Irma continued to cast himself as the long-suffering workhorse of the army group – indispensable, but overlooked. On 5 September he wrote: 'As Leeb just told me, I'll probably have to help [Colonel-General Georg von] Küchler [commanding the Eighteenth Army] again. If I ask for something, however, I'm turned down. They know that I can still look after myself.'[122] While Hoepner had a better understanding of the war from a strategic perspective, he still desperately sought the acclaim of a major triumph and eyed Leningrad as his prize. Thus, when he was reassigned to Army Group Centre for Operation Typhoon, which would deny him the acclaim for the anticipated fall of the city, Hoepner was crestfallen and speculated it was all a malevolent plot by the army leadership. 'We are again deprived of the outward appearance of a victory. [...] One could assume that the senior authorities want to keep for themselves the glory of taking the city.'[123]

If Hoepner thought the high command might be stealing a march on him for the prestigious title of conqueror of Leningrad, he might also have looked to the ambitious corps commanders. It was Schmidt's XXXIX Motorised Army Corps that Hoth had to give up to aid Leeb and this convinced Schmidt that the capture of the city was now his responsibility.[124] As he wrote to Fridel on 24 August: 'I am currently in the midst of the attack on Petersburg, which the Führer entrusted to me.'[125] Schmidt was not answerable to Hoepner, having being subordinated to Busch's Sixteenth Army, and with Panzer Group 4 stalled to the south, Schmidt considered his own drive on Leningrad to be the decisive thrust. On 5 September he wrote to Fridel:

> As usual, I'm the closest to Petersburg. My forward-most units are located just 20 km from the centre of the city of Petersburg. I'm sitting by the Neva. We're merrily sinking warships and have been firing on Petersburg [...] Voroshilov [commanding the Soviet North-Western Direction] has focused on me as the most dangerous and has been attacking with ever new masses of troops for the last three days.[126]

Clearly, Schmidt saw himself as the principal besieger of Leningrad.

Reinhardt's letters told a contrasting story, which unsurprisingly emphasised his own decisive role in the thrust on Leningrad, but predictably he was hamstrung by the malicious high command. Reinhardt was contemptuous of the continued delays and expressed scorn for the flanking armies. As he wrote to Eva on 22 August:

> 'unfortunately', the worst thing is the hassle with the 'higher-ups', who are not supporting us at all, and with our neighbours on the left, who – one is almost tempted to believe it's out of ignorance or envy – act as though we ourselves were to blame for our difficult situation, because we had no cause to bolt ahead so far. That's bitter.[127]

When the panzer group did continue its advance, Reinhardt gave himself the credit and, just like Schmidt, claimed he was the main focus of Soviet counter-measures. Writing on 7 September, he told Eva: 'I've torn a big hole in the enemy in front of Petersburg, which has of course greatly benefited my neighbours, because it's drawn the enemy to us.'[128] Predictably, Reinhardt was incredulous that his advance was again halted to support the faltering advance on the flanks. In his opinion, precisely the opposite should happen. As Reinhardt continued:

> Unfortunately, we've again been stopped in full flow, once more 100 km ahead of everyone else, because they're afraid for us (we are never afraid!), instead of sending us reserves as quickly as possible!! It's the old story: we clear the way, and the higher-ups cannot exploit our successes, because they don't believe in our tempo or first have to get used to it![129]

Reinhardt emphatically believed he should be the focal point of the renewed attack, with priority for artillery and aircraft given to him, but this was not the case. Even Hoepner apparently expressed 'incomprehension' at Reinhardt's insistence. In the face of such a rebuff Reinhardt told Eva that his unsupported attack would simply have to prove such a success that the command would have no choice but to redirect everything to back his corps. 'Proud words, not typical of your Hansi', Reinhardt told Eva, 'but justified.' Yet Reinhardt already knew the proposed attack had succeeded, so he was establishing his supposed prescience, or as Römer might observe, building the foil into his narrative to underscore his superior military aptitude over and above others in the German command. Reinhardt then rejoiced in the achievement: 'My fantastic troops have not disappointed me. Should I not be gratefully moved?! Since yesterday evening, all higher authorities are naturally falling over themselves not only to congratulate us but also to fulfil every request that we have.'[130] According to Reinhardt's account, he had been correct all along and finally everyone recognised it. It was, however, too good to last and two days later, as the priority for the attack shifted again, Reinhardt returned to his melancholy commentary on the German command:

> In spite of new, major successes in battle, I was not and still am not happy; [...] It is enough to tell you that we are currently living in figures of speech such as: 'We're allowed to pull the chestnuts out of the fire for others,' or 'Others skim off the fat,' or, 'The Moor has done his duty, the Moor can go,'[131] and so on. You'll surely be able to sense from this hint how we, how I am feeling.[132]

Such an analysis of the letters reveals how potentially problematic they are when used as the only source for the purpose of reconstructing operational history. They do, however, tell us a great deal about the men who wrote them and the individualistic culture within the senior ranks of the *Panzertruppe*. It is striking how fixated the panzer generals were on being overlooked or bypassed by their own command. There is also a palpable sense of competition with fellow generals, who constantly threatened to outmanoeuvre them in the struggle for priority. It is as if each man believed his force and his conception of the campaign alone represented the key to victory on the Eastern Front. This led to interminable debate and rancour, which not only absorbed time and effort, but distracted attention from other issues. Explaining such behaviour probably requires further comparative study of generals outside of the *Panzertruppe*. My hypothesis would suggest the aggressive pursuit of individual career success by the panzer generals (as discussed in Chapter 3) was culturally unique within the army, which is not to suggest that such traits were not found in the infantry or other service arms, but not to the same degree. The ruthlessness with which the panzer generals pursued their own measure of success is seen not just in their readiness to cry foul and outmanoeuvre their fellow commanders in operational matters, but also in the fact that they showed a near total indifference to the strategic circumstances. At this point in the war there was probably no doubt in their minds that Germany would win in the East; the more pertinent question was who would reap the rewards.

The absence of a common command culture and shared strategic vision meant the Barbarossa campaign was prone to erratic changes in direction. Even when agreement existed, this was always subject to change based on individual opportunity. When Guderian appeared at the Wolf's Lair in August, he did not stand on principle over what he believed to be the correct axis of advance. He was not about to break with Hitler – the ultimate career-maker – over a question of strategy and any loyalty to his fellow generals was outweighed by the potential rewards of embracing Hitler's Ukrainian option. In Guderian's shrewd calculation, he could either win Hitler's favour or risk being seen as a recalcitrant. Worse still, opposition to Hitler over the matter might see him replaced entirely. Thus, Guderian quickly switched sides and was not plagued by a sense of betrayal towards the army because he could tell himself (and others) that he was simply following Hitler's orders, while no doubt protecting his own interests.

Hoepner longed for Guderian's level of prominence and notoriety, and hoped the investment of Leningrad would at last force him into the spotlight, but compared with Guderian he simply was not ruthless enough. From Guderian's firebrand perspective, Hoepner had mistakenly followed Leeb's halt orders and compliantly parcelled out his meagre reserves to aid Busch and Küchler. Guderian would have fought both tooth and nail. If he did not determine a course of action to be essential to his own objective, it was to be cast aside and resisted by all means necessary. Hoepner, however, showed a greater respect for the chain of command, even when he did not agree with the decisions at hand. Reinhardt also observed his orders, but subscribed to Guderian's firebrand school of generalship, which demanded a single-minded focus on the objective to the wilful exclusion of all else. His constant frustrations quickly boiled over into spiteful reproaches against his commanders. Reinhardt was not interested in any conception of the war other than the one he was fighting, which made him deeply mistrustful of the army command and, at times, resentful of his fellow generals. Schmidt's attitude is harder to judge since he refrained from discussing command decisions in his letters to Fridel, but he certainly believed himself to be personally chosen by Hitler for the investment of Leningrad; this led to a level of entitlement that scorned competing interests proposed by the army. Importantly, all four panzer generals were united by their desire to win personal success, which dominated the thinking of Guderian and Reinhardt and unquestionably influenced Hoepner and Schmidt.

Command, according to the *Panzertruppe's* school of thought, was often a zero-sum game in which to gain strength, someone else had to lose it, inducing rivalries and antagonism, but also driving cut-throat competition in which the panzer generals felt justified by their 'natural' superiority within the army.

Operational Silences

While the discord and friction surrounding strategic decision-making and resource allocation form a constant theme within the letters, it is interesting to note how little discussion is devoted to other factors undermining Germany's campaign in the East. Operation Barbarossa's well-known difficulties with logistics, for example, are hardly ever discussed. Throughout the four letter collections, there are only thirteen separate mentions of supply problems undermining operations, and only three of these are made before October. Hoepner makes the first such reference on 19 July when he tells Irma: 'We will have to advance at least to the Volga if we want to exploit the Russian economy. Unfortunately, there are few stores here. Supplying the troops is very hard at times. Either the Russians did not have large stockpiles or they were able to evacuate them before our arrival.'[133] Five days later Guderian also makes mention of supply problems, but only among a host of other factors: 'The long way and the various losses are very noticeable, as well as the fatigue, the horrendous dust scourge, the supply difficulties.'[134] The only other reference in the summer months was made by Hoepner on 15 August and it constitutes one of the more profound comments on the entire war: 'The campaign <u>has to</u> be over by late September due to the whole supply situation and the cold.'[135] This represents a rare example of profound strategic thinking about the campaign, but given the clear importance Hoepner ascribes to the supply of the *Ostheer*, it is interesting that he does not discuss it more often or in greater depth.

Guderian's letter of 11 October, as the autumn rains were about to transform much of the landscape to a sodden bog, exemplified his ignorance of the seasonal conditions in Russia at this time: 'As soon as the encirclement battle is concluded and we have sorted out our supply, things will hopefully happen quicker. [...] Now we're hoping for good, dry weather, at least for 14 days, then the main part is done; otherwise, it could last much longer.'[136] By the end of the month, Guderian had learned the hard way that his operations had to take account of climate and transportation issues, which had frustrated his plans. As he told Margarete: 'Our situation here is annoying [brought on] by scarcity of supply and heavy rainfall and the abysmal roads. Replenishment almost fails and the troops can only move with extreme slowness. We have nonetheless reached the southern outskirts of Tula, but we must close our ranks and take a deep breath before this important industrial city can be taken.'[137] For the first two weeks of November, Army Group Centre paused its Typhoon offensive, hoping to gain sufficient supplies finally to reach Moscow, but the difficulties persisted and the breathing space benefited the Red Army at least as much as the Wehrmacht.[138] Assessing the situation in early November, Hoepner wrote to Irma: 'Already now, I've no idea how I'll even secure the supply of provisions. For the new attack, the preparation of provisions for ten days is required. What's more, there's trouble with our superiors, who have no understanding for our situation.'[139] While allocating a good degree of blame to the high command was certainly justified, it would be wrong to assume that an alternative existed, even had the OKH and OKW understood the severity of the problem. There was simply no prospect of resuming major operations in November 1941 in a manner commensurate with Germany's strategic objectives. The panzer forces would be lucky to reach Moscow, to say nothing of encircling the city or maintaining such extended positions throughout the winter.

Whatever Guderian and Hoepner claimed to understand about their respective supply situations, they were both guilty of pushing their men beyond the limit of their resources. If the Red Army could not halt their advance, the lack of supplies surely would; the final 1941 offensive, for both generals, degenerated into a slow, grinding and costly attack. However deficient Guderian and Hoepner may have been, there is at least some awareness and discussion about the supply issue in their letters. From the correspondence of Reinhardt and Schmidt, on the other hand, both appeared utterly oblivious to the problem. This was not only true of their time as corps commanders, but also from October when Reinhardt himself commanded Panzer Group 3 and, from November, when Schmidt took over the Second Army. At best, their letters alluded to the immediate problems of movement in their own day-to-day experience, but they never took this further and considered the wider implications for their operations, to say nothing of

Figure 5.2 A column of Guderian's Panzer Group 2 improvising a crossing over a destroyed Soviet bridge on 30 June 1941

Germany's strategic objectives. On 25 September, for example, Schmidt wrote to Fridel:

> When we're on the move, we get stuck in the mud. Recently, I spent 14 hours in the car covering a distance that would otherwise be covered in a 3-hour drive. A prime mover finally had to pull us out and I had to go through the mud at night on foot for the last eight kilometres. The so-called roads are simply indescribable. Everything gets stuck. This area is simply impossible for us motorised units.[140]

Schmidt could always see the immediate impact, but failed time and again to relate the wider implication to the objectives of his army or Germany's campaign. Similarly, Reinhardt wrote to Eva on 19 November: 'We were the first to set off again, after the weather gods had forced us all to stop. Thanks to the exemplary work of my supply staff and the sacrifices made by all the drivers, who drove through thick and thin, day and night, three days ago we were largely replenished with the things we need for new hostilities.'[141] So long as Reinhardt could make the next push, the bigger picture eluded him, as did every indication of overextension. This only underlines the blinkered cult of the offensive among the *Panzertruppe* commanders and their limited understanding of modern warfare in a theatre the size of the Soviet Union.

Accounting for such seemingly wilful self-destructiveness returns us to the powerful cultural framework that underpinned the Wehrmacht and informed its offensive doctrine. Felix Römer's study of the Fort Hunt transcripts reveals how dominant the subject of command quality was for middle-ranked officers and how cut-throat the judgements were. According to Römer's analysis, officers 'could tirelessly hold forth about other officers, peers, superiors and generals like Model, Halder and Rommel. They thought some of them were "alright" and others, on the other hand, "not" – what counted for them first and foremost here was whether their fellow officers conformed to their military conceptions.'[142] This shows that the generals were rigorously evaluated not only from above and by their peers, but also by their subordinates. Pressure to perform therefore surrounded the generals and the accusation of timidity or indecisiveness was a far graver charge in the Wehrmacht than the accusation of attempting too much or even pushing the men too hard. As Römer again explained:

> When officers behaved 'too strictly', they forfeited at most their popularity, but did not automatically lose the respect of their men. The experienced Second Lieutenant Josef Heindl, for instance, criticised his regimental commander in the 2nd Panzer Division for 'hounding the men to their deaths too much!' He nonetheless attested that he 'knew his stuff' and was 'a real daredevil' – in the Wehrmacht, this was a compliment.[143]

Thus, the hard-nosed panzer general who brazenly charged forward, even at a considerable cost in blood, earned the respect of the men. The same might not be said of the 'intellectual' general who emphasised the 'bigger picture', was more interested in staff work and justified inaction on the basis of supply problems. Not surprisingly, therefore, the panzer generals aggressively took the fight to the enemy at every opportunity because, in their minds, that was how wars were won and everybody knew it.

While it appears remarkable that logistics could be so comprehensively discounted in an invasion of the largest country on earth, it was not the only topic curiously under-represented in the letters of the generals. One of the best indications of the insular world the German generals inhabited is their relative disinterest in the Red Army. It is not that the 'Russians', as they are referred to, are absent from the letters, but that the engagement with them is superficial and often reflects racialised concepts or national stereotypes. On only the second day of the war Hoepner wrote to Irma: 'Although we unleashed a gigantic firework display, which I personally watched from close by, the Russians offered stubborn resistance. They were Caucasians, and they made a wild impression when we captured them: yellowy-brown, slitted eyes, broad, crude skulls, close-cropped hair, strong, wiry bodies.'[144] Having just crossed the border into Byelorussia (modern Belarus), Guderian sought to characterise the inhabitants for Margarete, but represented them in contrasting, even contradictory, terms. 'Byelorussians are friendly and don't apparently attach much importance to the retention of the Soviets. But there are also fanatical people of another mindset, particularly among the troops, who are fighting tenaciously and bravely.'[145] Friendly, but fanatical; do not want the Soviets, but fight tenaciously for them – what exactly did Guderian understand about his enemy? Of course, just because these Soviet soldiers fought in Byelorussia did not make them Byelorussians, a point Guderian seemingly overlooked. German misconceptions about the East, and especially their Soviet enemy, pervaded the high command. Geoffrey P. Megargee has revealed the tendency to fill the void of information concerning the Soviet Union with cultural preconceptions and national stereotypes.[146] Central tenets of these highlighted further contradictions that dated back to the nineteenth century and cast the Russian empire in the opposing roles of an aggressive colossus looking to expand westward and an internally fractured state unable to resist an external attack.[147] Such contradictory, double-sided notions fitted well with National Socialist precepts allowing, on the one hand, convincing arguments for the pursuit of *Lebensraum* in the East, while also providing a 'foe image' which depicted the Soviet state as a threatening Godless enemy of 'cultured' Europe, providing a justification for war. Moreover, as Gerhard Weinberg has argued, the distorted ideological and racial world view that the generals expounded provided an added measure of confidence in casting their gaze to the East. Germany's most important and dangerous enemies were initially judged to have been in the West and the ease of their defeat only made the conquest of the Soviet Union appear all the more certain.[148] Such views gave the panzer generals confidence that Barbarossa could be ended quickly without any fear of a long and bitterly contested struggle.

Reinhardt showed no particular interest in the new Soviet enemy until his letter of 16 July, which revealed his surprise as well as a sudden interest in why the Red Army fought so well. Tellingly, however, his answer to the dilemma was, at least in part, himself. During the period of cooperation between the Reichswehr and the Red Army, Reinhardt had taught Soviet officers on exchange to Berlin,[149] which provided a satisfying, if ludicrously exaggerated, answer. As Reinhardt wrote to Eva:

> The Russians are making our work a bit more difficult than in previous campaigns. They're taking action! They're not raising their hands and surrendering so quickly and so often as they did in the First World War, or even like the French did last year. They're fighting doggedly and cunningly, and they have very good weapons of all kinds. (Even now, how dangerous that would have been for us, had we waited for them to declare war.)[150] And they have leaders. We might be laying down the law here, and they always have to take counter-measures, but they do take them, sometimes so swiftly and well that we're amazed. For us, this war is by far the most interesting in terms of command, and also the most exciting. We must be constantly at the ready, in order that we can respond with counter-strikes and repeatedly spoil their plans. Sometimes, I'm almost afraid that the fellows in my lessons learned too much. Because even if almost all my students are now dead,[151] they've been able to pass on for almost ten years what I taught them in Berlin.[152]

Even as the panzer generals surged forward in the early weeks of the campaign, the resistance of the Red Army did not go unnoticed, but this opposition was attributed to other factors. Hoepner believed Soviet resistance was being propped up by the poor infrastructure delaying the German advance as well as by the Red Army's own scorched-earth tactics. On 5 July he noted: 'On the few large roads, the Russians are offering stiff resistance and have blown up all bridges, so that the tempo has slowed significantly.'[153] A week later he returned to the same theme, telling Irma that the enemy were 'helped by the terrain', were again destroying bridges and that they 'burn everything'.[154] Similarly, on 19 July Guderian wrote to Margarete that the Russians 'are demonstrating their status as the old masters in destroying all bridges and burning down all towns, which naturally slows us down'.[155]

Soviet resistance was also attributed to simple mass, as Hoepner pointed to the formation of 'several reserve armies', but stressed that they 'are weak and poorly equipped'.[156] In his letter from 19 July Hoepner claimed the Soviet command was 'full of desperation' and then added, 'we captured convicts from Leningrad, a female battalion and four companies of young communists'.[157] The generals' letters acknowledge Soviet resistance, but without a real understanding of its substance or conviction. When Reinhardt toured recently captured Soviet positions, he wrote to Eva about being 'amazed' at the 'extremely elaborate' defensive system. As he detailed the scene: 'there are masses of trenches, huge anti-tank obstacles, bunkers of all kinds, barriers, landmines everywhere in between, even in villages [...]'.[158] Yet even such achievements were reduced to standard tropes commonly found in Nazi propaganda, which Reinhardt unquestioningly accepted. Returning to the subject of Soviet defences in his next letter, Reinhardt explained that tens of thousands of men, women and children had been forced to build them 'under the yoke of the commissars'.[159] There was no apparent understanding that Germany's war for conquest and empire in the East, which already entailed widespread hardship for civilians, might have adverse political and military implications. Instead, the generals thought only in terms of Bolshevik tyranny as the motivating force of Soviet resistance, and this despite their own brutal occupation methods that, by August, included the outright mass murder of whole Jewish communities, and which substantiated the most bombastic claims of Soviet propaganda.[160]

Schmidt took another angle in explaining Soviet resistance, which again illustrated an individualistic understanding of the war as well as pointing to the penchant for vanity among the panzer generals. For Schmidt, the tough combat conditions and hard fighting were unique to his experience because, in his view, he was always at the main flashpoint of the Eastern Front. Referring to the period 24 July to 8 August, Schmidt wrote to Fridel about leading 'one of the toughest defensive battles of my life' in which his corps was 'entirely alone against an oppressively superior Russian force'. Yet according to Schmidt's account, he dealt the enemy 'an enormous, costly defeat', and added, 'Only as a result of this was the encirclement of Smolensk possible.'[161] There can be no doubt Schmidt contributed to Germany's success at Smolensk, but he was hardly alone in making it happen and the fighting was just as fierce on other sections of the long encirclement front. This characterisation was, however, typical of Schmidt's view, which assumed his force was always deployed to the area of the hardest fighting. On 2 October, as Operation Typhoon was being launched towards Moscow in the centre of the Eastern Front, Schmidt neverthe-less claimed that his far smaller offensive as part of Army Group North was the real subject of Soviet attention: 'All the heavy Russian attacks are now concentrated on me.'[162] A week later he again made the ostentatious claim: 'I had to carry the can for the preparations of the great operation against Moscow and so had to withstand the entirety of Russian pressure.'[163] At the end of the month, without any real basis for comparison, Schmidt once again pronounced: 'I've unfortunately landed up in the worst and most difficult spot of the entire Eastern Front.'[164] Such an assumed mixture of self-importance and self-pity no doubt allowed Schmidt to believe that the Red Army was nowhere else as strong or as determined as against his forces. It was a convenient and appealing logic. If he succeeded against such odds, it was a remarkable achievement and, if he did not, the reason was obvious. Not surprisingly, Schmidt was not alone in making such claims. As Hoepner drove on Moscow in mid-October, he wrote to Irma: 'It's incredible. I've experienced the heaviest fighting near Mozhaisk, because on the motorway the build-up is stronger and the defence at its most courageous.'[165] This may have had some truth, given that Hoepner was advancing on the direct route to the Soviet capital, but in making such judgements he took no real interest in the forces con-fronting Reinhardt's panzer group in the north or Guderian's panzer army in the south. Thus, while the Red Army was often the subject of discussion in the letters of the panzer generals, they typically attributed its remarkable endurance to 'fanatical' elements or localised factors unique to their area of operations. There was no serious consideration of intrinsic motivating factors that might account for the unprecedented and unceasing resistance they were encountering.[166] As a result, no thought was spared for the nature of the war in which they were engaged and how that might contribute to, or detract from, Germany's military objectives. Of course, the panzer generals considered warfare in narrowly operational terms, which seemed to preclude even the most basic strategic deliberations.[167] The Red Army would simply have to be defeated by more of the same, and if their methods had not proven sufficient after five and a half months of relentless attacks, the panzer generals had nothing else to offer.

While partisan warfare is typically seen to be a feature of subsequent years on the Eastern Front, in 1941 unrest in the rear areas was less a reaction to German occupation than due to the simple fact that large elements of the Red Army had been trapped behind the advancing panzer groups.[168] The losses resulting from these rearward attacks were small, relative to those at the front, but the implications were disproportionate to the numbers, given the already tenuous and highly vulnerable logistical apparatus of the panzer groups. While the letters of the panzer generals acknowledged the attacks in the rear area, they did so fleetingly and never linked them to their strategic significance, nor did they contemplate how such an increasingly vast area of occupation might somehow be pacified. Guderian's only reference to the situation in the rear came early in the war when he wrote to Margarete on 29 June: 'The enemy continues to fiercely fight his little war behind the areas of penetration and thereby inflicts multiple losses on us. One of my orderly officers has been missing since yesterday. I hope we find him again.'[169]

Like Guderian, Hoepner appeared largely oblivious to the problem, aside from a single mention in his letters to Irma, which referenced both the scale of the problem in the rear and the fact that it was directly impacting his vital lines of communication. On 1 August Hoepner told of 'many Russian soldiers and partisans' setting explosives on railroads and engaging in nightly firefights with his headquarters' security detail.[170] Hoepner seemed to believe that the attacks were purposefully directed against his supply lines, not just any random target of opportunity, which might have posed troubling questions about a coordinated threat. Yet his letter did not dwell on this or even revisit the issue.

Reinhardt, as one of Hoepner's two corps commanders at this stage in the war, was more vocal about the frequency of attacks, but, like his more senior counterparts, did not consider any other repercussions. As he wrote to Eva on 13 August:

> Today is another day of crisis; the Russians are launching desperate attacks everywhere, at the front with new troops

that they've thrown against us, at the rear Russian troops, who have withdrawn into the woods in the face of our attacks and are hiding there, attempt to break out everywhere. There is shooting everywhere, even on those roads I travelled on yesterday; cries for help reach us from everywhere.[171]

Later in the same month, Reinhardt returned to the problem, telling Eva that enemy units were 'oozing out of the huge forests; some of them want to surrender, while some of them want to make life difficult for us far in our rear'.[172] That his panzer corps was vulnerable to these attacks was not lost on Reinhardt, who alluded to his helplessness in providing any remedy to the problem. 'I can do nothing but firmly believe that my men, wherever they are located, will stand and hold their positions and repel all attacks, and they're sure to do that.'[173] Such confidence, however, overlooked the essential point that these attacks cumulatively weakened the ever-lengthening German lines of supply and proved harder and harder to combat as the extent of the occupied area increased.

Narcissistic Command

As the summer months drew to a close and the cooler autumn days heralded the changing season, none of the panzer generals noted the ominous passing of Operation Barbarossa's timetable for victory or the looming proposition of campaigning into the winter. Hope was invested in the new offensive – Operation Typhoon – the drive on Moscow that would somehow end the war in Germany's favour. For the *Ostheer's* last great roll of the dice in 1941, the four panzer generals would eventually all find themselves concentrated together in Army Group Centre. Most of Panzer Group 4 was redeployed in the second half of September, but if Hoepner hoped the new operation might mean an end to the wrangling and bitterness that had blighted the push towards Leningrad he was soon disappointed. When one of his staff officers returned from an advanced planning session at Bock's headquarters, Hoepner wrote to Irma that 'there is again big trouble ahead'.[174] As Hoepner nonchalantly explained the dysfunction: 'OKW, the OKH, the army group and Kluge are at odds with each other. Only one thing seems certain, namely that everyone interferes in the details and wants to decide on things that are my concern. This means: a fight before the fighting has even started.'[175] Still, this did not especially worry Hoepner, probably because it was hardly out of the ordinary, and in his next letter on 21 September he even sounded a note of optimism: 'My new assignment is a good one. If I fulfil it, a lot will be gained.'[176] A lot had already been gained in Hoepner's last assignment, but what he was hoping for this time was personal recognition. The only threat to that was someone stealing his limelight and Hoepner was already eyeing a well-known rival for undermining him. As his letter continued: 'I've also been given sufficient forces, even if Guderian has once more deducted some for himself on the crook.'[177] Hoepner was not alone in his disapproval of Guderian. Even before Guderian's well-known clashes with high-ranking officers in the French and Soviet campaigns, Hitler's army adjutant, Major Gerhard Engel, noted that the dictator believed 'he [Guderian] had a lot of enemies amongst the generals'.[178] General of Panzer Troops Leo Geyr von Schweppenburg, one of Guderian's corps commanders in Panzer Group 2, related his impressions to Ulrich von Hassell, who noted in his diary: 'Low opinion of the character of Guderian.'[179] Likewise, General of Infantry Gotthard Heinrici, the commander of the XXXXIII Army Corps, which for a time was also subordinated to Guderian, noted in his diary on 19 December 1941: 'Today we moved from Guderian to Kluge. We are pleased about that, because until now the leadership was not clear and good.'[180] Former officers who worked under Guderian before the war were more specific about his character flaws: 'He had not the gift of listening calmly to his subordinates or men of his own rank, and allowing them to finish what they were about to say, before issuing his orders or decisions.'[181] Another stated: 'He lacked the psychological faculty of feeling and sensing his way which a "leading personality", such as a commander-in-chief, should possess.'[182] This final point was reiterated by Major-General Gerhard Bassenge, who described Guderian as 'a good tank man', but 'no great personality' because he was 'terrifically impulsive'.[183] As we have seen, Guderian did also have his supporters, but he was clearly a deeply divisive figure, whom many of his contemporaries, including Hoepner, viewed with a mixture of suspicion and animus.[184]

The earliest phase of Operation Typhoon was another great operational success for Army Group Centre, but that did not preclude bitter strategic disagreements over where to close the two encirclements, which became known as the battles of Briansk and Viaz'ma.[185] Hoepner had unsuccessfully argued for a larger encirclement in the north (at Viaz'ma), but was overruled and by 6 October believed himself to have been justified by the course of events. Accordingly, a resentful Hoepner wrote to Irma:

> The approach taken was not the one I suggested, otherwise more would have been captured. This has become clear to me and many others since the day before yesterday. Bock and Kluge are seeking to make up for the missed opportunity by constant hustle and bustle. I already had a run-in with Bock on 29 September. He's old now and unpredictable in his moods, evidently as a result of his illness.[186] Kluge also interferes in my affairs, which always causes trouble. This resulted in a clash yesterday. I wanted to call in sick today.[187]

Even in the course of inflicting one of its most disastrous defeats upon the Red Army, such was the acrimonious culture within the German high command that the same event was interpreted as a bitter lost opportunity. Hoepner's frustrations also led to a rare moment of reflection about the implications of the constant jostling for authority at the top and the stream of orders and counter-orders that followed from the absence of unity. As Hoepner explained:

> It's become commonplace for everyone to stick their oar in. I already experienced that with Kluge in the West, but I won't put up with it. The lower echelons no longer know what to do; they're constantly shoved about, today in one direction, tomorrow in the other. There's no regard for their needs. So far, Kluge's interventions have led three times to the exact opposite of what he actually intended. He's also not panic-proof.[188]

As Hoepner lamented the supposed short-sightedness of his immediate superiors, Reinhardt was telling Eva much the same story about Hoepner. On 22 September, as Panzer Group 4 was in the process of redeploying for Operation Typhoon, Reinhardt was stewing over his own perceived missed opportunity at Leningrad. This was not his first letter on the subject, but his anger had not dissipated and Hoepner had become the focus of Reinhardt's fury. It is important to note that there is almost no reason to believe that charging Reinhardt's remaining tanks directly into such a large city would have resulted in anything other than their becoming enmeshed in the urban defences and suffering heavy losses, but Reinhardt remained convinced he had been denied a major victory.[189] Recasting the events for Eva, Reinhardt erroneously stated, 'the Russians in front of us were destroyed' and 'experiencing elation over this breakthrough', he began 'assailing Hoepner to let us continue the advance'. Of course, Hoepner rejected every request, which only further infuriated Reinhardt: 'I already had a map of Petersburg on my desk; I was already in the process of distributing the roads on which we would march in, because we wanted to risk everything and would have been able to, as well; but we weren't allowed to.' Reinhardt then claimed that Hoepner had mistakenly misinterpreted an order from the high command: 'As it turned out, as a result of a misunderstanding, [...] Hoepner made us halt one line earlier than the highest authorities wanted.' Yet having seemingly pinned the blame on Hoepner, Reinhardt then denounced the high command, who, he stated, 'did not want my panzer corps to reap the fruits of our endeavours throughout the past weeks'. This probably accounts for the real source of Reinhardt's anger – his denial of a great prestige victory. Seemingly, this is what Reinhardt was assured by his new assignment within Army Group Centre, telling Eva: 'And – we are needed for "something new", another major task. You'll say that this is an honour for us, just as the higher-ups tell us, Leeb included, with whom I signed off yesterday; but it's still difficult.'[190]

A week later, when Reinhardt had learned what exactly would be required of his corps in Operation Typhoon, he struggled to see how he might replicate the opportunity he believed had existed at Leningrad, but by this point he had resigned himself to a less conspicuous role. As he wrote home on 28 September: 'Even our senior officers seem to doubt whether everything will proceed in the way that is demanded of us, especially as I've had a division taken from me. [...] Ultimately, it's not important that my corps reaps the fruits of victory, but rather that we all contribute to winning another major battle.'[191] As elementary as such a sentiment may appear, as we have seen, it was all too often absent within the *Panzertruppe*. If Reinhardt was at last prepared to prioritise the greater good, the temptation of a prominent public profile soon beckoned when news arrived that he had been selected to replace Hoth as the commander of Panzer Group 3 in early October.[192]

Reinhardt's gain came at the expense of Schmidt, who was passed over because he was told he could not be spared from the current combat situation in Army Group North. Schmidt's XXXIX Motorised

Figure 5.3 Erich Hoepner at the funeral of *SS-Gruppenführer* Arthur Mülverstedt, the first German divisional commander to be killed in the East (10 August 1941)

Army Corps was fighting defensive battles across the Neva River, south of Shlisselburg. By early October Hitler was pushing for a renewed offensive in the north,[193] which resulted in Schmidt being told by Bodewin Keitel from the Army Personnel Office that his relegation had been made necessary by 'the current combat situation, in particular by the impossibility of removing you from your current role, and in no way indicates an affront to your person'.[194] Whether Schmidt accepted this as such is hard to say because his letters make no mention of Hoth's departure or the appointment of his replacement. Of course, there were numerous subjects that Schmidt did not broach with Fridel. Nevertheless, observing Army Group Centre's much publicised advance, Schmidt wrote of his frustrations:

> The others always go to blessed fields, where they make smooth forward progress and earn fame and honour and barely have any losses. I am always sent into swamps and forests, where endlessly tough battles have to be endured, where the battles almost exceed human strength and I have to watch while my best men fall. The next imminent act will be pretty much the worst.[195]

Clearly, Schmidt had a very distorted view of what was happening on other sections of the Eastern Front. Given this, however, it seems logical that he might have felt a degree of resentment at being passed over for a higher command, especially one with such a potential for 'fame and honour' as Panzer Group 3.

There can be no denying Schmidt's assignment in the north was beyond his strength. Ostensibly, his weakened corps was supposed to link up with the Finnish Army east of Lake Ladoga, but just reaching the first major objective at Tikhvin was straining every resource at his disposal. Not surprisingly, this further encouraged Schmidt's self-centred view that his sector was the most dangerous and difficult. On 28 October he told Fridel: 'I am currently right up the creek like never before. I've unfortunately landed up in the worst and most difficult spot of the entire Eastern Front.'[196] Schmidt's corps finally occupied Tikhvin on 8 November, but it was exhausted by the effort and threatened by strong Soviet forces operating on the flanks. In itself, Tikhvin was a small, remote town of 16,000 inhabitants, but its strategic importance stemmed from the fact that it controlled the railway line to Lake Ladoga, the last Soviet line of supply to Leningrad.[197] In spite of his precarious position, which fell well short of his original objective, Schmidt was convinced, as he wrote to Fridel on 12 November, that he had 'achieved a great success'. He proudly noted Tikhvin's capture being mentioned in the *Sondermeldung* of 10 November and claimed 'congratulatory telegrams rained down from the top'.[198] There was no prospect of a further advance and Schmidt was aware that even holding Tikhvin would prove very difficult. Nevertheless, his mood had greatly improved, which was partly explained by the seizure of Tikhvin, but probably more by new orders from the OKH transferring him to the command of the Second Army in Army Group Centre. Not only was this a promotion to army command (at least temporarily as he was only standing in for Colonel-General Maximilian von Weichs who had reported ill),[199] but in Schmidt's mind he was leaving the most arduous sector of the Eastern Front. Somewhat disingenuously, given his past letters, Schmidt declared: 'It will be difficult for me to leave here.'[200] Yet by 24 November, Schmidt was enjoying his new army command, head-quartered in a major Soviet city (Orel) and discovering, as he told Fridel, that there was 'much less to do than with the corps'.[201]

If Schmidt thought he had at last reached the 'blessed fields' where he could make 'smooth forward progress', he was mistaken. The early hope that Operation Typhoon would lead to 'The Military End of the Bolsheviks', as the *Völkischer Beobachter* proclaimed on 10 October,[202] was not the experience of the other panzer generals leading Army Group Centre's advance. As Guderian informed Margarete on 24 October: 'It's now really no trivial affair to meet the demands of the leadership – which is disinclined to picture our exact situation, despite all the reports – with the number of increasingly weak divisions and the motor vehicles, which are now in a wretched state.'[203] The period of rapid victories had certainly passed, but the allocation of blame for the increasingly precarious position of the ill-equipped, poorly supplied and increasingly exposed German forces was only just beginning. Importantly, men like Guderian might well have privately acknow-ledged the wretched state of his forces, but, as he told Margarete, 'we want to succeed, and we must'.[204] If the generals at the OKH might rightly be reproached for their detached and aloof understanding of the conditions at the front, Guderian knew the situation far better, but ultimately drove his men on, exacerbating their exhaustion as well as their dangerous overextension. As Felix Römer's research confirmed, 'In the Wehrmacht [...] failure remained more damaging to one's reputation than cruelty.'[205] The imperative of avoiding failure, therefore, forced ever more downward pressure on subordinates to achieve increasingly unreal-istic goals. The sheer scale of what was being attempted in the East was never able to be questioned (nor would such questioning have been tolerated) and therefore failure had to have a more devolved form of explanation that usually scapegoated individual command decisions within the army for systemic problems.

As a case in point, at the end of November, Hoepner complained to Irma that his progress was slow because he had been stripped of forces by Kluge and Guderian.[206] Hoepner's claim once again ignored the Red Army's role in Panzer Group 4's difficulties. Even if Hoepner had been forced to give up some resources, his panzer group remained the best-resourced and numerically strongest concentration of armoured forces on the Eastern Front.[207] Crying poor was, therefore, a harder claim to make, but Hoepner's next allegation substituted his claim of insufficient strength with one of abandonment. As he told Irma on 29 November: 'Every day, I telephone with Bock and Kluge, in an attempt to persuade them to commence their attack, too. [...] The Russians are bringing up new forces from all sides. I stand alone.'[208] Just as Schmidt had earlier believed, Hoepner insisted that the Soviets were able to concentrate all their forces on him because Kluge's Fourth Army was supposedly refusing to take part in the attack.[209] As the German offensive slowed to a crawl in early December, Hoepner again took aim at Army Group Centre's two field marshals:

> I demanded that Kluge should also attack, so that not all Russian divisions and armoured brigades could be deployed against me. On 1 December, others attacked, too, but with entirely insufficient forces, and they were then withdrawn again yesterday. Instead, Bock took a division from me overnight, and one that I was just about to deploy at the focal point of my further attack. [...] the offensive power of my [leading] corps is at an end.[210]

Even at the point of admitting his defeat, one sees how blinkered Hoepner's understanding of events was. Kluge and Bock were hardly the difference between success and failure, when one considers how utterly insufficient German forces were for the stated objective of encircling Moscow. In fact, the two field marshals had from the beginning aggressively supported the offensive and continued it well beyond its strategic rationale. If anything, the problem was chronic overcommitment, not a lack thereof.

For all the accusations levelled within Army Group Centre, there was universal agreement among the panzer generals that the late autumn offensive needed to be pursued to the last possible moment. North of Moscow, Hoepner and Reinhardt had relentlessly driven their panzer groups forward, while Guderian attacked far to the south on multiple fronts.[211] Schmidt proved so aggressive that even after 5 December, when Army Group Centre finally called a halt to all offensive actions, the Second Army defied numerous orders in order to continue attacking.[212] No one could claim the panzer generals had been hounded into action and the consequences for their long-suffering men stand in stark contrast to their much-professed concerns. Yet almost as soon as the German offensive had been called off the recriminations began. As Guderian wrote to Margarete on 8 December:

> We are facing the sad fact that the senior leadership has over-done things, did not want to believe the reports of the troops' declining combat strength, only made demands, did not make provisions for the harsh winter and was now surprised by the Russian cold of minus 35 degrees. The strength of the troops was no longer sufficient to carry out the attack on Moscow, so that, with a heavy heart, I had to resolve on the evening of 5 December to break off the unwinnable battle, and to retreat to a previously selected, relatively short line, which I hope to just about be able to hold with the remainder of my forces.[213]

The emerging calamity overtaking Army Group Centre turned an already toxic command culture into a cut-throat survival of the fittest. Guderian was incredulous at the turn of events and told Margarete he 'never believed that such a positively radiant military situation' of early October could be so utterly squandered 'through sheer pig-headedness'.[214] Of course, it is only because Guderian so utterly failed to grasp the strategic factors overshadowing Germany's operational successes that he believed there was ever such a bright period in the Eastern campaign.

Hoepner's fury extended so far as to point the finger directly at Hitler, telling Irma: 'It provokes fierce rage to think that the whole thing would have worked out, if the carelessness of a gambler had not prevailed [...] a halt ought to have been called after the battle of Viaz'ma.'[215] Having decried the supposed inactivity of his fellow generals, as Hoepner led the charge to Moscow, the sudden change of heart accompanied by 'fierce rage' that the offensive had not been stopped after Viaz'ma seems extraordinary. Schmidt joined the chorus of disbelief at the change in fortunes, insisting the turn of events was 'simply astounding'.[216] The fact that the panzer generals were so blindsided by events not only raises many questions about their basic comprehension of the war, but also suggests that little had been learned from their previous experiences. Throughout 1941, the Soviets had time and again found reserves to reconstitute their shattered front, but, unwilling to consider that this might again follow Typhoon's early success, the panzer generals surged ahead heedless of the danger posed by a potential counteroffensive.

From 6 December the Soviet winter offensive steadily gathered pace, exerting more and more pressure on the weakened and exposed armoured forces, and causing the panzer generals to direct all of their anger and blame against the senior leadership. Bereft of support and fearing the rout of his panzer army, Guderian wrote to Margarete on 10 December that 'the higher-ups were still living in cloud cuckoo land'.[217] There was a good measure of truth in this, but Guderian's conversion from a similar realm of fantasy cannot be ignored. Reinhardt made the same embittered point to Eva: 'the higher-ups are still palming us off with appreciation, positively inexplicable trust in the capabilities of my troops, with empty promises that don't help us one bit and with ridiculous orders, which must have emerged from complete ignorance'.[218] Hoepner also lashed out at the high command, again targeting Bock and Kluge as the troublesome pair who, he said, were 'calling from behind, asking this and that, giving advice and issuing orders that cannot be carried out'.[219] Having exercised a great deal of independence during the five and a half months of the German offensive, rejecting any imposition on their authority and jockeying to be the first in line for the anticipated acclaim, the panzer generals then distanced themselves from any responsibility for the state of affairs.

While much is made of the camaraderie and companionship within the German army,[220] the officer ranks were marked by far less cohesion and cooperation. Felix Römer's review of the secretly recorded conversations of lower-ranked German officers at their Fort Hunt detention camp showed: 'It was not uncommon for officers to place themselves above each other when it came to conflicts when working together. Everyone blamed someone else – they all claimed to have done everything right.'[221] Given the cult of individualism within the Wehrmacht's command, where an officer was personally responsible to 'make things happen', often irrespective of circumstances, there existed far fewer 'explanations' for failure. Enemy strength, vast distances, lack of supplies, exhausted men were beside the point because success and failure were indivisible from the human factor; the

commander's 'will' to find a way predominated. That more than anything determined the course of events, which meant setbacks or adverse
results required identifying who had blundered. The need to find
a scapegoat for poor results was therefore commonplace, which not
only accounts for the furious attacks on the high command, but in turn
opened the panzer generals to attack from their own subordinates. After
5 December Reinhardt depicted the atmosphere within his command as
'a gruelling game' that required 'putting on a brave face to those below
and a very severe choice of words for those above'.[222] Appearing before
his men, Reinhardt admitted to feelings of guilt as well as unspoken
reproaches for leading his panzer group into such a dire situation. 'I
involuntarily brood on whether I have made mistakes,' he disclosed to
Eva. The tension stemming from all the events that surrounded him and
his own expectation to control the outcome was on full display when
Reinhardt asked, 'how much I am to blame for the unfortunate turn of
events in our advance?' Reinhardt feared the judgement of his men, who
had no doubt internalised the same set of cultural precepts.
Acknowledging his inability to control events, Reinhardt asked: 'Do
they condemn me for it?!' Having to return to his duties, Reinhardt
provided the answer to his own question, concluding his letter, 'now
I must face the music'.[223]

If Reinhardt feared his authority might be questioned by his
subordinates, Hoepner was openly confronted by a constant barrage
of damning critiques written by one of his corps commanders,
General of Infantry Hermann Geyer, commanding the IX Army
Corps.[224] Ironically, just as Hoepner had himself presented an all-
knowing prescience as to what should have happened in the Eastern
campaign, so too did his disgruntled subordinate. As Hoepner related
the series of complaints to Irma: 'Geyer is dreadful, always
a pessimist, knows it all better, foresees all misfortune, writes
a report every day, in which he makes accusations against me or
Beaulieu but praises his own leadership.' Hoepner, of course, saw
none of the irony and accepted none of the blame, responding with
a pointed letter that Geyer 'can take to heart over Christmas'.
Longer-term, Hoepner had another solution in mind: 'I'll ask for
him to be replaced.'[225]

Schmidt's December letters did not directly elaborate on his
relations with his subordinates, although one might imagine that,
being relatively new to his command, he avoided some of the bad

blood or past resentment that came to the fore in times of crisis. Yet Schmidt alluded to his helplessness in command, telling Fridel: 'I often feel utterly dejected by all the suffering and heroism of these brave troops, but I can't change it.' The inability to control events might also have undermined some of Schmidt's authority, especially without a long-standing relationship to his commanders. Not only was he new to his post, Schmidt was also concerned that, as a temporary stand-in for Weichs, his position may not have been afforded the same measure of respect. As he told Fridel: 'It's not easy at all. At any rate, it's considerably more difficult as a "representative" than if you are the proper leader.'[226] Authority in command during a crisis is paramount and if Schmidt felt Weichs left big shoes to fill, from 26 December he also inherited Guderian's larger Second Panzer Army.[227] As Schmidt admitted, the weight of this dual responsibility 'costs a great deal of nerve strain'.[228]

It is less surprising that Guderian's letters wasted no time on the views of his subordinates. Apart from the fact that he did enjoy unique popularity among the panzer generals, it seems that those under his command who doubted his abilities rarely made their opinions known to him. Even in the midst of the winter crisis, Guderian's inflated self-belief provided little scope for self-reflection or doubt, especially with regard to his own performance. Indeed, ever aware that the optics of career-building rested as much on the perception of military success as anything substantive, Guderian's instinct was immediately to control the narrative surrounding the withdrawal of his panzer army. Rather than simply complain to Margarete about the faults of the high command, on 10 December Guderian announced his intention to write to Schmundt (Hitler's chief military adjutant) and Bodewin Keitel (head of the Army Personnel Office) 'in order to remove any illusions they might still be under'.[229] At this point, Guderian shrewdly avoided blaming the OKH or OKW, to which Keitel and Schmundt respectively belonged, and took aim at his fellow army commanders. According to Guderian, the real problems were with Kluge's Fourth Army and Schmidt's Second Army on his northern and southern flanks. Their inability to manage the crisis was the real reason behind the Second Panzer Army's retreat. As Guderian explained, the problems 'intensify from day to day, less regarding my own army, which is still united and tightly managed, than the sometimes more seriously vulnerable neighbours, whose fate naturally continues to have an influence on my own'.[230] Guderian's letters to Schmundt and Keitel are not known to have survived, but this was how he explained the intended content to Margarete. Apart from removing himself from any blame and providing the necessary scapegoats, Guderian also hoped that his letters might prompt more decisive action from above. As he told Margarete: 'My letters will hopefully reach the correct addresses in time, because a clear realisation and a strong will could still help to save some things.'[231]

That Guderian tailored his message to win over his audience and was always prepared to turn on anyone is seen from his next letter to Margarete, in which his problems were no longer the result of his neighbouring army commanders, but once again caused by the baneful ignorance of the higher command. Not mincing his words, Guderian wrote: 'The people from the OKH and OKW, who have never seen the front, have no idea of these conditions; they merely wire impossible orders and reject all requests and submissions.'[232] Yet even this was not entirely true. After receiving Guderian's letter, Schmundt swiftly replied and even flew to Second Panzer Army's headquarters to write a first-hand report for Hitler. This impressed Guderian, who expressed more faith in Hitler finding a resolution to the crisis than any of his fellow generals.[233] Given the centrality of Hitler's hubris in dramatically over-estimating Germany's military commitments in the East, Guderian's continued faith that the dictator was the one solution to the *Ostheer*'s crisis, rather than its principal problem, is symptomatic of the panzer general's own deficient understanding of events.

While Guderian was clearly prepared to blame others for the problems within Army Group Centre, the reality was that the Second Panzer Army was initially much more exposed than Kluge's Fourth Army. Discussing the Second Panzer Army's position with Hoepner, Kluge expressed his concerns, but Hoepner was unsympathetic: 'G[uderian] wanted to operate lavishly and has now distributed all his divisions over large expanses [...] The Russians have now broken right through in three places and are threatening to encircle individual groups.'[234] This was much closer to the reality than Guderian's rendition of events to Margarete. Far from Kluge's problems impacting Guderian, the reverse was true; Guderian's shattered left flank left the Fourth Army exposed and open in the south.[235] For all the inherent danger of the situation, Hoepner's depiction of Guderian's predicament was both reproachful (Guderian 'wanted to operate lavishly') and also hypocritical, given Hoepner had himself advocated the offensive at every turn and likewise suffered major reverses as a result. To make matters worse, Kluge had left the Fourth Army to replace Bock as commander of Army Group Centre, but his own replacement, General of Mountain Troops Ludwig Kübler, had not yet arrived. 'It's an absolute mess,' Hoepner wrote to Irma, but, which is illustrative of the individualistic command culture, he was only too glad to avoid being Kluge's replacement. Not only was Hoepner keen to avoid inheriting the serious problems in the south, but also he judged that retaining command of Panzer Group 4 offered the best pathway for advancing his own career. As he told Irma: 'Thank God they haven't brought me in. Here, however, I have the strongest army on the Eastern Front, and I can only improve my title.'[236] Such vanity in the midst of a crisis says a lot about the sordid loyalties driving the senior ranks of the *Panzertruppe*.

While Bock was still in command of Army Group Centre, he established a novel method of dealing with the mercenary behaviour of his panzer commanders. As sections of the front crumbled, Bock naturally sought to transfer reserves, however limited, from stronger armies to more threatened sectors of the front. Hoepner's formidable panzer group was an obvious surplus target, especially when the neighbouring panzer group, commanded by Reinhardt, found itself in the path of the main Soviet attack north of Moscow. Yet it was not as a simple as Bock issuing the orders for the transfer of men or equipment. The panzer generals became single-mindedly protectionist and cried poor whenever asked to give up formations, even when nominally asked to support one of their own. As the crisis began, Hoepner wrote to Irma: 'While I face the adversity of withdrawing my corps in heavy fighting without leaving wounded and artillery lying there, my northern neighbour, Reinhardt, has caved in, in other words, a serious crisis has taken place. Everyone is crying out for help. I should release forces, they claim.'[237] Hoepner acknowledged Reinhardt had 'caved in' and was experiencing 'a serious crisis', but he still flatly refused to send help, resulting in what he dubbed 'a very serious dispute'. Bock's novel solution, therefore, was to subordinate Reinhardt's panzer group to Hoepner's command, making him responsible for the security of this section of the front. 'What a lovely task!'[238] Hoepner sarcastically reported to Irma. Yet the move had the desired effect because it appealed to the same self-centred impulse that forestalled cooperation in the first place; Hoepner's prestige and standing had grown again, he commanded more formations across a longer stretch of front and he potentially stood to gain by restoring the situation – not to mention avoiding a calamity on his immediate flank. This is not to say Hoepner was happy with the move, but Bock only cared that his recalcitrant panzer generals were at last responding to the crisis.

At considerable cost, Hoepner and Reinhardt survived the December onslaught; they had lost much ground as well as irreplaceable equipment, but none of their major formations were cut off or destroyed by the Soviet advance. Yet Hoepner was still not satisfied, seeing Reinhardt's difficulties as having adversely taxed his own strength. Aggravated at the imposition, on 23 December he wrote to Irma: 'Panzer Group 3 was subordinated to me on 8 December, at a time when it could no longer maintain itself. It is largely to blame for my misfortune.'[239] It was yet another example of the siloed compartmentalisation of the Eastern Front, in which the panzer generals expected to be left alone when others needed help, but demanded that the high command respond when they were in trouble. Not surprisingly, on 9 December when Reinhardt was being overwhelmed, he complained to Eva that his panzer group had been forced to 'fend for ourselves, as so often', and then continued: 'In spite of repeated exhortations and requests by us, we had not been supplied with sufficient forces, which we vitally needed in order to consolidate our successes.'[240] As the situation stabilised by the end of the month, both as a result of Hoepner's support and because of Soviet priorities shifting to other German armies, Reinhardt suddenly struck a very different tone. Having withdrawn to the relative security of the Lama River,[241] Reinhardt at last enjoyed a reprieve, but the crisis in Army Group Centre had only moved to Colonel-General Adolf Strauss's Ninth Army, directly north of Reinhardt. Suddenly, the shoe was on the other foot and Reinhardt was being expected to act in support of Strauss. Reinhardt, however, was indignant at the prospect. He expressed no sympathy for Strauss and, like Hoepner before him, showed no understanding that the security of the Ninth Army was directly tied to maintaining his own position on the Lama. Having so bitterly complained that the high command had ignored his previous pleas for help, Reinhardt felt no shame in writing to Eva on 28 December:

> Unfortunately, today was once more a very tense day, again due to problems for our neighbours, while my brave chaps at the front were able to repulse all Russian attacks outright. I therefore had to quarrel with the neighbouring commanders

and convince them that we will not be affected by their adversity. Hoepner, the other neighbour, was very reasonable and fully agreed with me, so that we established a united front against our superiors.[242]

Hoepner, of course, had never wanted to come to Reinhardt's aid, so he was vehemently opposed to helping Strauss as well – allowing the two panzer generals to suddenly find common cause in their mutual opposition. To make matters worse, Kübler's Fourth Army, to Hoepner's south, was haemorrhaging from its open southern flank, courtesy of Guderian's initial neglect and subsequent indifference to a Soviet breakthrough of his lines. Hoepner and Reinhardt were therefore resisting calls to send support south as well as north, arguing that the lateral movement of men and equipment was simply not possible in the conditions. Someone in the high command consulted with the institutional arm of the panzer corps and this body maintained that at least some movement would in fact be possible. Reinhardt was furious. He explained to Eva that his opposition was not based on obstinacy, but the tangible realities of the winter. 'Time and again, the two of us [including Hoepner] observe how little other commanders from the panzer branch know or want to know, that is, can in no way assess what we are capable of accomplishing and what we sometimes, like now in the snow, simply cannot accomplish!'[243] As previous events during the initial retreat had shown, and subsequent requirements in January 1942 further revealed, movement in the snow was slow but certainly possible. Reinhardt and Hoepner were simply determined to safeguard their own section of the front, which by the end of the year was scarcely under attack, leaving their besieged neighbours to their fate.

Having abandoned all responsibility for the crisis, Reinhardt even had the audacity to question whether Strauss and Kübler were somehow overstating their problems when even the most cursory glance at Army Group Centre's daily briefing maps showed the precipitous danger of the situation. As Reinhardt wrote to Eva on 31 December:

New Year's Eve! Full of tension, worry, work and frustration, unfortunately! That's not the state of affairs with us; on the contrary: yesterday, when I spent all day at the front, I could only delight in how steadily and spiritedly our troops are holding out in spite of all the difficulties we've experienced and in

spite of all the hardships inflicted on our troops by the enemy
and, even more so, the winter. Thank God that this is the case;
panzer troops have their own pride and their own merits. But
even the most virtuous cannot live in peace when the mean
neighbour is not satisfied! Both flanks are cause for concern
for us; we are always positioned between two fires, regardless of
whether we should help them by giving them the shirt off our
back, whether things are really so dire for our neighbour or
whether we ought to remain tough in order that we don't run
into danger ourselves. Furthermore, we are put under pressure
by those above us, who claim that we are in a position to help,
evidently because they have unlimited faith in the panzer troops.
You can imagine how gruelling this stressful game is; we can
only explain to our commanders that _we_ are not to blame for
this disharmony and have to constantly hope that everything
will turn out well with God's help.[244]

Having washed his hands of the matter and exempted himself from any
blame, Reinhardt's final letter of 1941 encapsulates so many of the
behaviours exhibited by the panzer generals in Operation Barbarossa:
the total abrogation of responsibility, the disregard for higher authority,
the pre-eminence of self-interest in decision-making and the potential
for ruthlessness, even towards one's own comrades. Robert Citino has
argued that the German 'way of war' was always built on a certain
headstrong independence of command,[245] but, as Michael Geyer argued,
the new age of machine warfare radicalised an already diffuse system
of command: 'Blitzkrieg pitted staffs and commanders against each other
in the quest for optimal performance in the planning and conduct of
warfare. It created competing operational bases and very often left
undecided which one would capture the initiative. [...] What was truly
novel, however, was the dissolution of the corporate professional unity of
the military leadership.'[246]

For all the endemic problems of the Wehrmacht and its corrup-
tion under National Socialism, the intellectual and cultural heritage of
the German army was already deeply problematic long before the Nazis
took power. The pre-1918 Imperial Army officer corps, in which the
panzer generals began their careers, was a long way from the popular
notion of a lucid, cohesive, professionalised and highly efficient 'military
brain'. The extreme conservatism fostered within the late imperial

officer corps and its long resistance to a world that was changing both socially and politically led to an increasing rupture with reality. This isolated the officer corps from the rest of Wilhelmine society and allowed an increasingly distorted and self-deceiving ideology to take root.[247] Not only was the army separated from civil society, but the rejection of any reform and inability to embrace change increasingly undermined its professional duties and transformed the officer corps into a self-perpetuating clique. Moreover, as Martin Kitchen has observed, 'Even after the total defeat of the German army [in the First World War] the officer corps was to emerge again with most of the fondest prejudices of the Wilhelmine period unchanged.'[248] Precisely what those 'prejudices' were is illustrated most clearly by Isabel Hull in her detailed study of German military culture from the late nineteenth and early twentieth centuries, providing a remarkable juxtaposition with the *Panzertruppe* in 1941. As Hull concluded:

> One of the most striking qualities of the imperial German military establishment was the combination of operative and tactical effectiveness with apparent irrationality: the inflated and exclusivist definition of victory (in the Clausewitzian sense of complete annihilation of the enemy forces); the rigid adherence to the tactic of offensive envelopment; the rejection of realistic planning for provisioning and maintenance; the inability to estimate the enemy's strengths (a product of the necessity to assume professional superiority); the tendency to repetitive actionism at the cost of disproportionate destruction and even self-annihilation; the inability to admit defeat or to learn from it; and the overreliance on officers' moral qualities of daring, foolhardiness and optimistic self-sacrifice.[249]

A longer-term institutional and cultural context for the German officer corps does not excuse, but it does help explain the actions and behaviour of the panzer generals. There could be no doubt a mercenary individualistic culture predominated within the *Panzertruppe*, a fact not unique to the end-of-year crisis in 1941, but certainly exacerbated by it. Problems and challenges were viewed, and responses formulated, from a position of near total self-regard. The army group command was, therefore, forced into 'negotiations' to cajole and convince the panzer generals to act on their orders. Unlike the lower ranks of the German army, where orders were seldom the subject of discussion or interpretation, the panzer generals insisted upon an unusual degree of autonomy that, especially in difficult situations, could be taken to extremes. It was therefore no surprise that Guderian was fired in late December after repeatedly failing to adhere to the most categorical orders to halt his retreat. That this was a cultural phenomenon, indicative of the *Panzertruppe*, is shown by the fact that Guderian's staff and subordinates were indignant that he could be dismissed and believed he should have been allowed to direct his panzer army as he saw fit.[250] Moreover, Schmidt, who took over Guderian's Second Panzer Army, had himself just conducted an unauthorised retreat for which he made no apology.[251] Less than two weeks later, Hoepner followed in Guderian's footsteps by undertaking an unsanctioned withdrawal, for which he was also fired from command. He too departed with the backing and support of his staff.[252] Reinhardt's unwillingness to help Strauss ended when he was subordinated to the Ninth Army. Shortly thereafter, Reinhardt began pressing Strauss to undertake unauthorised withdrawals, which Strauss refused to allow.[253] It all underpinned a well-established culture of headstrong insistence upon autonomous command, which no doubt benefited the panzer corps during its daring attack and exploitation phases, but for a long and difficult campaign it led to a host of serious problems that repeatedly undermined the German army's effectiveness.

For a supposedly integrated army that depended upon all its constituent parts for its coherence, the independence of the *Panzertruppe*, often mythologised for its audacious successes, also had a baneful influence upon the *Ostheer*'s command culture. The panzer generals fought the war on their own terms, leading to private agendas that meant they could not always be relied upon to follow orders. They prioritised their own self-aggrandisement and jealously competed with one another for military awards and public recognition. Such narcissistic command forsook the common good for personal prestige and individual ambition. The fact that the panzer generals could not see beyond their own selfish interests was a general failing of their corps and of the army that tolerated it.

CONCLUSION

In Nazi Germany advancing to the highest ranks of the army was not simply a mark of professional achievement; it brought personal enrichment (through Hitler's private payments) as well as public celebrity. No other arm of the Wehrmacht provided a better springboard for such advancement than the dynamic *Panzertruppe*. As we have seen, such career inducements were not immaterial factors in motivating the generals and, to no small extent, served to pervert their priorities and conduct as military men. Professional duties and service to the army clashed with the yearning for individual recognition and reward. The same pressures also shaped their reporting of events, with problems typically leveraged to denounce others in the high command, while serious issues presented by the Red Army, the Eastern climate or the poor infrastructure were ignored or underappreciated. Hitler, as the ultimate patron, was typically spared criticism and, when the occasion presented itself, the culture of embracing 'can-do' personalities, over pessimists and naysayers, prefaced what information was provided and how it was presented. Hence, when Guderian visited Hitler in August 1941, ostensibly to challenge the dictator's decision to attack into Ukraine, he instead disavowed his previous commitments to the other generals and abruptly adopted Hitler's view.[1] Such behaviour has often been ascribed to the power of the 'Führer myth', which certainly played a role, but the generals were also self-interested, and their ambition drove conformity. In this sense they were not just giving in to Hitler, they were giving in to their desire for advancement, which came even at the expense of their strictly professional judgements. The 'Führer myth' should not, therefore, simply be accepted as a reflection of Hitler's infallibility in the eyes of the generals, although this was sometimes the case.

The letters of the panzer generals also offer an intriguing insight into their distorted understanding of command. Perhaps here the predominance of the 'Führer myth' served another purpose, acting as an example of leadership that rejected collaborative decision-making and emphasised the imposition of a dominant will. This would have appeared as a natural extension of the panzer commander's role, whose cultural ethos already demanded that a commander impose himself upon his enemy and set the agenda. Any idea of collective decision-making probably smacked of weakness, compromise and delay, the very things they believed undermined a rapid war of manoeuvre. Of course, not everything resulted in disagreement within the higher ranks of German command and the early successes helped smooth relations, but importantly, when conflicts erupted the chain of command did not suffice to determine outcomes as much as personalities did. Germany's Eastern Front was therefore less a unified, cohesive command organisation than a competing arena of devolved commands, some more loyal to the central idea than others. Moreover, the trend intensified throughout 1941, as resources were stretched and pressures built, making the army, and especially the panzer group commanders, increasingly suspicious of centralised command and much more insistent upon localised, autonomous control. This shift emboldened the natural instincts of the panzer generals and, as the overall situation worsened, they saw no problem in disputing orders, either openly or through some form of subterfuge.

By contrast, there was a far greater unity of command in German occupation policies, especially in 1941. In fact, the pressure of scant resources made the exploitation of the Soviet civilian population, and the ruthless eradication of any opposition, a common goal. From the spring of 1942 Schmidt had begun taking a much more critical view of German practices in the East, not out of any altruistic concerns, but rather as a pragmatic longer-term solution to local shortages as well as to counteract the increasingly dangerous security situation in his rear area.[2] Reinhardt's Third Panzer Army followed suit as of summer 1943 with new orders stating that 'the requirements of total war demand the complete use of every individual. [...] the Russian population must be internally won over through correct treatment and be fully utilized.'[3] Of course, there can be little doubt that Schmidt and Reinhardt were compelled to change their views by the dual failures of Germany's iron-fisted rule coupled with the inability to break the Red Army's resistance. Importantly, none of the panzer generals opposed Germany's draconian methods when victory was anticipated in 1941 and records show they disproportionately implemented murderous policies such as the Commissar Order. Moreover, in the more than 50,000 words that make up their collective 1941 correspondence, there is not a word of pity, indignation or shame at the mass murder of Soviet Jews. Nor is there a critical word for Germany's occupation policy generally. Subsequent self-serving changes to their own local occupation policies, post-war denials of wrongdoing or participation in the July Plot does not expunge their record of complicity and compliance.

The ability to market themselves successfully on a public and political stage was, if anything, the most noteworthy and, until relatively recently, the most enduring achievement of the panzer generals. They continued to build their careers and profiles through the ever-changing worlds of Imperial Germany, the Weimar Republic, Hitler's dictatorship and West Germany. They were remarkably skilful at ingratiating themselves with influential members of the military and political establishments, while their unflinching self-confidence proved as convincing as it was disarming. In addition, they each seemed to understand that broader public relations, seeking to build their prominence and status among their soldiers as well as the general German population, was the cornerstone of the greatest possible success. Here Guderian was the quintessential visionary, manipulator and propagandist, ruthlessly and innovatively dedicated to advancing himself, uninhibited by military tradition, personal effrontery or ethical concerns. Not surprisingly, his career flourished, despite major setbacks, such as his ignominious dismissal from command in 1941, but even more remarkable was his post-war reinvention from a leading man in the National Socialist regime to a supposedly tragic German war hero. Guderian not only escaped any accountability or justice; he obtained a post-war celebrity that surpassed his wartime fame. With former rivals like Rommel out of the way, Guderian rewrote his role in the war and became not only the father of the *Panzertruppe*, but the sane voice of reason attempting to steer Hitler away from one bad decision after another. In his own narrative Guderian appeared as the brilliant and honourable man hopelessly outmatched by the tide of events and the dreadful people directing them. Of course, he was telling his captors what they wanted to hear and, in a secretly recorded conversation during his short period of internment after the war, Guderian told other senior officers of his admiration for Hitler and the National Socialist state and of his contempt for the allies.[4] Whatever Guderian privately believed, he knew which way the wind was blowing. Perhaps having learned the lesson of engaging Kernmayr as a biographer in 1941, he then dedicated himself to the task of writing his memoir. The result, *Panzer Leader*, was a commercial best-seller in both the United States and the United Kingdom, solidifying Guderian's reputation for decades to come.[5] Having achieved the pinnacle of his fame and popularity, even within former enemy countries, Guderian died at age sixty-five in May 1954.

Margarete Guderian's wartime activities involved being a member of a board for the German Red Cross (an organisation to which she had belonged since 1913).[6] Her letters only make mention of having to attend a single meeting for the supervision of a military hospital.[7] Most of her reported activities seemed to revolve around socialising. Margarete also belonged to the Nazi Party, the National Socialist Women's League and the National Socialist People's Welfare, but there is no evidence that these memberships entailed any actual responsibilities.[8] Aged just forty-eight in 1941, Margarete was by no means beyond working age. Already in 1940, some 41 per cent of Germany's workforce was made up of women and their representation only increased as the war went on.[9] Yet, consistent with her privileged status, Margarete, and the elite class to which she belonged, were basically exempt from war work. She certainly served to support her husband and sons by, as Claudia Koonz put it, 'normalizing a masculine world gone amok'.[10] There is no available information on Margarete's post-war life, but from 1948 she was reunited with Heinz (after his post-war internment) to enjoy their final years together. She survived him by eighteen years, dying in 1972 at age seventy-eight. Both of the Guderian sons survived the war: in 1956 Heinz Günther returned to join the new West German Bundeswehr, rising to the rank of Major-General and serving in his father's former position as Inspector of Panzer Troops. Heinz Günther died at the age of ninety in 2004. Kurt Guderian rose to the rank of Captain in the Second World War and died in 1984 at the same age as his father (sixty-five).

Like Guderian, Reinhardt enjoyed a similarly extraordinary transition from fanatical wartime loyalist to a thriving post-war success story. In his case, overcoming indictment and conviction at the High Command Trial, one of the subsequent Nuremberg trials, proved just how low one could sink before returning to a highly successful career. Reinhardt fought his conviction every step of the way, and even after being sentenced to fifteen years' imprisonment appealed on humanitarian grounds for early release. Reinhardt had no respect for the judgement against him, indignantly believing he was the victim of 'victor's justice'.[11] Given that he was found guilty of countless 'crimes against humanity' and 'war crimes' (two of the four counts he faced), there was a certain irony in his 'humanitarian' appeal, which he based upon a request to care for his psychotic adult daughter who had attempted suicide.[12] Reinhardt even enjoyed the support of the West German Chancellor, Konrad Adenauer,[13] while organisations of veterans forcefully campaigned for the release of what they dubbed 'so-called war criminals'.[14] Reinhardt's appeal was successful and in 1952 he was released. Having gained his freedom, Reinhardt took on the chairmanship of the recently established *Gesellschaft für Wehrkunde*, an association nominally dedicated to promoting German defence issues. The organisation also incorporated many former army officers and, through its numerous publications, helped further the many myths of the 'clean Wehrmacht'.[15] Reinhardt served in this role from 1954 until 1963 and for his long service was awarded the Order of Merit of the Federal Republic of Germany in November 1962. Just as his loyal service to the Nazi state qualified him for an army group command and the prodigious Swords to his Knight's Cross (awarded in May 1944), Reinhardt was able to throw off the stigma of his fascist sympathies and criminal past to achieve continued high-profile success in West Germany. He died aged seventy-six in November 1963, one year after Eva passed away.

Hoepner was killed in August 1944 for his part in the July Plot and his legacy was shaped almost entirely by his participation in the resistance, gaining a longevity that well surpassed his death. Until her own death in 1966, Irma advocated for her husband's memory, corresponding with former officers and public officials to advance Hoepner's reputation as one of Germany's heroic resistance fighters. There can be no question Hoepner's final role in the history of the Nazi state showed courage, which he continued to display at his show trial,[16] but it does

Figure 6.1 Georg-Hans Reinhardt (far right) at his Nuremberg trial of the German high command in February 1948

not expunge his past loyalty and service to the Nazi state.[17] The fact that his military career was terminated by Hitler provided its own impetus for an ambitious man to regain status and position under a new regime. In that sense Hoepner was no different from Guderian or Reinhardt, both of whom changed their allegiance when it best suited their circumstances and prospective career prospects.

Hoepner's post-war legacy has been eulogised in numerous histories of the July Plot. To the extent that his military career was considered, he was portrayed as having skilfully participated in Germany's early victories and then, in his greatest act of service, risked his life in the fight against Nazism. It was a simplistic narrative, but an effective one, and in a country desperate for anti-Nazi heroes, the German public asked few questions. In 1956, on what would have been his seventieth birthday, Hoepner's former high school (Kaiserin-Augusta Gymnasium) in Berlin was renamed 'Erich Hoepner Schule' in his honour. The dedication speech to students and staff by West Berlin Senator Julius Lipschitz claimed, 'we are allowed to declare that the lights of humanity did not go out in Germany's darkest epoch, you should be thankful for this [...] Erich Hoepner's legacy is fulfilled.'[18] The West German military followed suit in 1969, renaming their Saarburg Barracks in Wuppertal-Elberfeld 'Colonel-General Hoepner Barracks'. Hoepner had served at this barracks in 1938 as the commander of the 1st Light Division (later 6th Panzer Division).[19] Fortunately, Germany's ongoing reckoning with its National Socialist past ensured the barracks was renamed in 1994 and the school finally voted to drop the name in 2008, becoming the 'Heinz Berggruen Gymnasium'.[20] Yet at least three German streets are still named after him (in Düsseldorf, Neuss and Wuppertal)[21] and memorial plaques are found at the Bundeshaus in Berlin as well as outside his former residence in Wuppertal.

Schmidt was the exception to the rule among the panzer generals, spending most of his post-war life in Soviet captivity and gaining almost no post-war status. Unlike in the Anglo-American world, which, thanks to the public advocacy of men like Basil Liddell Hart, proved somewhat sympathetic to the plight of the imprisoned German generals,[22] the Soviet state had no such consideration. Arrested in 1947, Schmidt could not even write letters to his family until June 1955. He was not accorded any privileges of rank. Schmidt was forced to share a communal cell and given bed linen that was too small, but the prison authorities refused to exchange it.[23] In keeping with the practice of adapting to his new political environment, Schmidt proved himself a model prisoner with a Soviet report observing: 'During his stay in the detention centres, he did not violate the rules of the prison regime. He was not subjected to administrative punishments. He remained calm in the cell. He is friendly with the prison staff. He did not express his political views to the inmates.'[24] In 1955, aged sixty-eight, Schmidt's health deteriorated sharply. He complained of dizziness, headaches, physical weakness and lack of concentration and had trouble sleeping. Schmidt received months of treatment in the prison, but his condition did not improve.[25] In spite of his conviction for war crimes, in January 1956 Schmidt was included among the last of the German prisoners of war to be repatriated, having served more than eight years in a variety of Soviet prisons. Schmidt had regained his freedom, but not his health; he died fifteen months later in April 1957.

For all that the private letters of the panzer generals reveal about their wartime experiences, their most enduring legacy is not to be found anywhere in their writings, because it is not about the generals themselves but rather the consequences of their actions. Hundreds of thousands of German soldiers served under them, many until their deaths. An even greater number of Soviet soldiers opposed them, suffering untold casualties as a consequence of their service. Beyond the lives destroyed at the front, the advance of the panzer groups placed millions of vulnerable civilians under Nazi occupation, leading to atrocities on a scale that the world had scarcely believed possible. These countless miseries must also find a place in the legacies of Guderian, Hoepner, Reinhardt and Schmidt. At the end of the day, making their names, earning their promotions and winning their awards came at a horrific cost in human lives, but one they were always prepared to pay.

AFTERWORD

The original plan for this study was to conclude with a series of appendices reproducing each of the letter collections (including Margarete's) as unabridged and fully annotated documents. Unlike other material held by the German Federal Military Archive, reproducing private papers requires a check to see if any publishing constraints were stipulated by the family members who donated the material. In each of these cases no such prohibition existed. Upon that basis I started my work; however, the archival authorities soon expressed reservations. The letter collections were donated before formal questions were asked about what may be done with the donated material, and the fear was that the generals' descendants might challenge any publication. The result was a request that I sign an indemnity form undertaking all legal responsibility for any future prosecution based on a claim of misuse. I agreed to this. Many months passed before the archive had another change of heart. They were no longer satisfied with the indemnity and opted to invoke German copyright law, which stipulates that an author's work is protected from unauthorised publication for seventy years following their death. That immediately precluded all but Hoepner's letters being published in this volume. I decided it had to be all or nothing.[1]

The decision to impose copyright law upon these collections is unfortunate. The letters are currently publicly available documents, freely donated by the families without any conditions of use. They are of major public and historical interest, concerning men at the heart of Germany's largest and most costly war. Given the devastation wrought and criminality perpetrated, if the question then becomes who owns this history and who may decide what can be done with it, there are only two choices: empowering the generals' own descendants or recognising the wider public interest, which includes the countless non-German descendants of their victims. The German authorities placed the decision to publish, in each instance, at the discretion of family descendants.[2] This was no doubt the safer legal option, but takes no account of their moral obligation. After the post-war West German state failed to bring these men to justice and indeed rewarded them with privilege and status, the idea that state representatives choose to evoke copyright law (which none of the families stipulated) to safeguard the intellectual property of Nazi generals feels like a closed circle in which little has changed. The generals' descendants can agree or disagree with any conclusion drawn, but in my opinion, they can no longer control the information itself because it should no longer belong to them. These letters belong to a wider body of Nazi era documentation that charts not just German history, but the history of violence, repression, genocide and war.

NOTES

Introduction

1. There were four panzer groups in June 1941, but two of these were renamed panzer armies in October. The remaining two panzer groups received the same distinction at the start of 1942.
2. Guderian's school reports and grades. BArch N 802/9.
3. As cited in Kenneth Macksey, *Guderian: Panzer General* (London: Purnell Books, 1975), p. 18. See also Kenneth Macksey, 'Guderian' in Correlli Barnett (ed.), *Hitler's Generals* (London: Phoenix Giant, 1989), pp. 452–453 (p. 442).
4. Russell A. Hart, *Guderian: Panzer Pioneer or Myth Maker?* (Washington, DC: Potomac Books, 2006), pp. 10–11.
5. Macksey, *Guderian*, pp. 16–17.
6. Hart, *Guderian*, pp. 36–39.
7. Johannes Hürter, *Hitlers Heerführer: Die deutschen Oberbefehlshaber im Krieg gegen die Sowjetunion 1941/42* (Munich: Oldenbourg Wissenschaftsverlag, 2006), pp. 72–73.
8. Heinrich Bücheler, *Hoepner: Ein deutsches Soldatenschicksal des 20. Jahrhunderts* (Herford: Verlag E. S. Mittler and Sohn, 1980), pp. 36–37.
9. Hürter, *Hitlers Heerführer*, p. 632.
10. Bücheler, *Hoepner*, p. 48.
11. Hürter, *Hitlers Heerführer*, p. 129.
12. Bücheler, *Hoepner*, p. 69.
13. Klaus R. Woche, *Zwischen Pflicht und Gewissen: Generaloberst Rudolf Schmidt 1886–1957* (Berlin: AALEXX Druck, 2002), pp. 13, 18–23; Hürter, *Hitlers Heerführer*, pp. 32, 40 and 660.
14. Samuel W. Mitcham Jr., *The Men of Barbarossa: Commanders of the German Invasion of Russia, 1941* (Newbury, PA: Casemate, 2009), p. 124.
15. Hürter, *Hitlers Heerführer*, p. 145.
16. Ibid., p. 31.
17. Christoph Clasen, *Generaloberst Hans-Georg Reinhardt* (Stuttgart: Zeitungsverlag, 1996), pp. 21–22.
18. www.lexikon-der-wehrmacht.de/Personenregister/R/ReinhardtGH.htm.
19. Ibid.; Hürter, *Hitlers Heerführer*, pp. 108, 129, 144–145 and 655.

20. Some of those that have been published include: Hans Meier-Welcker, *Aufzeichnungen eines Generalstabsoffiziers 1939–1942* (Freiburg: Rombach, 1982); Horst Mühleisen (ed.), *Hellmuth Stieff Briefe* (Berlin: Siedler, 1991); Johannes Hürter (ed.), *Notizen aus dem Vernichtungskrieg: Die Ostfront 1941/42 in den Aufzeichnungen des Generals Heinrici* (Darmstadt: Wissenschaftliche Buchgesellschaft, 2016); Torsten Diedrich and Jens Ebert (eds.), *Nach Stalingrad: Walther von Seydlitz' Feldpostbriefe und Kriegsgefangenenpost 1939–1955* (Göttingen: Wallstein Verlag, 2018).
21. Kaspar von Greyerz, 'Ego-Documents: The Last Word?' in *German History* vol. 28, no. 3 (2010), pp. 273–282 (p. 281).

1 The Letters of the Panzer Generals

1. Macksey, *Guderian*, p. xi.
2. See the extensive discussion of Guderian in Ronald Smelser and Edward J. Davies II, *The Myth of the Eastern Front: The Nazi–Soviet War in American Popular Culture* (Cambridge: Cambridge University Press, 2008).
3. Karl J. Walde, *Guderian* (Frankfurt: Ullstein, 1976), p. 11.
4. Dermot Bradley, *Generaloberst Heinz Guderian und die Entstehungsgeschichte des modernen Blitzkrieges* (Osnabrück: Biblio-Verlag, 1986).
5. Ibid., pp. 226–235.
6. Hart, *Guderian*.
7. Bücheler, *Hoepner*.
8. Woche, *Zwischen Pflicht und Gewissen*, p. 10.
9. Ibid., pp. 9–10.
10. Clasen, *Generaloberst Hans-Georg Reinhardt*. Reinhardt's personal army file refers to him as 'Georg-Hans' (not Hans-Georg as Clasen's title suggests). The confusion probably stems from Reinhardt using simply 'Hans' with intimate acquaintances. Reinhardt's personal army file. BArch PERS 6/50, fol. 2.
11. Hürter, *Hitlers Heerführer*.
12. The only comparable work is that of Jörn Hasenclever, who provided rich biographical essays covering the leading German rear area commanders in 1941–1943. Jörn Hasenclever, *Wehrmacht und Besatzungspolitik: Die Befehlshaber der rückwärtigen Heeresgebiete 1941–1943* (Paderborn: Schöningh, 2010).
13. Consideration of the 'private space', and the extent to which it afforded honesty and freedom within the National Socialist state, is expertly explored in Elizabeth Harvey, Johannes Hürter, Maiken Umbach and Andreas Wirsching (eds.), *Private Life and Privacy in Nazi Germany* (Cambridge: Cambridge University Press, 2019).
14. Georg-Hans Reinhardt's letters to his wife Eva. BArch N 245/2 (7 December 1941).
15. Ibid.
16. The collection was subsequently transferred to the Federal Military Archive in 1972.
17. Margarete Guderian's letters to her husband Heinz. BArch N 802/47 (19 September 1941).
18. Guderian's letter from 15 October provides evidence that on occasion Margarete did send her correspondence through the usual army postal system. It is unclear if Guderian did the same.
19. Heinz Guderian's letters to his wife Margarete. BArch N 802/46 (31 October 1941).
20. Ortwin Buchbender and Reinhold Sterz (eds.), *Das andere Gesicht des Krieges: Deutsche Feldpostbriefe 1939–1945* (Munich: C. H. Beck, 1982), p. 15.
21. Katrin Kilian, 'Postal Censorship from 1939 to 1945' www.feldpost-archiv.de/eng lish/e11-zensur.html.

22. Christopher R. Browning and Jürgen Matthäus, *The Origins of the Final Solution: The Evolution of Nazi Jewish Policy 1939–1942* (London: Arrow Books, 2004), p. 283.
23. Peter Longerich, *The Unwritten Order: Hitler's Role in the Final Solution* (Stroud: Tempus, 2005), p. 118.
24. Hürter, *Hitlers Heerführer*, p. 139.
25. Erich Hoepner's letters to his wife Irma. BArch N 51/9 (27 November 1941).
26. Georg-Hans Reinhardt's letters to his wife Eva. BArch N 245/2 (19 June 1941).
27. Rudolf Schmidt's letter to Margarete Guderian. BArch N 823/24 (14 July 1941).
28. Ibid.
29. As Katrin A. Kilian has observed, the disproportionate availability of letters between the generals and their wives is reflective of the wider tend in German field post: 'About 24 per cent of the forces mail in the Second World War consisted of letters from men on active service, and 76 per cent of letters from home. This is not, however, reflected in the correspondence that has come down to us – there is a marked preponderance of letters from servicemen in the collection that are accessible to the public.' Katrin A. Kilian, 'Moods in Wartime: The Emotions Expressed in Forces Mail' in Militärgeschichtlichen Forschungsamt (ed.), *Germany and the Second World War. Volume IX/II. German Wartime Society 1939–1945: Exploitation, Interpretations, Exclusion* (Oxford: Oxford University Press, 2014), p. 254.
30. Reinhardt also wrote a lot in his letters from the second half of 1944, but that is the only period that comes close to June–December 1941.

2 The Private Generals

1. David A. Harrisville, *The Virtuous Wehrmacht: Crafting the Myth of the German Soldier on the Eastern Front, 1941–1944* (Ithaca, NY: Cornell University Press, 2021), pp. 23–26.
2. Thomas Kühne, *The Rise and Fall of Comradeship: Hitler's Soldiers, Male Bonding and Mass Violence in the Twentieth Century* (Cambridge: Cambridge University Press, 2017), pp. 70–72.
3. Lisa Pine, *Hitler's 'National Community': Society and Culture in Nazi Germany* (New York: Bloomsbury, 2017), p. 93.
4. Margarete Christine Franziska Goerne was born on 25 March 1893. She married Heinz Guderian in 1913.
5. Margarete Guderian's letters to her husband Heinz. BArch N 802/47 (31 August 1941).
6. An 1892 guide for young wives of German officers advised that ladies should not speak about themselves, which, it was emphasised, was especially to be observed in letters. Moreover, in everyday conversation the guide encouraged women to 'show a friendly interest' without overstepping the line into 'indiscreet curiosity'. Isa von der Lütt, *Die elegante Hausfrau: Mitteilungen für junge Hauswesen mit besonderen Winken für Offiziersfrauen 1892* (Bad Langensalza: Rockstuhl, 2012), pp. 140 and 209.
7. Margarete Guderian's letters to her husband Heinz. BArch N 802/47 (17 December 1941).
8. Ibid.
9. Heinz Guderian's letters to his wife Margarete. BArch N 802/46 (12 July 1941).
10. Letters were not addressed directly to a man's unit or even his area of deployment; in fact it was not necessary for the sender to know anything about his military

service or posting in order for a letter to reach him. A letter was simply addressed with his name and a five-numbered field post signature. Every unit had a unique number, which for security reasons could be changed at any time during the war.

11. Heinz Guderian's letters to his wife Margarete. BArch N 802/46 (24 July 1941).
12. Ibid. (19 July 1941).
13. Ibid. (24 October 1941).
14. Ibid. (11 October 1941).
15. Erich Hoepner's letters to his wife Irma. BArch N 51/9 (30 June 1941).
16. Ibid. (29 July 1941).
17. Ibid. (24 September 1941).
18. Ibid. (15 August 1941).
19. Hans-Georg Keitel was mortally wounded in July 1941 by a Soviet aircraft and died soon afterwards. The secret SD reports gauging German public opinion revealed: 'From the number of obituaries, under which many well-known names can be found (Gauleiter Leopold, the sons of leading men from the party, state and armed forces, etc.) [...], it is assumed with certainty that the losses are indeed higher than in previous campaigns.' Heinz Boberach (ed.), *Meldungen aus dem Reich: Die geheimen Lageberichte des Sicherheitsdienstes der SS 1938–1945*, Band 8 (Berlin: Pawlak, 1984), p. 2609 (31 July 1941). Among the other prominent commanders to lose sons in the East were Erich Manstein, whose eldest son was killed in October 1942. Friedrich Paulus had twin sons, with one being killed in the war (date unknown) and the other wounded at Stalingrad. One of Hermann Hoth's sons was reported missing in action in 1943. One of Wilhelm Leeb's sons was killed in Lvov during the 1939 Polish campaign.
20. Heinz Guderian's letters to his wife Margarete. BArch N 802/46 (19 July 1941).
21. Ibid. (24 July 1941).
22. Rudolf Schmidt's letter to Lieutenant-General Friedrich Paulus. BArch N 372/22 (29 July 1941).
23. Heinz Guderian's letters to his wife Margarete. BArch N 802/46 (31 July 1941).
24. Erich Hoepner's letters to his wife Irma. BArch N 51/9 (30 June 1941).
25. Ibid. (26 August 1941).
26. Heinz Guderian's letters to his wife Margarete. BArch N 802/46 (31 July 1941).
27. Erich Hoepner's letters to his wife Irma. BArch N 51/9 (24 September 1941).
28. Heinz Guderian's letters to his wife Margarete. BArch N 802/46 (17 November 1941).
29. Ibid.
30. Erich Hoepner's letters to his wife Irma. BArch N 51/9 (8 December 1941).
31. Margarete Guderian's letters to her husband Heinz. BArch N 802/47 (15 December 1941).
32. Ibid. (17 December 1941).
33. Ibid. (29 December 1941).
34. René Schilling, *'Kriegshelden': Deutungsmuster heroischer Männlichkeit in Deutschland 1813–1945* (Paderborn: Schöningh, 2002), p. 339.
35. Margarete Guderian's letters to her husband Heinz. BArch N 802/47 (5 November 1941).
36. Ibid. (26 October 1941). The name 'Spanke' was very difficult to read in the original handwritten letter and may not be spelled correctly.
37. Ibid. (4 December 1941).
38. Ernst Klink, 'The Conduct of Operations' in Militärgeschichtlichen Forschungsamt (ed.), *Germany and the Second World War. Volume IV: The Attack on the Soviet Union* (Oxford: Oxford University Press, 1998), pp. 525–763 (p. 619).

39. Margarete Guderian's letters to her husband Heinz. BArch N 802/47 (4 December 1941).
40. Ibid. (17 December 1941).
41. Ibid.
42. Ibid.
43. My thanks to Dr Jan Tattenberg for illuminating this point.
44. As cited in Elizabeth D. Heineman, *What Difference Does a Husband Make? Women and Marital Status in Nazi and Postwar Germany* (Berkeley, CA: University of California Press, 2003), p. 52. See also Jay W. Baird, *To Die for Germany: Heroes in the Nazi Pantheon* (Bloomington, IN: Indiana University Press, 1992), pp. 227–229.
45. As cited in Claudia Koonz, 'Mothers in the Fatherland: Women in Nazi Germany' in Renate Bridenthal and Claudia Koonz (eds.), *Becoming Visible: Women in European History* (Boston, MA: Houghton Mifflin, 1976), pp. 445–473 (p. 466).
46. Gudrun Schwarz, '"Herrinnen der Zukunft": SS-Offiziere und ihre Frauen' in Ursula Breymayer, Bernd Ulrich and Karin Wieland (eds.), *Willensmenschen: Über deutsche Offiziere* (Frankfurt am Main: Fischer, 1999), pp. 123–133 (p. 128).
47. Margarete Guderian's letters to her husband Heinz. BArch N 802/47 (17 December 1941).
48. Roger Moorhouse, *Berlin at War: Life and Death in Hitler's Capital, 1939–45* (London: The Bodley Head, 2010), pp. 251–253.
49. Georg-Hans Reinhardt's letters to his wife Eva. BArch N 245/2 (4 October 1941).
50. Ibid.
51. Angelika Tramitz, 'Nach dem Zapfenstreich: Anmerkungen zur Sexualität des Offiziers' in Ursula Breymayer, Bernd Ulrich and Karin Wieland (eds.), *Willensmenschen: Über deutsche Offiziere* (Frankfurt am Main: Fischer, 1999), pp. 211–226 (p. 214).
52. French L. Maclean, *The Unknown Generals: German Corps Commanders in World War II* (Fort Leavenworth, unpublished MA thesis, 1988), pp. 89–90.
53. The first statistical evidence of this is provided by Robert Kirchubel and Sorin Adam Matei, 'Blunting Barbarossa's Spear: Analyzing Army Group Center's Officer Losses during the Campaign's First Half' in *The Journal of Slavic Military History* vol. 34, no. 4 (2021), pp. 510–536. One of the best targeted operational studies to have charted this phenomenon is Adrian Wettstein, *Die Wehrmacht im Stadtkampf* (Paderborn: Schöningh, 2014), pp. 155–157.
54. Walter von Reichenau's letter to Lieutenant-General Friedrich Paulus. BArch N 372/22 (27 September 1941). See also Walter Görlitz, *Paulus and Stalingrad* (London: The Citadel Press, 1963), p. 139.
55. Maclean, *The Unknown Generals*, p. 92.
56. Heinz Guderian, *Panzer Leader* (New York: Da Capo Press, 1996), pp. 154–156.
57. Ibid., p. 204.
58. Ibid., p. 206.
59. Heinz Guderian's letters to his wife Margarete. BArch N 802/46 (2 September 1941).
60. Karl-Henning von Barsewisch's diary. BArch N 802/189, p. 3 (4 August 1941). There is different pagination at the top and bottom of Barsewisch's diary; all my references pertain to the bottom number.
61. Georg-Hans Reinhardt's letters to his wife Eva. BArch N 245/2 (12 September 1941).
62. 'Herbert von Blanckenhagen, Dolmetscher im Stabe Hoepner: Erinnerungen Manuskript' BArch MSG 2/1172, p. 120.

63. Erich Hoepner's letters to his wife Irma. BArch N 51/9 (23 June 1941). While some have expressed surprise at this arrangement, the *SS Totenkopf* was still in reserve at this stage and amenable to such a request. As we will see in Chapter 4, Hoepner had an especially close relationship with the SS in this area of operations.

64. Georg-Hans Reinhardt's letters to his wife Eva. BArch N 245/2 (12 July 1941).

65. Elke Fröhlich (ed.), *Die Tagebücher von Joseph Goebbels. Teil II: Diktate 1941–1945, Band 1, Juli–September 1941* (Munich: K. G. Saur, 1996), p. 100 (21 July 1941). Helmuth James von Moltke heard the same rumour, but believed it to be General of Panzer Troops Leo Geyr von Schweppenburg, one of Guderian's corps commanders in Panzer Group 2. Helmuth James von Moltke, *Letters to Freya: 1939–1945* (New York: Alfred A. Knopf, 1990), p. 149 (13 July 1941).

66. It is unclear exactly when Schmidt and Guderian first served together, but most likely it was as officers during the First World War, when they were both tasked with running new radio communication centres. Hürter, *Hitlers Heerführer*, p. 73, n. 12.

67. Rudolf Schmidt's letter to Margarete Guderian. BArch N 823/24 (14 July 1941).

68. Erich Hoepner's letters to his wife Irma. BArch N 51/9 (19 July 1941).

69. Ibid. Hoepner's letter actually refers to 'Lieutenant-General Schmidt', whereas Rudolf Schmidt had been a General of Panzer Troops since 1 June 1940. While there were numerous other generals by the name of Schmidt in the German high command (twenty-two in fact reached the rank of Major-General or above during the war), Rudolf Schmidt was the only recipient of the Oak Leaves by this stage of the war.

70. Klaus Woche's biography of Schmidt stated that Soviet and British reports had claimed Schmidt was killed in early July. In fact, he claimed that Fridel had been visited by at least one acquaintance who had heard the foreign radio address and had come to express condolences. Woche, *Zwischen Pflicht und Gewissen*, p. 108.

71. Rudolf Schmidt's letters to his wife Fridel. BArch N 823/24 (21 July 1941).

72. Ibid. (1 September 1941).

73. Heinz Guderian's letters to his wife Margarete. BArch N 802/46 (16 December 1941).

74. Guderian, *Panzer Leader*, p. 274.

75. Heinz Guderian's letters to his wife Margarete. BArch N 802/46 (12 August 1941).

76. Erich Hoepner's letters to his wife Irma. BArch N 51/9 (9 July 1941).

77. Ibid. (19 July 1941).

78. Ibid. (18 August 1941).

79. Georg-Hans Reinhardt's letters to his wife Eva. BArch N 245/2 (12 July 1941).

80. Fabian von Schlabrendorff, *Begegnungen in fünf Jahrzehnten* (Tübingen: Rainer Wunderlich, 1979), pp. 262–263.

81. There are other letters from Kluge dating from earlier and later years of the war, but for the campaign against the Soviet Union in 1941 this is all that is available.

82. Günther von Kluge's letters to his wife Mathilde. BArch MSG/2/11185 (12 July 1941).

83. Von Schlabrendorff, *Begegnungen in fünf Jahrzehnten*, p. 263.

84. Walther-Peer Fellgiebel, *Elite of the Third Reich: The Recipients of the Knight's Cross of the Iron Cross 1939–45: A Reference* (Solihull: Helion, 2003), p. 50.

85. Georg-Hans Reinhardt's letters to his wife Eva. BArch N 245/2 (23 July 1941).

86. Ibid. (28 August 1941).

87. Ibid.

88. Ibid. See also Clasen, *Generaloberst Hans-Georg Reinhardt*, pp. 300–301.

89. Rudolf Schmidt's letters to his wife Fridel. BArch N 823/24 (12 August 1941).

90. Erich Hoepner's letters to his wife Irma. BArch N 51/9 (29 July 1941).
91. Heinz Guderian's letters to his wife Margarete. BArch N 802/46 (24 July 1941).
92. Ibid. (7 August 1941).
93. David Stahel, *Operation Barbarossa and Germany's Defeat in the East* (Cambridge: Cambridge University Press, 2009), p. 270.
94. Heinz Guderian's letters to his wife Margarete. BArch N 802/46 (7 August 1941).
95. Ibid. (30 August 1941).
96. Georg-Hans Reinhardt's letters to his wife Eva. BArch N 245/2 (8 August 1941).
97. Klink, 'The Conduct of Operations', p. 635.
98. According to Chales de Beaulieu at Panzer Group 4, Reinhardt attempted to halt the advance after it had begun, but was overruled by Hoepner. Walter Chales de Beaulieu, *Leningrad: The Advance of Panzer Group 4, 1941* (Havertown, PA: Casemate Publishers, 2020), pp. 84–85.
99. Robert Kirchubel, *Hitler's Panzer Armies on the Eastern Front* (Barnsley: Pen and Sword, 2009), p. 140.
100. Georg-Hans Reinhardt's letters to his wife Eva. BArch N 245/2 (8 August 1941).
101. Robert P. Ericksen, 'Assessing the Heritage: German Protestant Theologians, Nazis and, the "Jewish Question"' in Robert P. Ericksen and Susannah Heschel (eds.), *Betrayal: German Churches and the Holocaust* (Minneapolis, MN: Fortress Press, 1999), pp. 22–30 (p. 22).
102. Hürter, *Hitlers Heerführer*, p. 28.
103. Erich Hoepner's letters to his wife Irma. BArch N 51/9 (13 July 1941).
104. Ibid. (27 November 1941).
105. Rudolf Schmidt's letters to his wife Fridel. BArch N 823/24 (12 August 1941).
106. Ibid. (12 November 1941).
107. Ibid. (28 January 1942).
108. Georg-Hans Reinhardt's letters to his wife Eva. BArch N 245/2 (4 October 1941).
109. Ibid. (9 December 1941).
110. As cited in Valerie Geneviève Hébert, *Hitler's Generals on Trial: The Last War Crimes Tribunal at Nuremberg* (Lawrence, KS: University Press of Kansas, 2010), p. 124.
111. Guderian's Panzer Group 2 was renamed Second Panzer Army on 5 October 1941.
112. Heinz Guderian's letters to his wife Margarete. BArch N 802/46 (8 December 1941).
113. Ibid. (2 September 1941).
114. Ibid. (6 November 1941).
115. Ibid. (11 October 1941).
116. Georg-Hans Reinhardt's letters to his wife Eva. BArch N 245/2 (23 October 1941).
117. Ibid. (19 November 1941).
118. Margarete Guderian's letters to her husband Heinz. BArch N 802/47 (1 October 1941).
119. Ibid. (17 December 1941).
120. Doris Bergen, *Twisted Cross: The German Christian Movement in the Third Reich* (Chapel Hill, NC: University of North Carolina Press, 1996), p. 125.
121. Doris Bergen, 'Storm Troopers of Christ: The German Christian Movement and the Ecclesiastical Final Solution' in Robert P. Ericksen and Susannah Heschel (eds.), *Betrayal: German Churches and the Holocaust* (Minneapolis, MN: Fortress Press, 1999), pp. 40–67 (p. 40).
122. https://encyclopedia.ushmm.org/content/en/article/the-german-churches-and-the-nazi-state.
123. Bergen, 'Storm Troopers of Christ', p. 41.

124. John A. Moses, 'The Rise and Fall of Christian Militarism in Prussia-Germany from Hegel to Bonhoeffer' in Stephan Atzert and Andrew Bonnell (eds.), *Europe's Pasts and Presents* (Unley, SA: Australian Humanities Press, 2004), pp. 113–125 (pp. 119–121).

125. Susannah Heschel, 'When Jesus Was an Aryan: The Protestant Church and Antisemitic Propaganda' in Robert P. Ericksen and Susannah Heschel (eds.), *Betrayal: German Churches and the Holocaust* (Minneapolis, MN: Fortress Press, 1999), pp. 68–89 (p. 84).

126. Wolfgang Gerlach, *Als die Zeugen schwiegen: Bekennende Kirche und die Juden* (Berlin: Institut Kirche und Judentum, 1987).

127. Bergen, 'Storm Troopers of Christ', p. 65; see also p. 46.

128. Robert P. Ericksen, *Complicity in the Holocaust: Churches and Universities in Nazi Germany* (Cambridge: Cambridge University Press, 2012), p. 127.

129. Bergen, *Twisted Cross*, p. 65.

130. Bergen, 'Storm Troopers of Christ', p. 44.

131. David A. Harrisville, 'Unholy Crusaders: The Wehrmacht and the Reestablishment of Soviet Churches during Operation Barbarossa' in *Central European History* vol. 52, no. 4 (2019), pp. 620–649.

132. Michael Burleigh, *Ethics and Extermination: Reflections on Nazi Genocide* (Cambridge: Cambridge University Press, 1997), p. 41.

133. Kurt Meier, 'Sowjetrußland im Urteil der evangelischen Kirche (1917–1945)' in Hans-Erich Volkmann (ed.), *Das Rußlandbild im Dritten Reich* (Cologne: Böhlau, 1994), pp. 285–321 (p. 312).

134. Even after the war, when leading German generals, including Reinhardt, had been tried and convicted for criminal activities, the Church joined the *Kirchliches Gefangenenhilfe* (Committee for Church Aid for Prisoners). This institution provided the war criminals with funds for legal counsel and public lobbyists to campaign more broadly on their behalf. Working together with other groups, they would eventually succeed in gaining reduced sentences for the convicted prisoners. Hébert, *Hitler's Generals on Trial*, pp. 54–55.

135. Georg-Hans Reinhardt's letters to his wife Eva. BArch N 245/2 (7 December 1941).

136. Hürter, *Hitlers Heerführer*, p. 52.

137. Irma was the daughter of the textile entrepreneur Julius Gebauer.

138. Koonz, 'Mothers in the Fatherland: Women in Nazi Germany', p. 455.

139. Craig W. H. Luther and David Stahel (eds.), *Soldiers of Barbarossa: Combat, Genocide, and Everyday Experiences on the Eastern Front, June–December 1941* (Guilford, CT: Stackpole Books, 2020).

140. Dagmar Herzog, 'Hubris and Hypocrisy, Incitement and Disavowal: Sexuality and German Fascism' in Dagmar Herzog (ed.), *Sexuality and German Fascism* (Oxford: Berghahn Books, 2004), pp. 1–21 (pp. 9–11).

141. Buchbender and Sterz (eds.), *Das andere Gesicht des Krieges*, p. 14.

142. Although, as Cornelie Usborne noted: 'The impact of official censorship on private correspondence is now generally held to have been slight.' Cornelie Usborne, 'Love Letters from Front and Home: A Private Space for Intimacy in the Second World War?' in Elizabeth Harvey, Johannes Hürter, Maiken Umbach and Andreas Wirsching (eds.), *Private Life and Privacy in Nazi Germany* (Cambridge: Cambridge University Press, 2019), pp. 280–303 (p. 294).

143. Heinz Guderian's letters to his wife Margarete. BArch N 802/46 (16 June 1941).

144. Ibid. (27 June 1941).

145. Margarete Guderian's letters to her husband Heinz. BArch N 802/47 (31 August 1941).

146. Heinz Guderian's letters to his wife Margarete. BArch N 802/46 (12 July 1941).

147. For numerous examples see Luther and Stahel (eds.), *Soldiers of Barbarossa*, pp. 25, 35, 38, 47, 62 and 74.

148. Heinz Guderian's letters to his wife Margarete. BArch N 802/46 (29 June 1941).

149. Ibid. (15 July 1941).

150. Ibid. (31 July 1941).

151. Margarete Guderian's letters to her husband Heinz. BArch N 802/47 (31 August 1941).

152. Michelle Mouton, *From Nurturing the Nation to Purifying the Volk: Weimar and Nazi Family Policy, 1918–1945* (Cambridge: Cambridge University Press, 2007), p. 63.

153. Peter Knoch, 'Kriegsalltag' in Peter Knoch (ed.), *Kriegsalltag: Die Rekonstruktion des Kriegsalltags als Aufgabe der historischen Forschung und der Friedenserziehung* (Stuttgart: J. B. Metzler, 1989), p. 226.

154. Heinz Guderian's letters to his wife Margarete. BArch N 802/46 (1 October 1941).

155. Margarete Guderian's letters to her husband Heinz. BArch N 802/47 (1 October 1941).

156. Schilling, *'Kriegshelden'*, p. 336.

157. Margarete Guderian's letters to her husband Heinz. BArch N 802/47 (26 October 1941).

158. Heinz Guderian's letters to his wife Margarete. BArch N 802/46 (15 October 1941).

159. Erich Hoepner's letters to his wife Irma. BArch N 51/9 (30 June, 9, 19 July, 18 August, 5, 12, 17, 21 September, 6, 19, 22, 30 October 1941).

160. Ibid. (5, 16 July, 26 August, 24 September, 5 November 1941).

161. Ibid. (23 June, 16 July, 17 September 1941).

162. Ibid. (30 June, 15 August, 12, 21 September, 19, 22 October 1941).

163. Ibid. (8 December 1941).

164. Ibid. (13 July, 1 August, 5, 27, 29 November 1941).

165. Ibid. (29 November 1941).

166. Walter Chales de Beaulieu, *General Erich Hoepner: A Military Biography* (Havertown, PA: Casemate Publishers, 2021), p. x.

167. Tramitz, 'Nach dem Zapfenstreich', p. 223.

168. Heinz Rahe, Museumsstiftung Post und Telekommunikation, Berlin, 3.2002.0985 (28 October 1941).

169. Georg-Hans Reinhardt's letters to his wife Eva. BArch N 245/2 (26 June 1941).

170. Rudolf Schmidt's letters to his wife Fridel. BArch N 823/24 (24 December 1941).

171. Ibid. (13 December 1941).

172. Rudolf Schmidt's letter to Lieutenant-General Friedrich Paulus. BArch N 372/22 (13 November 1941).

173. Sonja Hagelstam, 'Families, Separation and Emotional Coping in War: Bridging Letters between Home and Front, 1941–44' in Tiina Kinnunen and Ville Kivimäki (eds.) *Finland in World War II: History, Memory, Interpretations* (Boston, MA: Brill, 2012), pp. 277–312 (pp. 306–307).

174. Claus-Christian W. Szejnmann, '"A Sense of *Heimat* Opened Up during the War": German Soldiers and *Heimat* Abroad' in Claus-Christian W. Szejnmann and Maiken Umbach (eds.) *Heimat, Region, and Empire: Spatial Identities under National Socialism* (London: Palgrave, 2012), pp. 112–147 (pp. 136–137).

175. Christa Hämmerle, 'Gewalt und Liebe – ineinander verschränkt. Paarkorrespondenzen aus zwei Weltkriegen: 1914/18 und 1939/45' in Ingrid Bauer and Christa Hämmerle (eds.), *Liebe schreiben: Paarkorrespondenz im Kontext des 19. und 20. Jahrhunderts* (Göttingen: Vandenhoeck & Ruprecht, 2017), pp. 171–230 (p. 21).

176. Usborne, 'Love Letters from Front and Home', p. 303.

177. Hester Vaizey, *Surviving Hitler's War: Family Life in Germany, 1939–48* (New York: Palgrave, 2010), p. 79.

178. In fact, Schmidt wrote five letters to Fridel in this time, but I excluded the shortest from my calculation because it came to just eighteen words.

179. Heinz Guderian's letters to his wife Margarete. BArch N 802/46 (11 October 1941).

180. Ibid. (15 October 1941).

181. Ibid. (21 October 1941).

182. Margarete Guderian's letters to her husband Heinz. BArch N 802/47 (5 November 1941).

183. Heinz Guderian's letters to his wife Margarete. BArch N 802/46 (12 November 1941).

184. Ibid. (6 November 1941).

185. Ibid. (12 November 1941).

186. Rudolf Schmidt's letters to his wife Fridel. BArch N 823/24 (2 October 1941).

187. Ibid. (28 October 1941).

188. Ibid. (1 November 1941).

189. Ibid. (15 November 1941).

190. Ibid. (18 November 1941).

191. Ben Shephard, *A War of Nerves: Soldiers and Psychiatrists 1914–1994* (London: Pimlico, 2002), p. 300.

192. Erich Hoepner's letters to his wife Irma. BArch N 51/9 (22 October 1941).

193. Luther and Stahel (eds.), *Soldiers of Barbarossa*, p. 81.

194. Erich Hoepner's letters to his wife Irma. BArch N 51/9 (5 November 1941).

195. Fellgiebel, *Elite of the Third Reich*, p. 264.

196. David Stahel, *Operation Typhoon: Hitler's March on Moscow, October 1941* (Cambridge: Cambridge University Press, 2013), p. 85.

197. There is one passage in Reinhardt's diary from 14 November that explicitly mentions Guderian's pessimism. 'Guderian screams that he cannot do anything in winter. I think it still has to work.' Diary of Georg-Hans Reinhardt. BArch N 245/3, fol. 14 (14 November 1941).

198. Georg-Hans Reinhardt's letters to his wife Eva. BArch N 245/2 (16 November 1941).

199. Ibid. (23 November 1941).

200. Ibid. (7 December 1941).

201. Ibid.

202. Hagelstam, 'Families, Separation and Emotional Coping in War', p. 309.

203. Heinz Guderian's letters to his wife Margarete. BArch N 802/46 (17 November 1941).

204. Ibid.

205. Ibid.

206. Ibid. (21 November 1941).

207. Margarete Guderian's letters to her husband Heinz. BArch N 802/47 (27 November 1941).

208. Ibid. (4 December 1941).

209. Kilian, 'Moods in Wartime', p. 287.
210. Heinz Guderian's letters to his wife Margarete. BArch N 802/46 (31 October 1941).
211. 'Tagebuch Wolfram von Richthofen'. BArch N 671/8, fol. 144 (7 December 1941).
212. Heinz Guderian's letters to his wife Margarete. BArch N 802/46 (1 December 1941).
213. Ibid. (10 December 1941).
214. Ibid. (16 December 1941).
215. Ibid.
216. As cited in Earl F. Ziemke and Magna E. Bauer, *Moscow to Stalingrad: Decision in the East* (New York: Military Heritage Press, 1988), p. 95.
217. For a detailed account of Guderian's December campaign and dismissal see David Stahel, *Retreat from Moscow: A New History of Germany's Winter Campaign, 1941–1942* (New York: Farrar, Straus and Giroux, 2019).
218. Schmidt's new assignment in the Second Army was, however, only temporary. He was standing in for Colonel-General Maximilian von Weichs, who had reported ill and returned to Germany. Weichs resumed his command on 15 January 1942.
219. Rudolf Schmidt's letters to his wife Fridel. BArch N 823/24 (24 November 1941).
220. Ibid. (13 December 1941).
221. Ibid. (24 December 1941).
222. Erich Hoepner's letters to his wife Irma. BArch N 51/9 (8 December 1941).
223. Ibid. (12 December 1941).
224. Ibid. (17 December 1941).
225. Hermann Balck, *Order in Chaos: The Memoirs of General of Panzer Troops Hermann Balck* (Lexington, KT: University Press of Kentucky, 2015), p. 228.
226. Erich Hoepner's letters to his wife Irma. BArch N 51/9 (21 December 1941).
227. Georg-Hans Reinhardt's letters to his wife Eva. BArch N 245/2 (8 December 1941).
228. Ibid. (9 December 1941).
229. Ibid. (10 December 1941).
230. Ibid. (12 December 1941).
231. Ibid. (15 December 1941).
232. Ibid. (31 December 1941).
233. Such a conclusion was further confirmed by Jeff Rutherford and Adrian Wettstein, looking at individual cases of middle-ranked generals serving in the East. As they explained, their research 'shed light on an often forgotten issue of German command in the East: many officers simply burned out under the burden of command, especially as the war dragged on and the German situation became critical and finally desperate.' Jeff Rutherford and Adrian Wettstein, *The German Army on the Eastern Front: An Inner View of the Ostheer's Experiences of War* (Barnsley: Pen & Sword, 2018), p. 57.
234. Sebastian Haffner, *Germany Jekyll & Hyde: A Contemporary Account of Nazi Germany* (London: Abacus, 2008), pp. 108–109.

3 The Public Generals

1. Adelheid von Saldern, 'Innovative Trends in Women's and Gender Studies of the National Socialist Era' in *German History* vol. 27, no. 1 (2009), pp. 84–112 (p. 93).
2. Schilling, '*Kriegshelden*', p. 339.
3. Although the nobility comprised just 0.14 per cent of the German population, they made up 21.7 per cent of the army officers in 1920. F. L. Carsten, *The Reichswehr and Politics 1918 to 1933* (Oxford: Oxford University Press, 1966), p. 215.

4. One does need to be careful about overstating the commitment of the panzer corps to new ideas. There had been serious debate about the embrace of tanks and new technology in the 1920s. Moreover, the distribution of the more conservative-minded nobility was not even throughout the army, with the cavalry drawing some 50 per cent of its officers from aristocratic families. The reactionary element, however, did not suffice to challenge major reforms and was no doubt further enticed by the results, especially in 1940. See Mary Habeck, *Storm of Steel: The Development of Armor Doctrine in Germany and the Soviet Union, 1919–1939* (London: Cornell University Press, 2003), pp. 64–68.

5. Hürter, *Hitlers Heerführer*, p. 171.

6. Georg-Hans Reinhardt's letters to his wife Eva. BArch N 245/2 (26 June 1941).

7. Aristotle A. Kallis, *Nazi Propaganda and the Second World War* (New York: Palgrave Macmillan, 2005), p. 111.

8. Howard K. Smith, *Last Train from Berlin* (New York: Alfred A. Knopf, 1943), p. 102.

9. Heinz Guderian's letters to his wife Margarete. BArch N 802/46 (29 June 1941).

10. Today known as Kaunas, Lithuania.

11. Alternatively referred to as the Western Dvina River.

12. Erich Hoepner's letters to his wife Irma. BArch N 51/9 (30 June 1941).

13. *Die Wehrmachtberichte 1939–1945, Band 1: 1. September 1939 bis 31. Dezember 1941* (Munich: Deutscher Taschenbuch Verlag, 1985), p. 595 (29 June 1941).

14. Ibid., p. 596 (29 June 1941).

15. Kallis, *Nazi Propaganda and the Second World War*, p. 111.

16. Daniel Uziel, *The Propaganda Warriors: The Wehrmacht and the Consolidation of the German Home Front* (Bern: Peter Lang, 2008), pp. 69–71.

17. Omer Bartov, 'From *Blitzkrieg* to Total War: Controversial Links between Image and Reality' in Ian Kershaw and Moshe Lewin (eds.), *Stalinism and Nazism: Dictatorships in Comparison* (Cambridge: Cambridge University Press, 2003), pp. 158–184 (p. 183).

18. Ortwin Buchbender, *Das tönende Erz: Deutsche Propaganda gegen die Rote Armee im Zweiten Weltkrieg* (Stuttgart: Seewald Verlag, 1978), pp. 20–23 and 56. The German model was not necessarily unique. According to one American war correspondent, the US Eighth Air Force 'had set up a large public-relations staff – men from newspapers, publicity firms, advertising agencies – and made use of Hollywood celebrities'. As cited in Steven Casey, 'Reporting from the Battlefield: Censorship and Journalism' in Richard J. B. Boworth and Joseph A. Maiolo (eds.), *The Cambridge History of the Second World War. Volume II: Politics and Ideology* (Cambridge: Cambridge University Press, 2015), pp. 117–138 (p. 128).

19. Jochen Lehnhardt, *Die Waffen-SS: Geburt einer Legende: Himmlers Krieger in der NS-Propaganda* (Paderborn: Schöningh, 2017), pp. 102–103.

20. Felix Römer, *Comrades: The Wehrmacht from Within* (Oxford: Oxford University Press, 2019), p. 237.

21. Erich Hoepner's letters to his wife Irma. BArch N 51/9 (23 June 1941).

22. Ibid. (30 June 1941).

23. Ibid. (19 July 1941).

24. Ibid. (5 July 1941).

25. For the influence of these publications in the public discourse see David Stahel, 'The Battle for Wikipedia: The New Age of "Lost Victories"?' in *The Journal of Slavic Military History* vol. 31, no. 3 (2018), pp. 396–402.

26. As cited in Woche, *Zwischen Pflicht und Gewissen*, pp. 100–101.

27. Rudolf Schmidt's letters to his wife Fridel. BArch N 823/24 (21 July 1941).

28. Kühne, *The Rise and Fall of Comradeship*, p. 139.

29. Woche, *Zwischen Pflicht und Gewissen*, p. 98.

30. As cited in Ibid., pp. 104–107.

31. J. P. Stern, *Hitler: The Führer and the People* (Berkeley, CA: University of California Press, 1992), Chapter 7: 'Hitler's Ideology of the Will'.

32. Antulio J. Echevarria II, *After Clausewitz: German Thinkers before the Great War* (Lawrence, KS: University Press of Kansas, 2000), p. 110.

33. Oliver Storz, 'Die Schlacht der Zukunft', in Wolfgang Michalka, (ed.), *Der Erste Weltkrieg: Wirkung, Wahrnehmung, Analyse* (Munich: Piper, 1994), p. 258.

34. Thomas Flemming, '"Willenspotentiale": Offizierstugenden als Gegenstand der Wehrmachtspsychologie', in Ursula Breymayer, Bernd Ulrich and Karin Wieland (eds.), *Willensmenschen: Über deutsche Offiziere* (Frankfurt am Main: Fischer, 2000), pp. 111–122 (p. 111).

35. Jörg Muth, *Command Culture: Officer Education in the U.S. Army and the German Armed Forces, 1901–1940, and the Consequences for World War II* (Denton, TX: University of North Texas Press, 2011), pp. 97–98.

36. Georg-Hans Reinhardt's letters to his wife Eva. BArch N 245/2 (5 October 1941).

37. Marco Sigg's work on the example of command underlined this point. Marco Sigg, *Der Unterführer als Feldherr im Taschenformat – Theorie und Praxis der Auftragstaktik im deutschen Heer 1869 bis 1945* (Paderborn: Schöningh, 2014).

38. Stephen Morillo, *What Is Military History?* (Cambridge: Polity Press, 2018), pp. 49–50.

39. Given that the divisional commander did not change in this time (Major-General Heinrich Wosch commanded from 1 June 1941 to 1 October 1942), this may refer to the division's subordination to the LVI Army Corps in October (General of Panzer Troops Ferdinand Schaal). Thanks to Dr Roman Töppel for pointing this out.

40. This awkward sentence simply follows the original.

41. The division had received the order to force the Lama River and capture Gluchina. On 13 November 1941 the divisional war diary read: 'The good thing about the order is that the division has attacked again for the first time since July 1941 [...], instead of only being used for security or defensive purposes.' Thanks to Dr Roman Töppel for sharing this information.

42. Georg-Hans Reinhardt's letters to his wife Eva. BArch N 245/2 (23 November 1941).

43. Ibid. (12 July 1941).

44. Heinz Guderian's letters to his wife Margarete. BArch N 802/46 (15 July 1941).

45. For more on this see Stahel, *Operation Barbarossa*, pp. 193–194.

46. The announcement on Wednesday 17 September made no reference to the fighting in Ukraine or to Field Marshal Bock's forces. The announcement Margarete is referring to was delivered on Friday 19 September, the same day as her letter.

47. Margarete Guderian's letters to her husband Heinz. BArch N 802/47 (19 September 1941).

48. For a detailed discussion of these events see Stahel, *Operation Barbarossa*; David Stahel, *Kiev 1941: Hitler's Battle for Supremacy in the East* (Cambridge: Cambridge University Press, 2012).

49. *Die Wehrmachtberichte 1939–1945, Band 1*, p. 677 (21 September 1941).

50. Ibid., pp. 635 and 639 (6 and 7 August 1941).

51. Ibid., p. 633 (6 August 1941).

52. Erich Hoepner's letters to his wife Irma. BArch N 51/9 (18 August 1941).

53. It was not unusual for Germans to refer to Leningrad as 'Petersburg'.
54. Ibid. (12 September 1941).
55. *Blücher Kurznachrichten*, no. 37, 9 September 1941, p. 2.
56. Rudolf Schmidt's letters to his wife Fridel. BArch N 823/24 (5 September 1941).
57. *Die Wehrmachtberichte 1939–1945*, Band 1, p. 666 (8 September 1941).
58. Ibid. (13 September 1941).
59. Heinz Guderian, *Achtung – Panzer! The Development of Tank Warfare* (London: Cassell Military Paperbacks, 2002). On the success of the book see Macksey, *Guderian*, p. 69.
60. Guderian, *Achtung – Panzer!*, p. 25.
61. Ibid., pp. 176 and 212.
62. Ralf Georg Reuth, *Rommel: The End of a Legend* (London: Haus Books, 2005), Chapter 3: 'The Creation of Propaganda'.
63. On the success of *Infantry Attacks* see David A. Grossman, 'Maneuver Warfare in the Light Infantry – The Rommel Model' in Richard D. Hooker (ed.), *Maneuver Warfare: An Anthology* (Novato, CA: Presidio Press, 1993), pp. 316–333 (pp. 316–317).
64. Christian Adam, *Bestsellers of the Third Reich: Readers, Writers and the Politics of Literature* (Oxford: Berghahn Books, 2021), p. 246.
65. Römer, *Comrades*, p. 116.
66. On Kernmayr's life see Jörg Weigand, 'Einflussreicher Nationalsozialist, Papst-Biograph und Jugendbuchautor: Das Schriftstellerleben des Hans Gustl Kernmayr (1900–1977)' in *JMS-Report* April 2 (2009), p. 4; Hans Gustl Kernmayr, *Ein Volk kehrt heim! Österreichs Kampf und Befreiung* (Berlin: Deutscher Verlag, 1938).
67. Heinz Guderian's letters to his wife Margarete. BArch N 802/46 (4 July 1941).
68. Margarete Guderian's letters to her husband Heinz. BArch N 802/47 (19 September 1941).
69. Ibid.
70. Ibid.
71. Ibid.
72. Heinz Guderian's letters to his wife Margarete. BArch N 802/46 (25 September 1941).
73. Hitler's chief military adjutant.
74. Karl-Henning von Barsewisch's diary. BArch N 802/189, p. 2 (11–12 July 1941).
75. Heinz Guderian's letters to his wife Margarete. BArch N 802/46 (25 September 1941).
76. Ibid.
77. Roman Roček, *Glanz und Elend des P.E.N.: Biographie eines literarischen Clubs* (Vienna: Böhlau Verlag, 2000), p. 271.
78. Otto Sroka und Erich Landgrebe (eds.), *Mit den Panzern in Ost und West* (Berlin: Volk und Reich Verlag, 1942). An English translation of this book appeared in 2005, with no reference to the editors and a different title: *Blitzkrieg: In Their Own Words: First-Hand Accounts from German Soldiers 1939–1940* (St Paul, MN: Zenith Press, 2005).
79. *Blitzkrieg: In Their Own Words*, p. 9.
80. Geoffrey P. Megargee, *Inside Hitler's High Command* (Lawrence, KS: University Press of Kansas, 2000), p. 233.
81. On Model, see Steven H. Newton, *Hitler's Commander: Field Marshal Walther Model – Hitler's Favorite General* (Cambridge, MA: Da Capo Press, 2006); Marcel Stein, *A Flawed Genius: Field Marshal Walter Model. A Critical*

Biography (Solihull: Helion, 2010). On Rommel, see Ian F. W. Beckett (ed.), *Rommel Reconsidered* (Mechanicsburg, PA: Stackpole Books, 2013); Martin Kitchen, *Rommel's Desert War: Waging World War II in North Africa, 1941–1943* (Cambridge: Cambridge University Press, 2009); Bastian Matteo Scianna, 'Rommel Almighty? Italian Assessments of the "Desert Fox" during and after the Second World War' in *The Journal of Military History* vol. 82, no. 1 (2018), pp. 125–145. On Guderian, see Hart's *Guderian* and my past campaign histories detailing Guderian's role in Operations Barbarossa and Typhoon.

82. As their research showed: 'performance, while a necessary standard for acceptability into a rather large pool of officers from which the elite will emerge, is nonetheless a minor influence on promotion and becomes even less discriminating as an officer's career progresses, whereas visibility – the extent to which an individual has developed contacts with peers and superiors who can influence his movement in the organization – begins moderately and eventually becomes the dominant influence'. David W. Moore and B. Thomas Trout, 'Military Advancement: The Visibility Theory of Promotion' in *The American Political Science Review* vol. 72, no. 2 (June 1978), pp. 452–468 (p. 452).

83. Fabrice d'Almeida, *High Society in the Third Reich* (Cambridge: Polity Press, 2008), p. 232.

84. Fabrice d'Almeida, 'Luxury and Distinction under National Socialism' in Pamela E. Swett, Cory Ross and Fabrice d'Almeida (eds.), *Pleasure and Power in Nazi Germany* (London: Palgrave Macmillan, 2011), pp. 67–83 (p. 69).

85. BArch N 823/24 (12 May 1941 and 2 August 1940).

86. Erich Hoepner's letters to his wife Irma. BArch N 51/9 (19 October 1941).

87. Reinhardt's personal army file BArch PERS 6/50, fol. 16.

88. D'Almeida, 'Luxury and Distinction under National Socialism', p. 69.

89. Hildegard von Kotze (ed.), *Heeresadjutant bei Hitler 1938–1943* (Stuttgart: Deutsche Verlags-Anstalt, 1974), p. 15 (13 March 1938). For an English translation see Gerhard Engel, *At the Heart of the Reich: The Secret Diary of Hitler's Army Adjutant* (London: Greenhill Books, 2005), p. 35 (13 March 1938). Engel's 'diary' should not be accepted as such, given that it was written after the war from memory.

90. D'Almeida, 'Luxury and Distinction under National Socialism', p. 75.

91. Guderian's personal army file. BArch PERS 6/27, fol. 61. Hart, *Guderian*, pp. 84–85.

92. Sönke Neitzel (ed.), *Tapping Hitler's Generals: Transcripts of Secret Conversations, 1942–45* (St Paul, MN: Frontline Books, 2007), p. 238.

93. Bastiaan Willems, *Violence in Defeat: The Wehrmacht on German Soil, 1944–1945* (Cambridge: Cambridge University Press, 2021), pp. 127–128.

94. Hürter, *Hitlers Heerführer*, p. 604.

95. Joachim Fest, *Plotting Hitler's Death: The German Resistance to Hitler 1933–1945* (London: Weidenfeld & Nicolson, 1996), pp. 297–303.

96. Nor were Guderian and his fellow court members politically constrained to produce only one result. Lieutenant-General Hans Speidel was cleared by the court of complicity in the plot, in spite of the fact that the regime considered him guilty. As a result, he was never executed, but the Gestapo kept him in custody until liberation. Russell Hart, 'Hans Speidel', in David T. Zabecki (ed.), *Chief of Staff: The Principal Officers behind History's Great Commanders. Volume 2: World War II to Korea and Vietnam* (Annapolis, MD: Naval Institute Press, 2008), pp. 50–61 (p. 60).

97. Hart, *Guderian*, p. 110.
98. D'Almeida, 'Luxury and Distinction under National Socialism', p. 69.
99. Margarete Guderian's Private Papers. BArch N 802/3, fol. 36.
100. Macksey, *Guderian*, pp. 7–8. Interestingly, David Fraser's biography of Rommel makes a similar point about his wife Lucie-Marie. David Fraser, *Knight's Cross: A Life of Field Marshal Erwin Rommel* (London: Harper Collins, 1993), p. 117.
101. Hart, *Guderian*, p. 103; see also p. 69.
102. Margarete Guderian's letters to her husband Heinz. BArch N 802/47 (23 December 1941).
103. This is either Princess Elisabeth of Bentheim-Steinfurt (1886–1959) or her sister Princess Victoria of Bentheim-Steinfurt (1887–1961). Margarete Guderian's letters to her husband Heinz. BArch N 802/47 (27 November 1941).
104. Ibid.
105. Presumably Luise Kesselring, the wife of Field Marshal Albert Kesselring. Ibid. (10 November 1941).
106. Ibid. (30 October 1941).
107. Trischa Goodnow and James J. Kimble (eds.), *The 10 Cent War: Comic Books, Propaganda, and World War II* (Jackson, MS: University Press of Mississippi, 2016); Mark Fertig, *Take That, Adolf! The Fighting Comic Books of the Second World War* (Seattle, WA: Fantagraphics Books, 2017).
108. Von Saldern, 'Innovative Trends in Women's and Gender Studies', p. 94.
109. Haffner, *Germany Jekyll & Hyde*, p. 104.
110. The boy's letter is in the same file as Schmidt's letters to Fridel. BArch N 823/24.
111. Remembering his time in the Hitler Youth, Jurgen Herbst recalled: 'I now was and would forever be a soldier. I steeped myself in book after book on German military history. [...] I absorbed deeply into every fibre of my being the Prussian military code.' Jurgen Herbst, *Requiem for a German Past: A Boyhood among the Nazis* (Madison, WI: The University of Wisconsin Press, 1999), p. 99. Another memoir of growing up in Nazi Germany recalled from 1940: 'The boys in school eagerly followed the exciting events. There was no one who did not know the different types of planes. There was a contest in diagnosing the make of the [English] plane by the sound of its engines long before one could see it, and we were up to date on the latest score of enemy planes downed by our fighter pilots.' H. Peter Nennhaus, *Boyhood: The 1930s and the Second World War: Memories, Comments and Views from the Other Side* (Worcester, MA: Chandler House Press, 2002), pp. 116–117.
112. For an eyewitness account of this event, see Solomon Perel, *Europa Europa: A Memoir of World War II* (New York: Wiley, 1993), pp. 33–34; Albert Axell, *Russia's Heroes 1941–45* (New York: Carroll & Graf, 2001), Chapter 5: 'Stalin's Son'.
113. The 15 July 1941 edition of the *Völkische Beobachter* (Wiener Ausgabe) showed a picture of Schmidt on the front page with his Oak Leaves to the Knight's Cross. This may be viewed online at the Austrian National Library at https://anno .onb.ac.at/cgi-content/anno?aid=vob&datum=19410715&seite=1&zoom=33.
114. It was a front-page article for the *Völkische Beobachter* (Wiener Ausgabe) as well as numerous other newspapers on 24 July 1941. https://anno.onb.ac.at/cgi-content /anno?datum=19410724&zoom=33.
115. The newspaper article is in the same file as Schmidt's letters to Fridel. The article has been cut out, so there is no way of knowing which newspaper published it. BArch N 823/24.
116. As Reuth noted, 'Rommel was receiving fan mail by the sackful.' *Rommel*, p. 120.

117. Helga Schneider, *The Bonfire of Berlin: A Lost Childhood in Wartime Germany* (London: Vintage, 2006), p. 7.

118. Sven Keller (ed.), *Kriegstagebuch einer jungen Nationalsozialistin: Die Aufzeichnungen Wolfhilde von Königs 1939–1946* (Berlin: De Gruyter Oldenbourg, 2015), p. 107; Wolfhilde von König, *Wolfhilde's Hitler Youth Diary 1939–1946* (Bloomington, IN: iUniverse, 2013), p. 110.

119. Rommel was sent to Libya not Tunisia. Ursula Mahlendorf, *The Shame of Survival: Working Through a Nazi Childhood* (University Park, PA: Pennsylvania State University Press, 2009), p. 130.

120. Susan Campbell Bartoletti, *Hitler Youth: Growing Up in Hitler's Shadow* (New York: Scholastic, 2005), p. 78.

121. Galland sent the boy his autograph, but not on a photo.

122. The magazine first appeared in 1935 with the name *Morgen*, but changed in 1937 to *Der Pimpf* and was only intermittently published during the war, ending with a July–August issue in 1944.

123. 'Meldefahrt mit dem Tod im Nacken', *Der Pimpf* (November 1941). I am indebted to Professor Randall Bytwerk for sending me a lot of detail about these books, including photos of individual editions. An overview of his collection is available on his 'German Propaganda Archive' hosted by Calvin University: https://research .calvin.edu/german-propaganda-archive/pimpf.htm.

124. 'General Schirokko', *Der Pimpf* (August 1942), p. 4.

125. Richard Grunberger, *A Social History of the Third Reich* (London, Phoenix, 2005), p. 358.

126. Guderian wrote 'unprinted' postcards, but probably meant 'blank' postcards. In German *ungedruckt* (unprinted) is easily confused with *unbedruckt* (blank).

127. Heinz Guderian's letters to his wife Margarete. BArch N 802/46 (12 August 1941).

128. Rommel also made use of coloured postcards with his printed autograph. See Reuth, *Rommel*, p. 129.

129. Heinz Guderian's letters to his wife Margarete. BArch N 802/46 (6 November 1941).

130. Horst Scheibert, *Das war Guderian: Ein Lebensbericht in Bildern* (Friedberg: Podzun-Palas Verlag, 1989), p. 135.

131. Ibid., p. 137.

132. In addition to the panzer generals, my search revealed signed postcards from other generals and field marshals within the army, including Georg von Küchler, Ernst Busch, Wilhelm List and Kluge, as well as many more who signed photographs.

133. It is also possible that some of these photographs may have been signed and circulated by the subjects after the war. I have chosen not to include the websites of stores that trade in Wehrmacht memorabilia or forums that showcase these as 'collectibles'.

134. An example of what Hoth's symbol actually looked like may be found in Robert Kirchubel, *Operation Barbarossa: The German Invasion of Soviet Russia* (Oxford: Osprey Publishing, 2013), p. 260. Thanks to Robert Kirchubel for pointing me to this.

135. Römer, *Comrades*, p. 99.

136. Heinz Guderian's letters to his wife Margarete. BArch N 802/46 (12 November 1941).

137. Muth, *Command Culture*, pp. 162 and 190–191.

138. Dennis Showalter, *Hitler's Panzers: The Lightning Attacks That Revolutionized Warfare* (New York: Berkley Caliber, 2009), p. 27. Interestingly, Guderian taught military history in the 1920s, although his school grades in history were typically judged 'pass' or 'satisfactory'. Only in this last year did he progress to 'good'

266 / Notes to pages 106–112

(although the grading system included 'very good' and 'excellent'). Guderian's school reports and grades. BArch N 802/9.

139. A search for 'Hoepner' between June and December 1941 reveals no results because his name was routinely misspelled. 'Hoeppner' generates twelve results and 'Höppner' another ten.

140. See 'German Front Newspapers in WWII: Mobilizing Soldiers and Civilians for War'. www.servicenewspapers.amdigital.co.uk/Explore/Essays/JurgenForster.

141. Born on 14 September 1886, Hoepner turned fifty-five on this day.

142. Memories of Colonel-General Hoepner. BArch N 51/8, fol. 23–24.

143. Römer, *Comrades*, p. 244.

144. Mitcham Jr., *The Men of Barbarossa*, p. 123.

145. Woche, *Zwischen Pflicht und Gewissen*, pp. 107–108.

146. Mitcham Jr., *The Men of Barbarossa*, p. 100.

147. Rudolf Schmidt's letters to his wife Fridel. BArch N 823/24 (1 November 1941).

148. Ibid. (18 November 1941).

149. Chales de Beaulieu, *Leningrad*, p. 135.

150. Mitcham Jr., *The Men of Barbarossa*, pp. 130 and 132.

151. 'Herbert von Blanckenhagen, Dolmetscher im Stabe Hoepner: Erinnerungen Manuskript'. BArch MSG 2/1172, p. 50.

152. Peter M. Kaiser (ed.), *Mut zum Bekenntnis: Die geheimen Tagebücher des Hauptmanns Hermann Kaiser 1941/1943* (Berlin: Lukas, 2010), p. 500 (12 April 1943).

153. Erich Hoepner's photos. BArch N 51/10.

154. Georg-Hans Reinhardt's letters to his wife Eva. BArch N 245/2 (8 August 1941).

155. Ibid. (28 August 1941).

156. Ibid.

157. Macksey, *Guderian*, p. 7.

158. Hermann Hoth, *Panzer-Operationen: Die Panzergruppe 3 und der operative Gedanke der deutschen Führung Sommer 1941* (Heidelberg: Scharnhorst Buchkameradschaft, 1956), p. 101; Hermann Hoth, *Panzer Operations: Germany's Panzer Group 3 during the Invasion of Russia, 1941* (Havertown, PA: Casemate, 2017), p. 117.

159. See Stahel, *Operation Barbarossa*, Chapter 8.

160. Heinz Guderian's letters to his wife Margarete. BArch N 802/46 (11 October 1941).

161. Römer, *Comrades*, p. 99.

162. Reinhardt's letter of 30 October 1939. BArch N 245/21, p. 1.

163. By contrast, the Soviet Marshal Georgy Zhukov believed his own sudden appearance in the Soviet media in October 1941 was a ploy by Stalin to have a scapegoat should Moscow fall. Karel C. Berkhoff, *Motherland in Danger: Soviet Propaganda during World War II* (Cambridge, MA: Harvard University Press, 2012), p. 43.

164. For examples see the front pages of the *Völkische Beobachter* (Wiener Ausgabe) from 24 to 28 September. These may be viewed online at the Austrian National Library at http://anno.onb.ac.at/cgi-content/anno?aid=vob. Thanks to John Lynott for pointing me in this direction.

165. 'Wer sind die Träger der höchsten Auszeichnungen?' *Wacht im Osten*, no. 620, p. 3. (21 August 1941); 'Wer sind die Träger der höchsten Auszeichnungen?' *Wacht im Osten*, no. 621, p. 3. (22 August 1941). www.servicenewspapers.amdigital.co.uk /Explore/Essays/JurgenForster.

166. Erich Hoepner's letters to his wife Irma. BArch N 51-9 (19 July 1941).

167. Georg Meyer (ed.), *Generalfeldmarschall Wilhelm Ritter von Leeb: Tagebuchaufzeichnungen und Lagebeurteilungen aus zwei Weltkriegen* (Stuttgart: Deutsche Verlags-Anstalt, 1976), p. 327 (11 August 1941).

168. Grunberger, *A Social History of the Third Reich*, p. 189. For an example of this term being used in a report from 1941, see Woche, *Zwischen Pflicht und Gewissen*, p. 108.

169. Römer, *Comrades*, p. 95.

170. Underlining in original. Erich Hoepner's letters to his wife Irma. BArch N 51-9 (1 January 1942).

171. Fellgiebel, *Elite of the Third Reich*, p. 50.

172. Pine, *Hitler's 'National Community'*, p. 93.

173. Heinz Guderian's letters to his wife Margarete. BArch N 802/46 (31 July 1941).

174. Rudolf Schmidt's letter to Margarete Guderian. BArch N 823/24 (14 July 1941).

175. Ibid. This was the reason Schmidt was writing to Margarete, to request Heinz's field post number.

176. Interestingly, British intelligence invested heavily in acquiring German press reports and front newspapers about the war in the East, believing that when 'scientifically read' they offered 'a remarkably revealing and coherent picture of conditions'. Ben Wheatley, *British Intelligence and Hitler's Empire in the Soviet Union, 1941–1945* (London: Bloomsbury, 2018), p. 83.

177. Stahel, *Operation Barbarossa*, pp. 315–317.

178. Heinz Guderian's letters to his wife Margarete. BArch N 802/46 (31 July 1941).

179. Rudolf Hofmann, *German Efficiency Report System*, US Army Historical Division Study MS# P-134 (Washington, DC: Office of the Chief of Military History, 1952), p. 41.

180. Maclean, *The Unknown Generals*, p. 80.

181. There were 5,070 Knight's Cross recipients in the army and 486 of these went on to win the Oak Leaves. Ibid., p. 77.

182. A good selection of these photographs was published after the war in Scheibert, *Das war Guderian*.

183. Heinz Guderian's letters to his wife Margarete. BArch N 802/46 (12 August 1941).

184. Lieutenant-General Wilhelm von Dommes (1867–1959) was a German divisional commander in the First World War, and from 1932 until the death of Wilhelm II in 1941 the administrative head of the exiled Prussian royal house.

185. Erich Hoepner's letters to his wife Irma. BArch N 51-9 (30 October 1941).

186. Ibid. (23 December 1941).

187. Maiken Umbach, '(Re-)Inventing the Private under National Socialism' in Elizabeth Harvey, Johannes Hürter, Maiken Umbach and Andreas Wirsching (eds.), *Private Life and Privacy in Nazi Germany* (Cambridge: Cambridge University Press, 2019), pp. 102–131 (p. 115). See also Maiken Umbach, 'Selfhood, Place, and Ideology in German Photo Albums, 1933–1945' in *Central European History* vol. 48, no. 3 (2015), pp. 335–365.

188. Corey Ross, 'Radio, Film and Morale: Wartime Entertainment between Mobilization and Distraction' in Pamela E. Swett, Cory Ross and Fabrice d'Almeida (eds.), *Pleasure and Power in Nazi Germany* (London: Palgrave Macmillan, 2011), pp. 154–174 (pp. 158–159).

189. Heinz Boberach (ed.), *Meldungen aus dem Reich: Die geheimen Lageberichte des Sicherheitsdienstes der SS 1938–1945*, Band 4 (Berlin: Pawlak, 1984), p. 1284 (20 June 1940).

190. Heinz Boberach (ed.), *Meldungen aus dem Reich: Die geheimen Lageberichte des Sicherheitsdienstes der SS 1938–1945*, Band 7 (Berlin: Pawlak, 1984), p. 2563 (24 July 1941).

191. Randall L. Bytwerk, *Bending Spines: The Propagandas of Nazi Germany and the German Democratic Republic* (East Lansing, MI: Michigan State University Press, 2004), p. 92.
192. Lehnhardt, *Die Waffen-SS*, p. 98.
193. Erich Hoepner's letters to his wife Irma. BArch N 51-9 (6 October 1941).
194. Kay Hoffmann, '"Kämpfer und Künder". Die Propagandakompanien' in Peter Zimmermann and Kay Hoffmann (eds.), *Geschichte des dokumentarischen Films in Deutschland, Band 3: 'Drittes Reich' (1933–1945)* (Stuttgart: Reclam, 2005), pp. 649–662 (p. 662).
195. Results (as of October 2020) are available on the website of the Russian Archive of Documentary Film and Newsreels (also available in English): www.net-film.ru.
196. These episodes of the *Wochenschau* may be viewed by searching for 'Guderian' at www.net-film.ru.
197. Margarete Guderian's letters to her husband Heinz. BArch N 802/47 (17 December 1941).
198. Erich Hoepner's letters to his wife Irma. BArch N 51-9 (27 November 1941).
199. David Stahel, *The Battle for Moscow* (Cambridge: Cambridge University Press, 2015), pp. 287–288 and 295–296.
200. Georg-Hans Reinhardt's letters to his wife Eva. BArch N 245/2 (28 September 1941).
201. Rudolf Schmidt's letters to his wife Fridel. BArch N 823/24 (15 November 1941).
202. Ibid. (1 November 1941).
203. Ibid. (18 November 1941).
204. Rudolf Schmidt's letter to Margarete Guderian. BArch N 823/24 (14 July 1941).
205. Rudolf Schmidt's letters to his wife Fridel. BArch N 823/24 (19 December 1941).
206. Margarete Guderian's letters to her husband Heinz. BArch N 802/47 (27 November 1941).
207. Gerd R. Ueberschär and Winfried Vogel, *Dienen und Verdienen: Hitlers Geschenke an seine Eliten* (Frankfurt am Main: S. Fischer, 1999), pp. 72–73.
208. Norman J. W. Goda, 'Black Marks: Hitler's Bribery of His Senior Officers during WWII' in *The Journal of Modern History* vol. 72, no. 2 (June 2000), pp. 413–452 (pp. 418–419).
209. Heinz Guderian's letters to his wife Margarete. BArch N 802/46 (24 July 1941).
210. Adam Tooze, *The Wages of Destruction: The Making and Breaking of the Nazi Economy* (London: Viking, 2006), p. 141.
211. Heinz Guderian's letters to his wife Margarete. BArch N 802/46 (24 July 1941).
212. Ibid. (10 December 1941).
213. Margarete Guderian's letters to her husband Heinz. BArch N 802/47 (31 August 1941).
214. Heinz Guderian's letters to his wife Margarete. BArch N 802/46 (30 August 1941).
215. Ibid. (1 December 1941).
216. Margarete Guderian's letters to her husband Heinz. BArch N 802/47 (29 December 1941).
217. Underlining in original. Erich Hoepner's letters to his wife Irma. BArch N 51-9 (30 October 1941).
218. Ibid. (14 December 1941).
219. Chales de Beaulieu, *General Erich Hoepner*, p. 100.
220. On alcohol in the German army, see Edward B. Westermann, *Drunk on Genocide: Alcohol and Mass Murder in Nazi Germany* (Ithaca, NY: Cornell University Press, 2021), Chapter 7.

221. Von Schlabrendorff, *Begegnungen in fünf Jahrzehnten*, pp. 215–216.
222. Erich Hoepner's letters to his wife Irma. BArch N 51-9 (26 August 1941).
223. Ibid. (30 October).
224. Ibid. (29 November 1941).
225. As one soldier from Army Group North wrote after the war: 'Despite regulations against it, it was not uncommon for German soldiers to ship looted Russian property such as icons or artefacts back to Germany. Most of the time, however, troops sent back items taken from the battlefield or from captured Red Army troops such as Soviet pistols and decorations. In general, the military authorities closed their eyes to such behaviour. In my experience, parcels sent home were not even checked for stolen property.' William Lubbeck, *At Leningrad's Gates: The Story of a Soldier with Army Group North* (Philadelphia, PA: Casemate, 2006), p. 118.
226. Stahel, *Retreat from Moscow*, pp. 240–241.
227. Erich Hoepner's letters to his wife Irma. BArch N 51-9 (1 August 1941).
228. Ibid. (19 July 1941).
229. Ibid. (1 August 1941).
230. Ibid. (12 September 1941).
231. Ibid. (17 September 1941).
232. Arvid Fredborg, *Behind the Steel Wall* (London: George G. Harrap, 1944), p. 69.
233. Erich Hoepner's letters to his wife Irma. BArch N 51-9 (19 October 1941). For the shortages of tobacco on the Eastern Front, see Stahel, *Retreat from Moscow*, p. 249.
234. Erich Hoepner's letters to his wife Irma. BArch N 51-9 (29 November 1941).
235. Moorhouse, *Berlin at War*, pp. 79-88.
236. Margarete Guderian's letters to her husband Heinz. BArch N 802/47 (31 August 1941).
237. Heinz Guderian's letters to his wife Margarete. BArch N 802/46 (30 August 1941).
238. Ibid. (7 November 1941).
239. Moorhouse, *Berlin at War*, p. 81.
240. Heinz Guderian's letters to his wife Margarete. BArch N 802/46 (1 December 1941).
241. Georg-Hans Reinhardt's letters to his wife Eva. BArch N 245/2 (9 December 1941).
242. Revealingly, the secret recordings of German generals held in British captivity at Trent Park include some egregious examples of entitlement. When a Swiss representative visited to inspect their conditions, the generals hatched a plan to hide or play down their many privileges in order to gain even more. See Helen Fry, *The Walls Have Ears: The Greatest Intelligence Operation of World War II* (New Haven, CT: Yale University Press, 2019), pp. 126–127.
243. Martin Middlebrook and Chris Everitt, *The Bomber Command War Diaries: An Operational Reference Book 1939–1945* (New York: Viking Publishing, 1985), pp. 171–172, 176–177.
244. Rudolf Schmidt's letter to Margarete Guderian. BArch N 823/24 (14 July 1941).
245. Erich Hoepner's letters to his wife Irma. BArch N 51-9 (19 July 1941).
246. Ibid. (29 July 1941).
247. Ibid. (18 August 1941).
248. Ibid. (24 September 1941).
249. Ibid. (12 December 1941).
250. Ibid. (4 January 1942).
251. Heinz Guderian's letters to his wife Margarete. BArch N 802/46 (24 October 1941).

252. Margarete Guderian's letters to her husband Heinz. BArch N 802/47 (26 October 1941).
253. Ibid. (27 November 1941).
254. Ibid. (26 December 1941).
255. Ibid. (23 December 1941).
256. Erich Hoepner's letters to his wife Irma. BArch N 51-9 (27 November 1941).
257. Ibid. (29 November 1941).
258. Hart, *Guderian*, pp. 87–88.
259. Ibid., p. 83; Goda, 'Black Marks', p. 436.
260. Goda, 'Black Marks', p. 437.
261. As cited in Ueberschär and Vogel, *Dienen und Verdienen*, p. 170; see also pp. 224–225.
262. Ibid., p. 172.
263. Goda, 'Black Marks', p. 437.
264. Alexander Stahlberg, *Bounden Duty: The Memoirs of a German Officer 1932–45* (London: Brassey, 1990), p. 372.
265. Stahlberg's memoir casts Manstein in a near universally positive light, choosing to ignore his racial and political views as well as his ambivalence towards mass murder in the East. Whether Manstein was really so surprised, much less bothered, by the injustice perpetrated against a single Pole is therefore unknown. For a fuller account of Manstein's own criminal behaviour, see Oliver von Wrochem, 'Ein unpolitischer Soldat? Generalfeldmarschall Erich von Manstein' in Gerhard Hirschfeld and Tobias Jersak (eds.), *Karrieren im Nationalsozialismus: Funktionseliten zwischen Mitwirkung und Distanz* (Frankfurt: Campus Verlag, 2004), pp. 185–204.
266. Ueberschär and Vogel, *Dienen und Verdienen*, p. 172.
267. Neitzel (ed.), *Tapping Hitler's Generals*, p. 238. The same point is made by Hermann Kaiser in 1943; see Kaiser (ed.), *Mut zum Bekenntnis*, pp. 491, 526 (6 April and 12 May 1943).
268. Gerhard L. Weinberg, *Germany, Hitler & World War II* (Cambridge: Cambridge University Press, 1995), pp. 307–308.
269. Ulrich von Hassell, *The Ulrich von Hassell Diaries: The Story of the Forces against Hitler inside Germany* (London: Frontline Books, 2011), p. 194 (20 April 1943).
270. Neitzel (ed.), *Tapping Hitler's Generals*, p. 238.
271. D'Almeida, *High Society in the Third Reich*, p. 235.

4 The Criminal Generals

1. David A. Gerber, *Authors of Their Lives: The Personal Correspondence of British Immigrants to North America in the Nineteenth Century* (New York: New York University Press, 2006), pp. 99–100.
2. Likewise, some of Margarete's letters (31 August and 5 November) abruptly end, mid-sentence, at the bottom of a page with no further pages included. Perhaps the subsequent pages were merely lost, but it seems highly possible they could have been deliberately excluded from the record.
3. Hürter, *Hitlers Heerführer*, p. 89. On this period, see Peter Keller, *'Die Wehrmacht der Deutschen Republik ist die Reichswehr': Die deutsche Armee 1918–1921* (Paderborn: Schöningh, 2014).
4. Michael Mann, *Fascists* (Cambridge: Cambridge University Press, 2010), p. 153.
5. Hürter, *Hitlers Heerführer*, p. 90.

6. Erich von Manstein, *Aus einem Soldatenleben 1887–1939* (Bonn: Athenäum-Verlag, 1958), p. 63.
7. As cited in Bradley, *Generaloberst Heinz Guderian*, pp. 123–124.
8. Ibid., p. 119.
9. Ibid., p. 126.
10. As cited in Hürter, *Hitlers Heerführer*, p. 177.
11. Erich Hoepner's letters to his wife Irma. BArch N 51/9 (1 September 1939).
12. Ibid. (6 September 1939).
13. Reinhardt's post-war memoir. BArch N 245/22, p. 3.
14. Ibid., p. 6.
15. For an excellent assessment of German policy in Poland, see Alexander B. Rossino, *Hitler Strikes Poland: Blitzkrieg, Ideology, and Atrocity* (Lawrence, KS: University Press of Kansas, 2003).
16. As cited in Bradley, *Generaloberst Heinz Guderian*, p. 142.
17. Neitzel (ed.), *Tapping Hitler's Generals*, p. 238.
18. As cited in Hürter, *Hitlers Heerführer*, p. 129, n. 32.
19. John Wheeler-Bennett, *The Nemesis of Power: The German Army in Politics 1918–1945* (London: Macmillan, 1954), p. 585.
20. Erich Hoepner's letters to his wife Irma. BArch N 51/9 (26 September 1939).
21. Wheeler-Bennett, *The Nemesis of Power*, p. 407.
22. While many works in this area seek only to celebrate the achievements of the German resistance, there is a growing, and far more measured, body of evidence that helps contextualise their motives and activities. See Christof Dipper, 'Der Deutsche Widerstand und die Juden' in *Geschichte und Gesellschaft* vol. 9 (1983), pp. 349–380; Christian Gerlach, 'Men of 20 July and the War in the Soviet Union' in Hannes Heer and Klaus Naumann (eds.), *War of Extermination: The German Military in World War II 1941–1944* (New York/Oxford: Berghahn, 2006), pp. 127–145; Christian Gerlach, 'Hitlergegner bei der Heeresgruppe Mitte und die "verbrecherischen Befehle"' in Gerd R. Ueberschär (ed.), *NS-Verbrechen und der militärische Widerstand gegen Hitler* (Darmstadt: Primus Verlag, 2000), pp. 62–76; Johannes Hürter, 'Auf dem Weg zur Militäropposition. Tresckow, Gersdorff, der Vernichtungskrieg und der Judenmord. Neue Dokumente über das Verhältnis der Heeresgruppe Mitte zur Einsatzgruppe B im Jahr 1941' in *Vierteljahreshefte für Zeitgeschichte* vol. 52, no. 3 (2004), pp. 527–562; Matthew Olex-Szczytowski, 'The German Military Opposition and National Socialist Crimes, 1939–1944: The Cases of Stauffenberg, Tresckow, and Schulenburg' in *War in History* vol. 28, no. 2 (2019), pp. 380–404. Beyond the military membership in the resistance, a similar point has been made by Stephan Malinowski about the 'tiny noble minority who went against the grain of the overwhelming majority of their professional colleagues and their class'. Stephan Malinowski, *Nazis and Nobles: The History of a Misalliance* (Oxford: Oxford University Press, 2021), p. 264.
23. Felix Römer cautions against seeing the anti-Hitler conspirators as black-and-white characters and compares their evolution to the changing attitudes observed among some German soldiers: 'One feature of the flexibility of the world views of many Wehrmacht soldiers was also their adaptability. Typical for the majority of the soldiers was not a linear, but rather a procedural, oft broken development in their attitudes. This famously applied even to the conspirators of 20 July 1944, who gradually distanced themselves from the Nazi regime only after a, sometimes, torturous process of detachment, until they were ultimately prepared to take part

in a coup. Yet even firm National Socialists found their world view, in some cases, only in a roundabout way.' Römer, *Comrades*, p. 60.

24. Moriz von Faber du Faur, *Macht und Ohnmacht: Erinnerungen eines alten Offiziers* (Stuttgart: Hans E. Günther Verlag, 1953), p. 178; see also p. 130.
25. Fabian von Schlabrendorff, *The Secret War against Hitler* (New York: Hodder and Stoughton, 1966), p. 178.
26. Von Schlabrendorff, *Begegnungen in fünf Jahrzehnten*, p. 264.
27. Wassili S. Christoforow, Wladimir G. Makarow and Matthias Uhl (eds.), *Verhört: Die Befragungen deutscher Generale und Offiziere durch die sowjetischen Geheimdienste 1945–1952* (Berlin: De Gruyter Oldenbourg, 2015), p. 186.
28. Hürter, *Hitlers Heerführer*, pp. 602–603.
29. Chris Helmecke, 'Ein "anderer" Oberbefehlshaber? Generaloberst Rudolf Schmidt und die deutsche Besatzungsherrschaft in der Sowjetunion 1941–1943' in *Militärgeschichtliche Zeitschrift* vol. 75, no. 1 (2016), pp. 55–93 (p. 66).
30. Christoforow, Makarow and Uhl (eds.), *Verhört*, p. 185, n. 26.
31. Hartmut Mehringer (ed.), *Die Tagebücher von Joseph Goebbels. Teil II: Diktate 1941–1945, Band 8, April–Juni 1943* (Munich: K. G. Saur, 1993), p. 266 (10 May 1943).
32. Roman Töppel, *Kursk 1943: The Greatest Battle of the Second World War* (Warwick: Helion, 2018), pp. 22–24.
33. Christoforow, Makarow and Uhl (eds.), *Verhört*, pp. 185–186 and 283.
34. Kaiser (ed.), *Mut zum Bekenntnis*, p. 494 (6 April 1943).
35. Christoforow, Makarow and Uhl (eds.), *Verhört*, p. 185, n. 25.
36. Rudolf Schmidt's letters to his wife Fridel. BArch N 823/24 (2 August 1940).
37. As cited in Helmecke, 'Ein "anderer" Oberbefehlshaber?', p. 67, n. 60.
38. Ibid.
39. Von Schlabrendorff, *The Secret War against Hitler*, p. 178. See also Helmecke, 'Ein "anderer" Oberbefehlshaber?', p. 68.
40. Making this argument is Woche, *Zwischen Pflicht und Gewissen*.
41. Christoforow, Makarow and Uhl (eds.), *Verhört*, pp. 186–187. Another falsehood reported in von Schlabrendorff's account was that after his military career ended Schmidt took to farming near Göttingen (*Begegnungen in fünf Jahrzehnten*, p. 266).
42. Woche's biography suggests otherwise: 'He [Schmidt] was then allowed to write to his wife in West Germany, because on June 2, 1955, when asked by the prison administration, he stated that his wife's place of residence was also his permanent place of residence.' *Zwischen Pflicht und Gewissen*, p. 194.
43. As cited in Jens Brüggemann, *Männer von Ehre? Die Wehrmachtgeneralität im Nürnberger Prozess 1945/46. Zur Entstehung einer Legende* (Paderborn: Schöningh, 2018), pp. 201–202.
44. Reinhardt's letter of 30 October 1939. BArch N 245/21, p. 3.
45. Diary of Georg-Hans Reinhardt. BArch N 245/3, fol. 75 (20 July 1944).
46. Ibid. (21 July 1944).
47. Von Schlabrendorff, *The Secret War against Hitler*, p. 178.
48. Jana Richter (ed.), *Die Tagebücher von Joseph Goebbels. Teil II: Diktate 1941–1945, Band 13, Juli–September 1944* (Munich: K. G. Saur, 1995), p. 121 (15 July 1944).
49. Diary of Georg-Hans Reinhardt. BArch N 245/3, fol. 91 (7–9 June 1945).
50. Ibid., fol. 95 (27 July 1945).
51. Wolfram Wette, 'Juden, Bolschewisten, Slawen. Rassenideologische Rußland-Feindbilder Hitlers und der Wehrmachtgeneräle' in Bianka Pietrow-Ennker (ed.)

Präventivkrieg? Der deutsche Angriff auf die Sowjetunion (Frankfurt am Main: Fischer, 2011), pp. 40–58; Jürgen Förster, 'Zum Rußlandbild der Militärs 1941–1945' in Hans-Erich Volkmann (ed.), *Das Rußlandbild im Dritten Reich* (Cologne: Böhlau, 1994), pp. 141–163; Andreas Hillgruber, 'The German Military Leaders' View of Russia prior to the Attack on the Soviet Union' in Bernd Wegner (ed.), *From Peace to War: Germany, Soviet Russia and the World, 1939–1941* (Oxford: Berghahn Books, 1997), pp. 169–185.

52. Klaus Latzel, 'Feldpostbriefe: Überlegungen zur Aussagekraft einer Quelle' in Christian Hartmann, Johannes Hürter and Ulrike Jureit (eds.), *Verbrechen der Wehrmacht: Bilanz einer Debatte* (Munich: C. H. Beck, 2005) 171–181 (pp. 178–179); Klaus Latzel, 'Wehrmachtsoldaten zwischen "Normalität" und NS-Ideologie, oder: Was sucht die Forschung in der Feldpost?' in Rolf-Dieter Müller and Hans-Erich Volkmann (eds.), *Die Wehrmacht: Mythos und Realität* (Munich: Oldenbourg, 1999), pp. 573–588 (p. 586). For more general studies concerning German attitudes towards the East, see Vejas Gabriel Liulevicius, *The German Myth of the East: 1800 to the Present* (Oxford: Oxford University Press, 2011); Charles Ingrao and Franz A. J. Szabo (eds.) *The Germans and the East* (West Lafayette, IN: Purdue University Press, 2008); Michael Burleigh, *Germany Turns Eastwards: A Study of 'Ostforschung' in the Third Reich* (Cambridge: Cambridge University Press, 1988).

53. Michaela Kipp, *Großreinemachen im Osten: Feindbilder in deutschen Feldpostbriefen im Zweiten Weltkrieg* (Frankfurt: Campus Verlag, 2014).

54. Römer, *Comrades*, p. 52.

55. Guderian was in fact in Byelorussia.

56. Heinz Guderian's letters to his wife Margarete. BArch N 802/46 (1 July 1941).

57. Ibid. (24 July 1941).

58. Ibid. (15 October 1941).

59. Ibid. (10 December 1941).

60. Ibid. (8 December 1941).

61. Margarete Guderian's letters to her husband Heinz. BArch N 802/47 (17 December 1941).

62. Erich Hoepner's letters to his wife Irma. BArch N 51/9 (13 July 1941).

63. Rudolf Schmidt's letters to his wife Fridel. BArch N 823/24 (5 December 1941).

64. Ibid. (21 July 1941).

65. Georg-Hans Reinhardt's letters to his wife Eva. BArch N 245/2 (12 December 1941).

66. Ibid. (19 June 1941).

67. Ibid. (18 July 1941).

68. As cited in Hürter, *Hitlers Heerführer*, p. 365.

69. This designation would again be used with different units from 1942.

70. Neitzel (ed.), *Tapping Hitler's Generals*, p. 19.

71. Ibid., p. 308; Fry, *The Walls Have Ears*, p. 113.

72. Gerd von Rundstedt's letters to his wife Luise. BArch N 977/7, pp. 5–6 (7, 9, 17 and 26 July 1941).

73. Günther von Kluge's letters to his wife Mathilde. BArch MSG/2/11185 (12 July 1941).

74. As cited in Hürter, *Hitlers Heerführer*, p. 443. Manstein's letters are not publicly available and remain in the private possession of the family, although a future publication is being planned.

75. For general studies of the cooperation, see Ian Oha Johnson, *Faustian Bargain: The Soviet–German Partnership and the Origins of the Second World War*

(Oxford: Oxford University Press, 2021); Manfred Zeidler, *Reichswehr und Rote Armee, 1920–1933: Wege und Stationen einer ungewöhnlichen Zusammenarbeit* (Munich: Oldenbourg, 1993); Olaf Groehler, *Selbstmörderische Allianz: Deutsch–russische Militärbeziehungen 1920–1941* (Berlin: Vision Verlag, 1992); Sally W. Stoecker, *Forging Stalin's Army: Marshal Tukhachevsky and the Politics of Military Innovation* (New York: Westview Press, 1998), Chapter 4: 'The Clandestine Collaboration between the Reichswehr and the Red Army'.

76. Hürter, *Hitlers Heerführer*, pp. 105–106.

77. Von Manstein, *Aus einem Soldatenleben*, p. 159.

78. Georg-Hans Reinhardt's letters to his wife Eva. BArch N 245/2 (16 July 1941).

79. As cited in Hürter, *Hitlers Heerführer*, pp. 106–107.

80. Volker Ullrich, *Hitler: Downfall 1939–45* (London: The Bodley Head, 2020), pp. 157–160.

81. The GPU, short for 'State Political Directorate', was the successor of the Cheka – the original Russian state security organization.

82. Franz Halder, *Kriegstagebuch: Tägliche Aufzeichnungen des Chefs des Generalstabes des Heeres 1939–1942. Band II: Von der geplanten Landung in England bis zum Beginn des Ostfeldzuges (1.7.1940–21.6.1941),* Hans-Adolf Jacobsen (ed.) (Stuttgart: Kohlhammer, 1963), pp. 336–337 (30 March 1941). Hereafter cited as Halder, KTB II.

83. As cited in Hürter, *Hitlers Heerführer*, p. 7.

84. Halder, KTB II, p. 337 (30 March 1941).

85. Gerd R. Ueberschär and Wolfram Wette (eds.), *'Unternehmen Barbarossa': Der deutsche Überfall auf die Sowjetunion 1941* (Paderborn: Schöningh, 1984), p. 305 (Document Collection 5); Ueberschär (ed.), *NS-Verbrechen und der militärische Widerstand gegen Hitler,* Document 8, p. 162.

86. Markus Pöhlmann, *Der Panzer und die Mechanisierung des Krieges: Eine deutsche Geschichte 1890 bis 1945* (Paderborn: Schöningh, 2016), p. 495. See also Raffael Scheck, *Hitler's African Victims: The German Army Massacres of Black French Soldiers in 1940* (Cambridge: Cambridge University Press, 2006).

87. Hanna Diamond, *Fleeing Hitler: France 1940* (Oxford: Oxford University Press, 2007).

88. Heinz Guderian's letters to his wife Margarete. BArch N 802/46 (15 June 1940).

89. Clasen, *Generaloberst Hans-Georg Reinhardt*, p. 304.

90. For a more detailed account of the massacre, see Adrian Weale, *Army of Evil: A History of the SS* (New York: NAL Caliber, 2012), pp. 249–251.

91. Bücheler, *Hoepner*, pp. 109–110; Hürter, *Hitlers Heerführer*, p. 189.

92. As cited in Hürter, *Hitlers Heerführer*, pp. 219–220.

93. For the famous thesis espoused by the renowned British historian Ian Kershaw, see '"Working towards the Führer": Reflections on the Nature of the Hitler Dictatorship' in Ian Kershaw and Moshe Lewin (eds.), *Stalinism and Nazism: Dictatorships in Comparison* (Cambridge: Cambridge University Press, 2003), pp. 88–106.

94. The order is reproduced in Ueberschär and Wette (eds.), *'Unternehmen Barbarossa'*, pp. 306–307 (Document Collection 1); Erhard Moritz (ed.), *Fall Barbarossa: Dokumente zur Vorbereitung der faschistischen Wehrmacht auf die Aggression gegen die Sowjetunion (1940/41)* (Berlin: Deutscher Militärverlag, 1970), Document 97, pp. 316–318.

95. In spite of this, according to research by Regina Mühlhäuser, sexual violence by German soldiers within the occupied Soviet Union was by no means an exception. See Regina Mühlhäuser, *Eroberungen: Sexuelle Gewalttaten und intime*

Beziehungen deutscher Soldaten in der Sowjetunion 1941–1945 (Hamburg: HIS Verlag, 2010).

96. The order is reproduced in Ueberschär and Wette (eds.), *"Unternehmen Barbarossa"*, pp. 313–314 (Document Collection 1); Moritz (ed.), *Fall Barbarossa*, Document 100, pp. 321–323.

97. Felix Römer, 'The Wehrmacht in the War of Ideologies: The Army and Hitler's Criminal Orders on the Eastern Front' in Alex J. Kay, Jeff Rutherford and David Stahel (eds.), *Nazi Policy on the Eastern Front, 1941: Total War, Genocide, and Radicalization* (Rochester, NY: University of Rochester Press, 2012), pp. 73–100 (pp. 76–77).

98. Guderian, *Panzer Leader*, p. 152. Manstein made similar claims in his memoir; see Erich von Manstein, *Lost Victories* (Novato, CA: Presidio, 1994), pp. 179–180.

99. Ralf Raths, 'Vom "Typenkompass" zu "World of Tanks": Das populäre Bild der Panzerei der Wehrmacht' in Jens Westemeier (ed.), *'So war der deutsche Landser': Das populäre Bild der Wehrmacht* (Paderborn: Schöningh, 2019), pp. 169–189 (p. 176).

100. Felix Römer, *Der Kommissarbefehl: Wehrmacht und NS-Verbrechen an der Ostfront 1941/42* (Paderborn: Schöningh, 2008), p. 397.

101. Ibid.

102. Such data from the panzer groups underline Christoph Rass's research into a single infantry division, which points to the fallacy of distinguishing between 'front' and 'rear' in charting the dimensions of the *Ostheer*'s war of annihilation. As Rass explained: 'the analysis of the combat practices of an ordinary infantry division has made clear that differentiation between a conventional war at the front and a war of extermination in the rear cannot be made. [. . .] Nearly all elements of National Socialist warfare and extermination policies coincided in the world of these sol-diers.' Christoph Rass, *'Menschenmaterial': Deutsche Soldaten an der Ostfront. Innenansichten einer Infanteriedivision 1939–1945* (Paderborn: Schöningh, 2003), p. 410.

103. Hürter, *Hitlers Heerführer*, p. 189, n. 170.

104. Römer, *Der Kommissarbefehl*, p. 582.

105. Römer, *Comrades*, p. 316.

106. Heinz Guderian's letters to his wife Margarete. BArch N 802/46 (7 August 1941).

107. Peter Steinkamp, 'Die Haltung der Hitlergegner Generalfeldmarschall Wilhelm Ritter von Leeb und Generaloberst Erich Hoepner zur verbrecherischen Kriegsführung bei der Heeresgruppe Nord in der Sowjetunion 1941' in Gerd R. Ueberschär (ed.), *NS-Verbrechen und der militärische Widerstand gegen Hitler* (Darmstadt: Primus Verlag, 2000), pp. 47–61 (p. 49).

108. Ibid., pp. 50, 170.

109. Römer, *Der Kommissarbefehl*, p. 582.

110. Georg-Hans Reinhardt's letters to his wife Eva. BArch N 245/2 (22 August 1941).

111. Römer, *Der Kommissarbefehl*, p. 345, n. 59; Hürter, *Hitlers Heerführer*, p. 395.

112. Hürter, *Hitlers Heerführer*, p. 395, n. 161. Hoth employed the same strategy as Reinhardt, attempting to argue that, although he issued the Commissar Order, the figures from his panzer group were mostly fictitious. See also Hébert, *Hitler's Generals on Trial*, pp. 113–114.

113. Römer, *Der Kommissarbefehl*, p. 582.

114. Helmecke, 'Ein "anderer" Oberbefehlshaber?', pp. 73–74.

115. Römer, *Der Kommissarbefehl*, pp. 531–532. See also Hans Hertel, *Generation im Aufbruch: Im Herzen das Vaterland* (Preussisch Oldenburg: Schütz, 1977), p. 284.

116. Hürter, *Hitlers Heerführer*, p. 454.

117. Römer, *Der Kommissarbefehl*, pp. 604–605.
118. Hürter, *Hitlers Heerführer*, pp. 397–398; Felix Römer, '"Kein Problem für die Truppe"' in *Die Zeit Geschichte – Hitlers Krieg im Osten*, No. 2 (2011), pp. 42–45.
119. Römer, 'The Wehrmacht in the War of Ideologies', p. 77.
120. Hébert, *Hitler's Generals on Trial*, p. 88.
121. Römer, 'The Wehrmacht in the War of Ideologies', p. 84.
122. Richard Overy, *Interrogations: The Nazi Elite in Allied Hands, 1945* (London: Penguin, 2002), pp. 529–531.
123. Ibid., pp. 531–533.
124. According to Peter Hoffmann, Guderian had offered his support for an anti-Nazi coup as early as 1938. Peter Hoffmann, *The History of the German Resistance 1933–1945* (Montreal: McGill-Queen's University Press, 1996), p. 129.
125. Kaiser (ed.), *Mut zum Bekenntnis*, p. 565 (21 May 1943).
126. Bernd Freytag von Loringhoven, *In the Bunker with Hitler: The Last Witness Speaks* (London: Weidenfeld & Nicolson, 2007), p. 65.
127. Kaiser (ed.), *Mut zum Bekenntnis*, pp. 570, 580 (11 and 28 June 1943).
128. Neitzel (ed.), *Tapping Hitler's Generals*, p. 265.
129. As cited in Heinrich Schwendemann, 'Strategie der Selbstvernichtung: Die Wehrmachtführung im "Endkampf" um das "Dritte Reich"' in Rolf-Dieter Müller and Hans-Erich Volkmann (eds.), *Die Wehrmacht: Mythos und Realität* (Munich: Oldenbourg, 1999), pp. 224–244 (p. 224). According to Winfried Heinemann: 'How far such considerations were from the minds of those in Germany who were responsible for the conduct of the war was made clear to the remaining general staff officers next morning, when their newly appointed chief of staff, Heinz Guderian, addressed them, describing the widespread scepticism about the situation in the East as "defeatism and pessimism", threatening to arrest and shoot them, and dismissing the past work of the general staff as "completely negative".' Winfried Heinemann, 'Military Resistance Activities and the War' in Ralph Blank et al. (eds.), *Germany and the Second World War. Volume IX/I: German Wartime Society 1939–1945: Politicization, Disintegration, and the Struggle for Survival* (Oxford: Oxford University Press, 2004), pp. 771–925 (p. 796).
130. Vilmos Nagybaczoni Nagy, *The Fateful Years 1938–1945* (Reno, NV: Helena History Press, 2021), p. 199.
131. Guderian, *Panzer Leader*, p. 368.
132. Steinkamp, 'Die Haltung der Hitlergegner Generalfeldmarschall Wilhelm Ritter von Leeb und Generaloberst Erich Hoepner', p. 54.
133. Christian Streit, 'Das Schicksal der verwundeten sowjetischen Kriegsgefangenen' in Hannes Heer and Klaus Naumann (eds.), *Vernichtungskrieg: Verbrechen der Wehrmacht 1941 bis 1944* (Hamburg: Hamburger Edition, 1995), pp. 78–91 (p. 80).
134. Ueberschär (ed.), *NS-Verbrechen und der militärische Widerstand gegen Hitler*, Document 13, p. 170.
135. Hürter, *Hitlers Heerführer*, p. 481.
136. Hébert, *Hitler's Generals on Trial*, pp. 79–80.
137. Hürter, *Hitlers Heerführer*, p. 373, n. 68.
138. Overy, *Interrogations*, p. 529.
139. Ian Kershaw, *The End: The Defiance and Destruction of Hitler's Germany, 1944–1945* (New York: Penguin, 2011), pp. 390–391.
140. Nicholas Stargardt, 'Legitimacy through War' in Devin O. Pendas, Mark Roseman and Richard F. Wetzell (eds.), *Beyond the Racial*

State: Rethinking Nazi Germany (Cambridge: Cambridge University Press, 2017), pp. 402–429 (p. 416).

141. Claude Steele, 'The Psychology of Self-Affirmation: Sustaining the Integrity of the Self' in *Advances in Experimental Social Psychology* vol. 21 (1988), pp. 261–302.

142. Anna Merritt, Daniel Effron and Benoît Monin, 'Moral Self-Licensing: When Being Good Frees Us to be Bad' in *Social and Personality Psychology Compass* vol. 4 (2010), pp. 344–357.

143. For a useful discussion of male self-conception and its impact on criminality in the East, see Frank Werner, '"Hart müssen wir hier draußen sein": Soldatische Männlickeit im Vernichtungskrieg, 1941–1944' in *Geschichte und Gesellschaft* vol. 34 (2008), pp. 5–40.

144. Heinz Guderian's letters to his wife Margarete. BArch N 802/46 (4 November 1941).

145. David A. Harrisville, *Unrighteous Cause: The Moral World of the German Soldier on the Eastern Front and the Wartime Origins of the Wehrmacht Myth, 1941–1944* (PhD dissertation, University of Wisconsin-Madison, 2018), p. 17. Harrisville's PhD was subsequently published as *The Virtuous Wehrmacht: Crafting the Myth of the German Soldier on the Eastern Front, 1941–1944*; however, this particular passage was cut from the published version.

146. Erich Hoepner's letters to his wife Irma. BArch N 51/9 (1 August 1941).

147. Heinz Guderian's letters to his wife Margarete. BArch N 802/46 (29 June 1941).

148. Ibid. (8 September 1941).

149. Rudolf Schmidt's letters to his wife Fridel. BArch N 823/24 (24 November 1941).

150. Dieter Pohl, *Die Herrschaft der Wehrmacht: Deutsche Militärbesatzung und einheimische Bevölkerung in der Sowjetunion 1941–1944* (Munich: Fischer, 2008), p. 190.

151. Berkhoff, *Motherland in Danger*, p. 277.

152. Georg-Hans Reinhardt's letters to his wife Eva. BArch N 245/2 (12 July 1941).

153. Stahel, *Operation Barbarossa*, p. 134.

154. On the role of everyday German soldiers in these practices, see Alex J. Kay and David Stahel, 'Reconceiving Criminality in the German Army on the Eastern Front' in Alex J. Kay and David Stahel (eds.), *Mass Violence in Nazi-Occupied Europe* (Bloomington, IN: Indiana University Press, 2018), pp. 177–181.

155. Erich Hoepner's letters to his wife Irma. BArch N 51/9 (14 December 1941).

156. Heinz Guderian's letters to his wife Margarete. BArch N 802/46 (8 December 1941).

157. Rudolf Schmidt's letters to his wife Fridel. BArch N 823/24 (5 September 1941).

158. Erich Hoepner's letters to his wife Irma. BArch N 51/9 (21 September 1941).

159. Hébert, *Hitler's Generals on Trial*, p. 124.

160. On 5 October 1941 Reinhardt wrote of sleeping in a 'manor house', but makes no mention of sharing it with civilians.

161. Hébert, *Hitler's Generals on Trial*, p. 124.

162. Ibid., p. 148.

163. Ibid., p. 108.

164. Ibid., p. 95.

165. Erich Hoepner's letters to his wife Irma. BArch N 51/9 (1 August 1941).

166. For a copy of the order see Ueberschär and Wette (eds.), '*Unternehmen Barbarossa*', pp. 339–340 (Document Collection 20).

167. As cited in Hürter, *Hitlers Heerführer*, p. 584.

168. 'Kriegstagebuch Nr.2 XXXXVII.Pz.Korps. Ia 23.9.1941–31.12.1941' BArch RH 24-47/258, fol. 75 (6 November 1941).

169. 'A.O.K.4 Ia Anlagen B 20 zum Kriegstagebuch Nr.9. 28.11.-3.12.41' BArch RH 20–4, fol. 156 (2 December 1941).

170. Ueberschär and Wette (eds.), 'Unternehmen Barbarossa', p. 339.

171. Römer, Comrades, pp. 317–318; Timothy L. Schroer, 'Civilization, Barbarism, and the Ethos of Self-Control among the Perpetrators' in German Studies Review, vol. 35, no. 1 (February 2012), pp. 33–54 (p. 35).

172. Isabel V. Hull, Absolute Destruction: Military Culture and the Practices of War in Imperial Germany (Ithaca, NY: Cornell University Press, 2006), p. 123.

173. André Mineau, Operation Barbarossa: Ideology and Ethics against Human Dignity (Amsterdam: Rodopi, 2004), p. 99.

174. Ernst Fraenkel, The Dual State: A Contribution to the Theory of Dictatorship (Oxford: Oxford University Press, 2016), pp. 110–111.

175. Mark Mazower, 'Military Violence and National Socialist Values: The Wehrmacht in Greece 1941–1944' in Past and Present, no. 134 (February 1992), pp. 129–158 (p. 156).

176. As cited in Steinkamp, 'Die Haltung der Hitlergegner Generalfeldmarschall Wilhelm Ritter von Leeb und Generaloberst Erich Hoepner', p. 55.

177. As cited in Ibid. See also Hürter, Hitlers Heerführer, p. 414, n. 243.

178. As cited in Steinkamp, 'Die Haltung der Hitlergegner Generalfeldmarschall Wilhelm Ritter von Leeb und Generaloberst Erich Hoepner', p. 56.

179. Ibid., p. 57.

180. For a discussion about German preparations for gas warfare in the East, see Stahel, The Battle for Moscow, pp. 302–303.

181. International Military Tribunal, Trial of the Major War Criminals before the International Military Tribunal. Volume IV (Nuremberg: n.pub., 1947), pp. 470–471. For an online reference see www.loc.gov/rr/frd/Military_Law/pdf/NT_Vol-IV.pdf. See also Smelser and Davies II, The Myth of the Eastern Front, p. 106.

182. Overy, Interrogations, p. 531.

183. International Military Tribunal, Trial of the Major War Criminals Volume IV, pp. 467–468. For an online reference see www.loc.gov/rr/frd/Military_Law/pdf/NT_Vol-IV.pdf.

184. Ben Shepherd, Hitler's Soldiers: The German Army in the Third Reich (New Haven, CT: Yale University Press, 2016), p. 487.

185. Alex J. Kay, Empire of Destruction: A History of Nazi Mass Killing (New Haven, CT: Yale University Press, 2021), p. 272.

186. Guderian, Panzer Leader, p. 362; David K. Yelton, Hitler's Home Guard: Volkssturmmann Western Front, 1944–1945 (Westminster, MD: Osprey, 2006), pp. 7–8.

187. As cited in Hürter, Hitlers Heerführer, p. 440, n. 356.

188. Ibid., p. 369, n. 48.

189. As cited in Hébert, Hitler's Generals on Trial, p. 89.

190. Ibid., pp. 89–90.

191. Friedrich-Christian Stahl, 'Generaloberst Rudolf Schmidt' in Gerd R. Ueberschär (ed.), Hitlers militärische Elite. Band 2: Vom Kriegsbeginn bis zum Weltkriegsende (Darmstadt: Primus Verlag, 1998), pp. 218–225 (p. 223).

192. Christoforow, Makarow and Uhl (eds.), Verhört, pp. 274–276.

193. Ibid., pp. 777–280.

194. Ibid., pp. 426–430.

195. Hürter, Hitlers Heerführer, p. 437.

196. Helmecke, 'Ein "anderer" Oberbefehlshaber?'.

197. Hürter, Hitlers Heerführer, pp. 459–460, 462.

198. For the scope of Hitler's New Order, see Richard J. Evans, *The Third Reich at War: How the Nazis Led Germany from Conquest to Disaster* (London: Penguin, 2009), pp. 336–339, 373–375.

199. Memories of Colonel-General Hoepner. BArch N 51/8, fols. 23–24. See also Hoffmann, *The History of the German Resistance 1933–1945*, p. 520.

200. Erinnerungsbericht Major i. G. Joachim Hoepner vom 12 Juni 1945, copy held in Gedenkstatte Deutscher Widerstand (The German Resistance Memorial Center, Berlin, Germany). This information is found on page 7 (although the printed pagination is not correct). My thanks to Professor Johannes Tuchel and the memorial for sending me this information as a digitised file.

201. Johannes Tuchel, '... *und ihrer aller wartete der Strick': Das Zellengefängnis Lehrter Straße 3 nach dem 20. Juli 1944* (Berlin: Lukas, 2014), p. 63.

202. Alex J. Kay, 'Transition to Genocide, July 1941: Einsatzkommando 9 and the Annihilation of Soviet Jewry' in *Holocaust and Genocide Studies* vol. 27, no. 3 (Winter, 2013), pp. 411–442.

203. As cited in Timm C. Richter, 'Die Wehrmacht und der Partisanenkrieg in den besetzten Gebieten der Sowjetunion' in Rolf-Dieter Müller and Hans-Erich Volkmann (eds.), *Die Wehrmacht: Mythos und Realität* (Munich: Oldenbourg, 1999), pp. 837–857 (p. 846).

204. Ueberschär and Wette (eds.), *'Unternehmen Barbarossa'*, p. 339.

205. Harrisville, *The Virtuous Wehrmacht*, p. 246, n. 83.

206. For examples see Luther and Stahel (eds.), *Soldiers of Barbarossa*, pp. 34–35, 40, 52, 59, 67–68, 76, 84, 94, 171, 182, 185, 194–196, 218, 222, 233 and 245–246.

207. Römer, *Comrades*, p. 52.

208. Raul Hilberg, *The Destruction of the European Jews* (New York: Holmes and Meier, 1985), pp. 107–108.

209. As cited in Browning and Matthäus, *The Origins of the Final Solution*, p. 260.

210. As cited in Steinkamp, 'Die Haltung der Hitlergegner Generalfeldmarschall Wilhelm Ritter von Leeb und Generaloberst Erich Hoepner', p. 57.

211. Friedmann Bedürftig, *Drittes Reich und Zweiter Weltkrieg: Das Lexikon* (Munich: Piper, 2002), p. 347.

212. My recent study of the 1941–1942 winter campaign provides evidence of all four panzer generals disregarding orders; see Stahel, *Retreat from Moscow*. Such behaviour was hardly unique to this period, and my earlier books offer further examples, especially for Guderian. Character references also testify to forceful personality traits. Lieutenant-General Karl Spang, who served with Hoepner as a young general staff officer, told fellow officers: 'Hoepner is a very capable man, but he is one of those with a very strong will of his own, with very clear-cut ideas.' Cited in Neitzel (ed.), *Tapping Hitler's Generals*, p. 252. Field Marshal Kluge was even more direct about Guderian: 'I have the greatest respect for Colonel-General Guderian, and he is a fantastic commander, but he does not obey.' 'Kriegstagebuch Nr.1 (Band December 1941) des Oberkommandos der Heeresgruppe Mitte'. BArch RH 19-II/122, fol. 206 (25 December 1941).

213. Nicholas Stargardt, 'Private and Public Moral Sentiments in Nazi Germany' in Elizabeth Harvey, Johannes Hürter, Maiken Umbach and Andreas Wirsching (eds.), *Private Life and Privacy in Nazi Germany* (Cambridge: Cambridge University Press, 2019), pp. 81–101 (p. 101).

214. Helmut Heiber and David M. Glantz (eds.), *Hitler and His Generals: Military Conferences 1942–1945* (New York: Enigma Books, 2003), p. 483.

215. As cited in Frank Vossler, *Propaganda in die eigene Truppe: Die Truppenbetreuung in der Wehrmacht 1939–1945* (Paderborn: Schöningh, 2005), p. 162.
216. As cited in Hürter, *Hitlers Heerführer*, pp. 139 and 513, n. 15.
217. Browning and Matthäus, *The Origins of the Final Solution*, p. 259.
218. As cited in Hürter, *Hitlers Heerführer*, p. 543.
219. Count 2: War crimes by being responsible for murder, ill-treatment and other crimes against prisoners of war and enemy belligerents. Count 3: Crimes against humanity by participating in or ordering the murder, torture, deportation, hostage-taking, etc. of civilians in military-occupied countries.
220. As cited in Hébert, *Hitler's Generals on Trial*, p. 151.
221. Clasen, *Generaloberst Hans-Georg Reinhardt*, pp. 505–507.
222. As cited in Hébert, *Hitler's Generals on Trial*, pp. 265–266.
223. Helmecke's 2016 article ('Ein "anderer" Oberbefehlshaber?') is useful in assessing aspects of Schmidt's occupation policy as of 1942, but conspicuously avoids most of his role in 1941. Woche's biography (*Zwischen Pflicht und Gewissen*) is a complete whitewash.
224. The secret recordings of conversations by senior German commanders held at Trent Park attest to the casual antisemitism that coloured their worldviews. Fry, *The Walls Have Ears*, pp. 129, 210–230 and 248–251.
225. As cited in Stahl, 'Generaloberst Rudolf Schmidt', p. 218.
226. Johanna Ray Vollhardt and Maggie Campbell-Obaid, 'The Social Psychology of Genocide and Mass Atrocities' in Arthur G. Miller (ed.), *The Social Psychology of Good and Evil* (New York: Guilford, 2016), pp. 159–184 (p. 160).
227. Claudia Koonz, *Mothers in the Fatherland: Women, the Family, and Nazi Politics* (New York: St. Martin's Press, 1987), p. 420.
228. Ibid.
229. Schwarz, '"Herrinnen der Zukunft"', p. 128.
230. Pine, *Hitler's 'National Community'*, p. 106.
231. Koonz, 'Mothers in the Fatherland: Women in Nazi Germany', p. 466.
232. Margarete Guderian's letters to her husband Heinz. BArch N 802/47 (5 November 1941).
233. Gaby Zipfel, 'Wie führen Frauen Krieg?' in Hannes Heer and Klaus Naumann (eds.), *Vernichtungskrieg: Verbrechen der Wehrmacht 1941 bis 1944* (Hamburg: Hamburger Edition, 1995), pp. 460–474 (p. 469).
234. Schwarz, '"Herrinnen der Zukunft"', p. 131.
235. Margarete Guderian's letters to her husband Heinz. BArch N 802/47 (17 December 1941).
236. Ibid.
237. Stanley Milgram, *Obedience to Authority: An Experimental View* (New York: Harper and Row, 1974). Milgram's research is not without its detractors and more recently questions have been raised about the validity of his methods and conclusions. See Gina Perry, *Behind the Shock Machine: The Untold Story of the Notorious Milgram Psychology Experiments* (Brunswick, NJ: Scribe, 2012); George R. Mastroianni, *Of Mind and Murder: Toward a More Comprehensive Psychology of the Holocaust* (Oxford: Oxford University Press, 2018).
238. Arthur G. Miller, Amy M. Buddie and Jeffrey Kretschmar, 'Explaining the Holocaust: Does Social Psychology Exonerate the Perpetrators?' in Leonard S. Newman and Ralph Erber (eds.), *Understanding Genocide: The Social Psychology of the Holocaust* (Oxford: Oxford University Press, 2002), pp. 301–324 (p. 321).

239. Adelheid von Saldern, 'Victims or Perpetrators? Controversies about the Role of Women in the Nazi State' in David Crew (ed.), *Nazism and German Society, 1933–1945* (London: Routledge, 1994), pp. 141–165 (p. 158).
240. Koonz, *Mothers in the Fatherland*, p. 17.
241. Johannes Hürter, 'Hitler's Generals in the East and the Holocaust' in Alex J. Kay and David Stahel (eds.), *Mass Violence in Nazi-Occupied Europe* (Bloomington, IN: Indiana University Press, 2018), pp. 17–40 (p. 32).
242. As social psychologists have argued: 'As the moral exclusion of victim groups, as well as violence against them, progresses, new norms are established, and this violence is normalized in society. Additionally, people can become habituated to violence and desensitized after an initial period of shock and physical discomfort.' Vollhardt and Campbell-Obaid, 'The Social Psychology of Genocide and Mass Atrocities', p. 168.
243. As cited in Hürter, 'Hitler's Generals in the East and the Holocaust', p. 35; Hürter, *Hitlers Heerführer*, p. 599.

5 The Military Generals

1. Georg-Hans Reinhardt's letters to his wife Eva. BArch N 245/2 (19 June 1941).
2. Ibid.
3. Guderian's post-war account emphasises his supposed prescience concerning Soviet strength, which he claimed led him to see the coming campaign as an 'infinitely difficult task'. He also denigrated optimists in the high command, writing: 'All the men of the OKW and the OKH with whom I spoke evinced an unshakeable optimism and were quite impervious to criticism or objections.' Guderian, *Panzer Leader*, pp. 142–143. See also Overy, *Interrogations*, p. 533. In fact, according to Engel, when Guderian's opinion was asked for during the planning of the campaign, he presented an optimistic view of German superiority over the Red Army. Von Kotze (ed.), *Heeresadjutant bei Hitler 1938–1943*, p. 86 (10 August 1940); Gerhard Engel, *At the Heart of the Reich*, p. 96 (10 August 1940). For Guderian's views in 1941, see Hillgruber, 'The German Military Leaders' View of Russia prior to the Attack on the Soviet Union', pp. 181–182.
4. Heinz Guderian's letters to his wife Margarete. BArch N 802/46 (16 June 1941).
5. Ibid. (29 June 1941).
6. Ibid. (1 July 1941).
7. Ibid. (12 July 1941).
8. As cited in Bücheler, *Hoepner*, p. 131.
9. Erich Hoepner's letters to his wife Irma. BArch N 51/9 (26 August 1941).
10. Underlining in the original. Ibid. (15 August 1941).
11. Ibid.
12. Heinz Guderian's letters to his wife Margarete. BArch N 802/46 (10 December 1941).
13. Rudolf Schmidt's letters to his wife Fridel. BArch N 823/24 (5 September 1941).
14. Ibid. (5 December 1941).
15. Christoforow, Makarow and Uhl (eds.), *Verhört*, p. 160.
16. Ibid., pp. 426–427. That Schmidt had some sense of foreboding is supported by the memoir of Schmidt's orderly: Hertel, *Generation im Aufbruch*, p. 280.
17. Rudolf Schmidt's letter to Lieutenant-General Friedrich Paulus. BArch N 372/22 (29 July 1941).

18. Heinz Guderian's letters to his wife Margarete. BArch N 802/46 (8 December 1941).

19. Guderian, *Panzer Leader*, p. 261.

20. Heinz Guderian's letters to his wife Margarete. BArch N 802/46 (16 December 1941).

21. Guderian's counterpart in Army Group Centre, Hermann Hoth, stated after the war: 'I myself was of the opinion that Hitler was the leader recognised by all the people and that if you stood against Hitler, you were going against the will of the people. I still had full confidence in Hitler at the beginning of the Russian campaign in 1941.' As cited in Hürter, *Hitlers Heerführer*, p. 213.

22. Margarete Guderian's letters to her husband Heinz. BArch N 802/47 (17 December 1941).

23. Georg-Hans Reinhardt's letters to his wife Eva. BArch N 245/2 (17 December 1941).

24. Rudolf Schmidt's letters to his wife Fridel. BArch N 823/24 (26 December 1941).

25. Buchbender and Sterz (eds.), *Das andere Gesicht des Krieges*, p. 15.

26. As explored in Chapter 3, this is also why the public naming of generals in official media releases was significant. The rarity only heightened the prestige of being identified.

27. Kilian, 'Postal Censorship'.

28. Lubbeck, *At Leningrad's Gates*, p. 118.

29. Johannes Hamm was fighting in southern Ukraine as part of Panzer Group 1 on the Sea of Azov. Johannes Hamm, Museumsstiftung Post und Telekommunikation, Berlin, 3.2002.7184 (16 November 1941).

30. Erich Hoepner's letters to his wife Irma. BArch N 51/9 (30 June 1941).

31. Ibid. (13 July 1941).

32. Ibid. (16 July 1941).

33. Ibid. (13 July 1941).

34. Ibid. (13, 19 July, 1, 18 August, 5 September 1941).

35. Georg-Hans Reinhardt's letters to his wife Eva. BArch N 245/2 (12 July 1941).

36. Heinz Guderian's letters to his wife Margarete. BArch N 802/46 (15 July 1941).

37. Rudolf Schmidt's letters to his wife Fridel. BArch N 823/24 (24 October 1941).

38. Heinz Guderian's letters to his wife Margarete. BArch N 802/46 (4 July 1941).

39. Commander of the 18th Panzer Division.

40. Commander of the 10th Panzer Division.

41. Commander of the SS 'Reich' Division.

42. Heinz Guderian's letters to his wife Margarete. BArch N 802/46 (4 July 1941).

43. For a detailed discussion of changes in the German high command at this time, see Stahel, *Retreat from Moscow*, Chapter 6: 'Put to the Sword: The End of Brauchitsch'.

44. Commander of Army Group South until 1 December 1941.

45. Commander of Army Group Centre until 19 December 1941.

46. Erich Hoepner's letters to his wife Irma. BArch N 51/9 (20 December 1941).

47. Ibid. (21 December 1941).

48. Ibid. (23 December 1941).

49. Ibid. (14 December 1941).

50. This is further confirmed by the other available letter collections by senior German officers. See Hürter (ed.), *Notizen aus dem Vernichtungskrieg*; Diedrich and Ebert (eds.), *Nach Stalingrad*; Mühleisen (ed.), *Hellmuth Stieff Briefe*; Meier-Welcker, *Aufzeichnungen eines Generalstabsoffiziers 1939–1942*; Günther von Kluge's letters to his wife Mathilde, BArch MSG/2/11185. By contrast, after the war the

intelligence section of SHAEF (Supreme Headquarters Allied Expeditionary Force) studied the letters of Field Marshal Gerd von Rundstedt and concluded: 'Von Rundstedt writes comparatively little about military matters. He mentions operations as being "satisfactory" or "unsatisfactory", and though he sometimes mentions future locations as much as 8 days beforehand, this lack of security seems never to go beyond a certain point. He never once, for example, discloses any matter of vital importance, he mentions topical events in his own particular sector in vague terms only, and usually refers his wife to "special announcements" as a further source of information. During his stay in Russia, he never once mentioned any military or political event outside his own combat zone [...].' Gerd von Rundstedt's letters to his wife Luise. BArch N 977/7, pp. 1–2.

51. Rudolf Langhaeuser, *German Methods of Safeguarding Classified Military Information*, US Army Historical Division Study MS# P-140 (Washington, DC: Office of the Chief of Military History, 1955), pp. 12–13.

52. Ibid.

53. Erich Hoepner's letters to his wife Irma. BArch N 51/9 (26 May 1941). In another letter from 26 May 1941, Hoepner informed his mother of the coming campaign. Heinrich Bücheler, *Hoepner*, p. 130.

54. Already in 1934 Guderian had been the target of a successful spying operation in which his planning documents, tank blueprints and even the key to his safe had been compromised by agents of the Polish Intelligence Service. Christer Jörgensen, *Hitler's Espionage Machine: The True Story behind One of the World's Most Ruthless Spy Networks* (London: The Lyons Press, 2004), p. 35.

55. Heinz Guderian's letters to his wife Margarete. BArch N 802/46 (16 June 1941).

56. Georg-Hans Reinhardt's letters to his wife Eva. BArch N 245/2 (19 June 1941).

57. Mauerwald was located some twenty kilometres northeast of Hitler's 'Wolf's Lair' headquarters.

58. The Schmidt family home was in Münster, but after a number of British bombing raids in early July 1941, Fridel moved to Leipzig to stay with her cousin. It is not known how long she remained there.

59. This is another consequence of Reinhardt editing out the personal details from his letters. Most likely the family residence was in either Dresden or Berlin, where Reinhardt served during the interwar period.

60. Gerd von Rundstedt's letters to his wife Luise. BArch N 977/7, p. 2.

61. On 10 November 1941 she wrote to Heinz: 'Mrs Kesselring just rang (9:30 in the evening) to the effect that a courier will fly out tomorrow, so I want to quickly write my greetings to give to him.' Margarete Guderian's letters to her husband Heinz. BArch N 802/47 (10 November 1941).

62. As Guderian noted on 15 October: 'Your letter from 1 October from Kl[ein] W[anzleben] is still on the move somewhere with the field post, which now needs about three weeks.' Heinz Guderian's letters to his wife Margarete. BArch N 802/46 (15 October 1941).

63. Remarkably, the U.S. War Department's G-2 (intelligence) data card on Guderian listed him as being a bachelor. Muth, *Command Culture*, p. 28.

64. Gerd von Rundstedt's letters to his wife Luise. BArch N 977/7, p. 1.

65. Developed in the nineteenth century under the tutelage of Helmuth von Moltke the Elder (chief of the general staff 1857 to 1887), *Auftragstaktik* was 'a command method stressing decentralised initiative within an overall strategic framework' (definition by Günther E. Rothenberg). The concept sought to reduce 'friction' in the command process by making lower-level commanders responsible for set objectives and empowering them to make independent decisions, while freeing

the higher command from tactical details. Strictly speaking it is not a tactic, nor is it limited to the tactical level of command, rather *Auftragstaktik* is best understood as a leadership method.

66. Sigg, *Der Unterführer als Feldherr im Taschenformat*, pp. 240–246.
67. See Michael Geyer's comments in his review of Sigg, *Der Unterführer als Feldherr im Taschenformat*, in *German History*, vol. 26, no. 1 (2018), pp. 142–144 (pp. 143–144). Thanks to Dr Roman Töppel for pointing out this review.
68. The artillery firepower available to an army was certainly formidable, but, given that it was horse-drawn and typically unsupported by tanks or the Luftwaffe, reliance on artillery alone meant the ability to maintain an offensive, in the manner of the panzer groups, was seriously compromised. For a more detailed discussion, see Jeff Rutherford, *Combat and Genocide on the Eastern Front: The German Infantry's War, 1941–1944* (Cambridge: Cambridge University Press, 2014), pp. 61–63.
69. Heinz Guderian's letters to his wife Margarete. BArch N 802/46 (4 July 1941).
70. 'Kriegstagebuch Nr.2 XXXXVII.Pz.Korps. Ia 25.5.1941–22.9.1941' BArch RH 24–47/2. This war diary has no folio-stamped page numbers, so references must be located using the date (24 June 1941).
71. Joachim Lemelsen's diary. BArch N 910 5, fol. 21 (30 June 1941).
72. Heinz Guderian's letters to his wife Margarete. BArch N 802/46 (4 July 1941).
73. Joachim Lemelsen's diary. BArch N 910 5, fol. 27 (6 July 1941).
74. Stahel, *Operation Barbarossa*, pp. 178–180.
75. Joachim Lemelsen's diary. BArch N 910 5, fol. 2 (10 June 1941).
76. Ibid., fol. 3 (17 June 1941).
77. Georg-Hans Reinhardt's letters to his wife Eva. BArch N 245/2 (12 July 1941). See also Chales de Beaulieu, *Leningrad*, pp. 156–158.
78. Erich Hoepner's letters to his wife Irma. BArch N 51/9 (16 July 1941). See also Chales de Beaulieu, *General Erich Hoepner*, pp. 146–147.
79. Georg-Hans Reinhardt's letters to his wife Eva. BArch N 245/2 (23 July 1941).
80. Chales de Beaulieu, *General Erich Hoepner*, p. 150.
81. Georg-Hans Reinhardt's letters to his wife Eva. BArch N 245/2 (26 July 1941).
82. Chales de Beaulieu, *Leningrad*, pp. 64–65.
83. Erich Hoepner's letters to his wife Irma. BArch N 51/9 (1 August 1941).
84. 'XXXXI Pz. Korps KTB 21.4.1941–31.12.1941' BArch RH 24/41–6 (7–8 August 1941).
85. Georg-Hans Reinhardt's letters to his wife Eva. BArch N 245/2 (10 August 1941).
86. Chales de Beaulieu, *Leningrad*, p. 84.
87. Ibid., pp. 86–87; Kirchubel, *Hitler's Panzer Armies*, pp. 140–141.
88. Stahel, *Operation Barbarossa*, pp. 268–270.
89. Hoth, *Panzer-Operationen*, p. 97; Hoth, *Panzer Operations*, p. 113.
90. Heinz Guderian's letters to his wife Margarete. BArch N 802/46 (24 July 1941).
91. Hertel, *Generation im Aufbruch*, p. 293.
92. Rudolf Schmidt's letter to Margarete Guderian. BArch N 823/24 (17 July 1941).
93. Rudolf Schmidt's letter to Lieutenant-General Friedrich Paulus. BArch N 372/22 (29 July 1941).
94. Woche, *Zwischen Pflicht und Gewissen*, pp. 80–81.
95. Stahel, *Operation Barbarossa*, pp. 268, 283.
96. Rudolf Schmidt's letter to Lieutenant-General Friedrich Paulus. BArch N 372/22 (29 July 1941).
97. Heinz Guderian's letters to his wife Margarete. BArch N 802/46 (31 July 1941).
98. Ibid. (7 August 1941).
99. Ibid. Stahel, *Operation Barbarossa*, p. 339.

100. Heinz Guderian's letters to his wife Margarete. BArch N 802/46 (12 August 1941).
101. Von Loringhoven, *In the Bunker with Hitler*, p. 123.
102. Karl-Henning von Barsewisch's diary. BArch N 802/189, p. 2 (11–12 July 1941).
103. Ibid., p. 2 (7 July 1941).
104. Ibid., p. 3 (5, 6 and 7 August 1941).
105. Joachim Lemelsen's diary. BArch N 910 5, fol. 4 (17 June 1941).
106. As cited in Michael Jones, *The Retreat: Hitler's First Defeat* (London: John Murray, 2009), p. 234.
107. Heinz Guderian's letters to his wife Margarete. BArch N 802/46 (18 August 1941).
108. Underlining in the original. 'Kriegstagebuch Nr.1 (Band August 1941) des Oberkommandos der Heeresgruppe Mitte'. BArch RH 19II/386, pp. 371–372 (23 August 1941).
109. Guderian, *Panzer Leader*, p. 200.
110. Ibid.
111. Macksey, *Guderian*, pp. 145–147; Macksey, 'Guderian'.
112. Franz Halder, *Kriegstagebuch: Tägliche Aufzeichnungen des Chefs des Generalstabes des Heeres 1939–1942. Band III: Der Rußlandfeldzug bis zum Marsch auf Stalingrad (22.6.1941–24.9.1942)*, Hans-Adolf Jacobsen and Alfred Philippi (eds.) (Stuttgart: Kohlhammer, 1964), p. 195 (24 August 1941).
113. Guderian, *Panzer Leader*, p. 202.
114. Rudolf-Christoph von Gersdorff, *Soldat im Untergang* (Frankfurt: Ullstein, 1979), p. 96; Rudolf-Christoph von Gersdorff, *Soldier in the Downfall: A Wehrmacht Cavalryman in Russia, Normandy and the Plot to Kill Hitler* (Bedford, PA: The Aberjona Press, 2012), p. 69. See also Fedor von Bock, *Generalfeldmarschall Fedor von Bock: The War Diary 1939–1945*, Klaus Gerbet (ed.) (Munich: Schiffer Military History, 1996), pp. 291–292 (24 August 1941).
115. Heinz Guderian's letters to his wife Margarete. BArch N 802/46 (30 August 1941).
116. Guderian, *Panzer Leader*, p. 202.
117. Stahel, *Kiev 1941*, pp. 130–131.
118. Heinz Guderian's letters to his wife Margarete. BArch N 802/46 (2 September 1941).
119. Ibid. (8 September 1941).
120. Römer, *Comrades*, p. 295.
121. Erich Hoepner's letters to his wife Irma. BArch N 51/9 (18 August 1941).
122. Ibid. (5 September 1941).
123. Ibid. (12 September 1941).
124. For Hitler's role, see Nicolaus von Below, *Als Hitlers Adjutant 1937–45* (Mainz: Pour le Mérite, 1999), p. 289.
125. Rudolf Schmidt's letters to his wife Fridel. BArch N 823/24 (24 August 1941).
126. Ibid. (5 September 1941).
127. Georg-Hans Reinhardt's letters to his wife Eva. BArch N 245/2 (22 August 1941).
128. Ibid. (7 September).
129. Ibid.
130. Ibid. (10 September).
131. This is a reference to a fictional character called Muley Hassan, who was a Tunisian Moor, in Friedrich Schiller's play *Die Verschwörung des Fiesco zu Genua*.
132. Georg-Hans Reinhardt's letters to his wife Eva. BArch N 245/2 (12 September 1941).
133. Erich Hoepner's letters to his wife Irma. BArch N 51/9 (19 July 1941).
134. Heinz Guderian's letters to his wife Margarete. BArch N 802/46 (24 July 1941).
135. Underlining in the original. Erich Hoepner's letters to his wife Irma. BArch N 51/9 (15 August 1941).

136. Heinz Guderian's letters to his wife Margarete. BArch N 802/46 (11 October 1941).

137. Ibid. (31 October 1941).

138. For more on this see Stahel, *The Battle for Moscow*, pp. 127–142.

139. Erich Hoepner's letters to his wife Irma. BArch N 51/9 (5 November 1941).

140. Rudolf Schmidt's letters to his wife Fridel. BArch N 823/24 (25 September 1941).

141. Georg-Hans Reinhardt's letters to his wife Eva. BArch N 245/2 (19 November 1941).

142. Römer, *Comrades*, p. 245.

143. Ibid., p. 243.

144. Erich Hoepner's letters to his wife Irma. BArch N 51/9 (23 June 1941).

145. Heinz Guderian's letters to his wife Margarete. BArch N 802/46 (1 July 1941).

146. Megargee, *Inside Hitler's High Command*, p. 110.

147. Wette, 'Juden, Bolschewisten, Slawen', pp. 42–45; Hillgruber, 'The German Military Leaders' View of Russia prior to the Attack on the Soviet Union', pp. 169–170; Förster, 'Zum Rußlandbild der Militärs 1941–1945', pp. 144–145; Olaf Groehler, 'Goals and Reason: Hitler and the German Military' in Joseph L. Wieczynski (ed.), *Operation Barbarossa: The German Attack of the Soviet Union 22 June, 1941* (Salt Lake City, UT: Charles Schlacks, 1993), pp. 50–55.

148. Gerhard Weinberg, '22 June 1941: The German View' in *War in History*, vol. 3, no.2 (1996), pp. 228–229.

149. Hürter, *Hitlers Heerführer*, pp. 105–106.

150. This theory was spread in Nazi propaganda and has long been debunked. See Bianka Pietrow-Ennker, (ed.), *Präventivkrieg? Der deutsche Angriff auf die Sowjetunion* (Frankfurt am Main: Fischer, 2011); Evan Mawdsley, 'Crossing the Rubicon: Soviet Plans for Offensive War in 1940–1941' in *The International History Review* vol. 25, no. 4 (2003), pp. 818–865.

151. A reference to Stalin's purge of the Red Army. See Peter Whitewood, *The Red Army and the Great Terror: Stalin's Purge of the Soviet Military* (Lawrence, KS: University Press of Kansas, 2015).

152. Georg-Hans Reinhardt's letters to his wife Eva. BArch N 245/2 (16 July 1941).

153. Erich Hoepner's letters to his wife Irma. BArch N 51/9 (5 July 1941).

154. Ibid. (13 July 1941).

155. Heinz Guderian's letters to his wife Margarete. BArch N 802/46 (19 July 1941).

156. Erich Hoepner's letters to his wife Irma. BArch N 51/9 (15 July 1941).

157. Ibid. (19 July 1941). Given the detailed research on women serving in the Red Army, it appears highly unlikely that a battalion-sized female combat formation existed at this stage in the war. See Anna Krylova, *Soviet Women in Combat: A History of Violence on the Eastern Front* (Cambridge: Cambridge University Press, 2011), p. 28; Alexander Hill, *The Red Army and the Second World War* (Cambridge: Cambridge University Press, 2017), pp. 224–225.

158. Georg-Hans Reinhardt's letters to his wife Eva. BArch N 245/2 (13 August 1941).

159. Ibid. (22 August 1941).

160. German atrocities were a central theme of Soviet propaganda, with posters such as 'Death to the Child Murderers', featuring a dead girl with a pair of bloody, swastika-emblazoned, boots walking away. Other posters were clearly aimed at the soldiers of the Red Army, with slogans such as 'Shoot the Murderers of Our Wives and Children', 'Soldier, Save Me from Slavery' and 'Warrior of the Red Army Save Us'. As cited in Cathy Porter and Mark Jones, *Moscow in World War II* (London: Chatto & Windus, 1987), pp. 68–71.

161. Rudolf Schmidt's letters to his wife Fridel. BArch N 823/24 (13 August 1941).

162. Ibid. (2 October 1941).
163. Ibid. (8 October 1941).
164. Ibid. (28 October 1941).
165. Erich Hoepner's letters to his wife Irma. BArch N 51/9 (19 October 1941).
166. On this subject, see Roger R. Reese, *Why Stalin's Soldiers Fought: The Red Army's Military Effectiveness in World War II* (Lawrence, KS: University Press of Kansas, 2011).
167. In the early nineteenth century the Prussian War Academy had taught 'strategic-tactical considerations' and 'logic', but by 1891 both had been cut from the curriculum. See Daniel J. Hughes and Richard L. DiNardo, *Imperial Germany and War, 1871–1918* (Lawrence, KS: University Press of Kansas, 2018), p. 93.
168. Research has shown that Soviet defections were mainly a result of internal issues within the Red Army. See Mark Edele, *Stalin's Defectors: How Red Army Soldiers Became Hitler's Collaborators, 1941–1945* (Oxford: Oxford University Press, 2019), p. 111. On German methods to encourage defection see Buchbender, *Das tönende Erz.*
169. Heinz Guderian's letters to his wife Margarete. BArch N 802/46 (29 June 1941).
170. Erich Hoepner's letters to his wife Irma. BArch N 51/9 (1 August 1941).
171. Georg-Hans Reinhardt's letters to his wife Eva. BArch N 245/2 (13 August 1941).
172. Ibid. (29 August 1941).
173. Ibid.
174. Erich Hoepner's letters to his wife Irma. BArch N 51/9 (17 September 1941).
175. Ibid.
176. Ibid. (21 September 1941).
177. Ibid.
178. Von Kotze (ed.), *Heeresadjutant bei Hitler 1938–1943*, p. 70 (10 December 1939); Engel, *At the Heart of the Reich*, p. 82 (10 December 1939).
179. Von Hassell, *The Ulrich von Hassell Diaries*, p. 86 (27 March 1940).
180. Hürter, *Notizen aus dem Vernichtungskrieg*, p. 121 (19 December 1941). Kluge commanded the neighbouring Fourth Army. For further complaints by Heinrici about Guderian's leadership see Ibid., pp. 88–89, 97 and 121 (15 November, 1 and 22 December 1941).
181. As cited in Basil Liddell Hart, *The Other Side of the Hill: Germany's Generals: Their Rise and Fall* (London: Pan Books, 1999), p. 71.
182. Ibid.
183. Neitzel (ed.), *Tapping Hitler's Generals*, p. 248.
184. As a twenty-year-old cadet at a military school in Metz, Guderian often reflected on his difficulties in forming friendships. In November 1908 he wrote: 'If only I could find a real friend. The comrades are all very nice, but I don't have a friend among them, nobody I could rely on for anything.' The following month he continued: 'I shut myself off from my comrades because I haven't found a real friend until now.' Bradley, *Generaloberst Heinz Guderian*, pp. 27–28.
185. Stahel, *Operation Typhoon*, pp. 74–75.
186. Bock had had a long-standing stomach complaint and had been largely bed-ridden from September 1940 until February 1941.
187. Erich Hoepner's letters to his wife Irma. BArch N 51/9 (6 October 1941).
188. Ibid.
189. Reinhardt's conviction on this matter also runs contrary to his own experience. Two years earlier, when he commanded the 4th Panzer Division in the Polish campaign, he unsuccessfully ordered his armoured forces into Warsaw and was twice repelled by much weaker defenders than he would have encountered in

Leningrad in September 1941. See Adrian Wettstein, 'Urban Warfare Doctrine on the Eastern Front' in Alex J. Kay, Jeff Rutherford and David Stahel (eds.), *Nazi Policy on the Eastern Front, 1941: Total War, Genocide and Radicalization* (Rochester, NY: Rochester University Press, 2012), pp. 45–72 (p. 45).

190. Georg-Hans Reinhardt's letters to his wife Eva. BArch N 245/2 (22 September 1941).

191. Ibid. (28 September 1941).

192. Stahel, *Operation Typhoon*, pp. 84–85.

193. Klink, 'The Conduct of Operations', pp. 644, 648.

194. See document printed in Woche, *Zwischen Pflicht und Gewissen*, p. 253.

195. Rudolf Schmidt's letters to his wife Fridel. BArch N 823/24 (14 October 1941).

196. Ibid. (28 October 1941).

197. Evan Mawdsley, *Thunder in the East: The Nazi–Soviet War 1941–1945* (London: Bloomsbury, 2016), p. 88.

198. Rudolf Schmidt's letters to his wife Fridel. BArch N 823/24 (12 November 1941). See also Schmidt's letter of 18 November.

199. Weichs would resume his command on 15 January 1942, by which time Schmidt was commanding both the Second Army and the Second Panzer Army after Guderian's dismissal.

200. Rudolf Schmidt's letters to his wife Fridel. BArch N 823/24 (12 November 1941).

201. Ibid. (24 November 1941).

202. The 10 October 1941 edition of the *Völkische Beobachter* (Wiener Ausgabe). https://anno.onb.ac.at/cgi-content/anno?aid=vob&datum=19411010&seite=1&zoom=33.

203. Heinz Guderian's letters to his wife Margarete. BArch N 802/46 (24 October 1941).

204. Ibid.

205. Römer, *Comrades*, p. 243.

206. Erich Hoepner's letters to his wife Irma. BArch N 51-9 (27 November 1941).

207. Stahel, *The Battle for Moscow*, p. 52.

208. Erich Hoepner's letters to his wife Irma. BArch N 51-9 (29 November 1941).

209. Guderian made the same claim against Kluge in his memoir. Guderian, *Panzer Leader*, p. 258–259. For Kluge's actual role in the offensive see Stahel, *The Battle for Moscow*, pp. 287–290.

210. Erich Hoepner's letters to his wife Irma. BArch N 51-9 (4 December 1941).

211. See Stahel, *The Battle for Moscow*, Chapters 9 and 10.

212. Stahel, *Retreat from Moscow*, p. 27.

213. Heinz Guderian's letters to his wife Margarete. BArch N 802/46 (8 December 1941).

214. Ibid.

215. Erich Hoepner's letters to his wife Irma. BArch N 51-9 (17 December 1941).

216. Rudolf Schmidt's letters to his wife Fridel. BArch N 823/24 (26 December 1941).

217. Heinz Guderian's letters to his wife Margarete. BArch N 802/46 (10 December 1941).

218. Georg-Hans Reinhardt's letters to his wife Eva. BArch N 245/2 (17 December 1941).

219. Erich Hoepner's letters to his wife Irma. BArch N 51-9 (12 December 1941).

220. See Kühne, *The Rise and Fall of Comradeship*.

221. Römer, *Comrades*, p. 246.

222. Georg-Hans Reinhardt's letters to his wife Eva. BArch N 245/2 (17 December 1941).

223. Ibid. (10 December 1941).

224. For Geyer's post-war account of the campaign, see Hermann Geyer, *Das IX. Armeekorps im Ostfeldzug 1941* (Neckargemünd: Vowinckel, 1969).

225. Erich Hoepner's letters to his wife Irma. BArch N 51-9 (23 December 1941).

226. Rudolf Schmidt's letters to his wife Fridel. BArch N 823/24 (24 December 1941).

227. On Guderian's dismissal see Stahel, *Retreat from Moscow*, pp. 195–198.
228. Rudolf Schmidt's letters to his wife Fridel. BArch N 823/24 (3 January 1942).
229. Heinz Guderian's letters to his wife Margarete. BArch N 802/46 (10 December 1941).
230. Ibid.
231. Ibid.
232. Ibid. (16 December 1941).
233. Ibid.
234. Erich Hoepner's letters to his wife Irma. BArch N 51-9 (23 December 1941).
235. Stahel, *Retreat from Moscow*, pp. 94–96.
236. Erich Hoepner's letters to his wife Irma. BArch N 51-9 (23 December 1941).
237. Erich Hoepner's letters to his wife Irma. BArch N 51-9 (8 December 1941).
238. Ibid.
239. Ibid. (23 December 1941).
240. Georg-Hans Reinhardt's letters to his wife Eva. BArch N 245/2 (9 December 1941).
241. Stahel, *Retreat from Moscow*, pp. 82–83.
242. Underlining in the original. Georg-Hans Reinhardt's letters to his wife Eva. BArch N 245/2 (28 December 1941).
243. Ibid.
244. Ibid. (31 December 1941).
245. Robert M. Citino, *The German Way of War: From the Thirty Years' War to the Third Reich* (Lawrence, KS: University Press of Kansas, 2005), pp. 308–309.
246. Michael Geyer, 'German Strategy in the Age of Machine Warfare, 1914–1945' in Peter Paret (ed.), *Makers of Modern Strategy: From Machiavelli to the Nuclear Age* (Oxford: Clarendon Press, 1999), pp. 527–597 (p. 586).
247. Martin Kitchen, *The German Officer Corps 1890–1914* (Oxford: Clarendon Press, 1968), pp. 224–225.
248. Ibid., p. 227.
249. Hull, *Absolute Destruction*, p. 333. See also Geoffrey P. Megargee, 'The German Army after the Great War: A Case Study in Selective Self-Deception' in Peter Dennis and Jeffrey Grey (eds.), *Victory or Defeat: Armies in the Aftermath of Conflict* (Moss Vale, NSW: Big Sky Publishing, 2010), pp. 104–117.
250. Stahel, *Retreat from Moscow*, pp. 197–198.
251. Ibid., p. 197.
252. Ibid., p. 303.
253. Ibid., pp. 341–342.

Conclusion

1. Stahel, *Operation Barbarossa*, pp. 427–436.
2. Helmecke, 'Ein "anderer" Oberbefehlshaber?', pp. 71, 77–87.
3. As cited in Jeff Rutherford, 'Total War in 1943: Combat and Occupation around the Kursk Salient' in *The Journal of Military History* (forthcoming). My thanks to Jeff for allowing me access to his unpublished paper.
4. Hart, *Guderian*, p. 114.
5. See the extensive discussion about Guderian's legacy in Smelser and Davies II, *The Myth of the Eastern Front*.
6. Margarete Guderian's private papers. BArch N 802/3, fol. 36.
7. Margarete Guderian's letters to her husband Heinz. BArch N 802/47 (30 October 1941).
8. Margarete Guderian's private papers. BArch N 802/3, fol. 36.

9. Tooze, *The Wages of Destruction*, p. 358.
10. Koonz, *Mothers in the Fatherland*, p. 419.
11. Some historians continue to believe this; see Georg Meyer, *Adolf Heusinger: Dienst eines deutschen Soldaten 1915 bis 1964* (Berlin: Mittler & Sohn, 2001), pp. 441–442.
12. Hébert, *Hitler's Generals on Trial*, p. 190; Brüggemann, *Männer von Ehre?*, pp. 35–44.
13. Norbert Frei, *Vergangenheitspolitik: Die Anfänge der Bundesrepublik und die NS-Vergangenheit* (Munich: Beck, 1996), p. 288.
14. Jörg Echternkamp, *Postwar Soldiers: Historical Controversies and West German Democratization, 1945–1955* (New York: Berghahn Books, 2020), pp. 230–231.
15. There is a great deal of excellent literature on this topic, but for two overviews see Wolfram Wette, *The Wehrmacht: History, Myth, Reality* (London: Harvard University Press, 2006); Ben Shepherd, *Hitler's Soldiers*.
16. Lieutenant-General Heinrich Kirchheim's account in Neitzel (ed.), *Tapping Hitler's Generals*, p. 274.
17. In this regard Heinrich Bücheler's 1980 biography is a whitewash. More recently, the English-language publications of Chales de Beaulieu's *Leningrad: The Advance of Panzer Group 4* (2020) and *General Erich Hoepner: A Military Biography* (2021) reproduce a sanitised post-war view of Hoepner. This in itself is fine, as it preserves Chales de Beaulieu's original account and makes it accessible to the Anglo-American world, but the same cannot be said of the historical editor (Matthias Strohn), who does not challenge any of the claims made by Chales de Beaulieu in the introductory essays of either book. Moreover, there is not a word about Hoepner's criminal past, which might have been understandable in books published in the 1960s, but is not acceptable today.
18. BArch N 51/8, fol. 44.
19. Bücheler, *Hoepner*, p. 207.
20. https://hbgym.de/schule/unser-name/.
21. These can be viewed (sometimes with photos of the signs) in a search of Google Maps.
22. See the 1948 letter by Basil Liddell Hart to Guderian detailing his public campaign. BArch N 802/80, fol. 3.
23. Woche, *Zwischen Pflicht und Gewissen*, pp. 193–194.
24. As cited in Ibid.
25. Woche, *Zwischen Pflicht und Gewissen*, p. 194.

Afterword

1. Hoepner's letters will subsequently be published in *The Journal of Slavic Military Studies* and in future years, as the copyright expires, I shall endeavour to do the same for the other letter collections.
2. Of course, the German authorities cannot identify who exactly those descendants would be today, or how any differences of opinion among them might be resolved.

BIBLIOGRAPHY

Archival Sources

I.   Bundesarchiv–Militärarchiv, Freiburg im Breisgau (BArch)

BArch MSG 2/1172 Herbert von Blanckenhagen, translator on Hoepner's staff.
BArch MSG/2/11185 Günther von Kluge's letters to his wife Mathilde.
BArch N 51/8 Memories of Colonel-General Hoepner.
BArch N 51/9 Erich Hoepner's letters to his wife Irma.
BArch N 51/10 Erich Hoepner's photos.
BArch N 223/24 Rudolf Schmidt's letters to his wife Fridel.
BArch N 245/2 Hans-Georg Reinhardt's letters to his wife Eva.
BArch N 245/3 Diary of Hans-Georg Reinhardt.
BArch N 245/21 Reinhardt's letter 30 October 1939.
BArch N 245/22 Reinhardt's post-war memoir.
BArch N 372/22 Friedrich Paulus's personal papers.
BArch N 671/8 Wolfram von Richthofen's diary.
BArch N 802/3 Margarete Guderian's Private Papers.
BArch N 802/9 Guderian's school reports and grades.
BArch N 802/46 Heinz Guderian's letters to his wife Margarete.
BArch N 802/47 Margarete Guderian's letters to her husband Heinz.
BArch N 802/80 Guderian's Correspondence with Historians.
BArch N 802/189 Karl-Henning von Barsewisch's diary.
BArch N 910/5 Joachim Lemelsen's diary.
BArch N 977/7 Gerd von Rundstedt's letters to his wife Luise.
BArch PERS 6/27 Guderian's Personal Army File.
BArch PERS 6/50 Reinhardt's Personal Army File.

BArch RH 19-II/122 'Kriegstagebuch Nr.1 (Band December 1941) des Oberkommandos der Heeresgruppe Mitte'.

BArch RH 19-II/386 'Kriegstagebuch Nr.1 (Band August 1941) des Oberkommandos der Heeresgruppe Mitte'.

BArch RH 20–4 'A.O.K.4 Ia Anlagen B 20 zum Kriegstagebuch Nr.9. 28.11.– 3.12.41'.

BArch RH 24–41/6 'XXXXI Pz. Korps KTB 21.4.1941–31.12.1941'.

BArch RH 24–47/2 'Kriegstagebuch Nr.2 XXXXVII.Pz.Korps. Ia 25.5.1941– 22.9.1941'.

BArch RH 24–47/258 'Kriegstagebuch Nr.2 XXXXVII.Pz.Korps. Ia 23.9.1941– 31.12.1941'.

II.   Museumsstiftung Post und Telekommunikation, Berlin

3.2002.985 – Heinz Rahe (28 October 1941).

3.2002.7184 – Johannes Hamm (16 November 1941).

III.   Gedenkstatte Deutscher Widerstand, Berlin

Erinnerungsbericht Major i. G. Joachim Hoepner vom 12 Juni 1945.

Secondary Works

Adam, Christian, *Bestsellers of the Third Reich: Readers, Writers and the Politics of Literature* (Oxford: Berghahn Books, 2021).

Axell, Albert, *Russia's Heroes 1941–45* (New York: Carroll & Graf, 2001).

Baird, Jay W., *To Die for Germany: Heroes in the Nazi Pantheon* (Bloomington, IN: Indiana University Press, 1992).

Balck, Hermann, *Order in Chaos: The Memoirs of General of Panzer Troops Hermann Balck* (Lexington, KT: University Press of Kentucky, 2015).

Bartoletti, Susan Campbell, *Hitler Youth: Growing up in Hitler's Shadow* (New York: Scholastic, 2005).

Bartov, Omer, 'From Blitzkrieg to Total War: Controversial Links between Image and Reality' in Ian Kershaw and Moshe Lewin (eds.), *Stalinism and Nazism: Dictatorships in Comparison* (Cambridge: Cambridge University Press, 2003), pp. 158–184.

Beckett, Ian F. W. (ed.), *Rommel Reconsidered* (Mechanicsburg, PA: Stackpole Books, 2013).

Bedürftig, Friedmann, *Drittes Reich und Zweiter Weltkrieg: Das Lexikon* (Munich: Piper, 2002).

Below, Nicolaus von, *Als Hitlers Adjutant 1937–45* (Mainz: Pour le Mérite, 1999).

Bergen, Doris, 'Storm Troopers of Christ: The German Christian Movement and the Ecclesiastical Final Solution' in Robert P. Ericksen and Susannah Heschel (eds.), *Betrayal: German Churches and the Holocaust* (Minneapolis, MN: Fortress Press, 1999), pp. 40–67.

Bergen, Doris, *Twisted Cross: The German Christian Movement in the Third Reich* (Chapel Hill, NC: University of North Carolina Press, 1996).

Berkhoff, Karel C., *Motherland in Danger: Soviet Propaganda during World War II* (Cambridge, MA: Harvard University Press, 2012).

Blitzkrieg: In Their Own Words: First-Hand Accounts from German Soldiers 1939–1940 (St Paul, MN: Zenith Press, 2005).

Blücher Kurznachrichten, no. 37, 9 September 1941.

Boberach, Heinz (ed.), *Meldungen aus dem Reich: Die geheimen Lageberichte des Sicherheitsdienstes der SS 1938–1945*. Vols 4, 7 and 8 (Berlin: Pawlak, 1984).

Bock, Fedor von, *Generalfeldmarschall Fedor von Bock: The War Diary 1939–1945*, Klaus Gerbet (ed.) (Munich: Schiffer Military History, 1996).

Bradley, Dermot, *Generaloberst Heinz Guderian und die Entstehungsgeschichte des modernen Blitzkrieges* (Osnabrück: Biblio-Verlag, 1986).

Browning, Christopher R. and Jürgen Matthäus, *The Origins of the Final Solution: The Evolution of Nazi Jewish Policy 1939–1942* (London: Arrow Books, 2004).

Brüggemann, Jens, *Männer von Ehre? Die Wehrmachtgeneralität im Nürnberger Prozess 1945/46. Zur Entstehung einer Legende* (Paderborn: Schöningh, 2018).

Buchbender, Ortwin, *Das tönende Erz: Deutsche Propaganda gegen die Rote Armee im Zweiten Weltkrieg* (Stuttgart: Seewald Verlag, 1978).

Buchbender, Ortwin and Reinhold Sterz (eds.), *Das andere Gesicht des Krieges: Deutsche Feldpostbriefe 1939–1945* (Munich: C. H. Beck, 1982).

Bücheler, Heinrich, *Hoepner: Ein deutsches Soldatenschicksal des 20. Jahrhunderts* (Herford: Verlag E. S. Mittler and Sohn, 1980).

Burleigh, Michael, *Ethics and Extermination: Reflections on Nazi Genocide* (Cambridge: Cambridge University Press, 1997).

Burleigh, Michael, *Germany Turns Eastwards: A Study of 'Ostforschung' in the Third Reich* (Cambridge: Cambridge University Press, 1988).

Bytwerk, Randall L., *Bending Spines: The Propagandas of Nazi Germany and the German Democratic Republic* (East Lansing, MI: Michigan State University Press, 2004).

Chales de Beaulieu, Walter, *General Erich Hoepner: A Military Biography* (Havertown, PA: Casemate Publishers, 2021).

Chales de Beaulieu, Walter, *Leningrad: The Advance of Panzer Group 4, 1941* (Havertown, PA: Casemate Publishers, 2020).

Carsten, F. L., *The Reichswehr and Politics 1918 to 1933* (Oxford: Oxford University Press, 1966).

Casey, Steven, 'Reporting from the Battlefield: Censorship and Journalism' in Richard J. B. Boworth and Joseph A. Maiolo (eds.), *The Cambridge History of the Second World War. Volume II: Politics and Ideology* (Cambridge: Cambridge University Press, 2015), pp. 117–138.

Christoforow, Wassili S., Wladimir G. Makarow and Matthias Uhl (eds.), *Verhört: Die Befragungen deutscher Generale und Offiziere durch die sowjetischen Geheimdienste 1945–1952* (Berlin: De Gruyter Oldenbourg, 2015).

Citino, Robert M., *The German Way of War: From the Thirty Years' War to the Third Reich* (Lawrence, KS: University Press of Kansas, 2005).

Clasen, Christoph, *Generaloberst Hans-Georg Reinhardt* (Stuttgart: Zeitungsverlag, 1996).

d'Almeida, Fabrice, *High Society in the Third Reich* (Cambridge: Polity Press, 2008).

d'Almeida, Fabrice, 'Luxury and Distinction under National Socialism' in Pamela E. Swett, Cory Ross and Fabrice d'Almeida (eds.), *Pleasure and Power in Nazi Germany* (London: Palgrave Macmillan, 2011), pp. 67–83.

Diamond, Hanna, *Fleeing Hitler: France 1940* (Oxford: Oxford University Press, 2007).

Diedrich, Torsten and Jens Ebert (eds.), *Nach Stalingrad: Walther von Seydlitz' Feldpostbriefe und Kriegsgefangenenpost 1939–1955* (Göttingen: Wallstein Verlag, 2018).

Die Wehrmachtberichte 1939–1945, Band 1: 1. September 1939 bis 31. Dezember 1941 (Munich: Deutscher Taschenbuch Verlag, 1985).

Dipper, Christof, 'Der Deutsche Widerstand und die Juden' in *Geschichte und Gesellschaft* vol. 9 (1983), pp. 349–380.

Echevarria II, Antulio J., *After Clausewitz: German Thinkers before the Great War* (Lawrence, KS: University Press of Kansas, 2000).

Echternkamp, Jörg, *Postwar Soldiers: Historical Controversies and West German Democratization, 1945–1955* (New York: Berghahn Books, 2020).

Edele, Mark, *Stalin's Defectors: How Red Army Soldiers Became Hitler's Collaborators, 1941–1945* (Oxford: Oxford University Press, 2019).

Engel, Gerhard, *At the Heart of the Reich: The Secret Diary of Hitler's Army Adjutant* (London: Greenhill Books, 2005).

Ericksen, Robert P., 'Assessing the Heritage: German Protestant Theologians, Nazis, and the "Jewish Question"' in Robert P. Ericksen and Susannah Heschel (eds.),

Betrayal: German Churches and the Holocaust (Minneapolis, MN: Fortress Press, 1999), pp. 22–30.

Ericksen, Robert P., *Complicity in the Holocaust: Churches and Universities in Nazi Germany* (Cambridge: Cambridge University Press, 2012).

Evans, Richard J., *The Third Reich at War: How the Nazis Led Germany from Conquest to Disaster* (London: Penguin, 2009).

Faber du Faur, Moriz von, *Macht und Ohnmacht: Erinnerungen eines alten Offiziers* (Stuttgart: Hans E. Günther Verlag, 1953).

Fellgiebel, Walther-Peer, *Elite of the Third Reich: The Recipients of the Knight's Cross of the Iron Cross 1939–45: A Reference* (Solihull: Helion, 2003).

Fertig, Mark, *Take That, Adolf! The Fighting Comic Books of the Second World War* (Seattle, WA: Fantagraphics Books, 2017).

Fest, Joachim, *Plotting Hitler's Death: The German Resistance to Hitler 1933–1945* (London: Weidenfeld & Nicolson, 1996).

Flemming, Thomas, '"Willenspotentiale": Offizierstugenden als Gegenstand der Wehrmachtspsychologie', in Ursula Breymayer, Bernd Ulrich and Karin Wieland (eds.), *Willensmenschen: Über deutsche Offiziere* (Frankfurt am Main: Fischer, 2000), pp. 111–122.

Förster, Jürgen, 'Zum Rußlandbild der Militärs 1941–1945' in Hans-Erich Volkmann (ed.), *Das Rußlandbild im Dritten Reich* (Cologne: Böhlau, 1994), pp. 141–163.

Fraenkel, Ernst, *The Dual State: A Contribution to the Theory of Dictatorship* (Oxford: Oxford University Press, 2016).

Fraser, David, *Knight's Cross: A Life of Field Marshal Erwin Rommel* (London: Harper Collins, 1993).

Fredborg, Arvid, *Behind the Steel Wall* (London: George G. Harrap, 1944).

Frei, Norbert, *Vergangenheitspolitik: Die Anfänge der Bundesrepublik und die NS-Vergangenheit* (Munich: Beck, 1996).

Fröhlich, Elke (ed.), *Die Tagebücher von Joseph Goebbels. Teil II: Diktate 1941–1945, Band 1, Juli–September 1941* (Munich: K. G. Saur, 1996).

Fry, Helen, *The Walls Have Ears: The Greatest Intelligence Operation of World War II* (New Haven, CT: Yale University Press, 2019).

Gerber, David A., *Authors of Their Lives: The Personal Correspondence of British Immigrants to North America in the Nineteenth Century* (New York: New York University Press, 2006).

Gerlach, Christian, 'Hitlergegner bei der Heeresgruppe Mitte und die "verbrecherischen Befehle"' in Gerd R. Ueberschär (ed.), *NS-Verbrechen und der militärische Widerstand gegen Hitler* (Darmstadt: Primus Verlag, 2000), pp. 62–76.

Gerlach, Christian, 'Men of 20 July and the War in the Soviet Union' in Hannes Heer and Klaus Naumann (eds.), *War of Extermination: The German Military in World War II 1941–1944* (New York and Oxford: Berghahn, 2006), pp. 127–145.

Gerlach, Wolfgang, *Als die Zeugen schwiegen: Bekennende Kirche und die Juden* (Berlin: Institut Kirche und Judentum, 1987).

Gersdorff, Rudolf-Christoph von, *Soldat im Untergang* (Frankfurt: Ullstein, 1979).

Gersdorff, Rudolf-Christoph von, *Soldier in the Downfall: A Wehrmacht Cavalryman in Russia, Normandy and the Plot to Kill Hitler* (Bedford, PA: The Aberjona Press, 2012).

Geyer, Hermann, *Das IX. Armeekorps im Ostfeldzug 1941* (Neckargemünd: Vowinckel, 1969).

Geyer, Michael, review of '*Der Unterführer als Feldherr im Taschenformat: Theorie und Praxis der Auftragstaktik im deutschen Heer 1869 bis 1945*. By Marco Sigg. Paderborn: Ferdinand Schöningh. 2014' in *German History* vol. 26 no. 1 (2018), pp. 142–144.

Geyer, Michael, 'German Strategy in the Age of Machine Warfare, 1914–1945' in Peter Paret (ed.), *Makers of Modern Strategy: From Machiavelli to the Nuclear Age* (Oxford: Clarendon Press, 1999), pp. 527–597.

Glantz, David M. (ed.), *The Initial Period of War on the Eastern Front: 22 June– August 1941* (London: Frank Cass, 1997).

Goda, Norman J. W., 'Black Marks: Hitler's Bribery of His Senior Officers during WWII' in *The Journal of Modern History* vol. 72, no. 2 (June 2000), pp. 413–452.

Goodnow, Trischa and James J. Kimble (eds.), *The 10 Cent War: Comic Books, Propaganda, and World War II* (Jackson, MS: University Press of Mississippi, 2016).

Greyerz, Kaspar von, 'Ego-Documents: The Last Word?' in *German History* vol. 28, no. 3 (2010), pp. 273–282.

Groehler, Olaf, 'Goals and Reason: Hitler and the German Military' in Joseph L. Wieczynski (ed.), *Operation Barbarossa: The German Attack of the Soviet Union 22 June, 1941* (Salt Lake City, UT: Charles Schlacks, 1993), pp. 48–61.

Groehler, Olaf, *Selbstmörderische Allianz: Deutsch–russische Militärbeziehungen 1920–1941* (Berlin: Vision Verlag, 1992).

Grossman, David A., 'Maneuver Warfare in the Light Infantry – The Rommel Model' in Richard D. Hooker (ed.), *Maneuver Warfare: An Anthology* (Novato, CA: Presidio Press, 1993), pp. 316–333.

Grunberger, Richard, *A Social History of the Third Reich* (London, Phoenix, 2005).

Guderian, Heinz, *Achtung – Panzer! The Development of Tank Warfare* (London: Cassell Military Paperbacks, 2002).

Guderian, Heinz, *Panzer Leader* (New York: Da Capo Press, 1996).

Habeck, Mary, *Storm of Steel: The Development of Armor Doctrine in Germany and the Soviet Union, 1919–1939* (London: Cornell University Press, 2003).

Haffner, Sebastian, *Germany Jekyll & Hyde: A Contemporary Account of Nazi Germany* (London: Abacus, 2008).

Hagelstam, Sonja, 'Families, Separation and Emotional Coping in War: Bridging Letters between Home and Front, 1941–44' in Tiina Kinnunen and Ville Kivimäki (eds.), *Finland in World War II: History, Memory, Interpretations* (Boston, MA: Brill, 2012), pp. 277–312.

Halder, Franz, *Kriegstagebuch: Tägliche Aufzeichnungen des Chefs des Generalstabes des Heeres 1939–1942. Band II: Von der geplanten Landung in England bis zum Beginn des Ostfeldzuges (1.7.1940–21.6.1941)*, Hans-Adolf Jacobsen (ed.) (Stuttgart: Kohlhammer, 1963).

Halder, Franz, *Kriegstagebuch: Tägliche Aufzeichnungen des Chefs des Generalstabes des Heeres 1939–1942. Band III: Der Rußlandfeldzug bis zum Marsch auf Stalingrad (22.6.1941–24.9.1942)*, Hans-Adolf Jacobsen and Alfred Philippi (eds.) (Stuttgart: Kohlhammer, 1964).

Hämmerle, Christa, 'Gewalt und Liebe – ineinander verschränkt: Paarkorrespondenzen aus zwei Weltkriegen: 1914/18 und 1939/45' in Ingrid Bauer and Christa Hämmerle (eds.), *Liebe schreiben: Paarkorrespondenz im Kontext des 19. und 20. Jahrhunderts* (Göttingen: Vandenhoeck & Ruprecht, 2017), pp. 171–230.

Harrisville, David A., *The Virtuous Wehrmacht: Crafting the Myth of the German Soldier on the Eastern Front, 1941–1944* (Ithaca, NY: Cornell University Press, 2021).

Harrisville, David A., 'Unholy Crusaders: The Wehrmacht and the Reestablishment of Soviet Churches during Operation Barbarossa' in *Central European History* vol. 52, no. 4 (2019), pp. 620–649.

Harrisville, David A., *Unrighteous Cause: The Moral World of the German Soldier on the Eastern Front and the Wartime Origins of the Wehrmacht Myth, 1941–1944* (PhD dissertation, University of Wisconsin-Madison, 2018).

Hart, Russell A., *Guderian: Panzer Pioneer or Myth Maker?* (Washington, DC: Potomac Books, 2006).

Hart, Russell A., 'Hans Speidel' in David T. Zabecki (ed.), *Chief of Staff: The Principal Officers behind History's Great Commanders. Vol. 2: World War II to Korea and Vietnam* (Annapolis, MD: Naval Institute Press, 2008), pp.50–61.

Harvey, Elizabeth, Johannes Hürter, Maiken Umbach and Andreas Wirsching (eds.), *Private Life and Privacy in Nazi Germany* (Cambridge: Cambridge University Press, 2019).

Hasenclever, Jörn, *Wehrmacht und Besatzungspolitik: Die Befehlshaber der rückwärtigen Heeresgebiete 1941–1943* (Paderborn: Schöningh, 2010).

Hassell, Ulrich von, *The Ulrich von Hassell Diaries: The Story of the Forces against Hitler inside Germany* (London: Frontline Books, 2011).

Hébert, Valerie Geneviève, *Hitler's Generals on Trial: The Last War Crimes Tribunal at Nuremberg* (Lawrence, KS: University Press of Kansas, 2010).

Heiber, Helmut and David M. Glantz (eds.), *Hitler and His Generals: Military Conferences 1942–1945* (New York: Enigma Books, 2003).

Heineman, Elizabeth D., *What Difference Does a Husband Make? Women and Marital Status in Nazi and Postwar Germany* (Berkeley, CA: University of California Press, 2003).

Heinemann, Winfried, 'Military Resistance Activities and the War' in Ralph Blank et al. (eds.), *Germany and the Second World War. Volume IX/I: German Wartime Society 1939–1945: Politicization, Disintegration, and the Struggle for Survival* (Oxford: Oxford University Press, 2004), pp. 771–925.

Helmecke, Chris, 'Ein "anderer" Oberbefehlshaber? Generaloberst Rudolf Schmidt und die deutsche Besatzungsherrschaft in der Sowjetunion 1941–1943' in *Militärgeschichtliche Zeitschrift* vol. 75, no. 1 (2016), pp. 55–93.

Herbst, Jurgen, *Requiem for a German Past: A Boyhood among the Nazis* (Madison, WI: The University of Wisconsin Press, 1999).

Hertel, Hans, *Generation im Aufbruch: Im Herzen das Vaterland* (Preussisch Oldenburg: K. W. Schütz, 1977).

Herzog, Dagmar, 'Hubris and Hypocrisy, Incitement and Disavowal: Sexuality and German Fascism' in Dagmar Herzog (ed.), *Sexuality and German Fascism* (Oxford: Berghahn Books, 2004), pp. 1–21.

Heschel, Susannah, 'When Jesus Was an Aryan. The Protestant Church and Antisemitic Propaganda' in Robert P. Ericksen and Susannah Heschel (eds.), *Betrayal: German Churches and the Holocaust* (Minneapolis, MN: Fortress Press, 1999), pp. 68–89.

Heusinger, Adolf, *Dienst eines deutschen Soldaten 1915 bis 1964* (Berlin: Mittler & Sohn, 2001).

Hilberg, Raul, *The Destruction of the European Jews* (New York: Holmes and Meier, 1985).

Hill, Alexander, *The Red Army and the Second World War* (Cambridge: Cambridge University Press, 2017).

Hillgruber, Andreas, 'The German Military Leaders' View of Russia prior to the Attack on the Soviet Union' in Bernd Wegner (ed.), *From Peace to War: Germany, Soviet Russia and the World, 1939–1941* (Oxford: Berghahn Books, 1997), pp. 169–185.

Hoffmann, Kay, '"Kämpfer und Künder". Die Propagandakompanien' in Peter Zimmermann and Kay Hoffmann (eds.), *Geschichte des dokumentarischen Films in Deutschland. Band 3: 'Drittes Reich' (1933–1945)* (Stuttgart: Reclam, 2005), pp. 649–662.

Hoffmann, Peter, *The History of the German Resistance 1933–1945* (Montreal: McGill-Queen's University Press, 1996).

Hughes, Daniel J. and Richard L. DiNardo, *Imperial Germany and War, 1871–1918* (Lawrence, KS: University Press of Kansas, 2018).

Hull, Isabel V., *Absolute Destruction: Military Culture and the Practices of War in Imperial Germany* (Ithaca, NY: Cornell University Press, 2006).

Hürter, Johannes, 'Auf dem Weg zur Militäropposition: Tresckow, Gersdorff, der Vernichtungskrieg und der Judenmord. Neue Dokumente über das Verhältnis der Heeresgruppe Mitte zur Einsatzgruppe B im Jahr 1941' in *Vierteljahreshefte für Zeitgeschichte* vol. 52, no. 3 (2004), pp. 527–562.

Hürter, Johannes, 'Hitler's Generals in the East and the Holocaust' in Alex J. Kay and David Stahel (eds.), *Mass Violence in Nazi-Occupied Europe* (Bloomington, IN: Indiana University Press, 2018), pp. 17–40.

Hürter, Johannes, *Hitlers Heerführer: Die deutschen Oberbefehlshaber im Krieg gegen die Sowjetunion 1941/42* (Munich: Oldenbourg Wissenschaftsverlag, 2006).

Hürter, Johannes (ed.), *Notizen aus dem Vernichtungskrieg: Die Ostfront 1941/42 in den Aufzeichnungen des Generals Heinrici* (Darmstadt: Wissenschaftliche Buchgesellschaft, 2016).

Ingrao, Charles and Franz A. J. Szabo (eds.) *The Germans and the East* (West Lafayette, IN: Purdue University Press, 2008).

International Military Tribunal, *Trial of the Major War Criminals before the International Military Tribunal. Volume IV* (Nuremberg: n.pub., 1947).

Johnson, Ian Oha, *Faustian Bargain: The Soviet–German Partnership and the Origins of the Second World War* (Oxford: Oxford University Press, 2021).

Jones, Michael, *The Retreat: Hitler's First Defeat* (London: John Murray, 2009).

Jörgensen, Christer, *Hitler's Espionage Machine: The True Story behind One of the World's Most Ruthless Spy Networks* (London: The Lyons Press, 2004).

Kaiser, Peter M. (ed.), *Mut zum Bekenntnis: Die geheimen Tagebücher des Hauptmanns Hermann Kaiser 1941/1943* (Berlin: Lukas, 2010).

Kallis, Aristotle A., *Nazi Propaganda and the Second World War* (New York: Palgrave Macmillan, 2005).

Kay, Alex J., *Empire of Destruction: A History of Nazi Mass Killing* (New Haven, CT: Yale University Press, 2021).

Kay, Alex J., 'Transition to Genocide, July 1941: Einsatzkommando 9 and the Annihilation of Soviet Jewry' in *Holocaust and Genocide Studies* vol. 27, no. 3 (Winter, 2013), pp. 411–442.

Kay, Alex J. and David Stahel, 'Reconceiving Criminality in the German Army on the Eastern Front' in Alex J. Kay and David Stahel (eds.), *Mass Violence in Nazi-Occupied Europe* (Bloomington, IN: Indiana University Press, 2018), pp. 173–194.

Keller, Peter, *'Die Wehrmacht der Deutschen Republik ist die Reichswehr': Die deutsche Armee 1918–1921* (Paderborn: Schöningh, 2014).

Keller, Sven (ed.), *Kriegstagebuch einer jungen Nationalsozialistin: Die Aufzeichnungen Wolfhilde von Königs 1939–1946* (Berlin: De Gruyter Oldenbourg, 2015).

Kernmayr, Hans Gustl, *Ein Volk kehrt heim! Österreichs Kampf und Befreiung* (Berlin: Deutscher Verlag, 1938).

Kershaw, Ian, *The End: The Defiance and Destruction of Hitler's Germany, 1944–1945* (New York: Penguin, 2011).

Kershaw, Ian, '"Working towards the Führer": Reflections on the Nature of the Hitler Dictatorship' in Ian Kershaw and Moshe Lewin (eds.), *Stalinism and Nazism: Dictatorships in Comparison* (Cambridge: Cambridge University Press, 2003), pp. 88–106.

Kilian, Katrin A., 'Moods in Wartime: The Emotions Expressed in Forces Mail' in Militärgeschichtlichen Forschungsamt (ed.), *Germany and the Second World War. Volume IX/II: German Wartime Society 1939–1945: Exploitation, Interpretations, Exclusion* (Oxford: Oxford University Press, 2014), pp. 253–290.

Kipp, Michaela, *Großreinemachen im Osten: Feindbilder in deutschen Feldpostbriefen im Zweiten Weltkrieg* (Frankfurt: Campus Verlag, 2014).

Kirchubel, Robert, *Hitler's Panzer Armies on the Eastern Front* (Barnsley: Pen and Sword, 2009).

Kirchubel, Robert, *Operation Barbarossa: The German Invasion of Soviet Russia* (Oxford: Osprey Publishing, 2013).

Kirchubel, Robert and Sorin Adam Matei, 'Blunting Barbarossa's Spear: Analyzing Army Group Center's Officer Losses during the Campaign's First Half' in *The Journal of Slavic Military History* vol. 34, no. 4 (2021), pp. 510–536.

Kitchen, Martin, *Rommel's Desert War: Waging World War II in North Africa, 1941–1943* (Cambridge: Cambridge University Press, 2009).

Kitchen, Martin, *The German Officer Corps 1890–1914* (Oxford: Clarendon Press, 1968).

Klink, Ernst, 'The Conduct of Operations' in Militärgeschichtlichen Forschungsamt (ed.), *Germany and the Second World War. Volume IV: The Attack on the Soviet Union* (Oxford: Oxford University Press, 1998), pp. 525–763.

Knoch, Peter, 'Kriegsalltag' in Peter Knoch (ed.), *Kriegsalltag: Die Rekonstruktion des Kriegsalltags als Aufgabe der historischen Forschung und der Friedenserziehung* (Stuttgart: J. B. Metzler, 1989), pp. 222–252.

König, Wolfhilde von, *Wolfhilde's Hitler Youth Diary 1939–1946* (Bloomington, IN: iUniverse, 2013).

Koonz, Claudia, 'Mothers in the Fatherland: Women in Nazi Germany' in Renate Bridenthal and Claudia Koonz (eds.), *Becoming Visible: Women in European History* (Boston, MA: Houghton Mifflin, 1976), pp. 445–473.

Koonz, Claudia, *Mothers in the Fatherland: Women, the Family, and Nazi Politics* (New York: St. Martin's Press, 1987).

Kotze, Hildegard von (ed.), *Heeresadjutant bei Hitler 1938–1943* (Stuttgart: Deutsche Verlags-Anstalt, 1974).

Krylova, Anna, *Soviet Women in Combat: A History of Violence on the Eastern Front* (Cambridge: Cambridge University Press, 2011).

Kühne, Thomas, *The Rise and Fall of Comradeship: Hitler's Soldiers, Male Bonding and Mass Violence in the Twentieth Century* (Cambridge: Cambridge University Press, 2017).

Langhaeuser, Rudolf, *German Methods of Safeguarding Classified Military Information, U.S. Army Historical Division Study MS# P-140* (Washington, DC: Office of the Chief of Military History, 1955).

Latzel, Klaus, 'Feldpostbriefe: Überlegungen zur Aussagekraft einer Quelle' in Christian Hartmann, Johannes Hürter and Ulrike Jureit (ed.), *Verbrechen der Wehrmacht: Bilanz einer Debatte* (Munich: C. H. Beck, 2005), pp. 171–181.

Latzel, Klaus, 'Wehrmachtsoldaten zwischen "Normalität" und NS-Ideologie, oder: Was sucht die Forschung in der Feldpost?' in Rolf-Dieter Müller and Hans-Erich Volkmann (eds.), *Die Wehrmacht: Mythos und Realität* (Munich: Oldenbourg, 1999), pp. 573–588.

Lehnhardt, Jochen, *Die Waffen-SS: Geburt einer Legende. Himmlers Krieger in der NS-Propaganda* (Paderborn: Schöningh, 2017).

Liddell Hart, Basil, *The Other Side of the Hill: Germany's Generals: Their Rise and Fall* (London: Pan Books, 1999).

Liulevicius, Vejas Gabriel, *The German Myth of the East: 1800 to the Present* (Oxford: Oxford University Press, 2011).

Longerich, Peter, *The Unwritten Order: Hitler's Role in the Final Solution* (Stroud: Tempus, 2005).

Loringhoven, Bernd Freytag von, *In the Bunker with Hitler: The Last Witness Speaks* (London: Weidenfeld & Nicolson, 2007).

Lubbeck, William, *At Leningrad's Gates: The Story of a Soldier with Army Group North* (Philadelphia, PA: Casemate, 2006).

Luther, Craig W. H. and David Stahel (eds.), *Soldiers of Barbarossa: Combat, Genocide, and Everyday Experiences on the Eastern Front, June–December 1941* (Guilford, CT: Stackpole Books, 2020).

Lütt, Isa von der, *Die elegante Hausfrau: Mitteilungen für junge Hauswesen mit besonderen Winken für Offiziersfrauen 1892* (Bad Langensalza: Rockstuhl, 2012).

Macksey, Kenneth, *Guderian: Panzer General* (London: Purnell Books, 1975).

Macksey, Kenneth, 'Guderian' in Correlli Barnett (ed.), *Hitler's Generals* (London: Phoenix Giant, 1989), pp. 441–460.

Maclean, French L., *The Unknown Generals: German Corps Commanders in World War II* (unpublished MA thesis, United States Military Academy, Fort Leavenworth, KS,1988).

Mahlendorf, Ursula, *The Shame of Survival: Working Through a Nazi Childhood* (University Park, PA: Pennsylvania State University Press, 2009).

Malinowski, Stephan, *Nazis and Nobles: The History of a Misalliance* (Oxford: Oxford University Press, 2021).

Mann, Michael, *Fascists* (Cambridge: Cambridge University Press, 2010).

Manstein, Erich von, *Aus einem Soldatenleben 1887–1939* (Bonn: Athenäum-Verlag, 1958).

Manstein, Erich von, *Lost Victories* (Novato, CA: Presidio, 1994).

Mastroianni, George R., *Of Mind and Murder: Toward a More Comprehensive Psychology of the Holocaust* (Oxford: Oxford University Press, 2018).

Mawdsley, Evan, 'Crossing the Rubicon: Soviet Plans for Offensive War in 1940–1941' in *The International History Review* vol. 25, no. 4 (2003), pp. 818–865.

Mawdsley, Evan, *Thunder in the East: The Nazi–Soviet War 1941–1945* (London: Bloomsbury, 2016).

Mazower, Mark, 'Military Violence and National Socialist Values: The Wehrmacht in Greece 1941–1944' in *Past and Present*, no. 134 (February 1992), pp. 129–158.

Megargee, Geoffrey P., *Inside Hitler's High Command* (Lawrence, KS: University Press of Kansas, 2000).

Megargee, Geoffrey P., 'The German Army after the Great War: A Case Study in Selective Self-Deception' in Peter Dennis and Jeffrey Grey (eds.), *Victory or Defeat: Armies in the Aftermath of Conflict* (Moss Vale, NSW: Big Sky Publishing, 2010), pp. 104–117.

Mehringer, Hartmut (ed.), *Die Tagebücher von Joseph Goebbels. Teil II: Diktate 1941–1945, Band 8, April–Juni 1943* (Munich: K. G. Saur, 1993).

Meier, Kurt, 'Sowjetrußland im Urteil der evangelischen Kirche (1917–1945)' in Hans-Erich Volkmann (ed.), *Das Rußlandbild im Dritten Reich* (Cologne: Böhlau, 1994), pp. 285–321.

Meier-Welcker, Hans, *Aufzeichnungen eines Generalstabsoffiziers 1939–1942* (Freiburg: Rombach, 1982).

Merritt, Anna, Daniel Effron and Benoît Monin, 'Moral Self-Licensing: When Being Good Frees Us to Be Bad' in *Social and Personality Psychology Compass* vol. 4 (2010), pp. 344–357.

Meyer, Georg, *Adolf Heusinger: Dienst eines deutschen Soldaten 1915 bis 1964* (Berlin: Mittler & Sohn, 2001).

Meyer, Georg (ed.), *Generalfeldmarschall Wilhelm Ritter von Leeb: Tagebuchaufzeichnungen und Lagebeurteilungen aus zwei Weltkriegen* (Stuttgart: Deutsche Verlags-Anstalt, 1976).

Middlebrook, Martin and Chris Everitt, *The Bomber Command War Diaries: An Operational Reference Book 1939–1945* (New York: Viking Publishing, 1985).

Milgram, Stanley, *Obedience to Authority: An Experimental View* (New York: Harper and Row, 1974).

Miller, Arthur G., Amy M. Buddie and Jeffrey Kretschmar, 'Explaining the Holocaust: Does Social Psychology Exonerate the Perpetrators?' in Leonard S. Newman and Ralph Erber (eds.), *Understanding Genocide: The Social Psychology of the Holocaust* (Oxford: Oxford University Press, 2002), pp. 301–324.

Mineau, André, *Operation Barbarossa: Ideology and Ethics against Human Dignity* (Amsterdam: Rodopi, 2004).

Mitcham Jr., Samuel W., *The Men of Barbarossa: Commanders of the German Invasion of Russia, 1941* (Newbury, PA: Casemate, 2009).

Moltke, Helmuth James von, *Letters to Freya: 1939–1945* (New York: Alfred A. Knopf, 1990).

Moore, David W. and B. Thomas Trout, 'Military Advancement: The Visibility Theory of Promotion' in *The American Political Science Review* vol. 72, no. 2 (June 1978), pp. 452–468.

Moorhouse, Roger, *Berlin at War: Life and Death in Hitler's Capital, 1939–45* (London: The Bodley Head, 2010).

Morillo, Stephen, *What Is Military History?* (Medford, PA: Polity Press, 2018).

Moritz, Erhard (ed.), *Fall Barbarossa: Dokumente zur Vorbereitung der faschistischen Wehrmacht auf die Aggression gegen die Sowjetunion (1940/41)* (Berlin: Deutscher Militärverlag, 1970).

Moses, John A., 'The Rise and Fall of Christian Militarism in Prussia-Germany from Hegel to Bonhoeffer' in Stephan Atzert and Andrew Bonnell (eds.), *Europe's Pasts and Presents* (Unley, SA: Australian Humanities Press, 2004), pp. 113–125.

Mouton, Michelle, *From Nurturing the Nation to Purifying the Volk: Weimar and Nazi Family Policy, 1918–1945* (Cambridge: Cambridge University Press, 2007).

Mühleisen, Horst (ed.), *Hellmuth Stieff Briefe* (Berlin: Siedler, 1991).

Mühlhäuser, Regina, *Eroberungen: Sexuelle Gewalttaten und intime Beziehungen deutscher Soldaten in der Sowjetunion 1941–1945* (Hamburg: HIS Verlag, 2010).

Muth, Jörg, *Command Culture: Officer Education in the U.S. Army and the German Armed Forces, 1901–1940, and the Consequences for World War II* (Denton, TX: University of North Texas Press, 2011).

Nagybaczoni Nagy, Vilmos, *The Fateful Years 1938–1945* (Reno, NV: Helena History Press, 2021).

Neitzel, Sönke (ed.), *Tapping Hitler's Generals: Transcripts of Secret Conversations, 1942–45* (St Paul, MN: Frontline Books, 2007).

Nennhaus, H. Peter, *Boyhood: The 1930s and the Second World War: Memories, Comments and Views from the Other Side* (Worcester, MA: Chandler House Press, 2002).

Newton, Steven H., *Hitler's Commander: Field Marshal Walther Model – Hitler's Favorite General* (Cambridge, MA: Da Capo Press, 2006).

Olex-Szczytowski, Matthew, 'The German Military Opposition and National Socialist Crimes, 1939–1944: The Cases of Stauffenberg, Tresckow, and Schulenburg' in *War in History* vol. 28, no. 2 (2019), pp. 380–404.

Overy, Richard, *Interrogations: The Nazi Elite in Allied Hands, 1945* (London: Penguin, 2002).

Perel, Solomon, *Europa Europa: A Memoir of World War II* (New York: Wiley, 1993).

Perry, Gina, *Behind the Shock Machine: The Untold Story of the Notorious Milgram Psychology Experiments* (Brunswick, NJ: Scribe, 2012).

Pietrow-Ennker, Bianka (ed.), *Präventivkrieg? Der deutsche Angriff auf die Sowjetunion* (Frankfurt am Main: Fischer, 2011).

Pine, Lisa, *Hitler's 'National Community': Society and Culture in Nazi Germany* (New York: Bloomsbury, 2017).

Pohl, Dieter, *Die Herrschaft der Wehrmacht: Deutsche Militärbesatzung und einheimische Bevölkerung in der Sowjetunion 1941–1944* (Munich: Fischer, 2008).

Pöhlmann, Markus, *Der Panzer und die Mechanisierung des Krieges: Eine deutsche Geschichte 1890 bis 1945* (Paderborn: Schöningh, 2016).

Porter, Cathy and Mark Jones, *Moscow in World War II* (London: Chatto & Windus, 1987).

Rass, Christoph, *'Menschenmaterial': Deutsche Soldaten an der Ostfront. Innenansichten einer Infanteriedivision 1939–1945* (Paderborn: Schöningh, 2003).

Raths, Ralf, 'Vom "Typenkompass" zu "World of Tanks": Das populäre Bild der Panzerei der Wehrmacht' in Jens Westemeier (ed.), *'So war der deutsche Landser': Das populäre Bild der Wehrmacht* (Paderborn: Schöningh, 2019), pp. 169–189.

Reese, Roger R., *Why Stalin's Soldiers Fought: The Red Army's Military Effectiveness in World War II* (Lawrence, KS: University Press of Kansas, 2011).

Reuth, Ralf Georg, *Rommel: The End of a Legend* (London: Haus Books, 2005).

Richter, Jana (ed.), *Die Tagebücher von Joseph Goebbels. Teil II: Diktate 1941–1945, Band 13, Juli–September 1944* (Munich: K. G. Saur, 1995).

Richter, Timm C., 'Die Wehrmacht und der Partisanenkrieg in den besetzten Gebieten der Sowjetunion' in Rolf-Dieter Müller and Hans-Erich Volkmann (ed.), *Die Wehrmacht: Mythos und Realität* (Munich: Oldenbourg, 1999), pp. 837–857.

Roček, Roman, *Glanz und Elend des P.E.N.: Biographie eines literarischen Clubs* (Vienna: Böhlau Verlag, 2000).

Römer, Felix, *Comrades: The Wehrmacht from Within* (Oxford: Oxford University Press, 2019).

Römer, Felix, *Der Kommissarbefehl: Wehrmacht und NS-Verbrechen an der Ostfront 1941/42* (Paderborn: Schöningh, 2008).

Römer, Felix, '"Kein Problem für die Truppe"' in *Die Zeit Geschichte – Hitlers Krieg im Osten* No. 2 (2011), pp. 42–45.

Römer, Felix, 'The Wehrmacht in the War of Ideologies: The Army and Hitler's Criminal Orders on the Eastern Front' in Alex J. Kay, Jeff Rutherford and David Stahel (eds.), *Nazi Policy on the Eastern Front, 1941: Total War, Genocide, and Radicalization* (Rochester, NY: University of Rochester Press, 2012), pp. 73–100.

Ross, Corey, 'Radio, Film and Morale: Wartime Entertainment between Mobilization and Distraction' in Pamela E. Swett, Cory Ross and Fabrice d'Almeida (eds.), *Pleasure and Power in Nazi Germany* (London: Palgrave Macmillan, 2011), pp. 154–174.

Rossino, Alexander B., *Hitler Strikes Poland: Blitzkrieg, Ideology, and Atrocity* (Lawrence, KS: University Press of Kansas, 2003).

Rutherford, Jeff, *Combat and Genocide on the Eastern Front: The German Infantry's War, 1941–1944* (Cambridge: Cambridge University Press, 2014).

Rutherford, Jeff, 'Total War in 1943: Combat and Occupation around the Kursk Salient' in *The Journal of Military History* (forthcoming).

Rutherford, Jeff and Adrian Wettstein, *The German Army on the Eastern Front: An Inner View of the Ostheer's Experiences of War* (Barnsley: Pen & Sword, 2018).

Saldern, Adelheid von, 'Innovative Trends in Women's and Gender Studies of the National Socialist Era' in *German History* vol. 27, no.1 (2009), pp. 84–112.

Saldern, Adelheid von, 'Victims or Perpetrators? Controversies about the Role of Women in the Nazi State' in David Crew (ed.), *Nazism and German Society, 1933–1945* (London: Routledge, 1994), pp. 141–165.

Scheck, Raffael, *Hitler's African Victims: The German Army Massacres of Black French Soldiers in 1940* (Cambridge: Cambridge University Press, 2006).

Scheibert, Horst, *Das war Guderian: Ein Lebensbericht in Bildern* (Friedberg: Podzun-Palas Verlag, 1989).

Schilling, René, *'Kriegshelden': Deutungsmuster heroischer Männlichkeit in Deutschland 1813–1945* (Paderborn: Schöningh, 2002).

Schlabrendroff, Fabian von, *Begegnungen in fünf Jahrzehnten* (Tübingen: Rainer Wunderlich, 1979).

Schlabrendorff, Fabian von, *The Secret War against Hitler* (New York: Hodder and Stoughton, 1966).

Schneider, Helga, *The Bonfire of Berlin: A Lost Childhood in Wartime Germany* (London: Vintage, 2006).

Schroer, Timothy L., 'Civilization, Barbarism, and the Ethos of Self-Control among the Perpetrators' in *German Studies Review*, vol. 35, no. 1 (February 2012), pp. 33–54.

Schwarz, Gudrun, '"Herrinnen der Zukunft": SS-Offiziere und ihre Frauen' in Ursula Breymayer, Bernd Ulrich and Karin Wieland (eds.), *Willensmenschen: Über deutsche Offiziere* (Frankfurt am Main: Fischer, 1999), pp. 123–133.

Schwendemann, Heinrich, 'Strategie der Selbstvernichtung: Die Wehrmachtführung im "Endkampf" um das "Dritte Reich"' in Rolf-Dieter Müller and Hans-Erich Volkmann (eds.), *Die Wehrmacht: Mythos und Realität* (Munich: Oldenbourg, 1999), pp. 224–244.

Scianna, Bastian Matteo, 'Rommel Almighty? Italian Assessments of the "Desert Fox" during and after the Second World War' in *The Journal of Military History*, vol. 82, no. 1 (2018), pp. 125–145.

Shephard, Ben, *A War of Nerves: Soldiers and Psychiatrists 1914–1994* (London: Pimlico, 2002).

Shepherd, Ben, *Hitler's Soldiers: The German Army in the Third Reich* (New Haven, CT: Yale University Press, 2016).

Showalter, Dennis, *Hitler's Panzers: The Lightning Attacks That Revolutionized Warfare* (New York: Berkley Caliber, 2009).

Sigg, Marco, *Der Unterführer als Feldherr im Taschenformat – Theorie und Praxis der Auftragstaktik im deutschen Heer 1869 bis 1945* (Paderborn: Schöningh, 2014).

Smelser, Ronald and Edward J. Davies II, *The Myth of the Eastern Front: The Nazi–Soviet War in American Popular Culture* (Cambridge: Cambridge University Press, 2008).

Smith, Howard K., *Last Train from Berlin* (New York: Alfred A. Knopf, 1943).

Stahel, David, *Kiev 1941: Hitler's Battle for Supremacy in the East* (Cambridge: Cambridge University Press, 2012).

Stahel, David, *Operation Barbarossa and Germany's Defeat in the East* (Cambridge: Cambridge University Press, 2009).

Stahel, David, *Operation Typhoon: Hitler's March on Moscow, October 1941* (Cambridge: Cambridge University Press, 2013).

Stahel, David, *Retreat from Moscow: A New History of Germany's Winter Campaign, 1941–1942* (New York: Farrar, Straus and Giroux, 2019).

Stahel, David, *The Battle for Moscow* (Cambridge: Cambridge University Press, 2015).

Stahel, David, 'The Battle for Wikipedia: The New Age of "Lost Victories"?' in *The Journal of Slavic Military History* vol. 31, no. 3 (2018), pp. 396–402.

Stahl, Friedrich-Christian, 'Generaloberst Rudolf Schmidt' in Gerd R. Ueberschär (ed.), *Hitlers militärische Elite. Band 2: Vom Kriegsbeginn bis zum Weltkriegsende* (Darmstadt: Primus, 1998), pp. 218–225.

Stahlberg, Alexander, *Bounden Duty: The Memoirs of a German Officer 1932–45* (London: Brassey, 1990).

Stargardt, Nicholas, 'Legitimacy through War' in Devin O. Pendas, Mark Roseman and Richard F. Wetzell (eds.), *Beyond the Racial State: Rethinking Nazi Germany* (Cambridge: Cambridge University Press, 2017), pp. 402–429.

Stargardt, Nicholas, 'Private and Public Moral Sentiments in Nazi Germany' in Elizabeth Harvey, Johannes Hürter, Maiken Umbach and Andreas Wirsching (eds.), *Private Life and Privacy in Nazi Germany* (Cambridge: Cambridge University Press, 2019), pp. 81–101.

Steele, Claude, 'The Psychology of Self-Affirmation: Sustaining the Integrity of the Self' in *Advances in Experimental Social Psychology* vol. 21 (1988), pp. 261–302.

Stein, Marcel, *A Flawed Genius: Field Marshal Walter Model. A Critical Biography* (Solihull: Helion, 2010).

Steinkamp, Peter, 'Die Haltung der Hitlergegner Generalfeldmarschall Wilhelm Ritter von Leeb und Generaloberst Erich Hoepner zur verbrecherischen Kriegsführung bei der Heeresgruppe Nord in der Sowjetunion 1941' in Gerd R. Ueberschär (ed.), *NS-Verbrechen und der militärische Widerstand gegen Hitler* (Darmstadt: Primus Verlag, 2000), pp. 47–61.

Stern, J. P., *Hitler: The Führer and the People* (Berkeley, CA: University of California Press, 1992).

Stoecker, Sally W., *Forging Stalin's Army: Marshal Tukhachevsky and the Politics of Military Innovation* (New York: Westview Press, 1998), pp. 252–279.

Storz, Oliver, 'Die Schlacht der Zukunft', in Wolfgang Michalka (ed.), *Der Erste Weltkrieg: Wirkung, Wahrnehmung, Analyse* (Munich: Piper, 1994).

Streit, Christian, 'Das Schicksal der verwundeten sowjetischen Kriegsgefangenen' in Hannes Heer and Klaus Naumann (eds.), *Vernichtungskrieg: Verbrechen der Wehrmacht 1941 bis 1944* (Hamburg: Hamburger Edition, 1995), pp. 78–91.

Szejnmann, Claus-Christian W., '"A Sense of *Heimat* Opened Up during the War": German Soldiers and Heimat Abroad' in Claus-Christian W. Szejnmann and Maiken Umbach (eds.), *Heimat, Region, and Empire: Spatial Identities under National Socialism* (London: Palgrave, 2012), pp. 112–147.

Tooze, Adam, *The Wages of Destruction: The Making and Breaking of the Nazi Economy* (London: Viking, 2006).

Töppel, Roman, *Kursk 1943: The Greatest Battle of the Second World War* (Warwick: Helion, 2018).

Tramitz, Angelika, 'Nach dem Zapfenstreich: Anmerkungen zur Sexualität des Offiziers' in Ursula Breymayer, Bernd Ulrich and Karin Wieland (eds.), *Willensmenschen: Über deutsche Offiziere* (Frankfurt am Main: Fischer, 1999), pp. 211–226.

Tuchel, Johannes, '... *und ihrer aller wartete der Strick': Das Zellengefängnis Lehrter Straße 3 nach dem 20. Juli 1944* (Berlin: Lukas, 2014).

Ueberschär, Gerd R. and Winfried Vogel, *Dienen und Verdienen: Hitlers Geschenke an seine Eliten* (Frankfurt am Main: S. Fischer, 1999).

Ueberschär, Gerd R. and Wolfram Wette (eds.), *'Unternehmen Barbarossa': Der deutsche Überfall auf die Sowjetunion 1941* (Paderborn: Schöningh, 1984).

Ullrich, Volker, *Hitler: Downfall 1939–45* (London: The Bodley Head, 2020).

Umbach, Maiken, '(Re-)Inventing the Private under National Socialism' in Elizabeth Harvey, Johannes Hürter, Maiken Umbach and Andreas Wirsching (eds.), *Private Life and Privacy in Nazi Germany* (Cambridge: Cambridge University Press, 2019), pp. 102–131.

Umbach, Maiken, 'Selfhood, Place, and Ideology in German Photo Albums, 1933–1945' in *Central European History* vol. 48, no. 3 (2015), pp. 335–365.

Usborne, Cornelie, 'Love Letters from Front and Home: A Private Space for Intimacy in the Second World War?' in Elizabeth Harvey, Johannes Hürter, Maiken Umbach and Andreas Wirsching (eds.), *Private Life and Privacy in Nazi Germany* (Cambridge: Cambridge University Press, 2019), pp. 280–303.

Uziel, Daniel, *The Propaganda Warriors: The Wehrmacht and the Consolidation of the German Home Front* (Bern: Peter Lang, 2008).

Vaizey, Hester, *Surviving Hitler's War: Family Life in Germany, 1939–48* (New York: Palgrave, 2010).

Vollhardt, Johanna Ray and Maggie Campbell-Obaid, 'The Social Psychology of Genocide and Mass Atrocities' in Arthur G. Miller (ed.), *The Social Psychology of Good and Evil* (New York: Guilford, 2016), pp. 159–184.

Vossler, Frank, *Propaganda in die eigene Truppe: Die Truppenbetreuung in der Wehrmacht 1939–1945* (Paderborn: Schöningh, 2005).

Walde, Karl J., *Guderian* (Frankfurt: Ullstein, 1976).

Weale, Adrian, *Army of Evil: A History of the SS* (New York: NAL Caliber, 2012).

Weigand, Jörg, 'Einflussreicher Nationalsozialist, Papst-Biograph und Jugendbuchautor: Das Schriftstellerleben des Hans Gustl Kernmayr (1900–1977)' in JMS-Report April 2/2009, p. 4.

Weinberg, Gerhard L., *Germany, Hitler & World War II* (Cambridge: Cambridge University Press, 1995).

Weinberg, Gerhard, '22 June 1941: The German View' in *War in History*, vol. 3, no. 2 (1996), pp. 225–233.

Werner, Frank, '"Hart müssen wir hier draußen sein": Soldatische Männlickeit im Vernichtungskrieg, 1941–1944' in *Geschichte und Gesellschft* vol. 34 (2008), pp. 5–40.

Westermann, Edward B., *Drunk on Genocide: Alcohol and Mass Murder in Nazi Germany* (Ithaca, NY: Cornell University Press, 2021).

Wette, Wolfram, 'Juden, Bolschewisten, Slawen. Rassenideologische Rußland-Feindbilder Hitlers und der Wehrmachtgeneräle' in Bianka Pietrow-Ennker (ed.) *Präventivkrieg? Der deutsche Angriff auf die Sowjetunion* (Frankfurt am Main: Fischer, 2011), pp. 40–58.

Wette, Wolfram, *The Wehrmacht: History, Myth, Reality* (London: Harvard University Press, 2006).

Wettstein, Adrian, *Die Wehrmacht im Stadtkampf* (Paderborn: Schöningh, 2014).

Wettstein, Adrian, 'Urban Warfare Doctrine on the Eastern Front' in Alex J. Kay, Jeff Rutherford and David Stahel (eds.), *Nazi Policy on the Eastern Front, 1941: Total War, Genocide and Radicalization* (Rochester, NY: Rochester University Press, 2012), pp. 45–72.

Wheatley, Ben, *British Intelligence and Hitler's Empire in the Soviet Union, 1941–1945* (London: Bloomsbury, 2018).

Wheeler-Bennett, John, *The Nemesis of Power: The German Army in Politics 1918–1945* (London: Macmillan, 1954).

Whitewood, Peter, *The Red Army and the Great Terror: Stalin's Purge of the Soviet Military* (Lawrence, KS: University Press of Kansas, 2015).

Willems, Bastiaan, *Violence in Defeat: The Wehrmacht on German Soil, 1944–1945* (Cambridge: Cambridge University Press, 2021).

Woche, Klaus R., *Zwischen Pflicht und Gewissen: Generaloberst Rudolf Schmidt 1886–1957* (Berlin: AALEXX Druck, 2002).

Wrochem, Oliver von, 'Ein unpolitischer Soldat? Generalfeldmarschall Erich von Manstein' in Gerhard Hirschfeld and Tobias Jersak (eds.), *Karrieren im Nationalsozialismus: Funktionseliten zwischen Mitwirkung und Distanz* (Frankfurt: Campus Verlag, 2004), pp. 185–204.

Yelton, David K., *Hitler's Home Guard: Volkssturmmann Western Front, 1944–1945* (Westminster, MD: Osprey, 2006).

Zeidler, Manfred, *Reichswehr und Rote Armee, 1920–1933: Wege und Stationen einer ungewöhnlichen Zusammenarbeit* (Munich: Oldenbourg, 1993).

Ziemke, Earl F. and Magna E. Bauer, *Moscow to Stalingrad: Decision in the East* (New York: Military Heritage Press, 1988).

Zipfel, Gaby, 'Wie führen Frauen Krieg?' in Hannes Heer and Klaus Naumann (eds.), *Vernichtungskrieg: Verbrechen der Wehrmacht 1941 bis 1944* (Hamburg: Hamburger Edition, 1995), pp. 460–474.

Internet Sources

Austrian National Library: ANNO (Austrian Newspaper Online)
http://anno.onb.ac.at/cgi-content/anno?aid=vob
Calvin University: 'German Propaganda Archive'
https://research.calvin.edu/german-propaganda-archive/pimpf.htm
German Front Newspapers in WWII: Mobilizing Soldiers and Civilians for War
www.servicenewspapers.amdigital.co.uk/Explore/Essays/JurgenForster

The Heinz Berggruen Gymnasium website (the renaming of 'Erich-Hoepner-Oberschule').
https://hbgym.de/schule/unser-name/
Katrin Kilian, 'Postal Censorship from 1939 to 1945'
www.feldpost-archiv.de/english/e11-zensur.html
Lexikon der Wehrmacht.de
www.lexikon-der-wehrmacht.de/Personenregister/R/ReinhardtGH.htm
Media Rep (Open Access Repository for Media)
https://mediarep.org
Net Film Archive (Russia)
www.net-film.ru
Trial of the Major War Criminals before the International Military Tribunal. Volume IV
www.loc.gov/rr/frd/Military_Law/pdf/NT_Vol-IV.pdf
The United States Holocaust Memorial Museum: 'The German Churches and the Nazi State'
https://encyclopedia.ushmm.org/content/en/article/the-german-churches-and-the-nazi-state

INDEX